Narrative, Violence, and the Law

Law, Meaning, and Violence

The scope of Law, Meaning, and Violence is defined by the wide-ranging scholarly debates signaled by each of the words in the title. Those debates have taken place among and between lawyers, anthropologists, political theorists, sociologists, and historians, as well as literary and cultural critics. This series is intended to recognize the importance of such ongoing conversations about law, meaning, and violence as well as to encourage and further them.

Series Editors:

Martha Minow, Harvard Law School
Michael Ryan, Northeastern University
Austin Sarat, Amherst College

Narrative, Violence, and the Law: The Essays of Robert Cover, edited by Martha Minow, Michael Ryan, and Austin Sarat

Narrative, Authority, and Law, by Robin West

The Possibility of Popular Justice: A Case Study of Community Mediation in the United States, edited by Sally Engle Merry and Neil Milner

Legal Modernism, by David Luban

Surveillance, Privacy, and the Law: Employee Drug Testing and the Politics of Social Control, by John Gilliom

Lives of Lawyers: Journeys in the Organizations of Practice, by Michael J. Kelly

Narrative, Violence, and the Law

The Essays of Robert Cover

Edited by

Martha Minow, Michael Ryan, and Austin Sarat

Ann Arbor

THE UNIVERSITY OF MICHIGAN PRESS

First paperback edition 1995
Copyright © by the University of Michigan 1993
All rights reserved
Published in the United States of America by
The University of Michigan Press
Manufactured in the United States of America

1998 1997 1996 1995   4 3 2 1

A CIP catalogue record for this book is available from the British Library.

Library of Congress Cataloging-in-Publication Data

Cover, Robert M.
    Narrative, violence, and the law : the essays of Robert Cover /
edited by Martha Minow, Michael Ryan, and Austin Sarat.
      p.   cm. — (Law, meaning, and violence)
    Includes bibliographical references and index.
    ISBN 0-472-09495-5 (alk. paper). — ISBN 0-472-06495-9 (pbk.:
alk. paper)
    1. Law—United States. 2. Human rights. 3. Justice. 4. Jewish
law. I. Minow, Martha, 1954– . II. Ryan, Michael, 1951– .
III. Sarat, Austin. IV. Title. V. Series.
KF213.C63 1992
348.73'2—dc20
[347.3082]   92-30307
                              CIP

Acknowledgments

Grateful acknowledgment is made to the following publishers and journals for permission to reprint previously published material.

The American Enterprise Institute for "Origins of Judicial Activism in the Protection of Minorities," which was originally presented at the American Enterprise Institute Conference on the Role of the Judiciary, December 1979. Reprinted with the permission of the American Enterprise Institute for Public Policy Research, Washington, D.C.

Capital University Law Review for "The Folktales of Justice: Tales of Jurisdiction," 14 *Capital University Law Review* 179 (1985).

The Catholic University of America for "Obligations: A Jewish Jurisprudence of the Social Order." Copyright © 1986 by The Catholic University of America. Professor Cover presented this paper at the Columbus School of Law as his contribution to the Symposium "The Religious Foundations of Civil Rights Law" on April 19, 1986. The Symposium was sponsored by the Interdisciplinary Program in Law and Religion. "Obligations: A Jewish Jurisprudence of the Social Order" was first published in 5 *Journal of Law and Religion* 65 (1987). Reprinted with permission.

The Harvard Law Review Association for "Nomos and Narrative," which first appeared as "The Supreme Court, 1982 Term—Foreword: Nomos and Narrative," in 97 *Harvard Law Review* 4 (1983). Copyright © 1983 by the Harvard Law Review Association.

The New York Times Company for "Your Law-Baseball Quiz," *New York Times,* April 5, 1979. Copyright © 1979 by The New York Times Company. Reprinted by permission.

William and Mary Law Review for "The Uses of Jurisdictional Redundancy: Interest, Ideology, and Innovation," 22 *William and Mary Law Review* 639 (1981).

The Yale Law Journal Company for "The Origins of Judicial Activism in the Protection of Minorities," 91 *Yale Law Journal* 1287–1316 (1982); and for "Violence and the Word," 95 *Yale Law Journal* 1601–29. Reprinted by permission of The Yale Law Journal and Fred B. Rothman and Company.

Every effort has been made to trace the ownership of all copyrighted material in this book and to obtain permission for its use.

Preface

Aviam Soifer

It was wonderful to learn with Robert Cover. Yet Bob Cover did not stand out as a teacher in the classic sense. He was hardly a dazzling orator; he did not adopt the entertainer's role for his audience, nor did his classroom zing with the tension of the so-called Socratic method done well. His classes and even his style on the lecture platform mirrored his probing, open-minded, everyday conversations. In those conversations, Bob Cover turned everyone—family, children, law students, friends, workers, and other scholars—into his fellow students.

To talk with Bob Cover on virtually any subject was to be swept along by his irresistible curiosity, wild flights of ideas, broad learning, and cascades of creative analogies and paradoxical arguments. Bob's talk was sometimes absurd, often cryptic, frequently wise, and always fun. How fitting that the name "Cover" is the transliteration of the Hebrew word *chaver* 'friend', the very term used for the person with whom one engages in the intense collegial relationship of studying Talmud.[1]

Bob Cover's words were like a dazzling new kind of intellectual jazz. He truly valued the collaborative process, but his solos soared. His amazing riffs and sparkling sense of the outlandish managed to

---

1. In a tribute to his student and friend, Joseph Lukinsky points out how the style of learning connected to studying Talmud illuminates Cover's work. According to Lukinsky, this collegial approach involves interactive thought across generations in pursuit of "multiperspectival, dialogic, simultaneous debate on contemporary issues" (Lukinsky, "Law in Education: A Reminiscence with Some Footnotes to Robert Cover's 'Nomos and Narrative,'" 96 *Yale Law Journal* 1836, 1837 [1987]. "[T]he task of education," Lukinsky summarizes, "is to use what scholars say to get back to that world which existed before they said it" [1859]).

remain grounded somehow in his belief that, through the very process of argument and irreverent imaginings with others past and present, it might actually be possible to make new, better worlds together. Steeped in history, Bob Cover looked to the future. Proudly Jewish and unusually sophisticated about Jewish sources, he admired the integrity of other groups, other norms, other ways to bridge reality's aching chasms of injustice.

This volume is a singularly worthwhile project. Bob Cover's work has had a remarkable impact across many genres already, but his articles addressed a diverse range of subjects and were scattered in many different types of journals. The additional new essays by Professors Minow, Ryan, and Sarat offer provocative interpretations and suggestions for further analysis and debate about topics Bob Cover explored in his short life. Yet this book also presents a double danger.

First, publication of most of Bob's most significant articles in a single volume surely will increase the tendency, already well underway, for scholars to consider Bob's published work *canonical* in several of the senses in which canonical is now in vogue. But Bob wrote many things in many places. He sometimes repeated himself, occasionally criticized his earlier work, and was nearly always cryptic and elliptical. We might, instead, read this book as Bob read. He was a remarkably eclectic and careful reader. For all his care about texts, however, this textualist always tried to get beyond the text. Perhaps this collection ought to be considered somewhat analogous to a trove of recordings by a great jazz innovator. What is between the book's covers merits close attention. But the articles only hint at the context; they underscore the need to consider how Bob, and those he played with and for, struggled to use and to break out of old patterns.

A second danger lies in the other meaning of canonization: the process of sainthood. Bob Cover was no saint. Instead, he was often wickedly, hilariously irreverent. And he was hardly a person of faith in any orthodox sense. But, because he talked, wrote, and thought with such an incomparable blend of learning, provocation, and creativity about the most important issues—and because he was a mensch who died so tragically young—there is a tendency to assume a reverential approach to his memory and to his work. Bob would have been amused and tickled by canonization in either sense, of course. But then he would have responded with some skeptical verbal zinger.

This is not to say that Bob Cover lacked either personal or intellectual ambition, far from it. He wanted to learn the essence of all the underlying legal rules, for example, and to show that he had conquered their deep structure. He was particularly intrigued by gaps: the clear biblical rule that the eldest son should inherit, for example, which was contradicted by every famous story of fathers and sons, or rules that encouraged disputation among the great Rabbis, but then prescribed the death penalty for anyone so insistent about his own position as to urge others to follow him. Such an insistent dissenter was to be executed as a rebellious elder (although the punishment actually was usually "only" banishment or excommunication). The core scholarly jurisdiction Bob assigned himself was trying to figure out when the time had come to break the rules.

Bob's work concentrated on the need to bridge past and future. Understanding the reality check that history painfully supplies is inextricably a part of the quest for the myths we will need to generate a better future. Ends and means will not be severed. Both process and goal require creative, feisty engagement and kinetic, collegial elaboration by people willing to treat one another—and even their predecessors who merit it—as *chaverim*, as friends.

Bob kept returning to an inquiry about what it takes for any person to "speak truth to power." In addition to the obvious dangers, he noted, there is also always the danger of being thought mad and, perhaps, of being mad. So Bob wanted to know what motivated past exemplars and what happened to them. He was a virtuoso about the words and deeds—and even more, the failures to act—of past masters. But his concern consistently was to change the future. To do that, Bob surely did not abjure the use of violence nor did he seek or even imagine a world without law. He sought nothing less than using law to invite new worlds.

Aware of his privileged position, Bob Cover nevertheless stood for persistent and direct challenges to hierarchy. Like the very best judges, rabbis, and scholars, Bob was astute in identifying a paradox and comfortable in living with it. Yet his keen appreciation of paradox did not translate into embracing the status quo. Bob pursued justice as he saw it, in deeds as well as in words. When he was a Princeton undergraduate, for example, as an SNCC volunteer, Bob went on a hunger strike and was beaten by his fellow prisoners in the Albany, Georgia, jail. As a law student at Columbia, he produced an important jurisdictional theory on behalf of welfare recipients. When he was a faculty member at Columbia and Yale, Bob could be found on picket lines such as those mounted by university workers and by anti-apartheid students seeking divestment of university funds invested in South Africa.[2]

Still, Bob was nobody's knee-jerk anything. Thus, to the amazement and even the horror of many of his closest friends, he declared, a few months before his death, that he was not an abolitionist concerning capital punishment. He also stepped forward to defend a Yale student accused of homophobic expression in an early confrontation about hate speech and the limits of freedom of expression on the college campus. Serious scholar and theoretical thinker that he surely was, Bob nevertheless decided to move his office into the chaotic din of the Legal Services Organization at Yale. There, in the clinic, he could enjoy the hubbub and he even might be able to help students with civil procedure or other lawyering problems. Taking part in the good legal fight was obligatory.

There is much truth in Bob's description of himself as an anarchist who loved law. Despite his emphasis on the violence done by judicial words and his insight into the particularly jurispathic qualities of the law of any state, one might learn with him the importance of thoughts pursued seriously and expressed with precision and courage. In any event, the very effort to upset established forms and to rethink fundamentally the roles of jurisdiction, sovereignty, and law was worthwhile in itself.

In his last few years, Bob concentrated on Jewish sources and on the issue of messianism through law. In significant ways, his own concern with legal, mystical, and messianic thinking echoed Joseph Caro and the work of Gershom Scholem.[3] But as he explored "true

---

2. Bob Cover's friend, Stephen Wizner, described these and other examples of Bob's active engagement in social issues in his memorial tribute, published at 96 *Yale Law Journal* 1707 (1987). Other memorial tributes in that issue offer additional details about Cover's ability to range and to move others between "is," "ought," and "might be made to be."

3. The basic biographical source on Joseph Caro (or Karo) in English remains R. J. Zwi Werblowsky, *Joseph Karo: Lawyer and Mystic* (1962). In the sixteenth

jurisdiction," Bob insisted that "sacred aspiration" could only be realized through the legal civilization of particularistic communities. He
did not seek the end of days, but, rather, realization of a very human,
earthbound community where there could be rules, but no rulers.

Law might cut across national boundaries. Law might protect
communities against state power. Conceivably, legal norms, working
primarily by consent rather than by coercion, could instill a sense
of obligation along with tolerance of diversity and even recognition
of basic rights. Bob Cover lived mightily in this and many other
senses. After a sabbath dinner, for example, Bob often picked away
at a cake he had decided not to eat and soon he had devoured it
entirely, all the while concentrating fully on utopia, the Red Sox, the
reasons he hated English novels, or some other topic of pressing,

---

century, Caro's *Shulhan Arukh* codified rabbinic law, and it remains the basic sum-
mation of the rules for Orthodox Judaism. Yet Caro, a learned scholar famous for
his more detailed *Beit Yosef* as well, was also a famous mystic. *Maggid Mesharim*,
an extraordinary diary of fifty years of dream visitations and automatic dictation by
a kind of angel-teacher, is apparently convincingly attributed to Caro. Caro was also
one of the group of rabbis in the town of Safed in the Galilee in 1538 who—in an
act Cover termed "supreme juridical chutzpah"—decided to reinstate the rabbinic line
broken for over a thousand years. Caro and his colleagues thereby touched off and
ultimately lost a great controversy with the rabbis of Jerusalem.

Cover had begun to concentrate on the context and content of this 1538 debate.
He focused on the issue of what was at stake in trying to use law to hasten the
coming of the Messiah. Fragments of Cover's translation, annotation, and interpre-
tation of the 1538 dispute were published posthumously as "Bringing the Messiah
Through Law: A Case Study," *Nomos XXX: Religion, Morality, and the Law*
(R. Pennock and J. Chapman eds., 1988).

Gershom Scholem, the great scholar of mysticism and false messiahs, came to
his subject from a strong German rationalist tradition. As a young man, Scholem
described his concept of justice as "action in deferment" to his friend, the critic Walter
Benjamin and to Benjamin's wife, Dora. They goaded Scholem as to why he did not
adopt the Orthodox way of life. Scholem recalled responding that he could not accept
"the concretization of the Torah in a false, premature sphere," but had to "maintain
the anarchic suspension." This instinct, he said, later helped lead him to kabbalistic
considerations (G. Scholem, *Walter Benjamin: The Story of a Friendship* 72 [H. Zohn
transl., 1981]).

Suzanne Stone elaborated what she called Cover's obsession with Caro and
explored the roots of a kind of restorative or realistic messianism. See Stone, "In
Pursuit of the Countertext: The Reclaiming of Jewish Sources in Modern American
Legal Scholarship," paper presented at the Conference on Jews and the Law in the
United States, Madison, Wisconsin, November, 1991. Nomi Stolzenberg tied Cover's
work to that of Caro and Gershom Scholem in "Jews, Jurisdiction, and Judicial
Review: Un-Covering the Tradition of Jewish 'Dissimilation,'" presented at the same
conference.

fervent interest. Yet this somewhat absentminded, largely impractical scholar brought people along with him with much more than his unusual personal style, obvious intellectual power, and shy boyish smile. Encounters with Bob Cover might provide glimpses of what a more collegial, more interesting, and less phony world might be like.

In Bob's "Your Law-Baseball Quiz" (see Coda), we learn—after noting the sexism inherent in both baseball and law—why John Marshall surely was the Babe Ruth of his day, but why Felix Frankfurter most nearly resembled Bobby Murcer. More telling was Bob's assertion that, despite all the more famous stars surrounding them, Earl Warren and Yogi Berra were the most valuable players on their respective teams. Neither player allowed excessive thought to interfere with clutch performance. Neither did Bob Cover.

This book gives us the chance to appreciate anew some of the greatest hits by a funny, challenging, marvelously irreverent, and deeply serious dreamer who played at the top of his game. We can learn with Bob Cover from generation to generation.

Contents

Introduction: Robert Cover and Law, Judging, and Violence

Martha Minow

While a student in the 1960s, Robert Cover actively participated in civil rights work and antiwar protests. He watched protesters defend against civil and criminal sanctions and he watched judges announce that they were helpless to respond to the protesters' avowed moral justifications for breaking laws. These observations prompted Cover's historical and jurisprudential inquiry into the work of pre–Civil War judges who enforced the fugitive slave laws despite their own privately expressed opposition to slavery. Cover's inquiry produced *Justice Accused: Antislavery and the Judicial Process* (New Haven: Yale University Press, 1975), a stunning exploration of how powerful men could assert they had no power to resist doing what they believed was wrong. Cover tried to explain why a group of judges pursued a mechanistic interpretation of the fugitive slave law and of law itself in direct opposition to their moral understandings.[1]

Justice Accused exposes the philosophical and psychological tensions between law and morality. Cover's later work embraces plural sources of beliefs and values with their accompanying conflicts and power struggles. Indeed, he coined the term *jurispathic* to refer to the power and practice of a government that rules by displacing,

---

1. The early version of the fugitive slave law, adopted in 1793, implemented Article IV, section 2 of the Constitution. It provided for the seizure and sentencing of escaped slaves and returned them to their owners even if the slave had successfully journeyed to a state that forbade slavery. As amended in 1850, the law imposed stricter standards and punished U.S. marshals who failed to seize fugitives or citizens who aided them. It also paid the judge double for returning a slave compared with the fee earned if the individual went free.

suppressing, or exterminating values that run counter to its own. Yet Cover placed at the center of law the communal groups that would seem peripheral if the government's own worldview were the starting point.[2] In so doing, Cover set in motion three captivating arguments: (1) government should be understood as one among many contestants for generating and implementing norms; (2) communities ignored or despised by those running the state actually craft and sustain norms with at least as much effect and worth as those espoused by the state; and (3) imposition of the state's norms does violence to communities, a violence that may be justifiable but is not to be preferred a priori.

On initial reflection, it makes good sense for the author of *Justice Accused* to advance this vision of plural normative worlds. If only the antebellum judges had felt more profoundly committed not only to the positive law but also to competing sources of their moral intuitions, perhaps they, as judges, could have reshaped the scope of the fugitive slave law or, instead, as persons of conscience, simply refused to enforce it. At another level, however, the conflict among normative sources seemed responsible for the antebellum judges' rigidity and assertions of their own powerlessness.[3] I will explore here, briefly, connections and tensions between the ideas in *Justice Accused* and Robert Cover's later works collected in this volume.

Justice Accused

Cover located his inquiry in the white society of the antebellum period of the United States. In the decade preceding the Civil War, anti-

---

2. This shift for Cover would transform even the details of historical narratives; thus, he criticized the court-centered language of a Supreme Court opinion describing the period after *Brown v. Board of Education* as a time of stress and anguish. That it was for the Court, reasoned Cover, but for the civil rights movement greater stress and anguish preceded the Court's decision (Robert M. Cover, "Nomos and Narrative," n. 193).

3. It is possible that plural normative worlds mean something very different for someone comfortably situated within one than they do for someone poised between several, and it is the latter person who most risks cognitive dissonance. Yet, at least in contemporary society, even the most insular communities have trouble shielding their members from some exposure to competing worlds. Perhaps the danger of cognitive dissonance explored by Cover in *Justice Accused* arises because of the clash between fidelity to an official role and personal belief, so it is particular to the situation of a public official. Cover explored the possibilities of justice if judges had no official power (see "The Folktales of Justice"). At times, his work held out the hope that even judges with official power could engage in committed, constitutional creation (see "Nomos and Narrative").

slavery agitators and defenders of slavery clashed. Their clash revealed contrasting religious, geographic, and ideological affiliations. Among those tugged by competing affiliations were the judges asked to enforce the fugitive slave laws. Cover examined how leading judges revealed, in their private letters and diaries, their basic sympathies with efforts to abolish slavery, and how the same men proceeded to demand that federal law protect the property interests of slaveholders by returning the slaves who had escaped into free states or territories.

Cover showed how the judges, at least before 1850, could have forged available legal materials into arguments for abolishing slavery.[4] The puzzle Cover poses is why they did not do so. Why, instead, did the judges announce their powerlessness to resist implementing the fugitive slave law? Why did they say that only legislative change by the states or the federal government could alter their task?[5] As his answer, Cover unearths the contemporaneous legal rules about slavery and about choice of law, the concepts of law and of the role of the judge available to these officials, and the psychological processes likely to have been at work in their lives.

Cover depicts a complex picture. First, a federal law commanded that even judges in free states use a summary procedure in a case involving the fugitive slave law. Thus, when presented with the claim of a slaveholder that the individual before the court was a runaway slave, the judge was to be presented only with the name of the alleged slave. Over time, courts ruled against allowing state antikidnapping laws to be used as defenses. Courts ruled against the use of a jury and against the use of habeas corpus—the classic writ for challenging constraints on an individual's liberty.[6] Thus, federal law seemed to command a judge to render the alleged slave to the slaveholder. Yet two other sources of law remained available. Each state had its own rules about when it should recognize and defer to the law of a sister state, including the general law of slavery and more specific rules about how to establish the identity of a given slave. And present in the minds of judges and lawyers then—as it is now in a different form—were ideals of natural law, preexisting the governments made by men. These sources of law offered resources for crafting results contrary to the fugitive slave law.

---

4. E.g., Cover, *Justice Accused*, 8–21 (natural law and language of liberty would proscribe slavery).

5. Cover, *Justice Accused*, 93.

6. See Cover, *Justice Accused*, 207–8.

But, as Cover vividly exposes, the judges' understandings of the nature of law and especially of the role of a judge led them to feel constrained. They could describe a sense of their own powerlessness to reach antislavery results. The judges exhibited what Cover called the "judicial can't," a rhetorical move indicating that the judge could do nothing but apply and enforce the command of the fugitive slave law.[7] The judges treated the matter as if law simply specified rules of the game, rules that narrowly specified the judge's own latitude for action. Accordingly, a judge simply could not do other than to enforce the fugitive slave law. To do otherwise would fall outside the judicial role.[8] The judges accompanied this role concept with statements about the high stakes, about the mechanistic quality of law, and about the proper assignment of blame for slavery to the legislature or the Constitution, but not to the judges or their actions.

Even these undestandings of law's nature and judicial role could not silence competing moral objections to slavery. Here, for Cover, was the heart of the matter.

> The antislavery judge experienced a pervasive, but more or less latent, conflict between two potentially inconsistent prescriptive systems: law and (antislavery) morality. Neither system had a wholly satisfactory accommodation mechanism for the potentially inconsistent principles or rules of the other.[9]

Such conflicts produced a kind of dissonance inside the judges' minds.[10] A particular psychological dynamic, Cover postulated, would then emerge.

> The dissonance hypothesis predicts that the judges who were most troubled by a result that favored slavery, but who nevertheless decided to be faithful to the judicial role where it seemed to require such a result, would be most likely to exhibit some form of behavior that reduced the distance that was consequence of such a difficult choice.[11]

---

7. Cover, *Justice Accused*, 119.

8. Cover, *Justice Accused*, 123–25.

9. Cover, *Justice Accused*, 225.

10. Cover, *Justice Accused*, 227 (offering the theory of cognitive dissonance as a heuristic device).

11. Cover, *Justice Accused*, 229.

As a result, an influential group of judges tended to respond with avowed helplessness and exaggerated formalism. They acted as if they were followers of the legal system rather than innovators. In the process, they selected the strand of their traditions that called for enforcing the slave laws rather than the strands that would have supported resistance to them.[12] They revealed and then shaped their own characters as obedient servants rather than leaders.[13]

Cover implicitly maintained that the antebellum judges he studied were not unusual. Most judges, he suggested, would similarly respond to the plural dimensions of normative argument by selecting the most rigid thread and, at the same time, denying their own responsibility for that choice. Although he did not discuss whether legislators in a plural normative universe undergo similar internal struggles with similar results, the fugitive slave law provides at least one supporting piece of evidence on this score. Stemming from compromises made by the drafters of the Constitution,[14] the law directing the return of escaped slaves in Cover's terms "represent[ed] a general policy of accommodation to divergent systems within the constitutional structure," a policy to assure union and a policy upon which union depended.[15] Here was a rule directing the mutual coexistence of people and states with incompatible views about slavery; mutual toleration required the free states to help the slave states protect slavery.

Coordination, Activism, and Redundancy

The coordination needed to sustain union among the states seemed to tether moral and political opposition to slavery until a Civil War threatened the union itself; certainly the new coordination erected after the war leashed the vanquished to the normative vision of the victors. In "The Origins of Judicial Activism in the Protection of Minorities," Cover examined the role of the federal courts in protecting minorities after the Civil War. In particular, he considered the irony that active monitoring and intrusion of federal judges seemed

---

12. See Cover, *Justice Accused*, 257–59.

13. Cover, *Justice Accused*, 259: "If a man makes a good priest, we may be quite sure he will not be a great prophet."

14. See, generally, Michael Kammen, *A Machine That Would Go of Itself: The Constitution in American Culture* (New York: Vintage Books, 1987), 47, 97.

15. Cover, *Justice Accused*, 208.

less intrusive than other options in combatting the legacies of slavery and racism. Endorsing this federal role, Cover did not, however, deny the cost to state sovereignty and to regional self-determination. Competing normative orders cannot be coordinated without doing violence to at least one of them.

A similar attentiveness to the collisions among competing normative orders animates Cover's next article, "The Uses of Jurisdictional Redundancy: Interest, Ideology, and Innovation." Restricting his scope here to the courts established by the states and the federal government, Cover detailed the concurrency—and the seeming redundancy—among judiciaries able to hear the same cases or issues. Unlike many scholars, however, especially unlike those who decry inefficiency, Cover celebrated this redundancy. According to Cover, the availability of multiple judicial settings offers a check against errors, a guard against bias, a challenge to ideological blinders, and an opportunity for innovation. Yet even in this celebration of redundancy, Cover retained a clear sense of its price in terms of conflicts and uncertainty. The costs of order imposed even temporarily upon such a field of conflict and uncertainty riveted Cover's attention in his next works.

"Nomos and Narrative"

Acknowledgment of the violence of imposed order animates part of a stanza from a poem by Wallace Stevens that Robert Cover used to begin his article "Nomos and Narrative," published eight years after *Justice Accused.* Stevens wrote:

A. A violent order is disorder; and/
B. A great order is an order. These/
Two things are one. (Pages of Illustrations).[16]

For both Stevens and Cover, order means at least some violence. When we try to imagine desirable relationships among communities and governments, for example, violence is an unavoidable feature. Producing one orderly system from divergent and conflicting com-

---

16. Wallace Stevens, "Connoisseur of Chaos," in *The Collected Poems of Wallace Stevens* 215 (1954) (quoted in Robert M. Cover, "The Supreme Court, 1982 Term—Foreword: Nomos and Narrative," 97 *Harvard Law Review* 4 [1983]). Cover once said that he went to law school to make the world safe for poetry.

munities means violence. Some views will trump others. Some groups will prevail over others, at least for some time. A search for harmony is no salvation. Nor, ultimately, is pure anarchy. Cover understood the need for some degree of order for plural communities to thrive. But order imposed by the state could exact too high a cost from those plural communities. We must acknowledge violence in the acts of judicial interpretation and we must also nurture the communities threatened by those acts: these are the themes recurring in Cover's articles. What could be a dark and even despairing view is rescued because Cover also offered glimpses of the possibility of redemption. He suggested ways to replace the known reality with a fundamentally different reality,[17] and the possibility of correction within the system if repeated challenges to its errors are heard and addressed.[18] Those glimpses included retellings of the abolition struggle that had been implicit in his *Justice Accused.* Yet Cover faced up to the fact that some of the particular visions and norms rejected by the state may themselves be at odds with his own notions of human equality and liberty.

In "Nomos and Narrative," Cover presented, without flinching, a legacy of the Civil War that ultimately freed not only the slaves but also the antislavery judges from their bondage. He examined continuing conflict over the significance of the Reconstruction amendments to the Constitution adopted to eliminate slavery.[19] And he considered the specific conflict of a white, fundamentalist Christian university, Bob Jones University, with the desegregation norm imposed by the national government.

The university had withdrawn its rule denying admission to any unmarried African-American person when the federal government threatened to revoke its favorable tax status. The university retained, however, its rule against interracial dating and marriage and against groups that advocate those practices. Cover attended to the danger of coercion of the university community by the state's antidiscrimination norm. He worried that his own evaluation of the views of Bob Jones University conflicted with his commitment to the flourish-

---

17. "Nomos and Narrative," 34–35.
18. See especially "The Uses of Jurisdictional Redundancy."
19. See Cover, *Justice Accused,* 17–18 (Americans share a national text in the amendments but not an authoritative narrative about their significance). Some might disagree by noting that native Americans do not even share the national text.

ing of minority communities. He believed that the activity of rendering the world a meaningful place by generating narratives and
norms requires space for groups of people gathered apart from the
state and bound to come into conflict with it.[20] For Cover, the state's
judges must continue to act on the basis of a "committed constitutionalism," but they must do so in a world in which each of many
communities also acts out of its committed beliefs and prepares to
resist the world imposed by the judges.[21]

Cover therefore elaborated a vision of group engagement with
the project of creating and nurturing norms regardless of state
approval. Especially when it comes to education of young people,
Cover celebrated autonomy for groups. For if a community cannot
choose how to constitute the world for its children, it cannot engage
in the enterprise of teaching its norms and its meanings.[22]

But should this autonomy be enjoyed by a community that
espouses a view of racial difference abhorred by a civil rights activist?
Should a white, segregationist community receive deference from a
scholar outraged by judges more than a century after they failed to
resist the fugitive slave law? Robert Cover, civil rights activist and
scholar, worked hard to present the situation of Bob Jones University
with sympathy, although he criticized its leaders for backing off and
not putting much on the line. He reserved his harshest criticism for
the Supreme Court justices who failed to venture commitment themselves, "to project their understanding of the law onto the future."[23]
The Court asserted a compelling governmental interest in eradicating
racial discrimination;[24] the Court shaped a narrative that pitted the
cause of racial justice against the religious community's claim of
insularity.[25] Racial justice won, but not as an assertion of constitutional command. The Court did not rule that the Constitution itself
forbade the kind of subordinating practices advanced by Bob Jones
University, but only that, since the Internal Revenue Service disap-
proved and Congress silently acquiesced, the community's practice
stood in the way of favorable tax status. Therefore, the justices failed,

20. Cover, *Justice Accused*, 28.
21. Cover, *Justice Accused*, 57 n. 158.
22. Cover, *Justice Accused*, 60–62.
23. Cover, *Justice Accused*, 67.
24. Cover, *Justice Accused*, 65.
25. Cover, *Justice Accused*, 65.

in Cover's view, to inscribe the narrative of redemption into law. Instead, they rested on political authority and jurisdictional superiority.[26] Because the state had adopted racial equality as a "public policy," the state could trump the insular community. This is a trump asserted by reference to rules and implemented by gestures to power; it shows no engagement with the vision of inclusion. It shows no honor to the insular communities. Instead, it threatens them with other invasions in the name of public policy.[27]

For Robert Cover, the state's norms are not necessarily superior.[28] Certainly, they are not superior simply because they are the state's. The backing of force and the power to suppress simply mean that the government's norms are capable of killing off the norms of other communities.[29] His criticism of judges who acted in both the nineteenth and twentieth centuries reveals his belief—his hope—that people within the legal system may, despite their roles and positions, themselves be engaged in normative activity. He predicted that resisters to the rules of the state are the ones who will generate normative advances; they will be less timid and also less invested in order and privilege.[30] At the same time, Cover warned against mistaking the romance of rebellion for normative vision; that would be as much a mistake as confusing state power with constitutional meaning.[31]

He pursued the consequences of these predictions and warnings in his next works. "The Folktales of Justice: Tales of Jurisdiction" speculated about the possibilities of justice pursued as resistance to the state or to extralegal violence enacted in the name of the state.[32] "Violence and the Word" baldly articulated the disturbing claims that

---

26. It is not clear how a pronouncement in a constitutional register but dependent on the force of the state would avoid the "jurispathic" effects of state law. Perhaps Cover would not be worried about that, and would argue that, at least, if posed in constitutional terms the normative clash could be debated while a mere declaration of public policy seems more like a preclusive assertion of *raison d'état*.

27. Cover, *Justice Accused*, 65–67.

28. Cover, *Justice Accused*, 30.

29. See also "Violence and the Word."

30. Cover, "Nomos and Narrative," 67–68.

31. Cover, *Justice Accused*; see also "The Folktales of Justice" (exploring what normative visions could be explored by judges who have no legal authority).

32. Exploring the same ground is Cover, "Bringing the Messiah Through the Law: A Case Study," 30 NOMOS: *Religion, Morality, and the Law* (R. Pennock and J. Chapman, eds., 1988) 201, which was published as an incomplete manuscript after his death.

legal interpretation by official judges occasions violence.[33] "Obligation: A Jewish Jurisprudence of the Social Order" elaborated the
concept of obligation as an organizing notion for law that contrasts
with the concept of rights so dominant in post-Enlightenment Western
secular societies. In so doing, he also shifted attention away from
what the state could or should assure to social solidarity founded on
mutual, reciprocal obligation. These three works, written just before
Cover's untimely death, convey his passionate, constructive vision
as well as his insistent examination of the tragedy and violence accompanying law. A self-proclaimed anarchist, Cover also loved the law;
an explorer of normative worlds beyond the government, Cover also
defended government force; a defender of rights, Cover also found
them limited compared to the solidarity of mutual obligation.

Cover would remind us that whatever our utopian visions, communities' beliefs will collide with one another and with the norms of
the government. Cover's work has only become more timely with the
breakup of the Soviet Union and the resurgence of national and ethnic
identities throughout the world. What structures of govrnment, what
political and economic theories will people now invoke for order?
Lawyers and law professors from the United States now consult with
groups around the world to devise constitutions and governing
schemes—a new export direct from this graying liberal democracy.
But what association among jurisdictions will work in Eastern Europe,
and for whom? Should a new version of lawful federalism remake
the relations between the Francophones and Anglophones in Canada,
or the communities in South Africa, Sri Lanka, or elsewhere? Robert
Cover warned us not to look at law per se but, instead, to an internal
sense of values honed by the constant awareness of violence. Coordination from this vantage point would be handled through "partly
principled, partly prudential rules of deference."[34]

Is there normative content or direction from this decidedly plu-
ralistic vision? Cover suggested that both principle and pragmatics
call for basic toleration of others, at least pending further struggles
to convert or dominate them.[35] No group, whether utopian com-

---

33. He explored the same themes with expanded attention to capital punishment
in an essay published after his death, "The Bonds of Constitutional Interpretation:
Of the Word, the Deed, and the Role," 20 *Georgia Law Review* 815 (1986).

34. Cover, "Nomos and Narrative," 30.

35. Compare, thus, the toleration of slavery by the Constitution and the resis-

munity or federal judges, can manage a total break from the legal understandings of other groups.[36] Whether through a principled commitment to tolerate others or a pragmatic commitment to survive, we who live in plural worlds must exhibit enough mutual respect at least to coexist. In so doing, we change one another.[37] Our efforts at mutual respect build a bridge between us and also between who we are and who we might become.

The image of a bridge appealed to Robert Cover. He used it to describe his chosen field of law: "Law may be viewed as a system of tension or a bridge linking a concept of reality to an imagined alternative."[38] He himself made a bridge. He connected the communal and the liberal, the religious and the secular, the moral and the legal. He inaugurated contemporary law school discussions of narrative and hermeneutics by reaching across time and space to the Talmudic discussions by people who never knew law could be separated from narrative and hermeneutics. Whether from principled deference to the contrasting parts of himself or pragmatic survival, Cover insisted that legal scholarship connect to the largest issues of spiritual and emotional meaning.

---

tance to it by the abolitionists. Cover treated, in both *Justice Accused* and "Nomos and Narrative," the contrast between Garrisonian abolitionists—who construed the Constitution to permit slavery and therefore renounced any obligation to it—and the radical constitutionalists who embraced a vision of the Constitution that forbade slavery and thus justified efforts to transform the world (see Cover, *Justice Accused*, 150–54; "Nomos and Narrative," 37–40).

36. Cover, "Nomos and Narrative," 33.

37. See Cover, "Nomos and Narrative," 30–31 (discussing the work of Carol Weisbrod exploring the interaction between Shaker and secular notions of contract). See, generally, James Clifford, *The Predicament of Culture* (Cambridge, Mass.: Harvard University Press, 1988) (cultures have mutual impact and constructed qualities rather than intrinsic and insular integrity).

38. Cover, "Nomos and Narrative," 9. There is a tension here with his view of the jurispathic dimensions of law and of its tendency to kill off competing normative visions. Cover was, however, no stranger to tensions of this sort and, indeed, placed paradox at the center of his own vision.

Chapter 1

The Origins of Judicial Activism
in the Protection of Minorities

I. Introduction: The Counter-majoritarian Difficulty

During the first third of the twentieth century, the Supreme Court
afforded constitutional protection to certain vaguely defined substantive interests that have since been loosely tied together under the label
of "substantive due process." Throughout that period, a rich and complex dissenting tradition was carried on first in the opinions of Holmes,
then Brandeis and, still later, Stone. That dissenting tradition—an
elaboration of the teachings of Professor James Thayer of Harvard
Law School—placed the majoritarian lawmaking process at the center
of constitutional theory. Judicial review was suspect insofar as it invalidated outcomes of this presumptively legitimate process.

The thrust of the Holmes, Brandeis, and Stone opinions was
largely negative at first. Though the three dissenters also attacked
the internal inconsistencies that any theory of substantive entitlements
will necessarily manifest, most often they emphasized the simple fact
that the Court was thwarting majoritarian mechanims of social
choice. Their delegitimation strategy revolved around the supposed
superiority of democratic—that is, legislative—choice mechanisms to
any judicially imposed theory of substantive rights.[1] Thus, they

This article is a slightly altered version of a paper presented at the American Enterprise
Institute Conference on the Role of the Judiciary, December 1979. Reprinted with
the permission of the American Enterprise Institute for Public Policy Research, Washington, D.C.

I wish to acknowledge a special debt to Louis Lusky, who taught me constitutional law fifteen years ago and first had me look through the lens of footnote
four. His fervor and commitment to the values of footnote four and his development
of its principles in his scholarship have been important guides to me and to others
through the years.

1. See, *e.g.*, Tyson & Brother v. Banton, 273 U.S. 418, 447 (1927) (Stone, J.,
dissenting); Truax v. Corrigan, 257 U.S. 312, 354 (1921) (Brandeis, J., dissenting);
Lochner v. New York, 198 U.S. 45, 74 (1905) (Holmes, J., dissenting).

attacked the exercise of judicial review with the blunt instrument that has become known as the "counter-majoritarian difficulty."[2]

In fact, none of the dissenters went so far in his opinion as to deny the due process clauses all substantive implications. Holmes and Brandeis went along with opinions striking down such "extreme" instances of state experimentation as the Kansas Industrial Court Act, which authorized compulsory arbitration not only for public utilities and transportation companies but for all industries relating to the production or distribution of food, clothing, shelter, and fuel.[3] And both joined the opinion in *Pierce v. Society of Sisters*[4] striking down Oregon's compulsory education law, which in effect outlawed private schools. Moreover, Holmes and Brandeis pioneered (in dissent) recognition of freedom of speech and of the press as liberties entitled to substantive protection under the due process clause of the fourteenth amendment.[5]

Nowhere in their opinions did the dissenters satisfactorily explain how even the limited substantive due process rights that they accepted could survive their own general attack with the heavy artillery of the counter-majoritarian difficulty. Indeed, some passages in the opinions of Justice Brandeis gave the impression that the dissenters' recognition of a limited role for substantive due process was tactical only and highly contingent. If there had to be a general doctrine of substantive entitlement under the due process clauses, Brandeis would have it protect free speech or education as more fundamental than the various property interests previously afforded protection.[6] His early attempts

---

2. The "counter-majoritarian difficulty" has spawned the central line of constitutional scholarship for the past thirty years. *See, e.g.,* A. BICKEL, THE LEAST DANGEROUS BRANCH (1962); C. BLACK, THE PEOPLE AND THE COURT (1960); L. HAND, THE BILL OF RIGHTS (1958); Wechsler, *Toward Neutral Principles of Constitutional Law,* 73 HARV. L. REV. 1 (1959). *But see* J. ELY, DEMOCRACY AND DISTRUST 43–72 (1980); L. TRIBE, AMERICAN CONSTITUTIONAL LAW (1978) (especially ch. 3).

3. Charles Wolff Packing Co. v. Court of Indus. Relations (I), 262 U.S. 522 (1922); Charles Wolff Packing Co. v. Court of Indus. Relations (II), 267 U.S. 552 (1925).

4. 268 U.S. 510 (1925). Holmes had dissented, however, in Meyer v. Nebraska, 262 U.S. 390 (1923) (holding unconstitutional state law proscribing teaching of German).

5. *See* Whitney v. California, 274 U.S. 357, 372 (1927) (Brandeis, J., concurring); Gitlow v. New York, 268 U.S. 652, 672 (1925) (Holmes, J., dissenting).

6. *See* Gilbert v. Minnesota, 254 U.S. 325, 334 (1926).

to extend substantive free speech protection against the states did not
resort to the methodology of substantive due process.[7]

The majoritarianism of Brandeis, Stone, and Holmes persisted
into the 1930s and lay at the heart of the New Deal critique of the
Court. Roosevelt's appointment of Hugo Black in 1937 established a
slim Court majority for majoritarianism. Where once it had been a
dissenting tradition, majoritarianism became more entrenched as a
dominant doctrine with each subsequent Roosevelt appointment.

But the doctrine proved more serviceable as a dissenting position
than as a reigning ideology. The Supreme Court must ultimately
justify the outcomes generated by polity and society, reconciling them
to the first principles of political structure. It must speak to those
questions that most urgently challenge the legitimacy of the social
and legal structure as a whole. And by the 1930s popular government
and the institutions of mass democracy had themselves become so
problematic that they could not, in and of themselves, serve to justify
outcomes that appeared intrinsically unjust. The manipulation of
mass politics had become for the twentieth century what "special
interest" politics had been for the age of the Robber Barons: a practical
and theoretical challenge to the sufficiency of popular government as
the governing constitutional principle.

If all or most substantive interests were to be subordinated to
the process principle of popular government, to majoritarianism, the
Court would have to explain how the virtues of popular government
were to triumph in the age that had seen the rise of bolshevism and
fascism, the orchestration of mass oppression of minorities, the cyn-
ical manipulations of elections, and the ascendancy of apparatus and
party over state and society. It was not that the dissenters of 1905–
1937 had failed to see these problems—although the problems had
become more obvious and pressing as the century advanced—but,
rather, that an idea can serve admirably as critique without being
even adequate as justification. Substantive due process applied to
economic regulation *was* properly subject to the criticism that it was
anti-democratic. But that did not mean that, in the age of Hitler,

---

7. Cover, *The Left, The Right and The First Amendment, 1918–1928*, 40 MD.
L. REV. 349, 377–81 (1981) (arguing that those attempts constitute highly original
and often misunderstood masterpieces).

majoritarianism itself would not require more in the way of justification than its professedly democratic nature.

II. Footnote Four and the Concept of Minorities

The terms of the modern debates on judicial activism were thus
spawned in the context of both the New Deal at home and totalitarianism abroad, emerging by 1937–38 in a decidedly contemporary
mode. It was then that the Court committed itself to the now familiar
dichotomy between the scope of review for economic legislation—a
nearly absolute majoritarianism—and that afforded legislation affecting a vague and dimly perceived set of other "personal" rights.[8] The
Court first articulated that dichotomy clearly in *United States v.
Carolene Products Co.*,[9] which upheld federal legislation that pro-

---

8. Almost simultaneously the Court conceded vast powers to Congress in economic matters, see *e.g.*, NLRB v. Jones & Laughlin Steel Corp., 301 U.S. 1 (1937),
while articulating several alternative theories by which judicial oversight of non-
economic personal rights would be retained. *Compare* Palko v. Connecticut, 302
U.S. 319, 324–25 (1937) (protecting rights deemed "implicit in the concept of ordered
liberty") *with* United States v. Carolene Prods. Co., 304 U.S. 144, 152 n.4 (1938).

9. 304 U.S. 144, 152–53 (1938). Cardozo's enunciation in *Palko* of rights "implicit
in the concept of ordered liberty" preceded footnote four, but did not speak to the
same issue of dichotomous review. The burden of *Palko* was to justify a different set
of distinctions: that among the varying treatments afforded different provisions in
the Bill of Rights when invoked against the states—that is, how to select for selective
incorporation. It is noteworthy that footnote four of *Carolene Products* does not
distinguish between review of state and federal legislation. The case itself, of course,
involved a federal statute; but the citations in footnote four involve, with one exception
(Farrington v. Tokushige, 273 U.S. 283 (1927), which invalidated a federal territorial
law), local statutes, regulations, and ordinances. Thus, while it is clear that footnote
four, as a method, cuts across state-federal lines, it might be supposed that the
"ordered liberty" notion of *Palko* is a method only for choosing among enumerated
rights those applicable against the states. The *Palko* idea is, however, susceptible to
being generalized in giving content to all relatively imprecise clauses in the Constitution, whether they be applied against state or federal legislation.

Although footnote four is the first, and, I believe, most convincing formulation
of the dichotomous standard for judicial review, it has not gone unchallenged. The
most direct attack upon the authority of the footnote is by Justice Frankfurter in his
concurring opinion in Kovacs v. Cooper, 336 U.S. 77, 89–92 (1949). Frankfurter, in
a single sentence that has about it the aura of the hysterical, makes three condemning
assertions: 1) a footnote is an inappropriate way to announce new doctrine; 2) it
did not purport to create new doctrine anyway; 3) and it did not have the concurrence
of a majority of the court. *Id.* at 90–91. Frankfurter's diatribe is contained within
an attack on a "preferred freedoms" approach to the First Amendment. Insofar as
his attack is premised on the idea that the doctrine "expresses a complicated process

hibited the shipment in interstate commerce of filled milk. After reiterating, with respect to economic matters,[10] the newly established deference to legislative judgments, Justice Stone gave us in footnote four the classic text that is the subject of this essay:

> There may be narrower scope for operation of the presumption of constitutionality when legislation appears on its face to be within a specific prohibition of the Constitution, such as those of the first ten Amendments, which are deemed equally specific when held to be embraced within the Fourteenth. See *Stromberg v. California*, 283 U.S. 359, 369–370; *Lovell v. Griffin*, 303 U.S. 444, 452.
>
> It is unnecessary to consider now whether legislation which restricts those political processes which can ordinarily be expected to bring about repeal of undesirable legislation, is to be subjected to more exacting judicial scrutiny under the general prohibitions of the Fourteenth Amendment than are most other types of legislation. On restrictions upon the right to vote, see *Nixon v. Herndon*, 273 U.S. 536; *Nixon v. Condon*, 286 U.S. 73; on restraints upon the dissemination of information, see *Near v. Minnesota ex rel. Olson*, 283 U.S. 697, 713–714, 718–720, 722; *Grosjean v. American Press Co.*, 297 U.S. 233; *Lovell v. Griffin, supra;* on interferences with political organizations, see *Stromberg v. California, supra*, 369; *Fiske v. Kansas*, 274 U.S. 380; *Whitney v. California*, 274 U.S. 357, 373–378; *Herndon v. Lowry*, 301 U.S. 242; and see Holmes, J., in *Gitlow v. New York*, 268 U.S. 652, 673; as to prohibition of peaceable assembly, see *De Jonge v. Oregon*, 299 U.S. 353, 365.
>
> Nor need we enquire whether similar considerations enter into the review of statutes directed at particular religious, *Pierce v. Society of Sisters*, 268 U.S. 510, or national, *Meyer v. Nebraska*, 262 U.S. 390; *Bartels v. Iowa*, 262 U.S. 404; *Farrington v.*

---

of constitutional adjudication by a deceptive formula," *id.* at 96, Frankfurter seems more on target with respect to the first paragraph of the footnote than with respect to paragraphs two and three.

10. The text of *Carolene Products* to which footnote four is appended affords judicial deference to "legislative facts," whether explicitly or implicitly found by the legislature. The presumption is that legislation rests upon "some rational basis within the knowledge or experience of the legislator." 304 U.S. at 152.

Tokushige, 273 U.S. 484 [*sic*]; or racial minorities, *Nixon v.
Herndon, supra; Nixon v. Condon, supra:* whether prejudice
against discrete and insular minorities may be a special condition,
which tends seriously to curtail the operation of those political
processes ordinarily to be relied upon to protect minorities, and
which may call for a correspondingly more searching judicial
inquiry. Compare *McCulloch v. Maryland*, 4 Wheat. 316, 428;
South Carolina v. Barnwell Bros., 303 U.S. 177, 184, n. 2, and
cases cited.[11]

Footnote four combined a textual and a functional justification
for the differing standards of review. The textual touchstone in the
first paragraph—apparently added by Chief Justice Hughes to the
clearer, purely functional justification in the original Stone draft[12]—
requires a more rigorous standard of scrutiny for rights specifically
enumerated or mentioned in the Constitution.[13]

The functional justifications in the second and third paragraphs
of the footnote accept the general terms of the counter-majoritarian
difficulty, extending the scope of judicial review not in terms of the
special *value* of certain rights[14] but in terms of their *vulnerability* to

11. *Id.* at 152–3.
12. For a good account of the authorship of footnote four, see A. MASON,
HARLAN FISKE STONE, PILLAR OF THE LAW 513–15 (1956). The authorship in the first
instance of paragraphs two and three of the footnote is usually attributed to Louis
Lusky, Stone's clerk in 1938. Professor Lusky has never denied that authorship, but
has qualified it by insisting upon the fact that whatever the Justice accepted as a part
of an opinion must be regarded as his own. *Id.* at 513. That Stone knowingly embraced
footnote four is evidenced by the fact that he, more than any other justice, used it
as authority in later cases. Moreover, he used it sensitively to designate its implicit
structural values, not as a simple citation for a "preferred freedoms" doctrine. *See,
e.g.*, Skinner v. Oklahoma *ex rel.* Williamson, 316 U.S. 535, 544 (1942) (Stone, J.,
concurring); Minersville School Dist. v. Gobitis, 310 U.S. 586, 606 (1940) (Stone, J.,
dissenting). Only Justice Murphy approached Justice Stone in his use of the footnote
as authority. As this article went to press, Professor Lusky published a new and
important article that treats the history and meaning of the footnote. *See* Lusky,
Footnote Redux: A Carolene Products Reminiscence, 82 COLUM. L. REV. 1093 (1982).
13. This approach, which would later form the basis of Justice Black's jurisprudence, has, to be sure, its functional justifications at a different and perhaps deeper
level; but the justifications for textualism (or interpretivism) are not part of textualism's
methodology. *See* J. ELY, *supra* note 2, at 1–41, for a sensitive discussion of the basis
of what he labels the interpretivist approach. Ely, quite rightly, sees paragraphs two
and three of the *Carolene Products* footnote as complementing paragraph one. J. ELY,
supra note 2, at 76 ("[T]he objection to interpretivism is that it is incomplete.")
14. These paragraphs do, of course, designate certain rights or types of rights

perversions by the majoritarian process. They do not require that one accept on any authority the privileged character of any specific interest. Rather, paragraphs two and three offer a justification that is entirely responsive to the political theory premises of the counter-majoritarian difficulty itself.

A. Paragraph Two: Protecting the Vitality of the Political Process

The second paragraph suggests that "legislation which restricts those political processes which can ordinarily be expected to bring about repeal of undesirable legislation" should be subject to "more exacting judicial scrutiny." In other words, the footnote acknowledges that those representatives enjoying office, its power, and its perquisites may con-

---

as occupying a "preferred" position in claims for judicial protection. But citation of the footnote for a "preferred freedoms" doctrine engenders the confusion Stone was trying to avoid. There is a vast conceptual gulf between saying that the Court is charged with protecting whatever interests and rights are more valuable, precious, or important in some ultimate ethical sense and saying that the court is charged with protecting interests and rights that entail predictable perversions of majoritarian government. The first position rests conceptually on a distrust of democratic choices, on a willingness to reverse them if they are too wrong. The second position rests upon the premise that the mechanisms of government may pervert and destroy the substance of democractic choices in predictable ways.

Though the conceptual bases of these positions are quite different, the practical results may often converge. As a result, practical people may choose to pursue their ends with both theories, interchanging them as they see fit for rhetorical purposes. Footnote four has frequently been cited for a "preferred freedoms" position, and Justice Frankfurter attacked it as such. See Kovacs v. Cooper, 336 U.S. 77, 90-92 (1949); *see also supra* note 8. Stone's identification with a "preferred freedoms" position can most plausibly be related to his dissenting opinion in Jones v. Opelika, 316 U.S. 584, 608 (1942) ("The First Amendment is not confined to safeguarding freedom of speech and freedom of religion against discriminatory attempts to wipe them out. On the contrary, the Constitution . . . has put those freedoms in a preferred position.") But Frankfurter mentions this dissent only in passing, *see* 336 U.S. at 93, although he concedes that it is the place where the adjective "preferred" is first used in this context. The point Stone is making in the *Jones* dissent—that the First Amendment must be read as creating a certain space free of regulation of speech and religion, even if the regulation is not specifically and discriminatorily directed at speech or religion—seems defensible. It is consistent with footnote four's functional justification for judicial enforcement of the freedom of the public political space. What is essential in footnote four is not that certain rights are designated "preferred" but the reasons for the preference. Here, of course, paragraph one gives a textual justification and rests on a different basis from paragraphs two and three. For the idea that paragraphs two and three do not rest on a single consistent foundation, see *infra* pp. 1310-12.

spire to entrench themselves and to defeat the very majoritarian processes that render the acts of legislatures presumptively more legitimate
than the acts of judges. The footnote gives as examples of such legislation restrictions on voting rights, on dissemination of information,
on political organization, and on peaceable assembly. The premise of
the paragraph seems to be that a politically free citizenry and honest,
suitable mechanisms for transforming public politics into governmental
action are prerequisites for majoritarian choice.[15]

In contemporary terms—and given the hindsight of forty years—
I would paraphrase the danger: incumbency may degenerate into
"apparatus," manipulating the formal machinery of choice in elections,
districting, and control of public benefits. We also fear that the political
society will degenerate into the party, circumscribing the space for
free, unconstrained public politics and allowing no "natural" political
life, antecedent and superior to the party and the state, to survive.

The footnote suggests that these dangers must be met from two
angles. First, the incumbents must not be permitted to manipulate
or to control unchecked the machinery that links public choices to
representation. For if they could, even wholesome public politics
would not avail. Second, the incumbents must not be permitted to
orchestrate public choice. The space for politics in the Greek sense
must be ample and unencumbered. For were the party able to orchestrate mass politics, even honest elections would not avail.[16]

I believe paragraph two of the footnote captures, in a marvelously
concise sentence with a few suggestive citations, the lesson of twentieth century perversions of the majoritarian forms of politics. In
1938 it was, of course, no wonder that such perversions attracted
attention.[17] The footnote neatly captures the concern both for devel-

---

15. The unsavory character of political bossism was occupying the Court more
and more in the late 1930s as private individuals, unions, and the federal government
began to seek ways to challenge the structure of local and state fiefdoms. *See, e.g.,*
United States v. Classic, 313 U.S. 299 (1941); Hague v. CIO, 307 U.S. 496 (1939).

16. For a contemporaneous treatment of legal problems associated with total-
itarian techniques in the orchestration of politics, see, e.g., Riesman, *Democracy and
Defamation: Control of Group Libel,* 42 COLUM. L. REV. 727 (1942); Riesman, *Democ-
racy and Defamation: Fair Game and Fair Comment* (pts. 1 & 2), 42 COLUM. L.
REV. 1085, 1282 (1942); *see also* Lusky, *Minority Rights and the Public Interest,* 52
YALE L.J. 1, 32–38 (1942).

17. In his exhaustive biography of Justice Stone, Alpheus Thomas Mason quotes
a letter written by Stone and dated the day after *Carolene Products* came down:
I have been deeply concerned about the increasing racial and religious intolerance

oping totalitarianism abroad and for the less virulent but more immediate perversions of democracy at home.

B. Paragraph Three: Protecting Minorities

While paragraph two concerns itself with the question of perversion
of democratic forms, paragraph three concerns itself with the limits
of permissible democratic purposes. Minorities, in the sense of that
paragraph and in the sense we use the term today—religious, ethnic,
national, and racial minorities—became a special object of judicial
protection only with footnote four, which was written at almost the
exact moment when majoritarianism became the dominant constitutional perspective.[18]

Many constitutional sources from before 1938 speak of judicial
protection of minorities. But they use the phrase in an obviously
different sense: to refer to losing factions in political struggles[19] or,

---

which seems to bedevil the world, and which I greatly fear may be augmented
in this country. For that reason I was greatly disturbed by the attacks on the
Court and the Constitution last year, for one consequence of the program of
'judicial reform' might well result in breaking down the guaranties of individual
liberty.

A. MASON, *supra* note 12, at 515 (quoting letter from Stone to Judge Irving Lehman,
April 26, 1938).

Moreover, some of the defenders of the Supreme Court in the court-packing
fight of 1937 had strongly linked the objective of maintaining the independence of
the judiciary from political retaliation to the struggle against totalitarianism. At least
one prominent witness at the Senate Judiciary Committee hearings on the court-
packing legislation had raised the experience of Nazi Germany and fascist Italy as
cautionary spectres for those considering Roosevelt's scheme for the discipline of the
Court. Dorothy Thompson, renowned columnist and journalist, testified in part as
follows:

I am not an expert on constitutional law, . . . I have been for some years, as a
foreign correspondent, an observer at the collapse of constitutional democracies.
You might say I have been a researcher into the mortality of republics. The
outstanding fact of our times is the decline and fall of constitutional democracy.
A great need of our time is for more accurate analysis of the pathology of
constitutional government. . . .

*Reorganization of the Federal Judiciary: Hearings before the Comm. on the Judiciary
of the United States Senate on S. 1391,* 75th Cong., 1st Sess. 859 (1937).

18. I have chosen to consider footnote four as the watershed. Obviously, the
choice is not written in stone. The justification appears within.

19. Madison thought that the tyranny of the majority would be most likely to
occur at the local and state level. He was not sanguine about the possibility of
effective judicial protection against such a "tyranny" and advocated the more radical

more importantly, to broad sectional or economic interests that may
be at a majoritarian political disadvantage.[20] In this latter sense the
term was current coin among the Framers. One of their solutions to
this "minority" problem was judicial review. We also find cases prior
to 1938 that do in fact extend judicial protection to minority groups
in our sense of the word.[21] But these cases present no theory that it
is this characteristic of the group—its "minorityness"—that requires
special judical solicitude. They justify constitutional protection by
the substantive character of the rights involved rather than by the
nature of the groups protected.[22]

---

measure of a congressional "negative" on state legislation. *See* 10 THE PAPERS OF
JAMES MADISON 206–19 (1840) (letter from James Madison to Thomas Jefferson, October 24, 1787). The problem of protecting the public interest, individuals, and minorities (in a most general sense) from a majority faction preoccupied Madison. His
classic essay on the subject, THE FEDERALIST No. 10, characteristically relies upon the
enlargement of the political space as the major counterforce to majority tyranny. In
effect, Madison argues that appeal to a sufficiently large and heterogeneous political
constituency makes it unlikely that the forces of passion and interest will prevail.
For a now classic critique of this argument, see R. DAHL, A PREFACE TO DEMOCRATIC
THEORY 128–29 (1956). *See also* G. WILLS, EXPLAINING AMERICA xv–xxi, 208–215
(1981).

    20. Madison saw economic interests as the primary determinants of "faction."
From the protection of different and unequal faculties of acquiring property,
the possession of different degrees and kinds of property immediately results;
and from the influence of these on the sentiments and views of the respective
proprietors, ensues a division of the society into different interests and parties.
    . . . But the most common and durable source of factions, has been the various
and unequal distribution of property.
THE FEDERALIST No. 10, at 131 (J. Madison) (B. Wright ed. 1961). Note the depth
of the point Madison makes: property not only is itself an interest over which groups
struggle, but also is an "influence" on the "sentiments and views" of its holders.
    The critical place of property in giving rise to "factions" is compounded in our
constitutional history by the identification of certain kinds of property interests with
certain sections of the nation. The South has always been identified with slave
property, and the Northeast with mercantile and shipping interests. For consideration
of the structural protection of such "minority" interests in a national scheme, see
S. LYND, CLASS CONFLICT, SLAVERY, AND THE UNITED STATES CONSTITUTION (1967)
(especially chs. 7, 8, & 10).

    21. *See, e.g.*, Nixon v. Herndon, 273 U.S. 536 (1927) (striking down state statute
requiring white primary); Pierce v. Society of Sisters, 268 U.S. 510 (1925) (invalidating
Oregon statute requiring children to attend public schools); Buchanan v. Warley, 245
U.S. 60 (1917) (invalidating city ordinance requiring, in effect, residential segregation);
Guinn v. United States, 238 U.S. 347 (1915) (striking down grandfather clauses).

    22. Some of the cases prior to 1938—Pierce v. Society of Sisters, 268 U.S. 510
(1925), and Buchanan v. Warley, 245 U.S. 60 (1917), for example—were substantive
due process cases protecting rights held by any and all individuals from a form of

Perhaps this generalization needs to be qualified with a word concerning the earlier understanding of the Reconstruction Amendments. The *Slaughter House Cases*, to prevent the fourteenth amendment from being a comprehensive source of rights against the state, made use of the common knowledge that the Amendments were designed to ameliorate the condition of Blacks.[23]

This view of constitutional law and history did perceive Negroes as a special object of protection.[24] Had the pattern of decisions over the ensuing fifty years taken a very different turn from its actual course, this assertion, from which there has never been real dissent, might have proven the starting point for articulating a special judicial role in protecting minorities, or at least in protecting the most important minority in American experience. But an observation about the purpose of a constitutional text is not in terms a theory about the role of the judiciary. And the massive retreat from protecting Black rights between the 1870s and the 1920s—a retreat led by the Court in many instances—eliminated any chance of inferring such a role from practice.[25] Thus, the explicit articulation of a special judicial

---

prohibited state interference. It just happened in each case that the probable motive or precipitating factor for the interference was a scheme of persecution against a "minority group." Strictly speaking, in each case that fact was legally irrelevant. Indeed, *Pierce's* companion case, Pierce v. Military Academy, 268 U.S. 510 (1925), involved no element of a "minority group," though the claim presented was otherwise in all respects identical to that of the Society of Sisters.

In *Buchanan*, the racial character of the zoning did have a plausible relevance to the case, but in a direction precisely opposite to what would be expected under modern equal protection law. For the state contended, in effect, that its affirmative interests in segregation of the races under its police power justified a restriction on property alienation and use that would normally constitute an infringement of due process rights.

23. Slaughter House Cases, 83 U.S. (16 Wall.) 36, 81 (1872) ("The existence of laws in the States where the newly emancipated negroes [*sic*] resided, which discriminated with gross injustice and hardship against them as a class, was the evil to be remedied by this [equal protection] clause, and by it such laws are forbidden.")

24.
It [the 14th Amendment] was designed to assure to the colored race the enjoyment of all the civil rights that under the law are enjoyed by white persons, and to give to that race the protection of the general government, in that enjoyment, whenever it should be denied by the States. . . .
Id.

25. A brief, useful narrative of all the important cases on race and civil rights may be found in L. MILLER, THE PETITIONERS (1966). For the period of massive retreat, see, especially, chapters 11–13. The most important legal history of the race cases in the progressive period to appear in some time is the excellent recent work of Benno

role with respect to minorities and their rights awaited the constitutional reconstruction of 1937–38.

Paragraph three of the footnote rescued that lost opportunity by
identifying discrimination against racial minorities as a characteristic
vice of majoritarianism in the twentieth century. The paragraph purported to address the most serious of "imperfections" in majoritarian
politics—"imperfections" that were highlighted in 1938.

"Discrete and insular" minorities are not simply losers in the
political arena, they are perpetual losers. Indeed, to say that they lose
in the majoritarian political process is seriously to distort the facts:
they are scapegoats in the real political struggles between other groups.
Moreover, in their "insularity" such groups may be characteristically
helpless, passive victims of the political process. It is, therefore, because of the discreteness and insularity of certain minorities (objects
of prejudice) that we cannot trust "the operation of those political
processes ordinarily to be relied upon to protect minorities." A more
searching judicial scrutiny is thus superimposed upon the structural
protections against "factions" relied on by the original Constitution—
the diffusion of political power and checks and balances.[26]

If anything, paragraph three, coming as it did just before the
worst excesses of organized racism were to burst upon the world,
somewhat understated the significance of racism in majoritarian politics.[27] While it clearly expressed the risks in relying upon majoritarian

Schmidt, Jr. See Schmidt, *Principle and Prejudice: The Supreme Court and Race in
the Progressive Era* (pts. 1–3), 82 COLUM. L. REV. 444 (1982), 82 COLUM. L. REV.
646 (1982), 82 COLUM. L. REV. 835 (1982).

26. The Court did not develop the reasons for considering racial, religious, or
ethnic minorities to be different from other minorities. But those reasons have been
elaborated somewhat by such thoughtful and, in a sense authoritative, *see supra* p.
1291 interpreters of footnote four as Professor Louis Lusky. As Lusky stated in the
earliest of his publications on the minorities problem:

> The minorities problem springs from the existence of fairly well defined 'out-
> groups' disliked by those who control the political and other organs of power
> in society. Such dislike arises not because the members of the groups have done
> or threatened acts harmful to the community, but because membership in the
> group is itself considered a cause for distrust or even hostility.

Lusky, *supra* note 16, at 2. Lusky later emphasized what he called kinship as the
necessary element in making representative government work: the absence of empathy
as to certain groups removes the element of self-restraint and fair dealing in pursuing
majoritarian interests. *See* L. LUSKY, By What Right? 12 (1975).

27. Decided on April 24, 1938, *Carolene Products* preceded the Krystalnacht
by seven months.

politics to preserve a minority's rights, it did not allude to the distorted shadows that the organized scapegoating of minorities cast upon other elements of politics. In this sense, the concerns of paragraphs two and three of the footnote converge. For organized baiting of minorities has been one of the levers for manipulating masses since the advent of modern politics. It represents, thus, a failure of politics not only in the nonprotection of the victim group, but also in the deflection and perversion of other public purposes. There are ways to block a message besides arresting the speaker, and one of them is to cry nigger.[28]

In effect, therefore, footnote four suggests two reasons for judicial protection of minorities. The clearest reason is contained in paragraph three: a discrete and insular minority cannot expect majoritarian politics to protect its members as it protects others. Less clearly stated is the additional argument of paragraph two that prejudice and race hatred are also levers of manipulation in the mass political arena.

---

28. By the late 1930s, a literature on the methods of contemporary tyrannies had developed that stressed "hate-mongering" as a typical lever for manipulation of the masses. This interest grew through the war years and became the subject of massive social science research through the 1940s and early 1950s. For important work in the legal literature on this subject, see Loewenstein, *Legislative Control of Political Extremism in European Democracies* (pts. 1 & 2), 38 COLUM. L. REV. 591, 725 (1938); Loewenstein, *Militant Democracy and Fundamental Rights* (pts. 1 & 2), 31 AM. POL. SCI. REV. 417, 638 (1937); Riesman, *Democracy and Defamation: Fair Game and Fair Comment* (pts. 1 & 2), *supra* note 16, at 1085, 1282.

Whether systematic hate campaigns against minorities are part of a common political phenomenon that can be labeled "totalitarianism" remains a subject of controversy among theorists. For an overview of the "totalitarianism" debate, compare H. ARENDT, THE ORIGINS OF TOTALITARIANISM (1966) (totalitarianism is a distinct form of government, politics, and social organization that cuts across "Left" and "Right") with A. MAYER, DYNAMICS OF COUNTERREVOLUTION IN EUROPE 1870–1956 (1971) (asserting that the concept of "totalitarianism" permitted Western liberal intellectuals to *obscure* the dynamics of and differences between revolution and counterrevolution).

The notion that race hatred could be manipulated to deflect constructive political change is a persistent theme in the history of the American South. *See, e.g.,* W. CASH, THE MIND OF THE SOUTH (1941); H. HELPER, THE IMPENDING CRISIS (1857); V. KEY, SOUTHERN POLITICS IN STATE AND NATION (1949); L. SMITH, KILLERS OF THE DREAM (1963); C. VANN WOODWARD, THE STRANGE CAREER OF JIM CROW (1974). The history of Southern populism is replete with observations of the deflection of innovation via a quite conscious, manipulated reversion to racism to incite the white masses and prevent a political coalition of Blacks and Whites from advancing to power. *See* L. GOODWYN, DEMOCRATIC PROMISE, THE POPULIST MOVEMENT IN AMERICA 276–306, 533–34 (1976); C. VANN WOODWARD, *supra*, at 78.

III. Majoritarian Politics and the "Minorities Problem"

Further analysis of the significance of the Court's pronouncement of judicial protection for minorities must await a brief consideration of the origins of the term "minorities" itself. For that history suggests a proper understanding of the theory behind and the problems within the footnote.

A. The Theory of Minorities

No important innovation is without antecedents. In the case of this new use of the term "minorities," the antecedents were so pervasive as to make the novelty barely perceptible. First, beginning in the nineteenth century and proliferating after the peace settlement at Versailles, treaties and conventions invoked the idea of international "protection of minorities" from the domestic political processes of certain nations.[29] The term "minorities" was used in these international agreements to include "racial, linguistic or religious minorities."[30] Moreover, this concern for protecting minorities carried with it an increasing recognition of a need for judicial protection. As Julius Stone wrote in 1932: "It was in the jurisdiction given [under the League of Nations scheme] to the Permanent Court of International Justice that there appeared the only completely new contribution of the postwar settlement to the machinery of minorities protection."[31] Thus, by the 1930s, "minorities" in the footnote four sense was already an accepted term of art with a recognized technical meaning in international law. Furthermore, the premise for this international protection was that the nation-state, ordinarily dominated by a single racial, religious, or ethnic group, might fail to afford the benefits of its

---

29. For brief accounts of the histories of such treaties, see, e.g., L. MAIR, THE PROTECTION OF MINORITIES 30–36 (1928); J. STONE, INTERNATIONAL GUARANTEES OF MINORITY RIGHTS 3–31 (1934). For a comprehensive account of the minorities treaties, see C. MACARTNEY, NATIONAL STATES AND NATIONAL MINORITIES (1934); for an interesting hypothesis concerning the ideological and political context for such treaties, see H. ARENDT, supra note 28, at 269–290.

30. "The country concerned agrees that the stipulations in the foregoing articles, so far as they affect persons belonging to racial, linguistic or religious minorities, constitute obligations of international law. . . ." J. STONE, supra note 29, at 273 (quoting League of Nations Council Resolution of Oct. 22, 1920).

31. Id. at 8.

political processes to the racial, religious, or ethnic minorities within the state. The international law system thus tacitly acknowledged that the twentieth-century nation-state was characteristically built upon the consolidation of a particular racial or ethnic group's political hegemony over a territory that included a mixed population.[32]

Second, the term "minority" had also assumed legal and institutional significance in a purely domestic context. The massive increase of federally administered programs during the New Deal required specific attention to the reciprocal impact between these programs and various racial patterns in different parts of the nation. In some programs, such as the Civilian Conservation Corps, federal administration acquiesced to racist local patterns.[33] In other programs, such as the National Youth Administration, a persistent effort was made to influence localities in the direction of equal treatment.[34]

The significant element in both the international law antecedent and the New Deal experience was the conceptualization of a *"minorities* problem" that cut across the contingent experiences of any particular minority group. The denomination of a "Jewish problem," a "Negro problem," or an "Indian problem" suggests that the "problem" is peculiar to the group's history, beliefs, or actions as they intersect with the history, beliefs, and actions of others. To generalize to a "minorities problem" suggests the *irrelevance* (or subordinate character) of any group's particular experience. All minority groups are deemed to have a common element of dominating significance, observable in social structure and social process as they affect politics.

---

32. More precisely, the break-up of the Turkish, Austro-Hungarian, and Russian Empires forced the European nation-state system to confront directly the question avoided through much of the nineteenth-century state-building: what relation does the nation bear to the state. Versailles' purposeful creation, at a stroke, of new states, the demand that these states be of a viable size, and the conflicting claims to hegemony all made it quite impossible to ignore the imperfect fit of population and territorial dominance. While it would be absurd to suggest that such "imperfections" were not noticed in the consolidations of Germany and Italy, they were renewed and accentuated in the process of drawing lines on a map at Versailles.

33. An Office of Minority Affairs was set up in the National Youth Administration under Mary McLeod Bethune. *See* G. Rawick, The New Deal and Youth: The Civilian Conservation Corps, the National Youth Administration and the American Youth Congress 137–170 (1957) (unpublished Ph.D. dissertation, University of Wisconsin); *see also* Salmond, *The Civilian Conservation Corps and the Negro,* in The Negro in Depression and War 78–92 (B. Sternsher ed. 1969).

34. *See* Bethune, *My Secret Talks with FDR,* in The Negro in Depression and War, *supra* note 33, at 53–65.

All groups that are minorities in the footnote four sense—and in the sense of the international law guarantees protecting minorities—share certain characteristics: they are isolated in the social structure; they occupy positions relatively resistant to change (in particular, resistant to the solvent of shifting interest alignments); and they are vulnerable to attack by others. The belief that there is a similarity or identity of social and psychological processes and structures at work in the otherwise widely different historical experiences of Jews, Blacks, Indians, ethnics (and perhaps women) represents a great intellectual step associated with twentieth-century theories of sociology and social psychology.[35] It is also a step of dubious validity.

Prior to footnote four our constitutional categories were historically determined. The Constitution clearly creates historically specific, contingent categories, such as "religions," and does not speak at all in the psychological or sociological terms of "prejudice" or "outgroups." There were free exercise and non-establishment rights of religious minorities because of the actual historical experiences of a particular set or group.

One might, therefore, imagine an innovator in constitutional law arguing as follows in 1938: The developing sociological perspective on intergroup relations and the rapidly developing inquiries into the social-psychological processes of "prejudice" support the view that a single phenomenon or family of phenomena is involved in prejudice against "minorities," whatever the particular history of a given group. It would be irrational to attempt to deal with these common phenomena, with their common structural implications for politics, solely by means of a set of divergent constitutional phrases that were shaped, in a less scientific age, to meet specific, purely contingent instances of prejudice.[36]

---

35. One of the most frequently cited sociological articles on "minorities" is Wirth, *The Problem of Minority Groups*, in The Science of Man in the World Crisis (R. Linton ed. 1945). Wirth defines a minority "as a group of people who, because of their physical or cultural characteristics, are singled out from the others in the society in which they live for differential and unequal treatment, and who therefore regard themselves as objects of collective discrimination." *Id.* at 347. For a brief account of the development of a set of related ideas that have been important in analyzing "minorities," see R. Merton, Social Theory and Social Structure chs. 8 & 9 (rev. ed. 1957).

36. Presumably, without a concept of "minorities" the treatment of a religious minority would be governed by the particular jurisprudence of the free exercise and

B. The Special Problem of Racial Politics

Whether Justice Stone had such an articulated view I do not know. His language (or that of Lusky[37]) in any event held these ideas implicit within it. For it is, otherwise, a peculiar notion indeed to suppose that the various situations alluded to by the citations in paragraph three of footnote four support a common response to related problems. In fact, as the next section of this essay suggests, the problems alluded to were sufficiently distinct in their implications to raise very different questions about the propriety of an active judicial role. Put simply, footnote four's paradigm of judicial intervention to avert the political products of prejudice easily accommodated the limited judicial interventions necessary to protect ethnic and religious groups from the legislative excesses associated with xenophobic hysteria or intolerance. But it could not answer the questions about the judicial role presented by the system of American Racial Apartheid—which was, indeed, a *system*.[38] Indeed, the questions associated with the Black experience in America raised, as no others could, the spectre of an internal conflict between the values of a free and open political life, protected by paragraph two of footnote four, and of fair treatment of "minorities," protected by paragraph three.[39]

---

establishment clauses; the treatment of immigrant and alien groups would be subject to the jurisprudence governing national powers over commerce, migration, and naturalization; and the treatment of Blacks would be governed by the jurisprudence of the Reconstruction Amendments. Of course, all such groups would be protected by such general clauses as due process and equal protection, but only in the same sense and to the same degree as everyone else. They would have no special position as "minorities."

37. In 1942 Lusky referred to "out-groups," though without reference to any specific sociological theory. Lusky, *supra* note 16, at 2. The dichotomous characterization of reference groups implicit in the in-group/out-group terminology is generally traced back to the we-groups/other-groups dichotomy of William Graham Sumner. W. SUMNER, FOLKWAYS 12–13 (1906); *see* R. MERTON, *supra* note 35, at 297. By the time Lusky wrote, of course, the idea and terminology were deeply embedded in the common intellectual culture. I am not suggesting that either Lusky or Stone was applying a specific sociological theory in footnote four, only that the generalization "minority group" as used there and as used previously in international law coincided with a sociological way of thinking about such problems.

38. For the classic presentation of the systematic character of American Apartheid, see G. MYRDAL, AN AMERICAN DILEMMA (1st ed. 1944). The date of the book makes it a particularly valuable source of observations of the system's operation made at roughly the same time as footnote four.

39. *See infra* pp. 1309–13.

Consider for a moment the extraordinary differences between the kinds of cases cited in paragraph three. All, apparently, involve "minorities" that are subsumed within the intent of the footnote. The note cites *Nixon v. Herndon*[40] and *Nixon v. Condon*,[41] two white primary cases, for the proposition that racial minorities may claim special judicial protection. Among the cases cited in the note, only these two involve massive political oppression against the minority. In other cases cited minorities are treated shabbily and may not, as the footnote suggests, be strong enough to defend themselves in the political arena. But here such a result is not left to chance. The suspect law denies to the minority access to the political arena itself. Thus, these two white primary cases are appropriately cited in both paragraphs two and three of the footnote.

It is not coincidental that these disenfranchisement cases involved Blacks. In modern America disenfranchisement has largely been confined to *racial* minorities.[42] Conversely, oppression of religious minorities (exemplified by *Pierce v. Society of Sisters*)[43] and of national minorities (exemplified by *Meyer v. Nebraska*,[44] *Bartels v. Iowa*,[45] and *Farrington v. Tokushige*),[46] though involving obnoxious, forced assimilation via the state's control over education and unseemly xenophobic

---

40. 273 U.S. 536 (1927).

41. 286 U.S. 73 (1932).

42. The mechanism used to disenfranchise orientals was denial of naturalization, which survived challenge throughout the relevant period of large-scale oriental immigration and attendant strong local prejudice.

I fear I am treading on dangerous ground with the statement in the text. Of course, in our early history many of the states relied upon property qualifications to restrict the franchise; for over a century, however, such devices have not been significant. More important, the franchise for women was not federally guaranteed until 1920. Whether or how women should be thought of as a "minority" group is a question I simply cannot attempt to answer within the scope of this essay. There is no indication that Stone intended to include women within the ambit of footnote four. Since I am arguing in part that constitutional responses ought to be somewhat more sensitive to the particular histories and contexts of the experiences of each group, and that the catch-all "minority" is not only an imprecise category but unworkably general as a guide for action with respect to those cases that clearly come within it, I am not troubled by having to treat the category "women" on its own terms and with respect to its particular history.

43. 268 U.S. 510 (1925).

44. 262 U.S. 390 (1923).

45. 262 U.S. 404 (1923).

46. 273 U.S. 284 (1927).

reactions to the disfavored foreigner and to his culture,[47] have not included exclusion from the political arena.

If we are to distinguish the laws burdening Catholics, such as those in *Pierce*, or those burdening German-Americans, in *Meyer*, from the regulations burdening bond-holders, creditors, and so on, it is only because the interest trod upon is more vital, authentic, or important in the one than in the other. For the cleavages between Catholic and non-Catholic, German ethnic and non-German have proven resistant to the solvent of self-interest only locally or in the short run. Catholics, for example, have almost always prevailed through political processes, to a degree acceptable to themselves, on this issue of public controls over parochial education. The courts have had little to do with it; *Pierce* itself came after many of the major political battles were over.[48] It is quite appropriate, therefore, to think

47. For a consideration of the struggle between native and immigrant groups over control of education, see D. RAVATCH, THE GREAT NEW YORK SCHOOL WARS (1975). For a sense of the importance of control over private and parochial education, see B. SOLOMON, ANCESTORS AND IMMIGRANTS ch. 3 (1956); *see also* J. HIGHAM, STRANGERS IN THE LAND 59–60, ch. 9 (2d ed. 1963) (describing struggle over education in 1880s, early 1900s). For an interesting contemporaneous account, see E. MEAD, THE ROMAN CATHOLIC CHURCH AND THE PUBLIC SCHOOLS (1890). For modern account stressing the assimilationist objectives of the kindergarten movement, see M. LAZERSON, ORIGINS OF THE URBAN SCHOOL: PUBLIC EDUCATION IN MASSACHUSETTS, 1870–1915 (1971). For an excellent, finely nuanced account of ethnicity and politics in the Midwest that includes attention to the problem of foreign language instruction, see P. KLEPPNER, THE CROSS OF CULTURE: A SOCIAL ANALYSIS OF MIDWESTERN POLITICS 1850–1900, at 158–61 (1970). For a good account of one extensive controversy that never reached the Supreme Court, see R. Ulrich, The Bennett Law of 1889: Education and Politics in Wisconsin (1965) (unpublished Ph.D. dissertation, University of Wisconsin).

48. Anti-Catholic feeling remained high in much of the Midwest and South throughout the 1920s, as the Smith campaign of 1928 indicated. But a prevalent pattern of relatively loose controls over parochial education had been established in the 1880s and 1890s, when the great expansion of parochial education took place. The revived Ku Klux Klan led a campaign against parochial schools in the 1920s. The Klan's single success in this campaign came in Oregon. There the outlawing of private schools was accomplished by direct democracy—an initiative that won a narrow victory after a vicious campaign.

Foreign-language instruction was another matter. There were two very distinct periods of effort to stop or limit the spread of foreign-language instruction; in both instances German was the primary target. In the late 1880s and early 1890s some midwestern states were concerned with the phenomenon of German Lutheran schools, and legislation was passed to outlaw or restrict the use of German as the principal language of instruction. *See* P. KLEPPNER, *supra* note 47, at 158; R. Ulrich, *supra*

in this context of judicial intervention as a limited adjunct to a political process that usually works.

If one asks why the political process has served Catholics (or Jews or Germans) despite significant prejudice and virulent hatred directed against them, the answer is that in a competitive political arena the votes of such groups will—rather sooner than later—appear too desirable a plum to leave unplucked. One or another party will befriend them and with their aid will entrench itself. This in fact was the strategy of Democratic machine politics in urban areas throughout the period of mass immigration.[49]

It was also the early Republican and early Populist strategy with respect to Blacks; but it failed.[50] The strategy failed because of white terror and the failure of will to control it.[51] But the strategy also failed because—for a time—too few southerners could perceive any issue or set of issues as more important than preventing Blacks from enjoying the advantages that would have come from full political participation. The temptations for a political solution have always been there, however, and are often quite strong. Whether in a one, two, or three-party system, the probable losers, who perceived an alliance with Blacks as the road to victory and power, confronted a powerful temptation to cheat on the White bargain. Precisely because that tension was present, racist domination required that the politics of the region be violent and extreme. In a more civilized context the bargain would not have been kept, as it has not been kept since 1965. Thus, terror has always been part of southern regional politics; and the "social" pressures among Whites, which are indispensable to the community politics paragraph two seeks to protect, rightly seemed ominous.

---

note 47. In World War I a quite different movement to restrict or outlaw the use of German was instituted. In the first case, despite overtones of particular prejudices, the legislation was intended to serve the goal of Americanization or assimilation. In the second, the objective of the legislation, which forbade even instruction in German as a second language, was a symbolic expression of hate for an enemy and obliteration of its culture. Meyer v. Nebraska, 262 U.S. 390 (1923), and Bartels v. Iowa, 262 U.S. 404 (1923), were both products of the second anti-German campaign.

49. See B. SOLOMON, supra note 47; J. HIGHAM, supra note 47.

50. For the Republican strategy during reconstruction, see L. COX & J. COX, POLITICS, PRINCIPLE AND PREJUDICE (1963); K. STAMPP, THE ERA OF RECONSTRUCTION, 1865–1877 (1965); A. TRELEASE, WHITE TERROR (1971) (especially introduction). For the populist strategy, see L. GOODWYN, supra note 28, at 276–306; C. VAN WOODWARD, supra note 28.

51. See A. TRELEASE, supra note 50.

Only in special circumstances and with an adequate animus can the requisite terror be organized to keep the political bargain from occurring. In the North, despite race hatred that has often exceeded that of the South and despite specific and effective violence against integrated housing, political violence has simply not been an issue. But in the South, until recently, conditions have been right for terrorism. Gunnar Myrdal brilliantly sketched them in 1944.[52] First, law enforcement was almost exclusively local, political, and nonprofessional. Second, organized political violence had been sufficiently frequent to bring with it cadres of white hoods who stood ready to act when change threatened. Third, and most important, the region had exhibited many characteristics of colonized areas. Like many colonies, the South expended a great deal of social energy in drawing and maintaining lines between master and servant classes. The distinction between White and Black, between colonist and native, was reinforced so prevalently that the political distinction seemed but part of a natural pattern. The resonance of society and politics in this respect was critical. It accounted in part for peculiar intransigence of the state-action problem.

In contrast to the deep societal roots of governmental action against Blacks—the close fit between private terror, public discrimination, and political exclusion, directed against Blacks for a century—action against other minorities has usually been sporadic, transitory, and local.[53] Other minorities are not systematically victimized by a widespread system of discrimination or by the politics that create and enforce it. As a result, instances of oppression of religious and national minorities have about them a sense of the extraordinary; they appear to be hysterical outbreaks attributable to special times (such as war, with its accompanying hysteria) or places.

C. The Dilemma of Racial Politics and Footnote Four

Why should it matter whether we distinguish between a minority subject to occasional mistreatment and one subject to a pervasive pattern of oppression? The answer should be obvious, arising as

---

52. G. MYRDAL, *supra* note 38.
53. Again, the oriental experience in the western states was closer to that of Blacks.

it does from the very considerations footnote four is designed to highlight. Intermittent judicial intervention may be justified in (and suited to) correcting oppression identified as an aberration, a single perversion of majoritarian politics. But when the oppression of a minority comes to constitute the essence of those politics or—still worse—when the constitutional structure for political activity has been arranged to facilitate the pattern of oppression,[54] judicial intervention will necessarily entail either inefficacy or a compromise of the constitutional structure itself. What starts as a modest principle justifying limited review will become the basis for bending general structural elements to fit the morally antecedent condition of nondiscrimination.

The ramifications of this distinction have, indeed, become manifest in post-1938 history. We can sketch, if you will, a line from *Pierce* and *Meyer* through footnote four to Stone's dissent in *Gobitis*,[55] to *Barnette*,[56] and on to *Sherbert v. Verner*[57] and *Yoder*.[58] In the forty years since footnote four none of these or of a host of other religion or nationality cases has entailed complex remedial questions, or dras-

---

54. At almost every critical juncture in our constitutional history, the structure of authority has been tailored to meet the contemporaneous needs of the prevailing patterns of racial domination. The three-fifths clauses, part of the North-South (or, more accurately, slave-free) compromise at the Convention of 1787, were the Constitution's most serious qualification of the principle of popular government, extending to the popular house of Congress itself. The fugitive-slave clause was an important limitation on state powers; the importation-and-migration clause, an unspeakable, unique limitation upon the commerce power of Congress. *See generally* S. LYND, *supra* note 20.

With the Reconstruction Amendments, the very idea of federalism became closely associated with race. The state-action limitation upon the Fourteenth Amendment, for example, was from the outset associated with impact upon patterns of racial domination. Most important, both the compromise of 1877, which created the political condition that encouraged the judicial retreat from Reconstruction in the late 1870s and 1880s, and the judicial retreat itself were informed by a vision of federalism whose central notion was the illegitimacy of the imposition of a national norm upon local patterns of racial domination. *See* Soifer, Book Review, 54 N.Y.U. L. REV. 651 (1979) (reviewing R. BERGER, GOVERNMENT BY JUDICIARY).

55. Minersville School Dist. v. Gobitis, 310 U.S. 586, 601 (1940).

56. West Virginia State Bd. of Educ. v. Barnette, 319 U.S. 624 (1943).

57. Sherbert v. Verner, 374 U.S. 398 (1963) (holding Seventh Day Adventist could not be denied unemployment compensation because of her refusal to take Saturday work).

58. Wisconsin v. Yoder, 406 U.S. 205 (1972) (holding state could not force Old Order Amish parents to send their children to public or private school after completion of eighth grade).

tic alterations of federalism or serious inroads on the requirement of state action, or dramatic confrontations between paragraph two's "political" values and paragraph three's protection of minorities.[59]

In sharp contrast, the protection of Blacks has entailed all of these elements. And a case of sorts could be made that the distinction was already clear before 1938. There were, at the time *Carolene Products* was written, three areas in which some changes had already occurred in the lamentable constitutional position of Blacks. One was housing. In 1917 the Court had held in *Buchanan v. Warley* that the property rights of White owners to sell to Blacks required invalidation of a Louisville racial zoning ordinance.[60] Since the Court refused to decide the case in terms of the rights of Blacks, *Buchanan* could hardly have been cited in footnote four, but it was one of the few areas in which the Court had already acted to protect Black interests, if not rights.[61]

Impartial administration of criminal justice was a second area of

---

59. The closest brushes with complex remedial problems or intensive interference with state schemes associated with religion have been with regard to public-school prayer and aid to parochial schools. These applications of the modern establishment clause have not involved judicial protection for religious minorities in any simple sense (unless atheists are so classified). The difficult remedial questions associated with the school-prayer cases arise primarily from the dilemma of enforcing a symbolic norm in the absence of a victim group. It has been, in many communities, a constitutional "victimless crime."

60. Buchanan v. Warley, 245 U.S. 60 (1917).

61. The Court had refused, however, to break the state-action barrier, apparently upholding the enforcement of restrictive covenants. Corrigan v. Buckley, 271 U.S. 323 (1926), *distinguished in* Shelley v. Kraemer, 334 U.S. 1 (1948). Actually, the Court stated only that the covenants themselves were not void as violative of the Constitution. Because the Court held it had no jurisdiction to review the judgment of a District of Columbia court in awarding specific enforcement of the decree, it did not reach the question of whether the enforcement of the covenant was itself valid. But since it affirmed the order of a court that thought it was deciding the question of enforcement in deciding the question of validity of the covenant, the natural conclusion was that the Supreme Court would not forbid enforcement of the restrictive covenant.

It might further be pointed out that petitioners explicitly argued that what was beyond the power of the legislature could not be rendered enforceable by judicial action. "This Court," petitioners argued, "has repeatedly included the judicial department within the inhibitions against the violation of the constitutional guaranties which we have invoked." 271 U.S. at 324-25 (reporter's summary of petitioner's argument—not part of opinion). The Court ignored these claims, perhaps because they were not raised in the lower courts. Whatever its *holding*, the *effect* of *Corrigan* was certainly to license restrictive covenants and their enforcement for another two decades. *See* C. VOSE, CAUCASIANS ONLY (1959).

limited progress. Although the Court had never treated them as race cases, there can be little doubt that the decisions in *Moore v. Dempsey*,[62] *Powell v. Alabama*,[63] and *Brown v. Mississippi*[64] made new criminal procedure law in part because the notorious facts of each case exemplified the national scandal of racist southern justice. This conclusion is reinforced by Holmes' famous letter to Laski, in which he replied to Laski's lament on the execution of Sacco and Vanzetti:

> Your last letter shows you stirred up like the rest of the world on the Sacco Vanzetti case. I cannot but ask myself why this so much greater interest in red than black. A thousand-fold worse cases of negroes [*sic*] come up from time to time, but the world does not worry over them.[65]

In a letter six days earlier Holmes had told of denying a writ in the Sacco-Vanzetti case, because it had not come within the rule of *Moore v. Dempsey*.[66] Of course, as Holmes' dissent in *Frank v. Mangum*[67] indicates, it was not the racial element in *Moore* that controlled his decision but the phenomenon of mob-dominated justice. Yet, in the letter to Laski, Holmes recognized that as a social fact such perversion of justice was a widespread epiphenomenon of Apartheid. The revolution in federal habeas that started with *Moore* should be viewed as at least undertaken with full knowledge of its racial implications.[68]

---

62. Moore v. Dempsey, 261 U.S. 86 (1923) (overturning mob-dominated conviction on due process grounds). For an interesting account of the underlying events in *Moore* (a riot in Helena, Arkansas), see A. WASKOW, FROM RACE RIOT TO SIT-IN, 1919 AND THE 1960's chs. 7 & 8 (1966).

63. Powell v. Alabama, 287 U.S. 45 (1932) (Scottsboro Boys case—applying to states constitutional right to counsel in some cases).

64. Brown v. Mississippi, 297 U.S. 278 (1936) (requiring, via Fourteenth Amendment, exclusion of coerced confessions by states). The defendant had been whipped, but, in the words of the deputy sheriff, "'not too much for a negro [*sic*].'" *Id.* at 284.

65. 2 HOLMES-LASKI LETTERS 974 (M. Howe ed. 1953) (letter of August 24, 1927).

66. *Id.* at 970.

67. 237 U.S. 309, 345 (1915) (did not involve Black petitioner).

68. The primary issue in *Frank* and *Moore* was the power of federal courts to exercise *collateral* review to pierce a record unobjectionable on its face to find the reality of mob domination. An expanded writ of habeas corpus was one of the primary strategies available for coping with a completely racist system of criminal justice that both worked unfairness against Black victims and defendants when no special political element was present and served as an adjunct to the political forces

The Court had also taken steps before 1938 to protect the franchise of Blacks, especially in the white primary cases. In 1915 the Court had invalidated the grandfather clause as a device for disenfranchisement of Blacks.[69] *Guinn v. United States* and its companion cases were in some respects the first since Reconstruction to protect Black rights.[70] The two *Nixon* cases later forged the principle that the *state* could not deny Blacks the opportunity to participate in a primary election. *Grovey v. Townsend*, however, upheld the white primary when it was the product of a party convention decision.[71] Thus, the Court, as in *Corrigan*, refused to pierce the state-action barrier that was the formal embodiment of a distinction between state and society—a distinction that was meaningless when custom and terror could be expected to enforce what the state could not.

Stone, as a participant in *Grovey*, was obviously aware of the magnitude of the lurking state-action problem, and even as he wrote footnote four he was apparently preparing to attack it. Stone's decision a year later in *United States v. Classic*[72]—though not a race case—was immediately understood to be a breakthrough for minority rights, and it was soon followed by renewed NAACP attacks on the rule of *Grovey*—attacks that ended with success in *Smith v. Allwright*.[73] Stone, then, was (or should have been) aware that such "neutral" dimensions of constitutional law as state action were at risk in pursuing the protection of Blacks to an extent that they were not at risk in the protection of other minorities.

In 1938, however, Stone may not have sensed the potentially

---

of Apartheid whenever necessary. For a discussion of more recent problems in supervising state criminal justice systems, see Amsterdam, *Criminal Prosecutions Affecting Federally Guaranteed Civil Rights: Federal Removal and Habeas Corpus Jurisdiction to Abort State Court Trial*, 113 U. Pa. L. Rev. 793 (1965); Cover & Aleinikoff, *Dialectical Federalism: Habeas Corpus and the Court*, 86 Yale L. J. 1035 (1977).

69. Myers v. Anderson, 238 U.S. 368 (1915); Guinn v. United States, 238 U.S. 347 (1915).

70. Isolated exceptions exist in the areas of discrimination in jury service and of peonage. *See, e.g.*, Carter v. Texas, 177 U.S. 442 (1900) (grand jury). *But cf.* Bailey v. Alabama, 219 U.S. 219 (1911); Franklin v. South Carolina, 218 U.S. 161 (1910). *Guinn*, however, is the first case that might be said to mark a new departure, a reversing of a trend. *Compare* Guinn v. United States, 238 U.S. 347 (1915) (protecting the franchise) *with* Giles v. Harris, 189 U.S. 475 (1903) (going to great lengths to find procedural basis for refusing to intervene to protect the franchise).

71. Grovey v. Townsend, 295 U.S. 45 (1935).

72. United States v. Classic, 313 U.S. 299 (1941).

73. Smith v. Allwright, 321 U.S. 649 (1944).

paradoxical relationship that paragraphs two and three of the footnote could bear to one another. On the one hand, part of the strategy of Apartheid was exclusion of Blacks from both political life and political machinery. When exclusion operated at the level of formal electoral machinery, the two paragraphs were mutually reinforcing: *Nixon v. Herndon* and *Nixon v. Condon* are cited in both paragraphs. At a different level of politics, however, such racial exclusions could also be understood to be exercised by individuals or groups operating within the autonomous political space protected by paragraph two. Guaranteeing the participation of minorities in all political organizations can hardly be understood as purely neutral regulation of the political process when the processes are mainly *about* the maintenance of Apartheid.[74] As we shall see, it could not have been clear in 1938 whether the objective of protecting minorities could be achieved without circumscribing the political space and cleansing the political machinery to free it of racist objectives.

IV. The Fate of Majoritarianism in the Programmatic Protection of Minorities

Footnote four coined the phrase "discrete and insular minorities" and staked out a territory for vigorous judicial action. The forty years since 1938 have repeatedly tested the meaning of the phrase and the strength of the Court's commitment to act. More often than not, the Court has had to measure its commitment to protection of minorities against its obligation to constitutional doctrines and values not, on their face, directly concerned with minorities at all. Thus, the Court has frequently tested its adherence to the values of local autonomy (implicit in federalism) and of distinguishing the state from society (implicit in the constitutional concept of state action). The clash of new commitment and old obligations defined the great "neutral principles" problem. It was a dilemma inherent in the commitment to protect Blacks, though not in the commitment to protect other minorities. For the apparently neutral structural characteristics of the Constitution had never been neutral concerning race.[75] It was therefore

---

74. *See* W. CASH, *supra* note 28; V. KEY, *supra* note 28; P. WATTERS & R. CLEGHORN, CLIMBING JACOB'S LADDER, THE ARRIVAL OF NEGROES IN SOUTHERN POLITICS (1967).

75. *See* S. LYND, *supra* note 20; *see also supra* note 54.

foreseeable that if judicial action were to be effective it would have to undo the structural underpinnings of Apartheid.

In *An American Dilemma*, Myrdal draws two conclusions from essentially the same facts, conclusions that make for an interesting juxtaposition. In his discussion of the "Inequality of Justice," Myrdal describes "[t]he American tradition of electing, rather than appointing, minor public officials" with the result of direct or indirect local political control over "[j]udges, prosecuting attorneys, minor court officials, sheriffs, the chief of police, . . . sometimes the entire police force. . . ."[76] This tradition, together with the jury system, Myrdal concludes, "turns out . . . to be the greatest menace to legal democracy when it is based on restricted political participation and an ingrained tradition of caste suppression. Such conditions occur in the South with respect to Negroes."[77] Myrdal also notes that: "The vote would be of less importance to groups of citizens in this country if America had what it does not have, namely, *the tradition of an independent and law-abiding administration of local and national public affairs.*"[78]

Thus, Myrdal points to the sociological dimension of basic constitutional law: the local political controls of federalism and the subjugation of administration to politics inherent in a national charter that carefully organized political government while barely suggesting that there might come to exist "departments" or "officers"[79] that would have to administer something. As Myrdal recognized, these elements supported and facilitated southern Apartheid. Nonetheless, in answering the question "is the South fascist?"—a question with a real bite in 1944—Mydral pointed to precisely the same characteristics of the political order to return a negative response: "The South entirely lacks the centralized organization of a fascist state. . . . The Democratic party is the very opposite of a state party in a modern fascist sense. It has no conscious political ideology, no tight regional or state organization and no centralized and efficient bureaucracy."[80]

This, then, is the paradox suggested to me by these Myrdal observations. Southern Apartheid was in large part a creation of

76. G. MYRDAL, AN AMERICAN DILEMMA 523 (20th anniv. ed. 1964).

77. *Id.* at 524.

78. *Id.* at 432.

79. Contrast the highly developed Article I of the Constitution with the very sketchy Article II.

80. G. MYRDAL, *supra* note 76, at 458.

fragmented, weak administration, of local autonomy and politics. To break the system necessarily meant destroying or vitiating this decentralized political structure. But it was precisely that structure that was inconsistent with fascism—and, by extension, with the other horrors of a centrally dominated party apparatus. Could the real political values inherent in local autonomy survive the penetration of national norms in the interest of destroying Apartheid? This question, I believe, had to be uppermost in the mind of any justice—if any justice there was—who understood footnote four not as a maxim but as a program.

Whether Stone or any of his colleagues had such a programmatic ambition in 1938, I am not prepared to say.[81] But developments after 1938 were surely informed by the tension between protection for Blacks and respect for the prevailing structures of political life. That tension revealed itself in several ways; the remainder of this paper presents two. The first was the competition between a "sanitized" political process and vigorous Black protest politics as the chief instrument for penetrating the political defenses of Apartheid. The second was the emergence of the federal judiciary as a co-ordinate form of federal pseudo-administration that, though capable of penetrating to a limited extent the local screen of lawless race politics, did not present any of the dangers of a centralized bureaucractic machinery that could be shaped to the uses of a party apparatus.

A. Competing Solutions to Political Apartheid

Shortly after footnote four, Justice Stone wrote the majority opinion in *United States v. Classic*,[82] which, emphasizing the integral part

---

81. Just a hint that some of the Court may have formulated an ambition to destroy Apartheid may be garnered from the fact that United States *ex. rel.* Gaines v. Canada, 305 U.S. 337 (1938) was decided the same term as *Carolene Products.* In *Gaines* the Court insisted that if a state were to provide separate but equal facilities, such facilities must be available regardless of demand; in the absence of equal facilities, Blacks would have a right of access to White facilities. Professor Gunther has called *Gaines* "[t]he first in the sequence of modern school segregation cases that culminated in Brown v. Board of Education. . . ." G. GUNTHER, CONSTITUTIONAL LAW 711 (9th ed. 1975). Of course, in 1938 *Gaines* had not revealed what was to follow. But Gunther is not alone in seeing *Gaines* as a turning point. *See* R. KLUGER, SIMPLE JUSTICE 213 (1975) ("*Gaines* was a tremendous milestone.")

82. 313 U.S. 299 (1941).

that primaries play in a state-regulated electoral scheme, upheld congressional power to punish fraud in a primary election for Congress. Three years later, *Smith v. Allwright*[83] relied on the reasoning of *Classic* to overrule *Grovey v. Townsend* and hold that a white primary violated the Fifteenth Amendment even when the racial restriction was imposed by the party, not by the state.[84]

But even *Allwright* proved susceptible to evasion; it was, in any event, inadequate to enfranchise Blacks in many places.[85] One response from those seeking to end Apartheid was an effort to require Black participation even at levels of politics antecedent to those constituting "state machinery." In *Terry v. Adams*,[86] a local association,

---

83. 321 U.S. 649 (1944).

84. "[R]ecognition of the place of the primary in the electoral scheme [as in *Classic*] makes clear that state delegation to a party of the power to fix the qualifications of primary elections is delegation of a state function that may make the party's action the action of the State." 321 U.S. at 660. For a good discussion of *Classic*, see Bixby, *The Roosevelt Court, Democratic Ideology, and Minority Rights: Another Look at* United States v. Classic, 90 YALE L.J. 741 (1981).

85. Actually, the ruling in *Smith v. Allwright* reversed a long-standing downward trend in Black voting in the South. A very substantial increase in Black registration and voting, concentrated mainly in the upper South and in large cities, occurred in the wake of *Allwright*. V. O. Key, a leading analyst of Southern politics, concluded that "[i]n one sense the most remarkable consequence of the decision has been the degree of its acceptance and the extent to which Negroes have come to vote." V. KEY, POLITICS, PARTIES AND PRESSURE GROUPS 612 (3rd ed. 1952). But Key goes on to document the evasion, resistance, and intimidation that took place in South Carolina, Alabama, and Mississippi. *See id.* at 612–616; *see also* V. KEY, *supra* note 28, ch. 29 (analyzing *Allwright* in still more detail).

In Georgia, where Blacks had substantial voting power in Fulton County (which included Atlanta), an extraordinarily liberal Governor, Ellis Arnall, was elected in 1942. Unable to succeed himself, Arnall supported another liberal, James Carmichael, who won a plurality of the popular votes in the election of 1946. Nonetheless, Carmichael was defeated by Eugene Talmadge under the Georgia "county unit" system of voting. Talmadge won through a combination of an appeal to White racial solidarity and a counting system that by 1960 afforded voters in the smallest rural counties as much as 100 times the voting power of voters in Fulton County. *See* V. KEY, *supra* note 28, at 128–29. The Georgia county unit system was declared unconstitutional in Gray v. Sanders, 372 U.S. 368 (1963). It was, needless to say, in the overrepresented rural counties to which *Smith v. Allwright* had not yet penetrated that White terror continued effectively to disenfranchise Blacks. *See* V. KEY, *supra* note 28, at ch. 29; P. WATTERS & R. CLEGHORN, *supra* note 74, at 26–27 (concluding that, after initial spurt, Black voting in South had actually begun to decline by early 1960s).

86. Terry v. Adams, 345 U.S. 461 (1953). *Terry* had something more than local significance. As Key shows, one possible strategy in the wake of *Allwright* was for a state to attempt to divest the primary of its "delegated state function" character

the Jaybirds, had held pre-primaries limited to white Democrats. Obviously, the whites had developed a "shadow" party to evade the formal line drawn by the Court in *Allwright*. What the Jaybirds regulated had no formal legal status at all; their success, so far as the record revealed, was entirely attributable to the acquiescence in their racist scheme of the great majority of the county's white voters in the subsequent official elections. To revert to the dichotomy alluded to at the outset, the problem with the Jaybird scheme lay not in a rigged electoral machinery but in a public politics perverted by racism. The decision to regulate the Jaybirds could not, in itself, bring the Republic down; but pursuit of the general strategy of attacking racist politics by regulating groups like the Jaybirds could have gone far along the road towards contradicting the political values expresssed in paragraph two of footnote four. Justice Minton, in dissent, struck this precise note:

> We have pressure from labor unions, from the National Association of Manufacturers, from the Silver Shirts, from the National Association for the Advancement of Colored People, from the Ku Klux Klan and others. Far from the activities of these groups being properly labeled as state action, . . . they are to be considered as attempts to influence or obtain state action.[87]

One might go even further than Minton. Only by protecting the right of these groups to associate, to communicate, and to seek to influence government can one have a community life that is antecedent and superior to the acts of the state. Without such non-governmenta! space for public politics, it is impossible to avoid the dangers addressed by paragraph two. If all political life must pass a test of healthfulness, those who control the testing apparatus have the means to substitute party and state for political society.

---

by ceasing to require or regulate it. Thus, in 1944 South Carolina repealed all laws relating to primaries. The lower federal courts nonetheless held exclusion of Negroes as a political party to be unconstitutional. Elmore v. Rice, 72 F. Supp. 516 (E.D.S.C. 1947), *aff'd*, 165 F.2d 387 (5th Cir. 1947), *cert. denied*, 333 U.S. 875 (1948). V. KEY, *supra* note 28, at 613. While the decision in *Terry v. Adams* came some years after the disappearance of any formal semblance of White primaries, a contrary holding might well have tempted some states to go the route South Carolina tried in the mid-40s.

87. 345 U.S. at 494 (1953).

But, on the eve of *Brown*, the possibility that a sanitized politics might be the only or the best hope for protecting minorities yet seemed reasonable. Black direct action had not yet begun, and Black participation in electoral politics, though in hindsight expanding, appeared to have reached a plateau.[88] It is during this same period that the Court upheld group libel laws in *Beauharnais v. Illinois*,[89] thus endeavoring to purify not only our political organizations but also our political discourse.

Although the Court never repudiated *Beauharnais* and *Terry*, neither has it pursued the directions they suggested.[90] Instead, the Court began protecting certain characteristic forms of renewed Black political organization. As Harry Kalven pointed out, it was the expansion of speech and associational freedoms against the state (in cases like *NAACP v. Alabama*,[91] *NAACP v. Button*,[92] *Shelton v. Tucker*,[93] and *New York Times v. Sullivan*)[94] that characterized the "Negro and the First Amendment" in the decade following *Brown*. Later there came a still more dramatic shift in emphasis from protecting the "minority," Blacks, to protecting the political activity and movements of that "minority."[95] This shift cannot be explained simply, but I should like to offer two observations.

---

88. P. WATTERS & R. CLEGHORN, *supra* note 74.

89. 343 U.S. 250 (1952). *Beauharnais* was analyzed at great length in an exquisite essay by the late Henry Kalven. *See* H. KALVEN, THE NEGRO AND THE FIRST AMENDMENT ch. 1 (1965).

90. The Supreme Court, in particular, has refused to forbid racial exclusion with respect to private clubs, even though they may well enclose the networks of personal political influence. *See* Moose Lodge No. 107 v. Irvis, 407 U.S. 163 (1972). While *Terry v. Adams* might well be decided today as it was in 1953, most commentators are convinced that *Beauharnais* would not be.

91. 357 U.S. 449 (1958) (holding unconstitutional state's demand that NAACP reveal names and addresses of Alabama members and agents).

92. 371 U.S. 415 (1963) (holding unconstitutional Virginia's ban against improper solicitation by lawyers as applied to NAACP's litigation campaign).

93. 364 U.S. 479 (1960) (holding unconstitutional Arkansas law requiring teachers to disclose all organizations to which they had belonged or contributed within five years).

94. 376 U.S. 254 (1964) (prohibiting state from imposing civil liability for publications concerning public figures unless published with actual malice, with knowledge of falseness, or in reckless disregard of whether false or not).

95. *See, e.g.*, Walker v. City of Birmingham, 388 U.S. 307 (1967); Cox v. Louisiana (II), 379 U.S. 559 (1965); Cox v. Louisiana (I), 379 U.S. 536 (1965); Hamm v. City of Rock Hill, 379 U.S. 306 (1965); Bell v. Maryland, 378 U.S. 226 (1964); Lombard v. Louisiana, 373 U.S. 267 (1963). For Kalven's discussion of many of these

The first derives from Hannah Arendt's long maintained—at least since her own experience as a refugee from Hitler—conviction that the most debilitating dimension of European Jewish self-consciousness was its insistence that anti-semitism was a wholly exogenous element of life, unrelated to anything save the existence of Jews.[96] As a result of this perspective, she reasoned, Jews did not understand their existence as political. They had relinquished responsibility for their political world. Arendt's view was the harsh one that the victims whose politics may well fail are nonetheless required to act if they are legitimately to stake a claim to the social world they inhabit.

In one sense Arendt's views strike me as having direct application to America. Without vigorous Black protest politics—a claim to be essential participants in the public choices of the day—American race politics might have become like the European Jewish question: politics about the victim group. Such a politics cannot help but betray, even at its best, a dehumanizing pattern. Fortunately, the spectre of some grotesque federalized extension of the doctrines approved in *Beauharnais* never constituted a serious threat.[97] For the civil rights movement instead confronted the courts with the problem of the limits of public protest, and in so doing reunited paragraphs two and three of the *Carolene Products* footnote.

A second observation derives from the vivid memory I have of the forceful image of the Mississippi Freedom Democratic Party in 1964. Of course, the Freedom Democratic Party and the Council of Federated Organizations never acquired in Mississippi the power that the Texas Jaybirds had in their little county; nor was the Party racially exclusive in character. But the extension of the power of scrutiny into shadow political parties and the development of a doctrine of vicarious state responsibility for their objectives and methods might well have provided a handle for harassment and destruction of one of the most dramatic symbols of the civil rights movement's struggle. It

cases, see H. KALVEN, *supra* note 89, at 123–214; Kalven, *The Concept of the Public Forum: Cox v. Louisiana*, 1965 SUP. CT. REV. 1.

96. H. ARENDT, *supra* note 28; *see* H. ARENDT, THE JEW AS PARIAH (1978).

97. Lest one dismiss too cavalierly such a possibility, consider carefully David Riesman's three articles, *Democracy and Defamation* (pts. 1, 2 & 3), 42 COLUM. L. REV. 727, 1085, 1282 (1942). Admittedly written amidst the war, they are, nonetheless, an imposing monument to the seriousness with which group libel was treated by a "new" generation of scholars. For a cautious rejection of Riesman, see Z. CHAFEE, 1 GOVERNMENT AND MASS COMMUNICATION ch. 5 (1947).

seems to me somewhat ironic that the vehicle for the second Reconstruction of Mississippi was itself a shadow political party that organized its own unofficial elections and hoped to transform them eventually into effective political power.[98]

B. The Federal Judiciary and Constrained Administration

The fear of damage to political values in the course of destroying Apartheid was, then, not entirely frivolous. It may be, of course, that a sanitized political discourse—one free of racist invective—and a hygienic principle of political organization that would not tolerate racial exclusion at any level would produce at least as good a political system as we now have. But, certainly, candor requires recognition of the risks entailed.

I feel a similar ambivalence about a second dimension of the judicial undertaking to protect minorities. Though we still do not have a national, law-oriented bureaucracy and administration—especially not in law enforcement, we are appreciably closer to such a goal (or fear) than we were when Myrdal wrote in 1944. It is certainly beyond my capacity to undertake a separation of cause and effect; but it seems that the changes in race relations are not unrelated to this increasing penetration of national administration in the past thirty-five years.

Despite the growth of national bureaucratic and administrative penetration, I would suggest that the judiciary's special, active role in protecting minorities may well have resulted in a less intrusive and pervasive centralized administration than would have been the case with other, alternative courses to integration. Put differently, *given* the objective of ending Apartheid, the activist federal judiciary as spearhead was the mode of action least likely to destroy the ultimate values served by fragmentation of political power and local political control over administration. Government by injunction[99]

---

98. *See* H. Zinn, SNCC, THE NEW ABOLITIONISTS (1965); *see also* P. WATTERS & R. CLEGHORN, *supra* note 74, at 289–92. The Mississippi Freedom Democratic Party achieved recognition by the national party in 1968, precipitating a recognition conflict within the state. *See* Riddell v. National Democratic Party, 508 F.2d 770 (5th Cir. 1975).

99. For starkly different attitudes to "government by injunction," compare F. FRANKFURTER & L. GREENE, THE LABOR INJUNCTION (1903) (treating the injunction as

may often appear highhanded, undemocratic, even tyrannical; but, in fairness, one must always ask compared to what. Representative bodies make decisions, but they do not carry them out. Political decisions to destroy Apartheid would necessarily have been made with less particularity and would have confronted the implementation dilemma in the most acute of forms: whether to entrust the job to locals—a virtual concession of defeat—or whether self-consciously to rule one region with natives of another.[100]

The transformation of the federal district courts into quasi-administrative bodies overseeing school desegregation and occasional other tasks[101] in the dismantling of Apartheid may appear from one perspective to have been a radical institutional step at the borderland of legitimacy;[102] and surely it did change the courts and their relation to their milieu. But from a different perspective it was, to paraphrase *Shelton v. Tucker,*[103] the least intrusive alternative. Because of the tradition of privately initiated law suits and case-by-case adjudication, the dismantling of Apartheid could and did proceed piecemeal over an extended period of time and with varying rates of speed

presumptively illegitimate device for shaping complex relations) with O. FISS, THE CIVIL RIGHTS INJUNCTION (1978) (injunction should often be favored remedy when underlying substantive claim is just). *See also* Chayes, *The Role of the Judge in Public Law Litigation,* 89 HARV. L. REV. 1281 (1976).

100. The traditional calumny against Reconstruction governments—"rule by Carbetbaggers, Negroes and Scalawags"—had a great deal of truth to it. And it is no accident that accusations of "outside agitation" continued to play an important part in White southerners perceptions of the civil rights movement. If federal administrators rather than the courts had cracked Apartheid, one may be sure that carpetbaggers and Negroes would have been prominent among them; and, by definition, any native White southerners who joined them would have become scalawags.

There is an important sense in which even the tasks of the courts were implemented by carpetbaggers. The lawyers who were initiators of litigation and who subsequently served as the courts' eyes and ears were frequently outsiders working either for the Justice Department or for the NAACP Legal Defense Fund.

101. The courts attempted to cope with the problem of recalcitrant registrars in a manner analagous to the school suits. This approach did not achieve notable success prior to 1965. Thereafter, the Voting Rights Act provided the courts with more powerful and blunter instruments of intervention. *See* P. WATTERS & R. CLEGHORN, *supra* note 74, chs. 8 & 9; C. HAMILTON, THE BENCH AND THE BALLOT (1973). For examples of complex remedies in voting rights, see, e.g., Hamer v. Campbell, 358 F.2d 215 (5TH CIR. 1966).

102. Professor Chayes sees the innovation as a harbinger of a new model of public litigation and does not view the legitimacy of the change as problematic. *See* Chayes, *supra* note 99.

103. 364 U.S. 479 (1960).

from state to state, county to county, and school district to school district. Of course, the role of the NAACP Legal Defense Fund rendered the process a good deal less fragmentary and more coordinated than a purely private-law model would predict.[104] But the civil rights movement itself was never controlled by the Fund, and litigation assumed a pace and character other than that planned in New York. The Justice Department also exercised a role in coordination of litigation, but not an overridingly important one until after 1964.[105]

Any legislatively imposed program creating or extending the administrative apparatus necessary for success would have been quicker, less sensitive to variations, and overwhelmingly coercive. When legislative programs finally did come, long after the ground had been broken and the worst shocks absorbed by the judiciary, they were more pervasive, evenhanded, and effective than the courts had been.[106] Had such programs been the spearheads of integration, it is doubtful whether they could have been as effective as the courts without becoming far more coercive.[107]

The federal courts proved to have some but not all of the defects that Myrdal attributed to local law enforcement. Loosely tied, administratively uncoordinated bodies, their personnel varied considerably

104. Much has been written of the Fund as grand strategist for landmark decisions. Too little has been written concerning its role in day-to-day financial suport and back-up work for "ordinary" litigation after *Brown*. To a large extent the initiative in such suits came from grass-roots people and local lawyers, though the Fund certainly had its targets and timetables. See Rabin, *Lawyers for Social Change: Perspectives on Public Interest Law*, 28 STAN. L. REV. 207, 216–17 (1976).

105. The Civil Rights Act of 1964 and the Voting Rights Act of 1965 gave the Department statutory powers to intervene and initiate law suits. The "standing" of the United States to initiate lawsuits to enforce the rights of specific persons in the absence of such statutory powers has long been doubtful. *Compare* United States v. United States Klans, 194 F. Supp. 897 (M.D. Ala. 1961) (upholding power) *with* United States v. Solomon, 516 F.2d. 1121 (4TH CIR. 1977) (denying power).

106. The Voting Rights Act of 1965 had an almost immediate, cataclysmic effect on areas where the numbers of Blacks voting had been particularly low. See C. HAMILTON, *supra* note 101, at vi; P. WATTERS & R. CLEGHORN, *supra* note 74, at ch. 9. A major watershed in public education was HEW's definition in 1968 of qualifying levels of integration for federal aid to education. These guidelines were considerably more effective than the courts had been; in advancing desegregation many school districts rushed to bring themselves into compliance. See G. ORFIELD, THE RECONSTRUCTION OF SOUTHERN EDUCATION (1969).

107. It is particularly doubtful whether HEW's carrot approach could have worked until after the principle of desegregation had already been established. After all, many communities in the South accepted substantial financial hardship during the period of "massive resistance" to preserve segregation.

in fidelity to the centrally promulgated norms. But the federal judges were politically more independent, identified with a more genteel elite, and better educated and professionally trained than local law enforcement.[108] They thus drew upon the prestige and values associated with what Weber called rule by "honoratiores."[109] Despite their prominence in destroying Apartheid (and, in a few cases, their obvious relish for the task) none of these judges was killed or seriously injured—a fact that probably is due in some measure both to the position of the judges in their communities and to the perception that such an act would have precipitated armed federal intervention.

Conclusion

Only with respect to Blacks could so dramatic and far-reaching a change in the judiciary's role and in its relation to state government be understood as a "least intrusive alternative." For only with respect to Blacks was it truly impossible to see the events generating the cases that reached the courts as isolated instances of impropriety or as transitory hysteria. Against hysterical politics it is necessary to offer protection, make amends, award compensation, but not to remake the political structure itself.[110]

Apartheid was not, however, hysteria. It was the governing system that pervaded half the country, and like any such system it was implicitly and explicitly supported by the Constitution. It is clear to me that when Stone wrote footnote four he intended to protect against transitory hysteria. It is not clear to me whether he knew he had also embarked on a program to rewrite the Constitution. The critical importance of *Brown v. Board of Education*[111] was that it removed any doubt about the Court's commitment to just such a program— whatever its implications. By 1964 Congress and the President had joined the battle against Apartheid. Judicial activism in support of the rights and interests of Blacks no longer would raise the special questions it once had.

---

108. For portraits of the southern federal bench, see SOUTHERN JUSTICE (L. Friedman ed. 1965).

109. *Max Weber on Law,* in ECONOMY AND SOCIETY 198–223 (M. Rheinstein ed. 1967).

110. I am not suggesting that the victims of an hysterical outbreak maintain equanimity with respect to the political system that spawned the attack.

111. 347 U.S. 483 (1954).

Each constitutional generaton organizes itself about paradigmatic events and texts. For my generation, it is clear that these events are *Brown v. Board of Education* and the civil rights movement and that the text is footnote four. For, whether or not the footnote is a wholly coherent theory, it captures the constitutional experience of the period from 1954 to 1964. And that experience, more than the logic of any theory, is the validating force in law.

Chapter 2

The Uses of Jurisdictional Redundancy: Interest, Ideology, and Innovation

The jurisdictional complexities of the American system of courts have occupied generations of scholars, perplexed generations of students, and enriched generations of lawyers.[1] Consider the enormity of it all. There are more than fifty separate systems of state courts, for most purposes largely independent of one another, but coordinated in important respects by the full faith and credit clause and by some dubious, specialized applications of due process.[2] Conflict of laws is a distinctive field of American jurisprudence—quite different from its private international law counterpart—because of those "loose" coordinating factors, enforced from time to time by the Supreme Court.[3]

I am thankful to the Marshall-Wythe School of Law and to the National Center for State Courts for providing the stimulating forum at which this paper was presented. The paper has benefitted greatly from the comments and criticisms of the other participants in the symposium. I am also grateful to Bruce Ackerman, Ed Dauer, Jan Deutsch, Drew Days, Don Elliott, John Ely, Joe Goldstein, Reinier Kraakman, Peter Schuck, and Aviam Soifer for reading and commenting on earlier drafts of the paper.

1. Jurisdictional rules may be viewed, from one perspective, as limitations upon the authority of public actors. Like other procedural principles designed to impose regularity upon public authority, jurisdictional rules may be manipulated to the strategic advantage of private parties and their lawyers. The more opaque the procedural principles are to discernible ends, the more their manipulation becomes an arcane province of lawyers to be used in a purely strategic manner. *See* Simon, *The Ideology of Advocacy: Procedural Justice and Professional Ethics*, 1978 Wis. L. Rev. 30–64, 91–113. The objective of this Article, to discern a set of principles justifying jurisdictional redundancy, leads to decisional principles in this area by which to judge the strategic demands of lawyers.

2. What is dubious about the application of due process is the use of the phrase to designate insufficient state authority to adjudicate quite apart from consideration of fairness to the parties. See the dissent of Justice Brennan in World-Wide Volkswagen Corp. v. Woodson, 444 U.S. 286, 299–313 (1980).

3. There seems to be a cyclical character to the Supreme Court's concern for

Under the applicable jurisdictional rules, many cases may be heard in the courts of more than one state.

Superimposed upon this array of state institutions is the separate system of federal courts. Since 1789 the overwhelmingly consistent element in the relationship between these federal courts and the state court systems has been concurrency or overlap of jurisdiction.[4] The federal courts have never been primarily tribunals vested with an exclusive special subject matter jurisdiction.[5] Rather they have been seized of classes of cases almost all of which could have been heard in the courts of one or more states.[6] While both the state and federal courts are subject to the appellate jurisdiction of the Supreme Court of the United States on matters of federal law, the independence of each of the state systems from one another and of all from the federal system has remained real and significant.[7] The possibilities of concurrency are thus both "vertical" (state-federal) and "horizontal" (state-state).

Two different emphases are possible in understanding this jurisdictional array. The first treats the complex patterns of concurrency as both an accident of history and an unavoidable, perhaps unfortunate incident of the formal logic of our system of states.[8] Political

coordination in conflicts. The last three years have witnessed an intensified concern with the imposition of limits upon state court jurisdiction combined with an apparent continuation of the longstanding trend of imposing few constraints upon choice of law. *Compare* Rush v. Savchuk, 444 U.S. 320 (1980), World-Wide Volkswagen Corp. v. Woodson, 444 U.S. 286 (1980), Kulko v. California Superior Court, 436 U.S. 84 (1978), *and* Shaffer v. Heitner, 433 U.S. 186 (1977), *with* Allstate Ins. Co. v. Hague, 49 U.S.L.W. 4071 (Jan. 13, 1981).

4. *See* H. FRIENDLY, FEDERAL JURISDICTION: A GENERAL VIEW 1–14. *Compare* H. HART & H. WECHSLER, THE FEDERAL COURTS AND THE FEDERAL SYSTEM 38–40 (1953), *with* ALI, STUDY OF THE DIVISION OF JURISDICTION BETWEEN STATE AND FEDERAL COURTS 99–104, 162–68, 366–69, 375–80 (1969).

5. The most important exception has been jurisdiction over federal crimes. Even that "exclusive" jurisdiction has become, in an important sense, concurrent in fact, if not in law. See notes 73–89 & accompanying text *infra* for a discussion of the implications of the creation of what are in effect concurrent crimes. Another apparent area of federal exclusivity, admiralty and maritime cases, has been rendered for many practical purposes concurrent with state jurisdiction by the "savings" clause. *See* H. HART & H. WECHSLER, *supra* note 4, at 373–74.

6. *See* P. BATOR, P. MISHKIN, D. SHAPIRO & H. WECHSLER, HART AND WECHSLER'S THE FEDERAL COURTS AND THE FEDERAL SYSTEM 309–438 (2d ed. 1973).

7. The systems may vary from one another in terms of recruitment and selection of judicial personnel, in terms of court organization, and in terms of procedure and administration.

8. *See* H. FRIENDLY, *supra* note 4, at 1–6.

fragmentation and imperfect administrative integration of the American nation in the late eighteenth century necessarily carried with it the malformed jurisdictional anomaly that we have endured, if not loved, for so long. The outline of our fractured jurisdictional mosaic, according to this view, was set in 1789 and, with the inertia characteristic of all institutions, persisted long after any functional basis had gone.[9] The Constitution embodied the recognition in some measure of the formal sovereignty of states, with the attendant formal independence of tribunals. Indeed, it may be this independence as much as any other feature which makes our states demonstrably *not* merely administrative units.[10]

But this emphasis upon etiology and formal sovereignty, however plausible as to origins, is weak in explaining the persistence of these complex patterns of concurrency of jurisdiction. Despite a civil war and a reconstruction which worked a partial revolution in some features of nation-state relations, despite developments in administration of welfare programs which, in fact, *have* made states and their agencies mere administrative units of the national government for many purposes,[11] despite massive changes in the substance and terms of federal court jurisdiction itself—the enlargement of federal question jurisdiction, the attack upon diversity,[12] which already have thoroughly reversed the pattern of caseload in the federal courts as categorized by substantive law[13]—despite all these changes, the structural

---

9. See ALI, Study of the Division of Jurisdiction between State and Federal Courts 99–110 (1969), for an example of the expression of this view concerning general diversity jurisdiction.

10. *Cf.* H. Hart & H. Wechsler, *supra* note 4, at 11 (where the authors write of the federal judicial power concerning "the general understanding [of the framers] that a government is not a government without courts").

11. Consider the detailed federal statutory and regulatory constraints on state administration in a typical federal/state program of "cooperative federalism." *See, e.g.,* 42 U.S.C. § 602 (1976); 45 C.F.R. §§ 200–282 (1980).

12. See the pending bill which would abolish diversity jurisdiction except for federal interpleader and would concomitantly remove the amount in controversy requirement for general federal question jurisdiction. H.R. 2404, 97th Cong., 1st Sess. (1981).

13. In 1951, of private civil actions in the United States district courts (those in which neither the United States nor a federal officer were parties), 6,062 were federal question cases, 12,772 were diversity, and 2,591 were admiralty. H. Hart & H. Wechsler, *supra* note 4, at 52. In 1978, of private civil actions, 59,271 were federal question cases, and 31,625 were diversity. Dir. Ad. Off. U.S. Courts Ann. Rep. 5 (1978). Of the 1951 federal question cases, 482 were habeas corpus for state

pattern of redundancy, of near total overlap in jurisdiction, has persisted.[14] Many of the formal attributes of the sovereignty of the states have bowed before the onslaughts of necessity and convenience time and again throughout our history while the crazy patchwork of jurisdiction, if anything, has become more complex and apparently anachronistic.[15]

An alternative emphasis is possible. Instead of viewing the persistence of concurrency as a dysfunctional relic, one may hypothesize that it is a product of an institutional evolution.[16] The persistence of the anomaly over time requires a search for a strong functional explanation. With such an approach, one makes the working asumption that the historical explanation of the origin of the structure of complex concurrency of jurisdiction, even if accurate, does not suffice to explain its persistence. It is this approach that I shall pursue here. But the objective of this paper will be a limited one—the exploration of a hypothesis. I shall attempt to identify the utility of the pattern or structure of jurisdiction that we have had for 200 years—not the justification for some particular rule or institution, but the justification for the very pattern itself. For it is the structure of overlap that has been constant, rather than the particular rules and areas of dispute. This argument will remain incomplete—a first step in a longer argument. The identification of functions that complex concurrency of jurisdiction may plausibly be said to serve constitutes neither a full explanation nor a justification for the structure. It does seem reasonable, however, to suggest that both a fuller causal explanation and an adequate justification of the structure must entail, at the least, an understanding of the utility of the pattern. The objective of this

---

prisoners, 122 were Civil Rights Act cases, and almost 3,000 were FELA and Jones Act cases (all personal injury cases of one sort or another). H. HART & H. WECHSLER, *supra* note 4, at 53. By 1978, that had changed: 16,969 were state prisoner petitions, 1,494 were FELA cases, and 4,843 were marine tort actions. DIR. AD. OFF. U.S. COURTS ANN. REP. 60 (1978).

14. The increase in federal question jurisdictional redundancy has corresponded to the growing importance of federal law.

15. See *Developments In the Law—Section 1983 and Federalism*, 90 HARV. L. REV. 1133 (1977), for a good overview of the growing complexity of one important area of federal jurisdiction.

16. I stress that the use of the "evolutionary" metaphor is only heuristic. I am by no means suggesting that such a process of institutional evolution necessarily occurs; but, it is permissible to set up such a conclusion as a hypothesis to be explored.

Article, then, is to take that first step. The Article will proceed to outline the functions of complex concurrency, largely ignoring, without thereby rejecting, the formal or historical arguments that might be said to explain or justify the system.

Dispute Resolution and Norm Articulation

The jurisdictional pattern we are dealing with concerns jurisdiction to adjudicate. An understanding of the significance of the pattern therefore requires an understanding of the adjudicatory act. Adjudication in the common law mold entails two simultaneously performed functions: dispute resolution and norm articulation. The work of comparativists and anthropologists should satisfy anyone that the intertwining of these two functions in the common law fashion is neither a logically necessary nor an empirically universal condition.[17] But there are deep cultural and contingent bases for the strong connection in American law. Moreover, these expectations are embodied in a series of formal norms with respect to the conduct of adjudication that forbid outright, or discourage in some contexts, the performance of one of these distinct functions without the other. For example, the requirement of "case and controversy" in the federal courts is a formal embodiment of the requirement that the norm articulation function not be performed apart from dispute resolution.[18] The converse requirement may also be found. It is true that there are many individual instances of literally inarticulate dispute resolution by courts.[19] Nevertheless, both court rules governing adjudicatory procedure and, in some cases, the Constitution's due process clauses require that dispute resolution be accompanied by reasons.[20] This requirement of

17. For an interesting exploration of other ways in which dispute resolution and norm articulation interact, see Eisenberg, *Private Ordering Through Negotiation: Dispute Settlement and Rulemaking*, 89 HARV. L. REV. 637 (1976).

18. The reasons behind the requirement have been rehearsed by almost every commentator and critic of court and Constitution. I continue to find Bickel's discussion the best starting point. A. BICKEL, THE LEAST DANGEROUS BRANCH, THE SUPREME COURT AT THE BAR OF POLITICS 111–98 (1962) (chapter entitled "The Passive Virtues").

19. Consider the now frequent, but very questionable practice of many appellate courts in rendering decisions without opinion. See, for example, Reynolds & Richman, *The Non-Precedential Precedent—Limited Publication and No-Citation Rules in the United States Courts of Appeals*, 78 COLUM. L. REV. 1167, 1173 (1978), for a discussion of the federal practice.

20. FED. R. CIV. P. 52; FED. R. CRIM. P. 23(c); Goldberg v. Kelly, 397 U.S. 254 (1970).

articulation, together with even a weak consistency requirement, over time, will necessarily entail the articulation of general norms. As Cardozo wrote, "as a system of case law develops, the sordid controversies of litigants are the stuff out of which great and shining truths will ultimately be shaped. The accidental and the transitory will yield the essential and the permanent."[21] It is important to realize that these *two* functions are normally performed simultaneously in adjudication. Moreover, devotees of the common law often attribute its genius to precisely this mix of dispute resolution and norm articulation.

The dual function of adjudication has repercussions for our consideration of jurisdictional patterns. The advantages and disadvantages of complex concurrency in a jurisdictional structure will often be differentially associated with the dispute resolution and norm articulation functions. That is, some particular characteristic of redundancy in the jurisdictional structure may be justified by reference to an acknowledged purpose which is peculiar either to dispute resolution or to norm articulation quite apart from the effect on the counterpart. For example, diversity jurisdiction is usually justified and explained as a device for avoiding partiality of local tribunals to local litigants. Partiality may be viewed as primarily a problem in dispute resolution.[22] The very significant area of concurrency of jurisdiction thereby established is justified by reference to a dispute

---

21. B. CARDOZO, THE NATURE OF THE JUDICIAL PROCESS 35 (1921).

22. One trenchant restatement and critique of the traditional justification is to be found in Wechsler, *Federal Jurisdiction and the Revision of the Judicial Code*, 13 L. & CONTEMP. PROB. 216, 234-40 (1948). *See also* Friendly, *The Historic Basis of Diversity Jurisdiction*, 41 HARV. L. REV. 483 (1928); Yntema & Jaffin, *Preliminary Analysis of Concurrent Jurisdiction*, 79 U. PA. L. REV. 869 (1931); Frankfurter, *A Note on Diversity Jurisdiction—In Reply to Professor Ynetma*, 79 U. PA L. REV. 1097 (1931). I confess that the battle of the late 1920s and early 1930s on this subject seems to remain more interesting than more recent controversy. One participant is constant. *See* H. FRIENDLY, *supra* note 4, at 139-52. *See also* Currie, *The Federal Courts and the American Law Institute*, 36 U. CHI. L. REV. 1 (1968).

Local prejudice may, of course, be demonstrated through norm articulation as well. Indeed, one might well conclude that the single most virulent form of prejudice against out of staters in today's world of ordinary state court adjudication is the home-party-biased choice-of-law methodology of "interest analysis." It is clear that one simple way to alleviate that problem is to extend the scope of jurisdictional redundancy by overruling *Klaxon Co. v. Stentor Elec. Mfg. Co.*, 313 U.S. 487 (1941), which requires federal courts sitting in diversity to apply the choice of law rules of the state in which they sit. *See* notes 114-115 & accompanying text *infra*.

resolution end. However, a significant tension is thereby set between the "normal" model of adjudication with intertwined dispute resolution and norm articulation and a concurrent jurisdiction that is erected to solve a dispute resolution problem only. The question arises: will the concurrency of competence with respect to dispute resolution carry with it concurrency of competence in norm articulation as well? That question, of course, constitutes the *Erie* problem.[23] The fact that the *Erie* problem has remained well-nigh intractable and capable of evoking heated scholarly debate throughout our history[24] testifies to the difficulty of separating the two dimensions of adjudication.

It has been no less problematic to construct complex structures of concurrency primarily to resolve norm articulation problems and then try to isolate that function from dispute resolution. For over fifty years special three-judge federal district courts heard cases in which the constitutionality of acts of Congress or of state legislation was called into question. These courts were set up because alternative forums were considered insufficient for articulation of norms of such consequence. However, the impulse to use three judges instead of one, which arose out of norm articulation concerns, ran counter to standards of efficient dispute resolution. Because of the case and controversy requirement, a total formal separation of norm articulation from dispute resolution was impossible; but complicated, unsatisfactory, and often inconclusive devices and standards were developed to separate the constitutional norm articulation act to the extent possible—either by dismissing the constitutional claim as a preliminary matter, or by resolving the legal claim and remanding most fact-finding to a single judge as a matter of remedy.[25]

---

23. [Ed. note: This is the problem of determining which state's law should be applied in a case involving multistate dimensions.] The relation between *Erie* and the fact of jurisdictional redundancy is well articulated in Wechsler, *supra* note 22, at 240–42.

24. *Compare* Warren, *New Light on the History of the Federal Judiciary Act of 1789*, 37 HARV. L. REV. 49 (1923), *with* Ely, *The Irrepressible Myth of Erie*, 87 HARV. L. REV. 693 (1974).

25. *See, e.g.,* Gonzales v. Automatic Employees Credit Union, 419 U.S. 90 (1974). The Act of Aug. 12, 1976, Pub. L. No. 94–381, § 3, 90 Stat. 1119, eliminated the three-judge court as a requirement in cases challenging the constitutionality of statutes, saving only the requirement that they be used in reapportionment cases. 28 U.S.C. § 2284(a) (1976). There are a few other provisions that may require such a court. *See* 42 U.S.C. §§ 1973b(a), 1973c, 1973b(c), (1976).

It may also be maintained that all appellate review, including a great deal of judicial review of administrative behavior, entails a special purpose of articulating norms with attendant devices for separating the articulation of the norm from the dispute resolution. Prospectivity in appellate review, because most explicit, is the most controversial of a series of such devices.[26]

These examples suggest that the jurisdictional solution to a mono-functional problem imposes a strain either upon the normal forms of adjudication or upon the remaining function of adjudication. If we are to distill "great and shining truths" out of "sordid controversies," it is surely a bit too much to expect that not only the system of case law, but also the crazy-quilt of concurrency in jurisdiction, will further this alchemy. Time and again one component of the jurisdictional array has been manipulated either for the purpose of resolving sordid controversies or for the purpose of polishing up shining truths with negative consequences in the other areas.

Complex Concurrency

The jurisdictional array that I have identified as the traditional and constant American structure of courts is a form of redundancy that I shall call complex concurrency. This structure exemplifies at least one of three important characteristics: strategic choice, synchronic redundancy, and diachronic or sequential redundancy. The first of these is nearly always present. The other two are manifestations of redundancy which are so costly that substantial and often successful efforts are made to avoid their effects. As a result they are frequently unrealized in the event.

Strategic choice is the pervasive attribute.[27] In the jurisdictional world of complex concurrency, it is usually possible for one of the parties in a law suit to choose the most favorable from among two or more forums in terms of expected return. And the United States is uncommon in the degree to which it multiplies the potential for forum shopping. The fifty-plus state jurisdictions reenact the inter-

---

26. See the discussion of prospectivity in A. Bickel, The Supreme Court and the Idea of Progress 55–58 (1978).

27. For a classic discussion of strategic behavior, see T. Schelling, The Strategy of Conflict (1960).

national order in many respects, while the potential choice between a state and federal forum squares the difficulties or opportunities. Moreover, perhaps because the United States is not composed of truly independent sovereignties, jurisdictional lines have not been of the bright-line variety.[28] Both the states exercising jurisdiction vis-à-vis one another and federal courts deciding upon the availability of the federal forum manipulate soft, imprecise standards subject to tremendous good faith, and bad faith, variations in interpretation.[29] The uncertainty of these standards contributes to the likelihood that alternative forums will be invoked as part of a pattern of strategic behavior.

The strategic behavior entailed in forum shopping is only one manifestation of complex concurrency. The structure of American jurisdiction presents the possibility of more than forum shopping. In some cases it is possible for more than one forum to be invoked simultaneously. I shall call this phenomenon "synchronic redundancy." Synchronic redundancy again is not unknown in the law of nations. But the American phenomenon is more widespread and complex. The principle of full faith and credit requires that most clear cases of synchronic redundancy ultimately abort. There may be two or more proceedings initiated, with two or more discovery stages, two or more trials, and more. But there will ordinarily be only one effective judgment. General principles of res judicata read into full faith and credit require this result. Other doctrines militate against synchronic redundancy by requiring deference on the part of one forum once another forum has started to act. The *Younger* doctrine,[30] the anti-injunction statute,[31] and the abstention doctrine[32] are but a few instances of such rules and principles.

Nevertheless, there are a number of situations in which the principles of res judicata do not apply in an unproblematic way. For example, the relation between two pending criminal prosecutions,

---

28. See Field, *The Uncertain Nature of Federal Jurisdiction*, pp. 683–724 *infra*.

29. *Id.* at 723–24.

30. Younger v. Harris, 401 U.S. 37 (1971). *See* Fiss, *Dombrowski*, 86 YALE L.J. 1103 (1977).

31. 28 U.S.C. § 2283 (1976).

32. *See, e.g.,* Field, *Abstention in Constitutional Cases: The Scope of the Pullman Abstention Doctrine*, 122 U. PA. L. REV. 1071 (1974).

arising out of the same conduct but properly within the legislative competence of two or more jurisdictions, will not be governed by res judicata.[33] And the application of full faith and credit to actions for injunctive relief is by no means straightforward.[34] Nevertheless, it must be said that synchronic redundancy is very seldom allowed to run its course, in the sense that multiple forums seized simultaneously of a matter proceed to judgment without adjusting for the judgments of the others.

A third pattern is somewhat more common than synchronic redundancy. The complex concurrency of the jurisdictional structure frequently permits recourse to the courts of another system after one system has adjudicated and reached a result. This diachronic or sequential redundancy is comparatively common. Federal habeas corpus constitutes a large and important instance of it.[35] But recourse to sister state courts in child custody and other domestic relations matters is also common.[36] In general, wherever res judicata is not absolute, so that sequential redundancy is a theoretical possibility in a unitary system, the concurrent complexity of the American jurisdictional structure affords a greater opportunity to realize the potential for relitigation.[37] Of course, not every dispute will lead a litigant to go to the lengths necessary to invoke a concurrent forum. In the case of federal habeas corpus the cost is small, given the plight of the petitioner.[38] In a child custody case, however, the price of the alternative forum may be an otherwise unplanned change in residence or domicile. For better odds for a child, some have paid the price.[39]

Strategic behavior in the choice of a forum, synchronic redun-

---

33. See United States v. Lanza, 260 U.S. 377 (1922); notes 73–91 & accompanying text infra.

34. See, e.g., Fall v. Eastin, 215 U.S. 1 (1909); Reese, Full Faith and Credit to Foreign Equity Decrees, 42 IOWA L. REV. 183 (1957).

35. Compare Cover & Aleinikoff, Dialectical Federalsim: Habeas Corpus and the Court, 86 YALE L.J. 1035 (1977), with Bator, Finality in Criminal Law and Federal Habeas Corpus for State Prisoners, 76 HARV. L. REV. 441 (1963).

36. See, e.g., Ferreira v. Ferreira, 9 Cal. 3d 824, 512 P.2d 304, 109 Cal. Rptr. 80 (1973).

37. The fact that relitigation is formally possible in a unitary system does not mean that it will likely produce a different result. A losing party, therefore, will often eschew relitigation. The alternative forum may afford a reason to believe that relitigation will be profitable to one side or the other.

38. See Friendly, Is Innocence Irrelevant? Collateral Attack on Criminal Judgments, 38 U. CHI. L. REV. 142 (1970).

39. Ferreira v. Ferreira, 9 Cal. 3d 824, 512 P.2d 304, 109 Cal. Rptr. 80 (1973).

dancy, and diachronic redundancy—all are manifestations of the complex concurrency of jurisdiction. It is time now to consider its uses.

Redundancy

The three possibilities discussed above emerge from the structural characteristic of forum or jurisdictional redundancy. This characteristic of redundancy in the design of other sorts of systems is now well understood to be essential to secure reliability. Everyone understands that if you wish to make sure that a physical structure is strong enough at certain points you put extra material or extra strong material at the given point. Or you may duplicate the critical beam or arch, using two components where one might do. Fairly early in the development of cybernetics as a separate discipline, it was also demonstrated that redundancy could provide a solution in principle to the problem of unreliability of components in information systems.[40] Since that time, sophisticated refinements in specification of necessary redundancy characteristics in information systems have been made.[41] Still more recently, political theorists have borrowed from cyberneticists and have argued that redundancy in a political design system may have some of the same positive characteristics as it has in inanimate decision systems.[42] Of course, in a real sense, the work of classical liberal political theory had already made many of these points, albeit without the technical jargon.[43]

In this section I shall review some specific arguments for the utility of redundancy in human decision systems in four important, related areas. I shall denominate these areas as Error, Interest, Ideology, and Innovation. Of these, the latter three will be shown to constitute justifications for the jurisdictional redundancy which characterizes our federalism.

---

40. The classic paper, I am told, is von Neumann, *Probabilistic Logics and the Synthesis of Reliable Organisms from Unreliable Components*, in AUTOMATA STUDIES 43–98 (C. Shannon & J. McCarthy eds. 1956). I confess that I understand only the general outline of the paper.

41. J. SINGH, GREAT IDEAS IN INFORMATIONAL THEORY LANGUAGE AND CYBERNETICS (1966), is a readable introduction.

42. J. STEINBRUNER, THE CYBERNETIC THEORY OF DECISION (1974); Landau, *Redundancy, Rationality and the Problem of Duplication and Overlap*, 29 PUB. AD. REV. 346 (1969); Shapiro, *Toward A Theory of Stare Decisis*, 1 J. LEGAL STUD. 125 (1972).

43. Landau makes this point nicely in Landau, *supra* note 42, at 351.

Error

The theoretical treatments of redundancy in artificial intelligence and in communication theory undertake to use this characteristic of a system to deal with "error." Error in a computer can be easily defined. It means that a gate is open when it should be shut or shut when it should be open. If all operations consist of combinations of binary positions, there is, in theory, a mechanically derivable *correct* position to all gates. The reliability of a component can be defined as its probability of being in the correct position. By appropriate levels of redundancy in the right places, it is possible to use a series of components, each of which is insufficiently reliable, and to construct with them a system with a much higher reliability coefficient.[44] With enough redundancy you can make that coefficient theoretically as high as you might wish.

A somewhat more mundane application of redundancy to deal with error in communication might elucidate its uses. Suppose one were confronted with the need to receive a very important message over a communication medium with a high level of static interference. It is essential that the message be received with a virtual certainty of accurate reception. One might imagine a company of three on the receiving end of the message making several possible arrangements. Suppose only one person can listen and there can be but one reception. Presumably the "best" listener will listen, and the group will ponder the lacunae or uncertain segments after the reception to figure out a plausible message. If there can be but one transmission, but no limit on listeners, the team will be better off with redundant receptions. All three will listen and transcribe independently. Several things might happen. Certain message components will be "confirmed." By this I mean that all three listeners, independently of one another, will receive the same message parts. It will be well to treat such message components as "correct." The reason is simple. Assume the probability of A having correctly received a message that he thinks he heard correctly to be .9. Assume the same for B and C. The probability of error for any single one is .1. It can then be shown that if A, B, and C all believe that they correctly heard a component

----

44. Singh's explanation of this principle is more accessible to the general reader than is von Neumann's proof. *See* J. Singh, *supra* note 41, at 39–58.

and independently agree upon it the probability of error is .0014,[45] a major increase in reliability.

Confirmation of the clearer parts of the message is only one small part of the benefit of the "redundant receiver" strategy. Suppose certain components are received by one but not the others of the listeners. It may be that the received component elicits subsequent acquiescence of the others. They may agree, "Yes, now that you say it that did sound like ' 'orse' with a cockney accent." Such confirmation is "weak confirmation." The subsequent acquiescence of the others is not independent of the reception being confirmed so that one cannot use the law of joint probabilities of mutually *independent* events. Nevertheless, the confirmation is worth something. The weakly confirmed message is certainly no less certain than the unconfirmed component received by only one listener. The three listeners may do more than confirm or weakly confirm one another. Suppose each receiver receives one or more components wholly *unconfirmed* by the others. These components, individually no more reliable than the single receiver case, may gain confirmation from context. But the potential for contextual confirmation increases with the amount of material for context that is provided. Whereas a single receiver might not provide sufficient context to confirm component X_n, the joint product of three receivers may provide X_m and X_o to flank X_n. Each of these three unconfirmed components may confirm each other indirectly by providing the context for one another within a larger message. Indeed, it is conceivable in an extreme case to find these unconfirmed components to be the links which indisputably make sense of the whole message.

Note that it is the redundancy of three independent centers of reception that makes possible all of these advances over the single receiver situation. Consider now the situation of redundant transmission as well as reception. It is clear that static interference randomly distributed over a message may sufficiently blot out the

---

45. This is the probability of error given the fact that all three *agree*. The prior probability of all three agreeing and being in error is $.1 \times .1 \times .1 = .001$. The prior probability of all three agreeing is $.9 \times .9 \times .9 + .001 = .730$. Given the fact that all three agree, the probability that all three are in error rather than all three being correct is $.001 \div .730 = .00137$. $P(U)$ is the probability of unanimity and $P(E)$ is the probability of error. We wish to calculate $P(E/U)$ or the conditional probability of E given U. The formula $P(E/U) = P(E+U) \div P(U) = .001 \div .73 = .00137$. For a more general formula, see note 51 *infra*.

message so that no amount of receptor redundancy will help. But repeated transmissions will, by the same law of joint probabilities of independent events, be quite likely to yield acceptable levels of clarity of more components than would a single transmission. There will again be confirmations, weak confirmations, and indirect confirmations of different components.[46]

Receptor redundancy and transmission redundancy still leave out one component in our highly simplified story. That component may be called "deliberative redundancy." If the message as a whole remains unclear even after confirmed components are put together with all the components received by even one of the listeners, then a problem of deduction remains. This problem will have cryptographic elements to it. It is the hypothesis of at least some decision theorists that small groups are better at resolving such tasks than is a single individual.[47] It is not clear that one would or should refer to the decision process characteristics of such a small group of people working together as entailing redundancy. But in some ways the term is not wholly inapposite. The problem-solving capacity of each of the individuals in the group is a dimension quite apart from the "reception" of information. That problem-solving capacity is backed up by the not identical and partly independent problem-solving capacity of the other actors. Moreover, almost all problems require the solver to bring information or experience to bear which is not communicated as part of the problem itself. The group of problem-solvers will bring, collectively, large amounts of information and experience to bear that a single individual would not.[48] There are, of course, limits to the size of a group that can effectively communicate. In any event, short of exceeding such size limits, the group of problem-solvers constitutes

---

46. "Redundancy may be said to be due to an additional set of rules, whereby it becomes increasingly difficult to make an undetectable mistake." C. CHERRY, ON HUMAN COMMUNICATIONS: A REVIEW, A SURVEY AND A CRITICISM 185 (1957), *quoted in* Shapiro, *Toward a Theory of Stare Decisis,* 1 J. LEGAL STUD. 125, 129 (1972).

47. *See* Lempert, *Uncovering "Nondiscernible" Differences: Empirical Research and the Jury-Size Cases,* 73 MICH. L. REV. 643 (1975). Contrast I. JANIS, VICTIMS OF GROUPTHINK: A PSYCHOLOGICAL STUDY OF FOREIGN-POLICY DECISIONS AND FIASCOES (1972).

48. This is to say, of course, that the additional decisionmakers are not really redundant. A more precise use of terms here might require that we state that multiple decisionmakers introduce a situation in which there is a high level of redundancy. The decisionmakers do replicate one another to a substantial extent, but the non-redundant information and abilities justify the practice.

a redundant array of solution potentials which may lead to quicker or better results.

Up to this point I have been speaking of the solution to a problem that has, in principle, a correct answer—the accurate reception of a message. The utility of redundancy lies arguably in the reduction of the probability of errors or of certain kinds of error. The applications of this use to our problems of adjudicatory jurisdiction are by no means straightforward. And yet, a most obvious, simplistic application must be made—subject to elaboration and revision in the sections which will follow.

It is an important element in the liberal theory of adjudication that decisions are rendered on the basis of correct determinations of *fact*. While everyone understands that the degree of certainty of correctness may vary greatly—with complex legal rules and institutions designed to attribute consequences to varying degrees of certainty in different kinds of cases—it is nonetheless supposed to be an approximation to a truth, in principle discoverable.[49] (Even the umpire who says, "They ain't nothin' till I call 'em," does not thereby claim that his calls are *independent* of the physical course of the ball.) It is therefore in order to ask whether redundancy in the design of the adjudicatory system furthers the desired end of reducing "error" defined simplistically as deviation of outcomes from those that would be predicated upon an accurate and truthful account of the event.

The answer to this question is an unqualified "yes." There are many redundancy features in procedure most of which are not jurisdictional. Trial testimony and exhibits go over the same ground covered by depositions, interrogatories, and document discovery. Multiple witnesses routinely testify to the same events. A given witness is asked essentially the same question in different ways by different lawyers. There are twelve or fewer jurors to hear, see, evaluate, and decide the same case on the same evidence. There is a judge who, along with the jurors, hears, sees, evaluates, and decides the case and possibly intervenes in the juror's decision. All of these devices may be said to entail a measure of redundancy for the purpose of correction of error or identification of areas of doubt and uncertainty. If several witnesses confirm one another's stories, we treat the *confirmation* as significant. If they contradict one another, we do not,

---

49. *See* H. Hart, Punishment and Responsibility (1968).

as system builders, regret that we permitted the redundancy element—multiple witnesses—that led to the contradiction. Rather, we pride ourselves that a problematic area of doubt has been identified.[50] Similarly, if trial testimony and discovery material are confirmatory, no problem arises. If a comparison reveals contradictions, we permit the deposition or interrogatory to be used for impeachment. Thus, we identify a potential *uncertainty* through redundancy. Likewise, cross-examination may reveal that we are less certain about something than we would have been had we relied upon direct examination alone.

Examples could easily be multiplied. The point is clear. Redundancy is in fact a critical strategy in procedural systems for purposes of confirming the "correct" and establishing the areas of uncertainty, that is, the areas of more probable "error" in any element of the proceeding. But, these uses of redundancy are not ordinarily jurisdictional. That is they do not entail the use of multiple potential or actual forums for disputes. It is, of course, possible to use multiple forums to deal with the potential of mere error,[51] and we do so

---

50. A principle function of syntactic redundancy is the identification of problematic parts of a message. Often, only higher levels of redundancy will identify the correct message. See J. SINGH, *supra* note 41, at 39–58; Shapiro, *Toward A Theory of Stare Decisis*, 1 J. LEGAL STUD. 125, 125–28 (1972).

51. Professor Bator in his classic article on habeas corpus seems to deny both of the premises of this section: that proceedings are based in any straightforward sense on correct determinations of fact; and, assuming they are so based, that redundancy produces significant gains in reliability. Bator, *supra* note 35, at 446–49. On the latter issue Bator seems to be wrong. If we have n independent iterations of an event with a probability of error $P(E)$ for each event, then the probability of *all* iterations producing erroneous results is $P(E)^n$. (We will assume that $P(E)$ is less than .5, otherwise there can be no acceptable level of certainty with one trial or with 1000.) The probability of all iterations producing correct results is $[1-P(E)]^n$. Obviously, the probability of agreement of all iterations, $P(A)$, is the sum of these two probabilities. $P(A) = P(E)^n + [1-P(E)]^n$. The probability of divergent results is $1 - P(A)$. The probability of any given array of divergent results, where exactly m outcomes are in error and $n-m$ results are correct, is determined by expanding the binomial. $P(E)_m$, the probability of error in m of the n trials, is

$$\frac{n!}{m! \, (n-m)!} \cdot P(E)^m \cdot [1-P(E)]^{n-m}.$$

The probability of exactly m of n trials being correct is, of course, simply the probability of $n-m$ being in error.

$$P(E)_{n-m} = \frac{n!}{m! \, (n-m)!} \cdot P(E)^{n-m} \cdot [1-P(E)]^m.$$

occasionally in providing for a de novo review. But, it is very expen-

---

The prior probability that outcomes will split so that there is a distribution in which exactly m outcomes diverge from the other $n-m$ is the sum of those two probabilities. The probability of a distribution of m outcomes of one sort and $n-m$ of the other, $P(D_{m, n-m})$, is $P(E)_m + P(E)_{n-m}$. This result is intuitive for the distribution occurs both when m outcomes are in error and $n-m$ are correct and when $n-m$ are in error and m are correct.

Once n trials have occurred and we know the distribution $(D_{m, n-m})$ which resulted, we will wish to know what the probability is that the m trials are in error as opposed to the $n-m$. The contingent probability that m trials are in error, given the distribution $(D_{m, n-m})$ is computed as follows. $P(E_m/D_{m, n-m})$, the contingent probability of error in m cases given the distribution $(D_{m, n-m})$ is

$$\frac{P(E_m)}{P(D_{m, n-m})} = \frac{P(E_m)}{P(E_m) + P(E_{n-m})} = \frac{P(E)^m \cdot [1 - P(E)]^{n-m}}{P(E)^m \cdot [1 - P(E)]^{n-m} + P(E)^{n-m} \cdot [1 - P(E)]^m}.$$

In the special case where $m=n$, that is where the results are in agreement in all trials the formula yields the result

$$P(E_n/D_{n,o}) = \frac{P(E)^n}{P(E)^n + [1 - P(E)]^n}.$$

The general formula yields other interesting patterns. In the special case where $m=n/2$, the probability of error in exactly m cases, given the distribution $(D_{m, m})$, becomes 1. Therefore, the outcome is not helpful in determining which of the results to adhere to. In all other cases, however, the formula yields a $P(E_m/D_{m, n-m})$ which is *at least* as informative as a single trial. Where $m=n-m+1$, $P(E_m/D_{m, m-1})=P(E)$. In general, where $n=m+(m-q)$ the formula simplifies so that

$$P(E_m/D_{m, m-q}) = \frac{P(E)^q}{P(E)^q + [1 - P(E)]^q}.$$

It will be recognized that this is the formula for the contingent probability of error in q trials, given the agreement of all q outcomes. The implications for Bator's rejection of redundancy are clear. Any odd numbers of trials will always yield as great or greater certainty than a single trial. A measurable *increase* in certainty over the outcome of a single trial is achieved whenever the number of trials with one outcome exceeds the number of trials with the opposite outcome by more than one. Even a spread of *one* achieves the same degree of certainty as a single trial.

If one takes a number such as .1 for $P(E)$ and 3 for n, this means that the prior probability of unanimity is .73. The probability of error given agreement is .0014. The probability of a 2-1 split is .27. And, given a 2-1 split, the probability of the two results in agreement being in error rather than the one being in error is .1. Thus, in 73% of the cases we are better off than with a single trial. In the other 27% we are no worse off. Note that in terms of the structure of a procedural system we can achieve the higher level of certainty of $n=3$ by routinely giving two trials of an event and providing a third only when the first two diverge, since in all cases in which the first two trials agree the third trial would only either confirm the first two

sive, and the coordination principles necessary to deal with inconsistent outcomes may become cumbersome. Within a single forum and proceeding, the contradictions among witnesses or between different statements of a single witness may be evaluated in a single act of judgment which encompasses a view of all the contradictory material. The output of a system of redundant forums, however, is either confirmatory or contradictory *verdicts*. Presented with such verdicts, one cannot easily pass judgment on questions of error in reconstructing events without first unpacking what might be called forum effects. The redundant forum causes us to focus on forum variables just as redundant testimony causes us to focus on testimony variables.

A commonplace observation supports this point. Ad hoc "jurisdictional" redundancy is commonly demanded when questions of factual error assume massive political significance. I have in mind special commissions or boards which might advise political leaders concerning the use of pardon or related powers in special political

or yield a 2-1 split with the first two trials providing the rule of decision. Such a structure is reminiscent of the structure imposed by federal habeas although the limited character of the federal court's jurisdiction and the limited scope of redundancy in fact-finding makes the analogy only suggestive.

If one assumes a fairly high $P(E)$ such as .2 a redundant regime of $n=3$ provides truly dramatic improvement. In 52% of the cases all three outcomes will agree. In those cases the probability that all three are in error will be .011. Thus in slightly over half of the cases we move from 20% chance of error down to a 1% chance of error. In the other 48% of the cases the outcomes will split 2-1. By deciding in accord with the two we run a 20% risk of being in error. Note, however, that *if* that risk is too high we may add contingent layers of redundancy thereby reducing the risk still further. An additional two trials in all such (2-1) cases would yield 4-1 splits after the five trials in 52% of these cases. As to these cases we would achieve the 1% error rate. As to the 48% of the original 48% (23% of the original population) there would remain a .2 probability of error. One could, in theory, continue to iterate in the problematic population until the number of such cases approached zero.

Of course, since we are not dealing with mere mechanical iterations with a constant $P(E)$ but with strategic interactions by "players" who learn from experience, the model cannot be useful without including the game theoretic implications of redundancy. Such a model is beyond the scope of this footnote. Professor Bator's rejection of redundancy, however, seems to be based on the simple notion that repetition achieves nothing. Given the demonstrable gains from repetition in the simplified case, the burden would appear to be on one who would deny its utility to show that the strategic interactions destroy any such gains.

Of course, nothing in this footnote provides an answer to the question of whether the gains from redundancy are worth its *costs*. On that issue, compare Cover & Aleinikoff, *Dialectical Federalism: Habeas Corpus and the Court,* 86 YALE L.J. 1035 (1977), with Bator, *Finality in Criminal Law and Federal Habeas Corpus for State Prisoners,* 76 HARV. L. REV. 441 (1963).

cases. The Sacco-Vanzetti case[52] called forth such a solution, as did the Dreyfus case.[53] The phenomenon attests to the naturalness of the impulse to invoke another forum when there is grave factual doubt based on political mistrust of the forum. The question that the rest of this paper addresses is whether this simple observation can be generalized to support current and long-standing practice.

The potential for simple error, then, justifies a measure of redundancy in the structure of procedural systems. But the coordination devices necessary for jurisdictional redundancy are awkward, and the bluntness of jurisdiction as a tool does not permit the redundancy to be focused upon particularly suspect issues and facts. But this does not mean that more systemic sources of divergence of outcomes are not best dealt with through jurisdictional solutions. The cleavage between jurisdictional systems of courts corresponds to more general political lines within our nation. The uses of jurisdictional redundancy, therefore, might best be sought by examining the kinds of problems associated with systematic political authority. There are three such areas that I have singled out for discussion here: Interest, Ideology, and Innovation. These terms are a shorthand for three general problems: (a) the self-interest of incumbent elites in a regime; (b) the more or less unconsciously held values and ways of seeing the world, reflected in the governing elites, which tend to serve and justify in general and longrun terms the social order which the elites dominate; and (c) the consciously determined policies of the authoritative elites, especially insofar as they depart from traditional, common cultural norms and expectations.

The proposition that I begin with is that different polities with differing constituencies, peopled by distinct governing elites, indeed will differ from one another in some measure with respect to all three areas. Clearly, the self-interest of the incumbents of one system is not necessarily furthered by the possibly corrupt pursuit of self-interest by the incumbents of another polity. Whether there are salient

---

52. Governor Fuller appointed a commission headed by Abbot Lawrence Lowell, President of Harvard, to investigate the case. The Lowell Committee found no unfairness. *See* G. JOUGHLIN & E. MORGAN, THE LEGACY OF SACCO AND VANZETTI, 298–309 (1948) (Chapter XI, "The Governor and His Committee").

53. After Dreyfus' conviction of treason in 1894, a period of five years of intense political struggle led to a second trial in 1899. A third proceeding occurred in 1906, which finally exonerated Dreyfus. *See* D. JOHNSON, FRANCE AND THE DREYFUS AFFAIR (1967).

ideological differences among governing elites in polities within a larger national and cultural entity is a more difficult question. It may well be argued that, on the whole, the United States has become sufficiently integrated economically and culturally so that distinct ways of understanding the world no longer tend to characterize our geographic regions nor to characterize the elites responsible to national as opposed to local constituencies. Mind you, I am here commenting on ideology rather than interest and policy. The different constituencies of different states and regions may well give rise to elites with differing interests and different policy objectives. But, so the argument might run, the pursuit of locally, regionally, or nationally oriented policy objectives all may proceed from a common epistemology, a common, if implicit, political economy, and a common ethic. I am inclined to believe that the very long-range trends are distinctly in the direction of rendering geography a less salient corollary of ideological differences. But I am also inclined to believe that this is a matter of degree and that there remain important ideological correlates to the political lines within America.[54] I am not prepared to prove or disprove this hypothesis, and the argument within proceeds upon the assumption that some such salient differences do remain.

The political subdivisions of America do indeed present a range of policy initiatives differing both in terms of conditions to be met and ways of meeting them. While it would be absurd to suggest that policy differentiation does not now occur among the several states and between the national and state levels of government, it is by no means absurd to suggest that the most significant policy questions are increasingly a function of a single, national-level decision and implementation process. If this is true and remains true, it does not destroy the argument that follows but reduces the significance of the conclusions that flow from it.

Each of these three areas must now be addressed separately and in detail. We proceed first to a discussion of "interest."

Interest

Let us take a most obvious case first—a case so obvious that the point seems to have been missed by ten federal judges—a district

_____

54. I am, of course, counting regional variations as correlating with the political divisions of America because it can be captured by groups of states, even though the differences among states within each group are ideologically insignificant.

judge and the nine Supreme Court Justices—who recently considered the matter. Suppose all the judges in a particular judicial system have a personal, financial interest in the subject matter of a law suit. Such would be the case if, for instance, the manner in which the judges are paid or the salary scale applicable to the system as a whole were in dispute.[55] The old maxim that no man shall be a judge in his own cause—reinforced by the Code of Judicial Conduct and in the federal system by the disqualification provisions of the judicial code[56]— requires that such a case, if possible, not be heard by the interested judges. If the case involves state court judges, the natural solution to the dilemma of self-interest is to hear the matter in the federal courts. Often, this may be possible. If the objection to a state judicial compensation scheme is that it fosters or constitutes partiality and unfairness, the objection may be cast in due process terms and heard by federal courts as an issue of federal constitutional law.[57] Conversely, any objections to a federal judicial compensation scheme may, in principle, be heard in state court in the first instance. For state courts are charged with the application of federal law and, as the Supreme Court never tires of informing us, are the tribunals of residual general jurisdiction in our system both for state and *federal* law.[58]

In fact, while federal courts have been used as forums for deciding cases in which state judges are interested parties, the absence of the converse is striking. In *United States v. Will*,[59] several federal judges

---

55. United States v. Will, 49 U.S.L.W. 4045 (Dec. 15, 1980) (holding that the timing of revocation of raises that would have accrued under the Executive Salary Cost-of-Living Adjustment Act violated the compensation clause of article III). *See also* Evans v. Gore, 253 U.S. 245 (1920).

56. 28 U.S.C. § 455 (1976).

57. *See, e.g.,* Tumey v. Ohio, 273 U.S. 510 (1927).

58. It is difficult to know what to make of the fact that no one seems to have suggested that a case like United States v. Will, 49 U.S.L.W. 4045 (Dec. 15, 1980), be decided in state court. Of course, the plaintiffs chose the federal forum, and, as a suit against the United States, there was a jurisdictional basis. The question is what kind of interaction there ought to be between jurisdiction and the so-called "Rule of Necessity." The court treats jurisdiction as a lexically prior step to its consideration of the Rule of Necessity. *Assuming* federal subject matter competence, there is no basis for recusal since all federal judges are equally interested. But the problem of direct and substantial self-interest might be understood, given the potential state forum, as a jurisdiction-blocking issue just as the deference implicit in the abstention doctrine blocks jurisdiction. Indeed, the Court might have conceived a special abstention doctrine for such cases.

59. *Id.*

sued, claiming, on a variety of theories, that the denial of raises to them over a period of years violated the compensation clause of article III. All of the federal judges who heard the case thought the Rule of Necessity permitted federal judges to sit and decide the case despite an interest inseparable from that of the plaintiffs.[60] The United States as defendant did not contest this application of the Rule of Necessity.

These somewhat extreme instances of system-wide self-interest would not, in themselves, go very far to justify an ongoing structure of redundancy. In such bald form they are too obvious and too infrequent. The Supreme Court had to wait sixty years between *Evans v. Gore*[61] and *United States v. Will*.[62] If we define "interest" in the narrow sense of a direct monetary stake in the outcome of litigation, it will be rare indeed for the whole system of judges to be "interested." However, there are less obvious and more insidious kinds of self-interest that are likely to infect a judicial system. The most common and disturbing phenomenon is the reality or suspicion of too strong linkage between the judiciary and political power. Reliable judges are terribly useful to political machines. They may be called upon to certify election results, to take appropriately lenient action when insiders are caught *en flagrante,* or to take appropriately stringent action when enemies of the machine must be punished. In short, their task is to clothe power in the cloak of law and favoritism in the garb of justice. The "interest" implicated in such regimes is simple enough. Judges who are chosen for their strong links to the regime in power may be expected to identify regime interest with their own self-interest. A carrot or a stick, or both, insure a generally adequate level of reliability on the part of such judges. It may be necessary at times to rely upon the less tangible and often less certain bonds of ideological identification, and many cases are intermediate areas between the judge who is a virtual hired hand of a machine and one who simply shares a world-view with the dominant elite in the

---

60. *See id.* at 4049. *See also* Will v. United States, 478 F. Supp. 621 (N.D. Ill. 1979) (issue not addressed by trial court).

61. 253 U.S. 245 (1920).

62. 49 U.S.L.W. 4045 (Dec. 15, 1980). There were sequellae to Evans v. Gore, 253 U.S. 245 (1920). See Miles v. Graham, 268 U.S. 501 (1925), and O'Malley v. Woodrough, 307 U.S. 277 (1939), both of which involved only individual judges rather than the full bench. *See also* O'Donoghue v. United States, 289 U.S. 516 (1933).

machine. Acknowledging that a continuum of positions exists between those two points, we shall treat one end of the continuum—that associated with direct, often corrupt, forms of self-interest—as the separable problem of "interest," while the other end of the continuum will be discussed in the next section as the problem of "ideology."

The kind of self-interest represented by the judicial compensation cases is so stark that it identifies itself. Even if the judges presume to decide the dispute despite their self-interest, they must discuss the issue and be accountable for their having decided it. The illegitimate self-interest of the machine judge does not proclaim itself though it may be notorious. Even if notorious, it may be unprovable. Moreover, it is often, though by no means always, difficult to know to which cases the interest extends. All of the above considerations militate against the use of conventional, ad hoc disqualification devices for the corrupt judge.

Jurisdictional redundancy is a structural solution that will frequently give relief.[63] It is the suspicion of corruption, so often unprovable, that leads a litigant to invoke a parallel forum. Even if *one* of the litigants expects to benefit from corruption and opts for the corrupt forum, the potential of a system of concurrency for synchronic redundancy inhibits the operation of corruption. The development of data to prove or reinforce the suspicion of corrupt complicity will be greatly aided by an independent forum, even if its outcomes must compete with those of the corrupt forum for ultimate implementation. To put it bluntly, if I am someone about to get railroaded by a corrupt system, I greatly value the opportunity to invoke a fair forum even if the corrupt forum's verdict does not bear its corruption on its sleeve and, thus, will compete with that of the fair forum for recognition. The concurrent forum does not provide a solution for the corrupt interest of judges, then, but rather

---

63. Madison supported an independent system of inferior federal tribunals in part on the ground that it is a structural solution to interested state courts. A federal appellate presence would not suffice.

"[U]nless inferior federal tribunals were dispersed throughout the Republic with *final* jurisdiction in *many* cases, appeals would be multiplied to a most oppressive degree." Besides, "an appeal would not in many cases be a remedy." "What was to be done after improper Verdicts in State tribunals obtained under the biased directions of a dependent Judge, or the local prejudices of an undirected jury?" H. HART & H. WECHSLER, *supra* note 4, at 17 (quoting 1 M. FARRAND, THE RECORDS OF THE FEDERAL CONVENTION OF 1787, at 124–25 (1937)).

a weapon with which to fight it. And this may be suggested as a general point about the utility of concurrency as a strategy. This structure is not in general useful for the imposition of determinate solutions. Rather, it facilitates conflicting answers and thus necessarily increases the area of indeterminacy. It is an approach to dilemmas of suspicion and uncertainty, not a formula for clear-cut answers.

Ideology

I have stated that the liberal conception of justice depends upon the idea that *in principle* there are relevant *facts* to be found. The success of such a system based upon the determination of facts depends upon the degree and scope of trust in the society. The philosopher, Michael Polanyi, has written:

> The widely extended network of mutual trust, on which the factual consensus of a free society depends, is fragile. Any conflict which sharply divides people will tend to destroy their mutual trust *and make universal agreement on facts bearing on the conflict difficult to achieve.* In France the Third Republic was shaken to its foundations by a question of fact: the question whether Captain Dreyfus had written the 'bordereau.' In Britain the dispute over the genuineness of the 'Zinoviev Letter,' as in the United States the trial of Alger Hiss, aroused popular conflicts which made it impossible to agree universally on the facts of these matters.[64]

Polanyi points to a disturbing, recurring phenomenon in liberal adjudicatory systems. But it may be argued that he somewhat understates the depth of the problem. For it is surely not the specific conflict, the facts of which are to be adjudicated, that is itself responsible for the chasms of mistrust that make it difficult or impossible for normal adjudicatory institutions to be trusted to reach reliable findings. Rather, certain specific conflicts are understood to lie upon a perceptual or conceptual fault line determined by the different and con-

<hr>

64. M. POLANYI, PERSONAL KNOWLEDGE TOWARDS A POST-CRITICAL PHILOSOPHY 241 (1958) (emphasis added).

flicting ideologies of the relevant social groups. Robert K. Merton summarizes the essence of this ideological perspective on thought:

> The sociology of knowledge takes on pertinence under a definite complex of social and cultural conditions. With increasing social conflict, differences in the values, attitudes and modes of thought of groups develop to the point where the orientation which these groups previously had in common is overshadowed by incompatible differences. Not only do there develop universes of discourse, but the existence of any one universe challenges the validity and legitimacy of the others. The co-existence of these conflicting perspectives and interpetations within the same society leads to an active and reciprocal *distrust* between groups.[65]

Thus, it is the existence of social groups in conflict which is the precondition for the development of conflicting "universes of discourse," while those conflicting universes of discourse serve to aggravate and create distrust. Put somewhat differently, for each group its "ideology" serves as a "template" to organize experience.[66] But the fact that different groups use different templates in organizing experience cannot but lead to distrust and conflict. For ultimately, the most profound determinants of our thought are those of which we are least conscious. And if even these dimensions of our epistemology are socially determined and only relative, we shall be beset by gravest anxiety and anger when we unwittingly come across a different and distinct epistemology. As Lippmann put it almost sixty years ago:

> Without the habit [of treating our own experience as necessarily filtered through our "stereotypes,"] we believe in the absolutism of our own vision, and consequently in the treacherous character of all opposition. For while men are willing to admit that there are two sides to a "question," they do not believe that there are two sides to what they regard as a "fact."[67]

And so we finally come back to adjudication. In a society such as

---

65. R. Merton, Social Theory and Social Structure 218 (1949).

66. *See* C. Geertz, *Ideology As a Cultural System,* in The Interpretation of Cultures 193–229 (1973).

67. W. Lippmann, Public Opinion 82 (1922).

ours, in which the social bases for diversity in total world-views is surely present, and in which there is persistent mistrust—though it fluctuates in intensity—adjudication can always become a ritualized enactment of the epistemological chasms between one class and another, one race and another, one gender and the other; between different generations, different nations; and between city and country, town and gown.[68]

When we challenge a verdict on ideological grounds—that is, on the ground that the decisionmaker's construction of reality was distorted by the social determinants of his mental world—we make what is both far more and much less than a claim of error. On the one hand we *may* (but need not) concede that the decisionmaker acted correctly within his or her frame of reference. Given his or her perceptual and conceptual apparatus, it was the "correct" decision. Presumably, if such is conceded, we may expect a like-equipped decisionmaker to reach the same result. The confirmation of an outcome by iteration of trials within a suspect apparatus only confirms the suspicion. So in one sense there is no claim of error at all. However, the very structure of the mind of the decisionmaker is challenged once one argues that it is a socially contingent apparatus and that it is functionally related to the needs and experiences of the group characterized by that structure.[69] For, if the dispute in question can be fairly understood as intergroup in some sense, then the question that begs for an answer is why does the ideology of *this* group, rather than that of its antagonist, determine the outcome.

Most of the forms of redundancy within a unitary system do not solve the dilemma of an ideological challenge. There is one marked exception. The overlapping domains of judge and jury speak to the issue. This overlap is unique in this respect and deserves to be treated with jurisdictional redundancy in any comprehensive functional

---

68. For an example of one commentator who would drive the logic of these chasms to their conclusion, see Note, *The Case for Black Juries,* 79 YALE L.J. 531 (1970).

    69.

    The distrust and suspicion which men everywhere evidence towards their adversaries . . . may be regarded as the immediate precursor of the notion of ideology. . . . [But we] begin to treat our adversary's views as ideologies only when we no longer consider them as calculated lies and when we sense in his total behaviour an unreliability which we regard as a function of the social situation in which he finds himself.

K. MANNHEIM, IDEOLOGY AND UTOPIA 61 (Wirth and Shils trans. 1936).

account.[70] On the other hand, redundancy across jurisdictional lines is admirably suited to speak to many of the dilemmas of ideological challenges. As our political lines continue to correspond less and less to differences in social systems and culture, this claim may become less valid, but it remains true today to an important degree.

Thus, to the extent that the jurisdictional alternatives differ with respect to the supposed salient social determinants of ideology, complex concurrency constitutes a strategy for coping with ideological impasse. If outcomes are confirmed by the courts of two or more different systems which vary with respect to supposed social determinants of knowledge and mind, this result would suggest some common epistemological ground with respect to the issue presented and with respect to its resolution. For a series of jurisdictional alternatives to present a plausible network of redundancy sufficient to "correct" ideological bias requires that those alternative forums arise out of widely varied political bases with attendant variations in the constituencies to which they speak. In terms of the American judicial systems, an approximation to this variation obtains in several ways. Most state court trial judges are drawn from local, provincial elites, while federal district court judges are more likely to be drawn from a national elite. Levels of education, bonds of loyalty, status, and even economic class may differ radically from one group to the other. Members of the national elite corps share a common education, a cosmopolitan reference group. Members of the state bench share provincial concerns, a local reference group, and ol' boy politics.

All judges, of course, can be presumed to be members of a professional elite. As such, regardless of jurisdictional redundancy, we could hardly expect too great a diversity of class identity—at least so long as one takes such gross factors as occupation and income as prime, if not sole, determinants of class. But neither class homogeneity in such terms nor the somewhat milder race or gender homogeneities found among judges is conclusive of the matter. Both in terms of their need for comprehensive ideological positions and in terms of their need for practical political allies, political elites can differ radically from one another.

Indeed, the differences between primary identification with local as opposed to national elites is a major theme in the literature of

---

70. *See* R. Merton, *supra* note 65, at 218.

modernization.[71] In the United States, no less than in more recently
developing countries, continental integration is a matter of degree.
The degree of identification of an officialdom with national rather
than local groups may often correlate with its attitudes on a series
of critical social, economic, and political questions. Indeed, in the
United States virtually all major ideological clashes of the past century
have had strong geopolitical correlates. Often they have pitted local
against national ideologies; frequently, they have presented urban-
rural conflicts or have set one region against another. We need not
answer the question of why this is so. Some would undoubtedly
argue that it is because geopolitical identification itself correlates with
a more fundamental variable—that is, degree of economic development with attendant class structure. But whatever the reason, if it is
the case that ideological conflicts correlate with geography, then
redundancy structured along such lines will be a relevant mechanism
for addressing many ideology-type claims. To put it more concretely,
a system of complex concurrency between a state court in Mississippi
and a federal court in New York[72] may not thereby capture in either
forum the class consciousness of the proletariat or peasant. But insofar
as the primary local elites of Mississippi grow out of and speak to
the experiences of a social structure radically different from that in
which a New York federal judge is located, they will bring to bear
conceptual and perceptual equipment which does differ with respect
to matters that are salient to industrial worker and poor farmer. While
neither court may be made up of anything but politically well-
connected elite lawyers, these elites may be faithful to and responsible
for different social orders. If one views judges primarily as enforcers
of and apologists for a social order, then the responsibility for different
orders and different dimensions of order will determine different mind
sets. Put more generally, it is both position in a social order and the
nature of the social order itself which determines ideology. Even if
judges in all systems have in common a somewhat privileged position
in their respective social orders, they do not, in a nation as diverse
as ours, necessarily share the same social order.

---

71. See, e.g., C. Geertz, The Integrative Revolution: Primordial Sentiments
and Civil Politics in the New States, in The Interpretation of Cultures 255–310
(1973).

72. The issue is not purely hypothetical. Consider the problem of libel through
the national media.

This paper does not attempt to establish the empirical data to support the proposition that American jurisdictional lines do correlate positively with diverse social orders. I should like rather to assume at least a weak case for that fact and proceed to consider its implications. The assumptions will be (1) that there are differences between state and federal judges in terms of relevant background, responsibilities, and reference groups sufficient to determine different ideologies, and (2) that there are differences among states or groups of states sufficient to determine different ideologies. For now, we need not take a position as to why those differences exist.

I have mentioned that the adjudicatory process entails both dispute resolution and norm articulation elements. Ideological distrust entails related challenges to both dimensions of adjudication. It implies skepticism about the reliability of a range of adjudicatory acts and orientations: ethical and practical judgment, capacity for critical or empathetic orientation to parties and witnesses, and appreciation for consequences. Thus, in its most blatant form, a system may be challenged because its judges cannot be expected to understand—to empathize with—"our" kind of people. They will literally not comprehend "us" without an act of translation, will not believe even when they understand what is foreign to them in the experience of "our" people, and will not appreciate the consequences to "us" of "their" standards.

Confusion and misunderstanding is most acute where there is an *apparent* convergence of discourse, when words and terms are the same or similar but meaning is different. However, when there is clear disagreement about relevant norms, expressed as such, it is possible to grapple with the differences directly. Thus, in the realm of dispute resolution, in precisely those cases in which relevant norms, as articulated, appear not to be subject to controversy, ideological differences may work their most insidious harm. For it is here that authority is seen not only as in conflict but as untrustworthy. Moreover, clear divergences in the articulation of norms, whether or not the result of the divergent ideologies, are readily susceptible to hierarchical solutions if a solution be desired. But the work of ideology in dispute resolution admits of no such easy hierarchical solution. If the problem is to be addressed *at all*, it must be addressed through one or another redundancy device. These points are best developed by an example.

a. Multiple Prosecutions Based on Mistrust of Forum

The general principle forbidding double jeopardy is held not to apply in instances where the same conduct constitutes a violation of state and federal criminal law.[73] Since the 1910s there has been a steady progression of criminalization on the federal level so that a very large number of crimes under state law constitute federal crimes as well.[74] Some of these statutes make the very same conduct criminal under federal law whenever the conduct has an interstate element to it.[75] Other federal statutes use a more indirect approach by taxing certain transactions which are criminal in most states.[76] The reporting and disclosure necessary to comply with the tax laws on the federal level entail high risk of prosecution on the state level. Therefore, these tax laws have the intended effect of a predictable pattern of noncompliance by those engaged in state criminal conduct. That pattern of noncompliance thus brings a federal enforcement and adjudication apparatus into service. Redundant federal criminalization is also very widespread where there is broad federal regulatory oversight, as in securities and banking,[77] or where there are federal instrumentalities, as in banking[78] or mail-related crimes.[79] Prostitution,[80] auto theft,[81] bootlegging,[82] kidnapping,[83] riot,[84] narcotics,[85] embezzlement,[86] bank

---

73. *E.g.*, Abbate v. United States, 359 U.S. 187 (1959) (federal prosecution following state prosecution); Bartkus v. Illinois, 359 U.S. 121 (1959) (state prosecution following federal prosecution).

74. *See* Schwartz, *Federal Criminal Jurisdiction and Prosecutors' Discretion*, 13 L. & CONTEMP. PROB. 64 (1948).

75. *See, e.g.*, The Interstate Racketeering Act, 18 U.S.C. § 1952(a)(2) (1976) (making a federal crime out of interstate travel or use of the mails to further any unlawful activity).

76. *See, e.g.*, United States v. Kahriger, 345 U.S. 22 (1953) (gambling); United States v. Sanchez, 340 U.S. 42 (1950) (marijuana).

77. *See* Securities Act of 1933, 15 U.S.C. §§ 77a–77aa (1976).

78. *See, e.g.*, Jerome v. United States, 318 U.S. 101 (1943); 18 U.S.C. § 2113 (1976).

79. 18 U.S.C. § 2114 (1976) (interference with the mail); 18 U.S.C. § 2115 (1976) (post offices).

80. *See* Hoke v. United States, 227 U.S. 308 (1913).

81. *See* 18 U.S.C. § 2312 (1976). *But see* United States v. Crawford, 466 F.2d 1155 (10th Cir. 1972).

82. *See* 18 U.S.C. §§ 1261–1265 (federal regulation of liquor traffic). *See also* Seaboard Air Line Ry. v. North Carolina, 245 U.S. 298 (1917).

83. *See* Brooks v. United States, 267 U.S. 432 (1925).

84. *See* 18 U.S.C. § 2101 (1976):

85. *See, e.g.*, United States v. Sanchez, 340 U.S. 42 (1950).

86. *See* 18 U.S.C. § 641 (1976).

robbery,[87] and mail frauds[88] are all necessarily or potentially federal as well as state crimes. In many instances the decision to develop or invoke the redundant criminal law forum is related to a mistrust of the alternative, a mistrust frequently arising out of considerations of interest or ideology.

For example, 18 U.S.C. § 241 makes criminal any conspiracy to "injure, oppress, threaten, or intimidate any citizen in the free exercise or enjoyment of any right or privilege secured to him by the Constitution or laws of the United States, or because of his having so exercised the same;" 18 U.S.C. § 242 similarly makes criminal any such deprivations "under color of any law." These statutes have been repeatedly used to remedy perceived deficiencies in local and state law enforcement and adjudication whether rooted in the racist or other suspect ideological characteristics of the locality, or in the entrenched powerful positions of the wrong-doers.

Justice Roberts wrote in *Screws v. United States:* "The only issue is whether Georgie alone has the power and duty to punish, or whether this patently local crime can be made the basis of a federal prosecution."[89] The answer to Roberts' question, that "local" crimes such as murder can be made the basis of federal prosecutions, has become more and more evident over the ensuing thirty-five years. And the clarity of the answer is related to clarification of the uses of redundancy to check distortions in the primary criminal justice system. In *Screws* itself, the Justice Department sounded what has become a general theme. The United States argued that the allegation of involvement of local officials in wrongdoing is itself a reason for invoking an independent system to guard the guardians. This use of redundancy to check the self-interest of law enforcement officials in failing to prosecute their own wrongful acts is by now almost uncontroversial, although there are those who prefer that the redundancy be incorporated as an epicycle within the unitary legal system.

b. Multiple Prosecutions Based on Ideological Differences

A somewhat more controversial practice has also developed: bringing federal prosecutions based upon ideological, rather than self-

---

87. *See* note 78 *supra.*
88. *See* 18 U.S.C. § 1342 (1976).
89. Screws v. United States, 325 U.S. 91, 139 (1945) (Roberts, J., dissenting).

interested, mistrust of the state forum or of its prosecutorial apparatus. It is now common to ask, for example, after a controversial
acquittal in a state trial prosecuting the issue of racism, whether a
federal civil rights prosecution will be brought. The uses of sections
241 and 242 for thirty years have been most prominent in the civil
rights arena; the crisis of ideology created by the civil rights movement is hardly unique. Indeed, the modern statement of the rule that
such sequential intersystemic prosecutions do not constitute double
jeopardy derives from the felt ideological necessities of a somewhat
different era. The gulf that separated wet from dry during the heyday
of the politics of prohibition entailed a complex of attitudinal differences encompassing much more than booze. In some parts of the
country local fervor for prohibition enforcement greatly exceeded that
of the federal government; in other states and localities, however,
that federal enforcement which did exist was met with considered
campaigns of nullification. Everywhere allegations of blatant corruption were common. The solution ratified by *United States v. Lanza*[90]
permitted separate state and federal prosecutions arising out of the
same conduct, thus recognizing that the mistrust engendered by a
too lax regime of enforcement might be mitigated by an adjudication
in the more "reliable" forum.[91]

    The relation of federal and state prosecutions in such instances
of mistrust based on ideology and/or interest is by no means simple.
It may be that the two jurisdictions will confirm one another. For
example, an alleged bootlegger might be acquitted by the courts of
New York, ideologically suspect to the dry's,[92] or an alleged Klan
killer of blacks might be acquitted by a state court in Mississippi. If
a subsequent federal prosecution in such cases confirms the acquittals,
it may remove some measure of the mistrust created by and directed
at the local verdict. The capacity of the federal court decision to
serve this function depends in part on its independence from factors
making the state court a target of suspicion. Are the federal judges
less tied to local elites? Are the federal juries drawn from a different
pool without the characteristics of the state jury pool? The alleviation

90. 260 U.S. 377 (1922).
91. *See* Schwartz, *supra* note 74, at 71.
92. For a view of the federal role during prohibition which confirms that which
I state here, see M. WILLEBRANDT, THE INSIDE OF PROHIBITION (1929).

of suspicion may be accomplished even if there is only a partial mitigation of ideologically biasing factors.

Reiterated acquittals mitigate suspicion on one side while reiterated convictions may serve to alleviate it on the other. The defendant is being shown, after all, that even the jurisdiction with leanings most in tune with the ideological claims of the accused perceives the defendant as the perpetrator of conduct not to be tolerated. Thus, for example, federal prosecutions directed at civil rights activists or southern state prosecutions directed at local white violence might have moral effects that the more predictable pattern of prosecution by the more hostile jurisdiction would not have.

The opportunities for mitigating distrust by confirmation of outcomes and of their implicit messages that are a product of complex concurrency is, however, only half the story (perhaps less than half), for the several systems seized of a matter may fail to confirm one another. Indeed, if we are to suppose that the common perceptions of lay observers, litigants, and lawyers alike have any basis in fact, the more different the public perception of various tribunals—that is, the more they are perceived to speak from different social bases— the more likely they are, in fact, to differ in adjudicating cases. Is there any value to the display of nonconfirming results in different tribunals?

If there is a chasm rendering the social reality of one group in our nation problematic to another, and if that problem of perception and apprehension is to arise in the work of adjudication, there is much to be said for making it explicit. Systematic differences in perception and apprehension by various court systems is not to be expected as a result of deviance and marginality alone. In some respects the ideological gulf separating the truly dispossessed of the society from its governing elites is not going to be bridged or displayed in the variations among state and federal tribunals. For despite recurring complaints about judicial salaries, no system has yet turned its bench over to its luftmenschen and beggars. But the political bases of the elites in different polities do vary remarkably and have varied historically still more. Filtered through the elites, we may thus perceive a modified and rationalized version—a tamed variation—of the naked interests of constituent groups.

In short, when we see the alternative forums reaching noncon-

firming, inconsistent results, we are watching the impasse between
the toned-down versions of social reality and right conduct held by
at least locally significant groups in the society. Of course, there must
be ways of dealing with an impasse. A defendant either will or will
not go to jail. But it may be very significant to be apprised of the
fact that this defendant goes to jail in consequence of an impasse
rule or goes free because of one, while another conviction or acquittal
has been confirmed without inconsistent results in two or more tribunals. Such knowledge might well affect prudential decisions relating
to the party, such as sentencing or pardoning, or might affect political
decisions with respect to future enforcement policy or subsequent
norm articulation. In effect, the disagreement of outcomes in redundant proceedings is a signal and an important one.

Innovation

One of the most familiar metaphors in federalism is that of the social
"laboratory." Both Brandeis and Holmes used the image often. As
Holmes wrote in *Truax v. Corrigan*, "There is nothing I more dep-
recate than the use of the Fourteenth Amendment beyond the absolute
compulsion of its words to prevent the making of social experiments
that an important part of the community desires, in the insulated
chambers afforded by the several states. . . ."[93] This simple figure of
speech can be fleshed out into an argument that innovation in norm
articulation is healthier in a federal system. Such an argument requires
only that there be a sizable number of polities, a sufficiently similar
set of experiences within each, and effective communication among
the political entities.[94] If these three conditions are met, one may
postulate that certain distinct advantages in terms of norm articulation will accrue.

If there were a unitary source for norm articulation over a given
domain, the costs of error or lack of wisdom in any norm articulation
would be suffered throughout the domain. Now consider the actual
state of affairs in the United States. There may be with respect to

---

93. Truax v. Corrigan, 257 U.S. 312, 344 (1921) (Holmes, J. dissenting).
94. Consider the analogous argument of Martin Shapiro that the 52 jurisdictions
constitute in some sense a single decentralized decision system for torts. Shapiro,
Decentralized Decision-Making In the Law of Torts, in POLITICAL DECISION-MAKING
44–75 (S. Ulmer ed. 1970).

many matters a potential for a unitary national norm. Congress or the Supreme Court could, perhaps, announce a uniform and exclusively federal rule—constitutional, common law, or statutory. However, more typically we rely upon a regime of polycentric norm articulation in which state organs and lower federal courts enjoy a geat deal of legislative autonomy. This multiplicity of norm articulation sources provides opportunities for norm application over a limited domain without risking losses throughout the nation. This proliferation of norm-generating centers also makes it more likely that at least one such center will attempt any given, plausible innovation. For, although one cannot know this with certainty without understanding the politics of each separate entity, it is likely as a practical matter, that the many centers will include among themselves norm articulators both more and less risk averse than would be a single national source.[95] With adequate communication, successful experience with an innovation will persuade others, slightly more risk averse, to follow suit. Thus, if one assumes a distribution of risk averseness among the "local" legislators, state and federal, which brackets the risk averseness of the sources for national norms, the result will be an important qualification upon the inertial quality of

---

95. Assume a very simplistic politics. Decisionmakers in each polity reflect risk averseness in their decisions according to the results of a poll of their constituents. A linear and continuous scale relating decisions to constituent responses to the poll exists. In the national polity the constituent response is simply the sum of all subentity constituent polls. Thus, it is clear that either the national constituent preference is identical with all subentity constituent preferences or there are some subentity preference patterns reflecting greater and lesser risk averseness. If decision patterns follow constituent preferences, the decisions will also have this characteristic. However, as I have indicated in the text, the politics of the various polities may differ. Thus, it may be the case that in the national polity, decisionmakers will be, on some issue, less closely linked to constituent preferences than would be local decisionmakers. This might be the case on a relatively low visibility item if lobbyists and special interests have concentrated on national decisionmakers. The "special interests" might be risk preferring on some issue. Because they are active only on the national level, they may influence decisions so that the national norm shows less risk averseness than any of the subentities. Even though the constituency at the national level is simply a sum of the subentities, national politics bear no such simple relation to state politics. Thus, one cannot say for certain that the elimination of local polities would leave a national polity more moderate than the extant extremes of the fifty-odd jurisdictions we know. The analysis in the text assumes, nonetheless, that an exclusively national rule would be more moderate. This is an assumption of the conventional wisdom even if it is not true. Pursuing the assumption at least demonstrates the logic of the conventional model of federalism.

the polity as a whole. The multiplicity of centers means an innovation is more likely to be tried and correspondingly less likely to be wholly embraced. The two effects dampen both momentum and inertia. Assuming a general readiness to take risks, the array of multiple norm articulation sources, some of which will not go so far in innovation, will then mitigate the damages suffered through risky experiments. All of these are familiar concepts. It justifies, at least in some areas, the existence of a system of polycentric norm articulation. Such a system is a prerequisite for, but does not itself justify, jurisdictional redundancy.

It is possible to specify more exactly the ways in which polycentric norm articulation operates, especially in a world in which the various jurisdictions are not chambers wholly insulated from one another. Such a specification will suggest some of the uses of jurisdictional redundancy as well.

a. Confirmatory Redundancy

If the several legislative authorities[96] articulate the same norm, the norm is, if anything, clarified and intensified. One of the characteristics of those prohibitory regulations often labeled *malum in se* is the fact that a wide variety of norm articulating sources, independent of one another, reinforces the prohibition. There are several ways in which the iteration of a norm operates to reinforce it. It first removes what might be called jurisdictional doubt. If the norm is found almost everywhere, then it is a safer inference that the norm will be applied even when it is unclear what norm articulation source operates over a given domain. Second, the fact that a variety of norm articulators have independently arrived at a given conclusion about some conduct reduces the likelihood that the conclusion is a product of local error or prejudice, ideology, or interest. If a large number of jurisdictions arrive *independently* at the conclusion that a certain kind of conduct is wrong or detrimental, then the conclusion is more apt to reflect the problematic character of the conduct than the problematic character of the norm articulation process.[97] Finally, the meaning of the

---

96. I use the term "legislative" here to mean all norm articulation work including that of legislatures and courts.

97. It is not important here to decide whether such a widespread norm reflects human nature or a broad cultural adaptation to a common environmental factor.

norm will be clarified by reiterating independently the "central core" conduct, which all jurisdictions include within the prohibition, while leaving less clear signals for the penumbral areas with respect to which controversy exists. It will be clearer that there is in fact an unproblematic core area of conduct to which the norm will be applied. The redundancy that establishes clarity through iteration, however, need not be cross-systemic. A unitary system may, over time, clarify by repetition as well. Density of contemporaneous utterances of equal authority then is simply a horizontal array performing a function similar to that of a body of precedent over time. Insofar as the array occurs over similar domains, the contemporaneous array has greater force as (redundant) repetition of a principle.

b. Nonconfirmatory Redundancy

If we turn from the very "simple" case of redundant articulation of a norm as confirmatory to the more complex instances of conflict or confusion among the sources of articulation, a very different image emerges. Nonconfirmatory articulation of norms by different polities may reflect, of course, different social conditions and/or ideologies. The prior sections have dealt with that result. However, there may be a more prosaic explanation. As law changes, it may change in different ways and at a different pace in different jurisdictions. The social laboratory metaphor does not tell us how the results of "experiments" in one lab come to claim the attention and deliberative energies of another.

Up to this point in the analysis, the distinctive and arguably advantageous characteristics of polycentric norm articulation have not required jurisdictional redundancy. Once we focus upon the overlapping effects of legislation outside the limited domains of individual states and districts, however, jurisdictional redundancy becomes central. If fifty-odd primary legislative authorities and several hundred coordinate judicial authorities are to pronounce upon the effects and limits of conduct which is entitled to and regularly does cross those political/jurisdictional lines, then there are two important advantages that flow from jurisdictional redundancy. First, the ensuing jurisdictional conflict may play a special role in communication among polities. Second, jurisdictional choice affords a kind of fairness to people whose affairs are caught in the vice of change—whose private lives and expectations are shaken by innovation.

(1) Communication

The advantages of polycentric norm articulation are greatest for little things.[98] Decision theorists have contrasted two paradigms for decisionmaking. One, variously denominated "synoptic"[99] and "analytic,"[100] posits a comprehensive choice between two alternative end-states with a complete cost-benefit analysis or similar mode of choice employed. Such a comprehensive comparison among options places an enormous burden on the decisionmaker. It may place impossible demands for information, analytic power, and attention upon the decision process.[101] Great decisions may possibly require that such demands be met. The demands will be met, *if possible,* if the matter is so important that few other decisions can compete for these resources. But more routine decisions cannot totally usurp the attention of the authoritative decisionmaker or the informational and analytic resources available. Systems must be structured to cope with such decisions more routinely. Different analysts have concentrated upon somewhat different dimensions of such routinized decisionmaking, labelling it alternatively "disjointed incrementalism"[102] or the "cybernetic paradigm."[103] In such systems the component act of decision focuses on a relatively small number of marginal changes in critical variables and responds to these with a repertoire of "programmed" responses. The insufficiency of such a set of responses to complex problems in a complex environment is obvious. But "under conditions of complexity, decisionmaking organizations arise which attempt to match the complexity of their environment by means of

---

98. *See* Shapiro, *Stability and Change in Judicial Decision-Making: Incrementalism or Stare Decisis?,* 2 L. TRANSITION Q. 134 (1965).

99. D. BRAYBROOKE & C. LINDBLOM, A STRATEGY OF DECISION; POLICY EVALUATION AS A SOCIAL PROCESS (1963).

100. J. STEINBRUNER, *supra* note 42, at 25–46.

101. *See id. See also* R. CYERT & J. MARCH, A BEHAVIORAL THEORY OF THE FIRM (1963); J. MARCH & H. SIMON, ORGANIZATIONS (1958). Both of these classic works in organization theory build from the point that limited decisional capacity requires modifications in the paradigm of comprehensive optimization decisions.

102. D. BRAYBROOKE & C. LINDBLOM, *supra* note 99.

103. J. STEINBRUNER, *supra* note 42, at 47–87.

an internal complexity which is not the property of a single decision maker, but rather of the collective."[104] The polycentric norm articulation of our court system is one such instance.

Today, courts may or may not be said to operate with a limited number of programmed responses to a few critical variables.[105] Unlike the kinds of organizations studied by Cyert and March,[106] by Steinbruner,[107] or by Simon,[108] they are typically uncontrolled by a top-level "management" which can integrate the decisions, whether analytically or by "sequential attention to goals."[109] The system, if it is to be successful, must have nonhierarchical solutions to the problem of integration of decisions, solutions which are themselves adequately complex.[110]

A large number of decision centers, simultaneously dealing with the same or similar problems, generates a density of experience that produces information quickly with simultaneous, interactive effects of decision and environment. At this point jurisdictional redundancy comes into play. The availability of alternative forums makes information, at least about pairs of jurisdictions, a matter of practical relevance to lawyers and litigants. Forum shoppers and those who oppose them thus become the carriers that polinate one system of courts with the information about another system's experience.[111] Moreover, where synchronic or diachronic redundancy is possible, each system must confront the potentially conflicting outcome *in the same case* of some other court with its alternative norms. Such a possibility makes second thoughts and adjustments more likely.

---

104. *Id.* at 69.

105. It might be argued that in a traditional system built on stare decisis each decision departs only marginally from preset responses, and then only in response to a very few salient variables in the situation. Whether that description ever fits appellate courts in the United States I do not know, but it seems far from an apt description of many appellate courts today.

106. *See* R. CYERT & J. MARCH, *supra* note 101.

107. *See* J. STEINBRUNER, *supra* note 42.

108. *See* J. MARCH & H. SIMON, *supra* note 101.

109. The term is that of R. CYERT & J. MARCH, *supra* note 101.

110. *See* Shapiro, *supra* note 94.

111. For a number of reasons this effect should be more pronounced in a system with jurisdictional redundancy than in one of a multiplicity of wholly independent decision centers. While in both cases adversaries might raise the law and experience of another jurisdiction, it is far more likely when those data have been part of the earlier strategic choices concerning the forum. Moreover, the vertical redundancy of the federal courts permits the neutral perspective on alternative norms.

Finally, such conflict of laws cases present a dramatic enactment of paired alternatives for future norm articulation. No longer is the court presented with an abstract choice of which rule to choose. Rather it is presented with at least two parties, each of whom claims as his own one of the alternative norm formulations. In short, acquiring information about other jurisdictions and their rules is a time consuming and costly process. It is in those cases in which a party claims another forum and/or its rule that a given court is forced to focus upon the other courts that compose this internally complex response to a complex environment.[112]

(2) Fairness

Innovating jurisdictions have a simple interest in externalizing the costs of the transition to whatever extent possible. While there are constitutional limits to what a state can do in externalizing such costs, those limits are very far from a comprehensive and effective bar.[113]

Moreover, it is by no means clear in many cases which of several different norms is the "innovation," and it is rarely if ever plain who ought to bear the costs of a transition. In short, a right answer to the question of how much of the cost can be imposed upon whom may be impossible to conceive. Nonetheless, there may be plain enough questions to be asked and some likelihood that different courts will answer them differently, not because of ideology or interest but because of differing views and commitments with respect to the policy issues at stake.

Jurisdictional redundancy can alleviate such problems in one of two ways. Most simply it may—as in the case of ideology—simply

---

112. There is another way of looking at this. Courts are much more likely to seriously encounter another court's law in an explicit choice of law situation. While such choice of law cases can arise whether or not there is jurisdictional redundancy, there is a strong positive correlation between the availability of multiple forums and the appearance of choice of law questions. The reason is simple enough. Many cases can appear to be domestic—the interstate element largely ignored—if it is natural and inevitable that they be heard only in the courts of the state with a particular relation to the subject. Once that jurisdiction link is established, several other relations become more salient and choice of law becomes problematic.

113. The "dormant" commerce clause is one of the chief limits. See L. TRIBE, AMERICAN CONSTITUTIONAL LAW 319–412 (1978).

facilitate fighting fire with fire. A party prejudiced by the policy commitments of Forum One will have an opportunity to try to invoke Forum Two with its contrary policy whether as an alternative to, a replacement or supplement for, or a sequel to Forum One. Alternatively, the concurrent jurisdiction may afford a neutral choice of law forum, a sort of Archimedean fulcrum above the commitments of either of two forums. The disinterested forum for choice of law might have developed out of diversity were it not for the *Klaxon* rule.[114] Moreover, the case could be made that, today, choice of law is one of the primary areas where some respectable state courts *do* systematically prejudice the out-of-staters.[115] So an anti-*Klaxon* rule would be consistent with the supposed office of diversity.

Not all problems of innovation in a coordinate system involve state-state choice of law questions. Lower federal courts and state courts stand on a par as expositors of federal law, including the Constitution. I have shown elsewhere, in detail, that the relation of state courts to lower federal courts in habeas corpus situations facilitates a creative dialogue in the ongoing work of articulating constitutional norms to govern the criminal process.[116] The fact of diachronic jurisdictional redundancy means that each system must attend closely to the articulations of the other. For each system can withhold from the other an element necessary to full success. If there is disagreement as to what the Constitution requires, federal courts may release prisoners and thus frustrate the specific objective of the state court. However, the state courts may persist in their independent and contrary view of the norm and, thus, in future cases, frustrate the norm the federal court seeks to impose.

In all such transition cases, civil or criminal, it is important to see the nature of the plight of the litigant. She appeals to "law" against law. It may be an appeal to law which one of several alternative forums calls no law. But so long as such a forum is only one of several, there is room, for awhile at least, for recognition of the truly open, tentative, and transitional status of norms which do not

---

114. Klaxon Co. v. Stentor Elec. Mfg. Co., 313 U.S. 487 (1941) (requiring that federal district courts sitting in diversity apply the choice of law rules of the state in which they sit).

115. This point is sharply and justifiably made by Brilmayer, *Interest Analysis and the Myth of Legislative Intent*, 78 Mich. L. Rev. 392 (1980).

116. Cover & Aleinikoff, *supra* note 35.

yet command common acquiescence among all relevant authoritative courts. Openness about such transitional norms might be useful in many ways. It might lead, for example, to compromise either upon the underlying claim or upon a third "neutral" forum.[117]

The Challenge to Coordination Rules

If jurisdictional redundancy has affirmative functional characteristics in these three, related areas of interest, ideology, and innovation, what consequences will follow with respect to the specific rules that govern coordination in a system of complex concurrency? These rules are of three sorts, involving: (a) rules and principles governing invocation of the forum, including rules governing in personam and subject matter competence, stays, abstention and other discretionary declinations of jurisdiction, *forum non conveniens*, and others; (b) rules and principles governing the law applied, involving largely choice of law and *Erie*; and (c) rules governing effects of determinations, such as res judicata, collateral estoppel, effects of judgments, and double jeopardy. Nothing of what I have written thus far provides a determinative answer to any question about specific coordination rules. Rather, I have presented a justification for the system as a whole with its characteristic need for coordination. Despite this lack of specific answers, several general principles are suggested that do have practical implications.

First, since the substantive battlefields upon which conflicts of interest, ideology, and innovation are fought change over time, it is not to be expected that effective coordination rules will be substance-neutral emenations of formal structure alone.[118] Rather, the areas of relatively unrestrained redundancy will change with the salient social conflicts. Thus, recourse to the federal forum in diversity was of utmost significance, in terms of both ideology and innovation, with respect to large scale equity receiverships and municipal bond litigation in the last half of the nineteenth century and with respect to labor in the 1920s and early 1930s. Access to the redundant federal

---

117. We do not often think of compromise as the judicial solution to conflict over norm articulation. Other cultures use compromise more fully than do we. *See* Eisenberg, *supra* note 17, at 640–46.

118. An example is the rule that a state must give the judgment of a sister state the same effect as it has in the state of rendition.

forum under sections 1983[119] and 1343[120] has been of equivalent concern in the 1960s and 1970s. When diversity, rather than civil rights jurisdiction, captures the relevant ideological differences, it will be with respect to diversity that coordination principles are highly articulated. The intricacies of diversity jurisdiction could occupy the scholars of the 1890s and 1920s with much the same degree of refinement as is now lavished upon section 1983.

Second, the political pressure for open avenues of redundancy comes about when effects are not random. Thus, to the extent that the redundant forum simply provides an avenue for forum shopping with no systematic differences arising from interest, ideology, or innovation, there will not be an identifiable and cohesive group prejudiced by the presence or absence of the alternative forum. When the forum becomes an issue to an identifiable group, it is because that group thinks that there is more than mere randomly distributed error at stake. This means that the very fact that significant groups have conflicting systematic preferences for a forum or type of forum as to some issue is a strong argument for relatively unrestrained redundancy.

Conclusion

This paper has been a plea for a nonsolution. For some time the jurisdictional structure of "our federalism" has struck me as comprehensible only as a blueprint for conflict and confrontation, not for cooperation and deference. It seems unfashionable to seek out a messy and indeterminate end to conflicts which may be tied neatly together by a single authoritative verdict. Unquestionably, my perverse perspective may be carried too far. I, ultimately, do not want to deny that there is value in repose and order. But the inner logic of "our federalism" seems to me to point more insistently to the social value of institutions in conflict with one another. It is a daring system that permits the tensions and conflicts of the social order to be displayed in the very jurisdictional structure of its courts. It is that view of federalism that we ought to embrace.

---

119. 42 U.S.C. § 1963 (1976).
120. 28 U.S.C. § 1343(a)(3) (Supp. III 1979).

Chapter 3

Nomos and Narrative

A. A violent order is disorder; and
B. A great disorder is an order. These
Two things are one. (Pages of illustrations.)
　　　　　　　　　　　—Wallace Stevens[1]

I. Introduction

We inhabit a *nomos*—a normative universe. We constantly create
and maintain a world of right and wrong, of lawful and unlawful,
of valid and void.[2] The student of law may come to identify the
normative world with the professional paraphernalia of social control.
The rules and principles of justice, the formal institutions of the law,
and the conventions of a social order are, indeed, important to that
world; they are, however, but a small part of the normative universe
that ought to claim our attention. No set of legal institutions or
prescriptions exists apart from the narratives that locate it and give

I wish to thank Boris Bittker, Robert Burt, Harlon Dalton, Mirjam Damaska, Perry
Dane, Owen Fiss, Jack Getman, Paul Gewirtz, Michael Graetz, Henry Hansmann,
Geoffrey Hazard, Leon Lipson, Jerry Mashaw, Peter Schuck, Avi Soifer, Harry Wellington, Stan Wheeler, and Steve Wizner for generous assistance at various stages in
the preparation of this Foreword. I also profited from comments by many colleagues
at a Yale Faculty work-in-progress session. I am indebted to Suhn-Kyoung Hong,
Yale J.D. 1985, and to Elyn Saks, Yale J.D. 1986, for research assistance in the
preparation of the Foreword.
　　1. W. STEVENS, *Connoisseur of Chaos*, in THE COLLECTED POEMS OF WALLACE
STEVENS 215 (1954).
　　2. On the idea of "world building" with its normative implications, see, for
example, P. BERGER, THE SACRED CANOPY (1967); P. BERGER & T. LUCKMANN, THE
SOCIAL CONSTRUCTION OF REALITY (1966); J. GAGER, KINGDOM AND COMMUNITY (1975);
K. MANNHEIM, IDEOLOGY AND UTOPIA (1936); *cf.* P. BERGER, *supra*, at 19 & *passim*
(invoking the idea of a "nomos" or "meaningful order").

it meaning.[3] For every constitution there is an epic, for each decalogue a scripture.[4] Once understood in the context of the narratives that give it meaning, law becomes not merely a system of rules to be observed, but a world in which we live.

In this normative world, law and narrative are inseparably related. Every prescription is insistent in its demand to be located in discourse—to be supplied with history and destiny, beginning and end, explanation and purpose.[5] And every narrative is insistent in its demand for its prescriptive point, its moral. History and literature cannot escape their location in a normative universe,[6] nor can prescription, even when embodied in a legal text, escape its origin and its end in experience, in the narratives that are the trajectories plotted upon material reality by our imaginations.[7]

---

3. I do not mean to imply that there is an official, privileged canon of narratives. Indeed, although some canons, like the Bible, integrate legal material with narrative texts, modern legal texts (with the possible exception of some court opinions) do not characteristically do so. It is the diffuse and unprivileged character of narrative in a modern world, together with the indispensability of narrative to the quest for meaning, that is a principal focus of this Foreword.

4. Prescriptive texts change their meaning with each new epic we choose to make relevant to them. Every version of the framing of the Constitution creates a "new" text in this sense. When the text proves unable to assimilate the meanings of new narratives that are nonetheless of constitutive significance, people do create new texts—they amend the Constitution. Thus, the adoption of the 13th, 14th, and 15th amendments may be seen as the creation of new texts to fit new constitutive epics. But other ways of creating texts may be less "official" and more dangerous. A deep division about the constitutive epics may lead to secessionist prescriptive texts—competing prescriptions to go with the competing narratives. *Compare* CONFEDERATE STATES OF AM. CONST. art. IV, § 2, CL. 1 (providing that a slave may not become free by transit in free territory), *with* U.S. CONST. art. IV, § 2, CL. 3 (fugitive slave clause). For the narrative context of this prescriptive conflict, see R. COVER, JUSTICE ACCUSED 86–88, 284 n. 10 (1975).

5. This point is similar if not identical to that made by the late Lon Fuller in L. FULLER, THE LAW IN QUEST OF ITSELF (1940).

6. *See, e.g.,* White, *The Value of Narrativity in the Representation of Reality,* in ON NARRATIVE 1, 20 (W. Mitchell ed. 1981) ("The demand for closure in the historical story is a demand, I suggest, for moral meaning, a demand that sequences of real events be assessed as to their significance as elements of a *moral* drama."); *see also id.* at 23 (suggesting that the demand for closure in the representation of "real events" "arises out of a desire to have real events display the coherence, integrity, fullness, and closure of an image of life that is and can only be imaginary").

7. There is a thick contextuality to all moral situations. *Cf.* C. GEERTZ, THE INTERPRETATION OF CULTURES 5 (1973) ("[M]an is an animal suspended in webs of significance he himself has spun."). For discussions of the "social texts" that form these contexts, see C. GEERTZ, NEGARA (1980); Fiss, *Objectivity and Interpretation,*

This *nomos* is as much "our world" as is the physical universe of mass, energy, and momentum. Indeed, our apprehension of the structure of the normative world is no less fundamental than our appreciation of the structure of the physical world. Just as the development of increasingly complex responses to the physical attributes of our world begins with birth itself, so does the parallel development of the responses to personal otherness that define the normative world.[8]

The great legal civilizations have, therefore, been marked by more than technical virtuosity in their treatment of practical affairs, by more than elegance or rhetorical power in the composition of their texts, by more, even, than genius in the invention of new forms for new problems. A great legal civilization is marked by the richness of the *nomos* in which it is located and which it helps to constitute.[9] The varied and complex materials of that *nomos* establish paradigms for dedication, acquiescence, contradiction, and resistance. These materials present not only bodies of rules or doctrine to be understood, but also worlds to be inhabited. To inhabit a *nomos* is to know how to *live* in it.[10]

---

34 STAN. L. REV. 739 (1982). On the agonistic circumstances of all interpretation, see H. BLOOM, THE ANXIETY OF INFLUENCE (1973). The thick context of literary and political theory is examined in Q. SKINNER, FOUNDATIONS OF MODERN POLITICAL THOUGHT (1978). On the central place of history and the human person in any account of law, see J. NOONAN, PERSONS AND MASKS OF THE LAW (1976).

8. *See, e.g.,* E. ERIKSON, CHILDHOOD AND SOCIETY 247 (1950); L. KOHLBERG, THE PHILOSOPHY OF MORAL DEVELOPMENT (1981); J. PIAGET, THE MORAL JUDGMENT OF THE CHILD (1932); J. PIAGET, PLAY, DREAMS AND IMITATION IN CHILDHOOD (1962). For an extended theoretical definition of the implications of "otherness," see 1–3 J. BOWLBY, ATTACHMENT AND LOSS (1969–1980), especially 1 *id.* at 177–298 (1969). It is instructive to note the structural similarity of theories of development, such as those of Piaget, Erikson, Bowlby, and Kohlberg, that include emotional, social, and moral components. All stress a system in which development is from a physiological, somatic dependence or interdependence to an awareness of abstract and cultural artifacts. A similar development is entailed in the acquisition of a concept such as space. *See, e.g.,* J. PIAGET & B. INHELDER, THE CHILD'S CONCEPTION OF SPACE (1967).

9. The Greek and Hebrew legal civilizations are remembered by us now chiefly for their magnificent use of narrative to explore great normative questions in relation to which the precise technical handling of an issue is of secondary importance. *See infra* pp. 19–25 (discussion of biblical texts). For one (perhaps idiosyncratic) view of the integration of Greek ideals of law and justice with other great cultural achievements of ancient Hellas, see 1–2 W. JAEGER, PAIDEIA (1939–1943), especially 1 *id.* (1939).

10. I mean here to suggest a rough correspondence to the Kuhnian understanding

The problem of "meaning" in law—of legal hermeneutics or interpretation—is commonly associated with one rather narrow kind of problem that confronts officials and those who seek to predict, control, or profit from official behavior.[11] A decision must be made about the incidence of a legal instrument. "Is an airplane or a baby carriage a 'vehicle' within the meaning of the statute prohibiting vehicles in the park?" "Is the statutory requirement of a minimum hourly wage a denial of liberty or property without due process of law?" There is a conventional understanding that a certain consequence follows from the instrument's classifying a thing as "X." There is a dispute about the appropriate criteria for classification.[12] Such problems of official application of legal precepts form one important body of questions about the meaning of law. But I want to stress a very different set of issues.

The normative universe is held together by the force of inter-

---

of "science" not as a body of propositions about the world nor as a method, but as paradigms integrating method, belief, and propositions—a doing. See T. KUHN, THE STRUCTURE OF SCIENTIFIC REVOLUTIONS (1962); M. POLANYI, PERSONAL KNOWLEDGE (1958).

11. The traditional problems are outlined in W. BISHIN & C. STONE, LAW, LANGUAGE AND ETHICS (1972). Even those who have expanded the concept of hermeneutics have often considered legal hermeneutics to be in large part addressed to a set of operational problems. See, e.g., H. GADAMER, TRUTH AND METHOD (G. Barden & J. Cumming trans. 1975). Gadamer, commenting on a practice I assume he thought characteristic of legal scholarship and dogmatics as practiced in its continental form, wrote: "Legal hermeneutics does not belong in this context [a 'general theory of the understanding and interpretation of texts'], for it is not its purpose to understand given texts, but to be a practical measure to help fill a kind of gap in the system of legal dogmatics." Id. at 289. The entire discussion of legal hermeneutics in Truth and Method is disappointingly provincial in several ways. First, it is entirely statist and therefore does not raise the question of the hermeneutic problems peculiar to all systems of objectified normative texts (statist and nonstatist alike). But it also inadequately addresses the question of the destruction of the hermeneutic in the necessarily apologetic functions of an officaldom. Finally, in Truth and Method, the problem of application is seen as the characteristic difficulty. Thus, even when Gadamer denies the possibility of a straightforward application of general laws to specific facts, he discusses the "problem" of legal hermeneutics as this problem. See, e.g., id. at 471 ("The distance between the universality of the law and the concrete legal situation in a particular case is obviously essentially indissoluble.").

Several of the problems addressed in this Foreword have been suggestively treated by James White, first in J. WHITE, THE LEGAL IMAGINATION (1973), and later in White, Law as Language: Reading Law and Reading Literature, 60 TEX. L. REV. 415 (1982). I am indebted to Professor White for the ways in which he has explored the range of meaning-constituting functions of legal discourse.

12. See W. BISHIN & C. STONE, supra note 11 (collecting cases and materials).

pretive commitments—some small and private, others immense and
public. These commitments—of officials and of others—do determine
what law means and what law shall be.[13] If there existed two legal
orders with identical legal precepts and identical, predictable patterns
of public force, they would nonetheless differ essentially in meaning
if, in one of the orders, the precepts were universally venerated while
in the other they were regarded by many as fundamentally unjust.[14]

I must stress that what I am describing is *not* the distinction
between the "law in action" and the "law in the books." Surely a
law may be successfully enforced but actively resented. It is a somber
fact of our own world that many citizens believe that, with *Roe v.
Wade*,[15] the Supreme Court licensed the killing of absolutely innocent
human beings. Others believe that the retreat from *Furman v. Georgia*[16] has initiated a period of official state murder. Even if the horror
and resentment felt by such persons fails to manifest itself in the
pattern of court decisions and their enforcement, the meaning of the
normative world changes with these events. Both for opponents of
abortion and for opponents of capital punishment the principle that
"no person shall be deprived of life without due process of law" has
assumed an ironic cast. The future of this particular precept is now
freighted with that irony no less than with the precedents of *Roe* and
Furman themselves.

Just as the meaning of law is determined by our interpretive
commitments, so also can many of our actions be understood only
in relation to a norm. Legal precepts and principles are not only
demands made upon us by society, the people, the sovereign, or God.
They are also signs by which each of us communicates with others.
There is a difference between sleeping late on Sunday and refusing
the sacraments,[17] between having a snack and desecrating the fast of

---

13. On commitment, see *infra* pp. 144–63.

14. We commonly express and sometimes confuse our sense of this difference
through a chronological projection of an ontological distinction. We speak of one
legal order as "decadent" or "crumbling" and often think that this quality will *make
a difference*—will cause a change over time. This projection onto chronology may
entail a serious prediction, of course, but I would suggest that it is as frequently a
metaphor (the propositions are so vague that they are never seriously testable) for
a deficiency we believe to inhere in a state of affairs.

15. 410 U.S. 113 (1973).

16. 408 U.S. 238 (1972).

17. *See, e.g.,* W. STEVENS, *Sunday Morning*, in THE COLLECTED POEMS OF
WALLACE STEVENS, *supra* note 1, at 66–70.

Yom Kippur,[18] between banking a check and refusing to pay your income tax. In each case an act signifies something new and powerful when we understand that the act is in reference to a norm. It is this characteristic of certain lawbreaking that gives rise to special claims for civil disobedients. But the capacity of law to imbue action with significance is not limited to resistance or disobedience. Law is a resource in signification that enables us to submit,[19] rejoice, struggle,[20] pervert, mock,[21] disgrace, humiliate, or dignify.[22] The sense that we make of our normative world, then, is not exhausted when we specify the patterns of demands upon us, even with each explicated by Hercules to constitute an internally consistent and justified package. We construct meaning in our normative world by using the irony of jurisdiction,[23] the comedy of manners that is *malum prohibitum*,[24]

---

18. This point is illustrated in Irving Howe's description of Yiddish radicalism on the Lower East Side:

> That the anarchists and some of the social democrats chose to demonstrate their freedom from superstition by holding balls and parades on Yom Kippur night, the most sacred moment of the Jewish year, showed not merely insensitivity but also the extent to which traditional faith dominated those who denied it.

I. HOWE, WORLD OF OUR FATHERS 106 (1976).

19. On domination and submission, see Hay, *Property, Authority and the Criminal Law*, in D. HAY, P. LINEBAUGH, J. RULE, E. THOMPSON & C. WINSLOW, ALBION'S FATAL TREE 17 (1975).

20. *See, e.g.*, R. KLUGER, SIMPLE JUSTICE (1975).

21. The story of Gary Gilmore provides a powerful example of the use of law for mockery. *See* N. MAILER, THE EXECUTIONER'S SONG (1979).

22. Law's expressive range is profound, and as with other resources of language, the relation of law's manifest content to its meaning is often complicated. Consider the question of using capital punishment to *express* the dignity of human life and its ultimate worth:

> This view of the uniqueness and supremacy of human life has yet another consequence. It places life beyond the reach of other values. The idea that life may be measured in terms of money . . . is excluded. Compensation of any kind is ruled out. The guilt of the murderer is infinite because the murdered life is invaluable. . . . The effect of this view is, to be sure, paradoxical: because human life is invaluable, to take it entails the death penalty. Yet the paradox must not blind us to the judgment of value that the law sought to embody.

Greenberg, *Some Postulates of Biblical Criminal Law*, in THE JEWISH EXPRESSION 18, 26 (J. Goldin ed. 1970) (footnote omitted).

23. *See, e.g.*, Marbury v. Madison, 5 U.S. (1 Cranch) 137 (1803). *Marbury* is a particularly powerful example of a general phenomenon. *Every* denial of jurisdiction on the part of a court is an assertion of the power to *determine* jurisdiction and thus to constitute a norm.

24. With the recognition, already well developed in ancient Greek thought, of

the surreal epistemology of due process.[25]

A legal tradition is hence part and parcel of a complex normative world. The tradition includes not only a corpus juris, but also a language and a mythos—narratives in which the corpus juris is located by those whose wills act upon it. These myths establish the paradigms for behavior. They build relations between the normative and the material universe, between the constraints of reality and the demands of an ethic. These myths establish a repertoire of moves— a lexicon of normative action—that may be combined into meaningful patterns culled from the meaningful patterns of the past. The normative meaning that has inhered in the patterns of the past will be found in the history of ordinary legal doctrine at work in mundane affairs; in utopian and messianic yearnings, imaginary shapes given to a less resistant reality; in apologies for power and privilege and in the critiques that may be leveled at the justificatory enterprises of law.

Law may be viewed as a system of tension or a bridge linking a concept of a reality to an imagined alternative—that is, as a connective between two states of affairs, both of which can be represented in their normative significance only through the devices of narrative.[26] Thus, one constitutive element of a *nomos* is the phenomemon George Steiner has labeled "alternity": "the 'other than the case', the counterfactual propositions, images, shapes of will and evasion with which we charge our mental being and by means of which we build the changing, largely fictive milieu for our somatic and our social existence."[27]

But the concept of a *nomos* is not exhausted by its "alternity"; it is neither utopia nor pure vision. A *nomos*, as a world of law, entails the application of human will to an extant state of affairs as well as toward our visions of alternative futures. A *nomos* is a present world constituted by a system of tension between reality and vision.

the relativity and essentially contingent character of much of the preceptual material in any society, there arises the possibility of making fun of the specific precepts of a society and especially of the heavy investment authority structures have in something bearing no necessary (*malum in se*) relation to the great and potentially tragic clashes of good and evil. When the devil is of our own creation, he becomes comic.

25. *See* G. GILMORE, THE AGES OF AMERICAN LAW III (1977) ("In Hell there will be nothing but law, and due process will be meticulously observed.").

26. *See* White, *supra* note 6.

27. G. STEINER, AFTER BABEL 222 (1975).

Our visions hold our reality up to us as unredeemed. By themselves the alternative worlds of our visions—the lion lying down with the lamb, the creditor forgiving debts each seventh year, the state all shriveled and withered away—dictate no particular set of transformations or efforts at transformation. But law gives a vision depth of field, by placing one part of it in the highlight of insistent and immediate demand while casting another part in the shadow of the millenium. Law is that which licenses in blood certain transformations while authorizing others only by unanimous consent. Law is a force, like gravity, through which our worlds exercise an influence upon one another, a force that affects the courses of these worlds through normative space. And law is that which holds our reality apart from our visions and rescues us from the eschatology that is the collision in this material social world of the constructions of our minds.

The codes that relate our normative system to our social constructions of reality and to our visions of what the world might be are narrative. The very imposition of a normative force upon a state of affairs, real or imagined, is the act of creating narrative. The various genres of narrative—history, fiction, tragedy, comedy—are alike in their being the account of states of affairs affected by a normative force field. To live in a legal world requires that one know not only the precepts, but also their connections to possible and plausible states of affairs. It requires that one integrate not only the "is" and the "ought," but the "is," the "ought," and the "what might be." Narrative so integrates these domains. Narratives are models through which we study and experience transformations that result when a given simplified state of affairs is made to pass through the force field of a similarly simplified set of norms.

The intelligibility of normative behavior inheres in the communal character of the narratives that provide the context of that behavior. Any person who lived an entirely idiosyncratic normative life would be quite mad. The part that you or I choose to play may be singular, but the fact that we can locate it in a common "script" renders it "sane"—a warrant that we share a *nomos*.[28]

In Part II of this Foreword, I first contrast an ideal form for the creation of a *nomos*—of a legal world conceived purely as legal

---

28. The warranty of sanity is worth only as much as the social processes that generate it. I perceive a difference, however, between the collective outrages that we sometimes label madness and the idiosyncratic act of an individual.

meaning—with the more familiar notion of law as social control. Next, I elaborate the unfamiliar idea of a *nomos* by providing an extended illustration through the use of biblical texts. I have chosen this material because the Bible constitutes a conventionally circumscribed corpus of integrated prescriptive and narrative material that can serve as an artificially simplified model. The sections that follow then apply the model to the more complex problems of creating constitutional meaning—problems that we meet in our own world—but concentrate on the creation of such meaning outside the official court. Two distinct versions of *nomos*—the insular and the redemptive—are explored. Part III then introduces the special role of commitment in living out legal meaning; it contrasts the nature of the commitments necessary on the part of communities that affirm a legal meaning opposed to that of the state with the nature of the commitment of official judges. Part IV concludes by offering a critique, based on the principles and methods developed throughout the Foreward, of *Bob Jones University v. United States.*[29]

II. Legal Worlds and Legal Meaning

The *nomos* that I have described requires no state. And indeed, it is the thesis of this Foreword that the creation of legal meaning—"jurisgenesis"—takes place always through an essentially cultural medium.[30] Although the state is not necessarily the creator of legal meaning, the creative process is collective or social. In the following Section, I shall suggest a social basis for jurisgenesis and a corresponding social basis for the process that destroys legal meaning in the interest of social control.

A. Jurisgenesis

According to one of Judaism's oldest rabbinic traditions

---

29. 103 S. Ct. 2017 (1983).

30. The state becomes central in the process not because it is well suited to jurisgenesis nor because the cultural processes of giving meaning to normative activity cease in the presence of the state. The state becomes central only because, as I shall argue in Part III, an act of commitment is a central aspect of legal meaning. And violence is one extremely powerful measure and test of commitment.

Simeon the Just [circa 200 B.C.E.] said: Upon three things the
world stands: upon Torah; upon the temple worship service; and
upon deeds of kindness.[31]

The "world" of which Simeon the Just spoke was the *nomos*, the
normative universe. Three hundred years later, after the destruction
of the Temple whose worship service was one of the pillars upon
which the "world" of Simeon the Just stood, Rabbi Simeon ben
Gamaliel said, "Upon three things the world [continues to] exist[]:
upon justice, upon truth, and upon peace."[32]

These two parallel aphorisms are reported within a single chapter
in the talmudic tractate *Aboth* and frame the chapter's contents. Of
the aphorisms, the great sixteenth century codifier, commentator, and
mystic, Joseph Karo, wrote the following:

[F]or Simeon the Just spoke in the context of his generation in
which the Temple stood, and Rabbi Simeon ben Gamaliel spoke
in the context of his generation after the destruction of Jerusalem.

---

31. MISHNAH, *Aboth* I:2. The exact identity and dates of Simeon the Just are
unknown. Most scholars now believe that he was the high priest Simeon II—son of
Onias II—who favored the Seleucids in their attempt to wrest Judea from the Ptolemaic
dynasty. *See* 14 ENCYCLOPAEDIA JUDAICA 1566–67 (1972). For a critical and historical
study of the aphorism of Simeon the Just, see Goldin, *The Three Pillars of Simeon
the Righteous*, 27 A.M. ACAD. FOR JEWISH RESEARCH PROC. 43 (1958).

The Hebrew word *Torah* was translated into the Greek *nomos* in the Septuagint
and in the Greek scripture and postscriptural writings, and into the English phrase
"the Law." "*Torah*," like "*nomos*" and "the Law," is amenable to a range of meanings
that serve both to enrich the term and to obscure analysis of it. In particular, all
three terms suggest Paul's polemic against the Law. The Hebrew "*Torah*" refers both
to law in the sense of a body of regulation and, by extension, to the corpus of all
related normative material and to the teaching and learning of those primary and
secondary sources. In this fully extended sense, the term embraces life itself, or at
least the normative dimension of it, and "*Torah*" is used with just such figurative
extension in later rabbinics. For a discussion of these senses of "*Torah*," see E. URBACH,
THE SAGES 286 (1979). The word *Torah* also connotes a canon of normatively authoritative material and its study. For the observation that, in contrast to the use of the
term in earlier scriptural sources, "*Torah*" is always singular in Deuteronomic writing
"in compliance with the notion of a canonized Torah," see M. WEINFELD, DEUTER-
ONOMY AND THE DEUTERONOMIC SCHOOL app. A at 338 (1972). Certainly in postbiblical
writings the appearance of "*Torah*" in the plural has an extraordinary, unusual, and
therefore expressive power. *See, e.g.*, "The Beraitha of Rabbi Jose," in BABYLONIAN
TALMUD, *Sanhedrin* 88b.

32. MISHNAH, *Aboth* I:18.

> Rabbi Simeon b. Gamaliel taught that even though the temple
> no longer existed and we no longer have its worship service and
> even though the yoke of our exile prevents us from engaging in
> Torah [study of divine law and instruction] and good deeds to
> the extent desirable, nonetheless the [normative] universe con-
> tinues to exist by virtue of these three other things [justice, truth,
> and peace] which are similar to the first three. For there is a
> difference between the [force needed for the] preservation of that
> which already exists and the [force needed for the] initial reali-
> zation of that which had not earlier existed at all. . . . And so,
> in this instance, it would have been impossible to have created
> the world on the basis of the three principles of Rabbi Simeon
> ben Gamaliel. But after the world had been created on the three
> things of Simeon the Just it can continue to exist upon the basis
> of Rabbi Simeon b. Gamaliel's three.[33]

Karo's insight is important. The universalist virtues that we have
come to identify with modern liberalism, the broad principles of our
law, are essentially system-maintaining "weak" forces. They are virtues that are justified by the need to ensure the *coexistence* of worlds
of strong normative meaning. The systems of normative life that they
maintain are the products of "strong" forces: culture-specific designs
of particularist meaning. These "strong" forces—for Karo, "Torah,
worship, and deeds of kindness"—*create* the normative worlds in
which law is predominantly a system of meaning rather than an
imposition of force.

Karo's commentary and the aphorisms that are its subject suggest
two corresponding ideal-typical patterns of combining corpus, discourse, and interpersonal commitment to form a *nomos*. The first
such pattern, which according to Karo is world-creating, I shall call
"paideic," because the term suggests: (1) a common body of precept
and narrative, (2) a common and personal way of being educated
into this corpus, and (3) a sense of direction or growth that is constituted as the individual and his community work out the implications of their law. Law as Torah is pedagogic. It requires both the

---

33. J. KARO, BEIT YOSEF AT TUR: HOSHEN MISHPAT 1 (translation by R. Cover).
For a useful biographical study of Karo, see R. WERBLOWSKY, JOSEPH KARO, LAWYER
AND MYSTIC (1962). On the significance of the *Beit Yosef*, see 5 ENCYCLOPAEDIA JUDAICA
195–96 (1971).

discipline of study and the projection of understanding onto the future that is interpretation. Obedience is correlative to understanding. Discourse is initiatory, celebratory, expressive, and performative, rather than critical and analytic. Interpersonal commitments are characterized by reciprocal acknowledgment, the recognition that individuals have particular needs and strong obligations to render person-specific responses. Such a vision, of course, is neither uniquely rabbinic nor ancient.[34] The vision of a strong community of common obligations has also been at the heart of what Christians conceive as the Church.

The second ideal-typical pattern, which finds its fullest expression in the civil community, is "world maintaining."[35] I shall call it "imperial."[36] In this model, norms are universal and *enforced* by institutions. They need not be taught at all, as long as they are effective. Discourse is premised on objectivity—upon that which is external to the discourse itself. Interpersonal commitments are weak, premised only upon a minimalist obligation to refrain from the coercion and violence that would make impossible the objective mode of discourse and the impartial and neutral application of norms.

Karl Barth, writing of Christian community and civil commu-

---

34. Indeed, some might question the application of what scholars have found to be a distinctly Greek concept to the very different Jewish civilization of the ancient world. *Cf.* W. JAEGER, EARLY CHRISTIANITY AND GREEK PAIDEIA (1961) (discussing interplay of Jewish and Greek intellectual traditions in early Christianity). For an application of the term "paideia" to the Torah-centered civilization of the Jews, see B. SEPTIMUS, HISPANO-JEWISH CULTURE IN TRANSITION: THE CAREER AND CONTROVERSIES OF RAMAH 3 (1982) (describing Ramah as a figure "[b]orn of the old aristocracy of Andalusia and educated in the best tradition of its Judeo-Arabic *paideia*").

35. I have borrowed the term but not the concept from Berger. *See* P. BERGER, *supra* note 2, at 29. Berger posits a social control function that attends upon the achievement of a socially constructed "world." The precarious "world" is threatened "by the human facts of self-interest and stupidity." *Id.* Without disputing Berger here, I would stress that the point I will be making is a bit different. The social bases of world construction are narrow, and we construct many "worlds." The problem of "world maintenance" is a problem of the *coexistence* of different worlds and a problem of regulating the splitting of worlds. *See infra* pp. 60–68.

36. The term "imperial" may not be ideal. I mean to suggest by it an organization of distinct nomic entities, just as an empire presupposes subunits that have a degree of juridical and cultural autonomy. Pluralism is obviously very close to what I am trying to convey. But a pluralism may be one of interests and objectives. It does not necessarily entail or even suggest a pluralism of legal meaning, which is my particular concern here. It is also the case that the slightly negative connotation of "imperial," its association with violence, is intended. I mean to give the virtues of "justice, truth, and peace" their due, but I also mean to suggest the price that is paid in the often coercive constraints imposed on the autonomous realization of normative meanings.

nity, stressed the absence in civil community of the strong forces of
normative world building that are present in the Church and, I would
add, in other paideic communities:

> The civil community embraces everyone living within its area.
> Its members share no common awareness of their relationship
> to God, and such an awareness cannot be an element in the legal
> system established by the civil community. No appeal can be
> made to the Word or Spirit of God in the running of its affairs.
> The civil community as such is spiritually blind and ignorant.
> It has neither faith nor love nor hope. It has no creed and no
> gospel. Prayer is not part of its life, and its members are not
> brothers and sisters.[37]

Barth emphasizes the absence from civil community of strong interpersonal bonds, of the common meanings found in shared ritual or
prayer, and of a common corpus—Torah, creed, or gospel—that is
taught, believed in, and recognized as the moving normative force
of the community.

Of course, no normative world has ever been created or maintained wholly in either the paideic or the imperial mode. I am not
writing of types of societies, but rather isolating in discourse the
coexisting bases for the distinct attributes of all normative worlds.
Any *nomos* must be paideic to the extent that it contains within it
the commonalities of meaning that make continued normative activity
possible. Law must be meaningful in the sense that it permits those
who live together to express themselves with it and with respect to
it. It must both ground predictable behavior and provide meaning
for behavior that departs from the ordinary.

Yet from the mundane flow of our real commonalities, we may
purport to distill some purer essence of unity, to create in our imaginations a *nomos* completely transparent—built from crystals completely pure. In this transparent *nomos*, that which must be done,
the meaning of that which must be done, and the sources of common
commitment to the doing of it stand bare, in need of no explication,
no interpretation—obvious at once and to all. As long as it stands

---

37. K. BARTH, *The Christian Community and the Civil Community*, in COM-
MUNITY, STATE AND CHURCH 149, 151 (1960).

revealed, this dazzling clarity of legal meaning can harbor no mere interpretation. The shared sense of a revealed, transparent normative order corresponds to the ideal type of the paideic *nomos.*

The divinely ordained normative corpus, common ritual, and strong interpersonal obligations that together form the basis of such a paideic legal order may indeed be potent. They combine to create precepts and principles enough to fill our lives, as well as to fit those precepts into the common narratives locating the social group in relation to the cosmos, to its neighbors, to the natural world. The precepts, then, not only are there—they are also infused with the full range of connotation that only an integrated set of narratives can provide.

But the very "jurispotence" of such a vision threatens it. Were there some pure paideic normative order for a fleeting moment, a philosopher would surely emerge to challenge the illusion of its identity with truth.[38] The unification of meaning that stands at its center exists only for an instant, and that instant is itself imaginary. Differences arise immediately about the meaning of creeds, the content of common worship, the identity of those who are brothers and sisters. But even the *imagined* instant of unified meaning is like a seed, a legal DNA, a genetic code by which the imagined integration is the template for a thousand real integrations of corpus, discourse, and commitment.[39] Such real integration occurs around particular

---

38. It may be argued that the strange machinery of indirection that Plato suggests in *The Laws* is, in fact, a device to deflect such a philosophical attack upon the cohesive meaning of integrated myths and precepts. *See* Pangle, *Interpretive Essay* on PLATO, THE LAWS OF PLATO 375 (T. Pangle trans. 1980).

39. The imagined "instant" is one in which the *nomos* is transparent. Such a vision may appear to be mystical, but it departs from the phenomenology of mysticism in its exoteric universalizability—that which makes it law and not experience. Theophany, as an essentially *legislative* event, may be perplexing and complex but cannot be esoteric or gnostic. It is no wonder that in the Jewish mystical traditions the divine manifestations in creation (*ma'aseh b'reishit*) and the manifestation in Ezekiel's vision of the chariot (*ma'aseh merkavah*) have played the central role in gnostic or esoteric mystical traditions, whereas the equally or even more dramatic revelation at Sinai stands at the heart of a predominantly exoteric, public interpretive tradition. On the esoteric traditions, see generally G. SCHOLEM, MAJOR TRENDS IN JEWISH MYSTICISM (rev. ed. 1946). For a magnificent collection of the exoteric midrashic tradition regarding Sinai, see S. AGNON, ATEM RE'ITEM (1958–1959). Sinai's position at the heart of an open exegetical tradition concerning narrative and its meaning is a fitting basis for the evolution of Jewish law (*halakah*), for "[h]alakah is an exoteric discipline." I. TWERSKY, RABAD OF POSQUIÈRES, A TWELFTH CENTURY TALMUDIST at xxiii (rev. ed. 1980).

constellations of creed and ritual—Torah and Temple worship—concurred in by a particular group of brothers and sisters. And to their common understanding of creed and ritual is added a common understanding of their relation to the primordial, imaginary, *true* unity that occurred in a vanished instant of long ago.

Thus it is that the very act of constituting tight communities about common ritual and law is jurisgenerative by a process of juridical mitosis. New law is constantly created through the sectarian separation of communities. The "Torah" becomes two, three, many Toroth as surely as there are teachers to teach or students to study.[40] The radical instability of the paideic *nomos* forces intentional communities—communities whose members believe themselves to have common meanings for the normative dimensions of their common lives—to maintain their coherence as paideic entities by expulsion and exile of the potent flowers of normative meaning.[41]

It is the problem of the multiplicity of meaning—the fact that never only one but always many worlds are created by the too fertile forces of jurisgenesis—that leads at once to the imperial virtues and the imperial mode of world maintenance. Maintaining the world is no small matter and requires no less energy than creating it. Let loose, unfettered, the worlds created would be unstable and sectarian in their social organization, dissociative and incoherent in their discourse, wary and violent in their interactions. The sober imperial mode of world maintenance holds the mirror of critical objectivity to meaning, imposes the discipline of institutional justice upon norms, and places the constraint of peace on the void at which strong bonds cease.

The paideic is an etude on the theme of unity. Its primary psychological motif is attachment. The unity of every paideia is being shattered—shattered, in fact, with its very creation.[42] The imperial

---

40. *See* BABYLONIAN TALMUD, *Sanhedrin* 88b. "Originally there were not many disputes in Israel. . . . But when the disciples of Shammai and Hillel who had not studied well enough increased [in number], disputes multiplied in Israel, and the Torah became as two Toroth." *Id.*

41. Consider, for instance, how the Massachusetts Bay Colony handled basic controversies during its first decades. The holistic integrity of the colony was maintained by exclusion and expulsion; the expulsion of Roger Williams and Anne Hutchinson are examples of this approach. *See* G. HASKINS, LAW AND AUTHORITY IN EARLY MASSACHUSETTS 47–51 (1960).

42. Consider the psychodynamics of attachment and separation as expressed in

is an etude on the theme of diversity. Its primary psychological motif
is separation.[43] The diversity of every such world is being consumed
from its onset by domination. Thus, as the meaning in a *nomos*
disintegrates, we seek to rescue it—to maintain some coherence in
the awesome proliferation of meaning lost as it is created—by unleash-
ing upon the fertile but weakly organized jurisgenerative cells an
organizing principle itself incapable of producing the normative meaning that is life and growth.

In the world of the modern nation-state—at least in the United
States—the social organization of legal precept has approximated the
imperial ideal type that I have sketched above, while the social organization of the narratives that imbue those precepts with rich significance has approximated the paideic. We exercise rigid social control
over our precepts in one fashion or another on a national level. There
is a systematic hierarchy—only partially enforced in practice, but
fully operative in theory—that conforms all precept articulation and
enforcement to a pattern of nested consistency. The precepts we call
law are marked off by social control over their provenance, their
mode of articulation, and their effects.[44] But the narratives that create
and reveal the patterns of commitment, resistance and understanding—patterns that constitute the dynamic between precept and mate-

---

the work of John Bowlby, *see* 1–3 J. BOWLBY, *supra* note 8. The family stands as a
metaphor for the inner intensity of the paideic mode. But the objectification that
accompanies nomizing activity shatters the strong psychic bonds.

43. *Cf.* 2 *id.* (1973) (explicating notion of separation as a stage of psychological
development). I am tempted at least to invite comparison between the psychological
dimension of the paideic/imperial distinction and the differences some scholars have
suggested exist betwen male and female psychologies of moral development. *See*
C. GILLIGAN, IN A DIFFERENT VOICE 5–23 (1980) (discussing the inadequacies of what
the author perceives to be the male-centered approach of the essays later collected
in L. KOHLBERG, THE PHILOSOPHY OF MORAL DEVELOPMENT (1981)).

44. The classic statement of the hierarchy of precepts and their pattern of nested
consistency is to be seen partly in J. GRAY, THE NATURE AND SOURCES OF THE LAW
(1909), which is to some extent a catalogue of types of controlled precepts, and in
H. L. A. HART, THE CONCEPT OF LAW (1961), especially chapters three and five,
which establish the nested character of "primary" and "secondary" rules. Dworkin's
critique of the "positivism" articulated by Hart does not deny the social control over
precept articulation that I am positing here. Though Dworkin disagrees with Hart
about how the judge, in particular, as one source of privileged precept articulation,
goes about his or her judicial task, Dworkin does not deny the special social control
exercised by virtue of the office. *See* R. DWORKIN, TAKING RIGHTS SERIOUSLY 81–82
(1977).

rial universe—are radically uncontrolled. They are subject to no formal hierarchical ordering, no centralized, authoritative provenance, no necessary pattern of acquiescence. Such is the radical message of the first amendment: an interdependent system of obligation may be enforced, but the very patterns of meaning that give rise to effective or ineffective social control are to be left to the domain of Babel.[45]

Authoritative precept may be national in character—or at least the authoritative text of the authoritative precepts may be. But the meaning of such a text is always "essentially contested,"[46] in the degree to which this meaning is related to the diverse and divergent narrative traditions within the nation. All Americans share a national text in the first or thirteenth or fourteenth amendment, but we do not share an authoritative narrative regarding its significance.[47] And even were we to share some single authoritative account of the framing of the text—even if we had a national history declared by law to be authoritative—we could not share the same account relating each of us as an individual to that history. Some of us would claim Frederick Douglass as a father, some Abraham Lincoln, and some Jefferson Davis. Choosing ancestry is a serious business with major implica-

---

45. I use the term Babel advisedly. It suggests not incoherence but a multiplicity of coherent systems and a problem of intelligibility among communities. If law is given meaning through mythos, and if the domain of mythos is characteristically narrower than that of precept, we are indeed in Babel. Dworkin's concerns converge in some ways with those expressed here. In his later work, Dworkin concedes the open character of the materials to which the "Herculean" judge appeals in reaching the "right answer." This openness is tantamount to the preconditions for the "Babel" I posit in text. See R. DWORKIN, supra note 44, at 105–30. Dworkin's chain novel analogy, see Dworkin, Law as Interpretation, 60 TEX L. REV. 527, 541–42 (1982), suggests the intelligibility, through retrospective harmonization, of any single interpretive effort even though it be interpersonal in character. But like the "Herculean" dimension of Dworkin's jurisprudence, the chain novel concept ignores the problem of interpenetrability or comprehensibility between interpretive efforts or traditions, each of which is independently defensible or even "right."

46. For an introduction to the notion of an "essentially contested concept," see W. GALLIE, PHILOSOPHY AND THE HISTORICAL UNDERSTANDING 157–91 (1964).

47. One obvious way in which tales can differ is in their beginning and ending points. The first amendment tale can begin with ancient Egypt, with 1776, or with 1789. The point is that constitutional scripture can be part of a sacred history that starts when God's church and man's earthly dominion coincide, or it can be a specific answer to a specific question raised about the national compromises struck between 1787 and 1789.

tions. Thus, the narrative strand integrating who we are and what we stand for with the patterns of precept would differ even were we to possess a canonical narrative text.

The conclusion emanating from this state of affairs is simple and very disturbing: there is a radical dichotomy between the social organization of law as power and the organization of law as meaning. This dichotomy, manifest in folk and underground cultures in even the most authoritarian societies, is particularly open to view in a liberal society that disclaims control over narrative. The uncontrolled character of meaning exercises a destabilizing influence upon power. Precepts must "have meaning," but they necessarily borrow it from materials created by social activity that is not subject to the strictures of provenance that characterize what we call formal lawmaking. Even when authoritative institutions try to create meaning for the precepts they articulate, they act, in that respect, in an unprivileged fashion.

Mark DeWolfe Howe argued this point almost twenty years ago when he pointed out that the Supreme Court had appropriated a singularly Jeffersonian, secular perspective on the establishment clause. Howe observed that the establishment clause could be understood as well, if not better, from an evangelical Christian perspective. He wrote:

> A frank acknowledgment that, in making the wall of separation a Constitutional barrier, the faith of Roger Williams played a more important part than the doubts of Jefferson probably seemed to the present Court to carry unhappy implications. Such an acknowledgment might suggest that the First Amendment was designed not merely to codify a political principle but to implant a somewhat special principle of theology in the Constitution— a principle, by no means uncontested, which asserts that a church dependent on governmental favor cannot be true to its better self.[48]

Howe combined his astute observation of distinct establishment clause narratives with a still more salient, if largely undeveloped, observation about the work of the Supreme Court:

---

48. M. HOWE, THE GARDEN AND THE WILDERNESS 7–8 (1965).

Among the stupendous powers of the Supreme Court of the United States, there are two which in logic may be independent and yet in fact are related. The one is the power, through an articulate search for principle, to interpret history. The other is the power, through the disposition of cases, to make it . . .

. . . I must remind you, however, that a great many Americans . . . tend to think that because a majority of the justices have the power to bind us by their law they are also empowered to bind us by their history. Happily that is not the case. Each of us is entirely free to find his history in other places than the pages of the *United States Reports*.[49]

The question Howe addressed concerned which narrative tradition should inform the Court's decisions. What he did not write with sufficient clarity is that, whichever story the Court chooses, alternative stories still provide normative bases for the growth of distinct constitutional worlds through the persistence of groups who find their respective meanings for the first amendment in the radically different starting points of Roger Williams and Thomas Jefferson. In this respect, as we shall see, the first amendment's religion clauses are not atypical.

B. The Thickness of Legal Meaning

One great strength and one great dilemma of the American constitutional order is the multiplicity of the legal meanings created out of the exiled narratives and the divergent social bases for their use. But before I address that situation, I shall elaborate in more concrete form the processes by which even a single self-enclosed world produces a system of normative meaning. To do so I shall take the highly simplified case of the Bible—simplified because the Bible is a literary artifact of a civilization and no more captures the full range of contested possibilities of ancient Israel than any similarly small composite of our texts would capture the full range of our normative potential. Still, I think the Bible has something to offer as an illustration of the ways in which precepts and narratives operate together to ground meaning.

---

49. *Id.* at 3–5.

Imagine two legal systems, each with identical precepts dictating private and official action: the oldest son is entitled to succeed his father as head of the family and to receive a double portion of the family inheritance. We might imagine one society in which such a precept is simply stated, routinely obeyed, and subject only to the ordinary tensions of human psychology and ingenuity.[50] Contrast such an imaginary legal order with the one we find pictured in the Bible. We know that throughout the ancient Near East, some such rule prevailed; that it is assumed in all the Pentateuchal narratives; and that it is expressed in Deuteronomy chapter 21, verses 15 through 17, in a somewhat particularized form:

> If a man has two wives, one loved and the other hated, and both the loved and hated have borne him sons, but the first born is the son of the hated wife—when he leaves his inheritance to his sons he may not prefer the son of the beloved wife over the elder son of the hated wife. He must acknowledge the first born son of the hated wife and give him the double portion. For he is the first fruit of his loins and to him is the birthright due.[51]

The very casuistic phrasing of this precept suggests an extremely

---

50. I do not know, in fact, whether it is psychologically realistic to suppose that such a precept can ever be unproblematic in the same way that precepts providing for the priority of secured creditors are unproblematic. But assume for a moment that such is the case. Perhaps in an untroubled society, younger children go off to conquer and rule provinces.

51. *Deuteronomy* 21:15–17. For the general legal rule, see Speiser, *Comment* on THE ANCHOR BIBLE: GENESIS at 210 (E. Speiser trans. 1964):

> Legally, the older son was entitled to a double and preferential share of the inheritance, especially in Hurrian society. But since the status of older son . . . could be regulated by a father's pronouncement, irrespective of chronological precedence, and since the legacy in this instance had been established by divine covenant, the emphasis of tradition on transfer of the birthright in a deathbed blessing—with Yahweh's approval . . . —can be readily appreciated.

Id. at 213. Whatever the specific Hurrian legal context, Speiser's analysis and all similar ones miss much of the point of the creation of meaning through law. The later, Davidic legal traditions of the Israelites did not recognize a right on the part of the patriarch to designate an "eldest" son. The stories, whatever their origin, were therefore used in the manner explicated in the text. The literary intentions of the author or redactor are sketched in an illuminating way in R. ALTER, THE ART OF BIBLICAL NARRATIVE 42–46 (1981).

problematic psychodynamic. But the narrative materials in which the precept is embedded present even more complex dimensions of apparent contradiction and complication.

The Deuteronomic material has been included in a biblical canon together with a rich set of accompanying narratives. Long before the final redaction of the canon, many of the texts and stories existed as parts of a common sacred heritage of the people who produced Deuteronomy.[52] These texts included: (1) the story of Cain and Abel, in whch God accepts the sacrifice of Abel, the younger son, rather than that of Cain, the elder, and in which Seth, the third born, ultimately becomes the progenitor of the human race;[53] (2) the story of Ishmael and Isaac, in which Ishmael, the first fruit of Abraham's loins, is cast out so that the birthright might pass to Isaac, the later son born of the preferred wife;[54] (3) the story of Esau, the first-born son of Isaac, who is denied his birthright by the trickery of Jacob, his younger brother;[55] and (4) the story of Joseph and his brothers, in which Joseph—a younger child of the preferred wife—is favored by his father, dreams of his own primacy, provokes retaliation, and comes to rule over his brothers in an improbable political ascendancy in another land.[56] Indeed, all of the stories of the patriarchs revolve around the overturning of the "normal" order of succession[57]—a pillar

---

52. *See* S. LEIMAN, THE CANONIZATION OF HEBREW SCRIPTURE (1976).

53. *Genesis* 4:1–5, 4:25–26.

54. *Id.* 21:1–14.

55. *Id.* 25:29–34, 27:1–40.

56. *Id.* 37:1–47:12. The motif also reappears almost gratuitously when Jacob crosses his hands in blessing Joseph's children Manasseh and Ephraim. *Id.* 48:8–20. The text provides no story of a dynamic between the two sons of Joseph, nor does it provide any background concerning Joseph's—or, for that matter, Jacob's—feelings for them. The incident seems to come out of the blue, but of course it fits the typology: when Jacob crosses his hands in blessing his grandchildren, he is not merely using what may or may not have been a legitimate legal technique for circumventing the general rule; he is also enacting, as Jacob the father, the typology that is so closely associated with Jacob the son and brother.

57. "[T]here is one theme that recurs frequently in the early books of the Bible: the passing over of the first-born son, who normally has the legal right of primogeniture, in favor of a younger one." N. FRYE, THE GREAT CODE 180–81 (1982). My discussion borrows heavily from Frye, who does not, however, see the significance of the theme as equally a matter of divine destiny, grace, and choice, on one hand, and a problem of the place of *law* in the human affairs that also constitute sacred history on the other. Frye's analysis does entail the theme of the sacrifice of the first born, which adds greater richness to the complexities I suggest here.

of the legal civilization that is formally enunciated in the code portions
of Deuteronomy itself.[58]

The motif continues to be prominent in stories beyond the patriarchal narratives; it appears, modified, in tales of political rather
than familial succession. Solomon's rise to the Davidic throne surely
recalls the theme,[59] as does the dominance of Moses over Aaron.[60]
Weaker forms of the motif appear in the Prophet Samuel's birth and
succession to the place of Eli the Priest as national leader,[61] and in
David's succession to the throne of Saul.[62] In both these cases, the
story involves a younger child's incorporation into a dynastic house-
hold and his ultimate ascendance over the older sons of the father,
the natural successors to power.

Now in order to understand any legal civilization one must know
not only what the precepts prescribe, but also how they are charged.
In the Bible there is no earthly or heavenly precept so heavily loaded
as that of Deuteronomy chapter 21, verses 15 through 17, because
there is no precept rendered so problematic by the narratives in which
the law is embedded. This does not mean that the formal precept
was not obeyed. Indeed, the narratives in question would lose most
if not all of their force were it not for the fact that the rule *was*
followed routinely in ordinary life.[63] What is distinctive about the
biblical narratives is that they can never be wholly squared either
with the formal rule—though some later rabbis tried to do so[64]—or

---

58. *See* M. WEINFELD, *supra* note 31, at 188.

59. 1 *Kings* 1:1–53.

60. *Exodus* 4:14–16.

61. 1 *Samuel* 3:11–21.

62. 2 *Samuel* 5:1–5.

63. A narrative concerning American life in the 1920s is not startling if it
describes characters sipping alcoholic drinks despite prohibition—for in fact that law
was routinely disobeyed, and what is portrayed is a simple fact of life, not the hand
of divine destiny or the specter of revolution.

64. "And Esau spurned the birthright." *Genesis* 25:34. "Scripture is testifying
to his wickedness in despising the worship of God." RASHI, at *Genesis* 25:34. Commentators supposed the birthright to have been associated with familial sacrificial
responsibilities, as well as (or rather than) with a double portion. "[He despised] also
this, the birthright, for he saw his father had no wealth." IBN EZRA, at *Genesis* 25:34.
The traditional commentators frequently combine disapproval of Jacob's method or
character with firm assertions of the unworthiness of Esau to be the inheritor of the
birthright. *See, e.g.*, N. LEIBOWITZ, STUDIES IN BERESHIT (GENESIS) 264–69, 275–78
(A. Newman trans. 2d ed. 1974) (collecting materials).

with the normal practice. It is tempting to reconcile the stories to the rule by creating exceptions or by positing circumstances that would remove the case from the rule. These strategies may be useful to the later legist whose concern is a consistent body of precepts. Life in the normative world of the Bible, however, required a well-honed sense of where the rule would end and why.

In a society in which the norm of succession is relatively unproblematic, compliance or noncompliance, resistance or acquiescence may vary according to the contingencies of each instance calling for application of the rule—the relative power of the parties, the emotions running among them, the possible outcomes presented. In ancient Israel such contingencies remain part of the narrative; the individual personalities and ambitions of Jacob and Joseph surely add much to our understanding of their stories. But in every instance in the Bible in which succession is contested, there is a layer of meaning added to the event by virtue of the fact that the mythos of this people has associated the divine hand of destiny with the typology of reversal of this particular rule. When Joseph recounts his dream to his brothers, we are confronted not only with a foreboding of a challenge to the rule, not only with a hint of a possible conflict over succession, but also, more importantly, with a claim to the divine role in destiny that accompanies such a challenge to the precept. To be an inhabitant of the biblical normative world is to understand, first, that the rule of succession can be overturned; second, that it takes a conviction of divine destiny to overturn it; and third, that divine destiny is likely to manifest itself precisely in overturning this specific rule.

In depicting the relationship between divine destiny and rules of succession, the biblical narratives reveal and reinforce a great fault line in the normative topography of the Israelites. It is natural to identify the later-born brother with the latecoming tribe or nation or church. Stories relating the travail of siblings who are unambiguously eponymous suggest the war of neighbors. If Jacob is Israel and Esau is Edom, there is an implicit correspondence between the private law norm of familial succession—rendered problematic by the divine hand of destiny (aided by human deceit)—and an "international" law regulating relations among those who have long been well settled and those who are self-proclaimed wanderers or newcomers. One must know the narratives to live as the problematic latecomer and usurper but bearer of destiny nonetheless, to have the fine-tuned sense of a horizon of will and of divine destiny at which the objective, universalized norm ceases to operate.[65]

The problem addressed by these biblical narratives is also an instance of a still more general problem of political legitimacy. Every legal order must conceive of itself in one way or another as emerging out of that which is itself unlawful. This conception is the mythic or narrative restatement of the positivist's concept of the rule of recognition or *Grundnorm*. The discontinuity that is appealed to may be purely fictitious, wholly mythic, or scientifically historical. We may point to a theophany, a revolution, a migration, a catastrophe. But whether the narrative device is that of Robinson Crusoe, the Pilgrim Fathers, the conquest of Canaan, or Mount Sinai, the sacred beginning always provides the typology for a dangerous return. Revelation and (to a lesser extent) prophecy are the revolutionary challenges to an order founded on revelation.[66] Secession is the

---

65. Robert Alter's discussion of the relationship between norms and destiny seems sensible to me:

If one insists on seeing the patriarchal narratives strictly as paradigms for later Israelite history, one would have to conclude that the authors and redactor of the Jacob story were political subversives raising oblique but damaging questions about the national enterprise. Actually, there may be some theological warrant for this introduction of ambiguities into the story of Israel's eponymous hero, for in the perspective of ethical monotheism, covenantal privileges by no means automatically confer moral perfection....

R. ALTER, *supra* note 51, at 45–46. If I may rephrase the point, the eternal conflict between the "lawful" on one hand and destiny and purpose on the other is thus exemplified on the canvas of this law and its eponymous protagonists.

66. This insight is the basis of many of the great works of religious literature, such as the "Grand Inquisitor" chapter of F. DOSTOEVSKY, THE BROTHERS KARAMAZOV (1880). Another well-known instance is the story of *Achnai's Oven* in rabbinic literature, in which the disputing rabbis reject the call of a voice from heaven intervening in the argument on the side of one of the parties. *See* BABYLONIAN TALMUD, *Baba Metzia* 59. According to one plausible interpretation of the story, God rejoiced when his "children" (the Sages) vanquished him through a legal argument rejecting divine intervention. A very useful discussion that also serves to introduce the vast rabbinic literature on the story may be found in England, *Majority Decision vs. Individual Truth: The Interpretations of the "Oven of Achnai" Aggadah*, TRADITION, Spring–Summer 1975, at 137. The issues raised by this *midrash* are connected to the theoretical, philosophical, and theological disputes that raged in Judaism for hundreds of years concerning the relative authority of law and prophecy. *See, e.g.,* A. REINES, MAIMONIDES AND ABRABANEL ON PROPHECY (1970). The extraordinary trial of Anne Hutchinson in Massachusetts Bay in 1637 also demonstrates the dangerous character of a return to revelation in a legal world founded on revelation. *See, e.g.,* C. ADAMS,

revolutionary response to an order founded on consent or social contract.[67] The return to foundational acts can never be prevented or entirely domesticated. As we remember the special discontinuities that endow foundational acts with their authority, we cannot but risk drawing the inference that they are exemplary. There are a host of techniques for fending off such a conclusion, but they are not foolproof; nor are they persuasive to a person sufficiently convinced of the destiny or providence that marks him or her as its agent.

The biblical narratives always retained their subversive force— the memory that divine destiny is not lawful. So it was that Paul could put the narratives to the service of a revolutionary allegorical extension of the typology in his Epistle to the Galatians.[68] There the Jews with their law are compared to Hagar and Ishmael, the firstcomers, whose claim is based on law. The new Christian Church is Sarah and Isaac, the later comers, who lack any legal entitlement but who hold the divine promise of destiny. The whole edifice of law is thus torn down through an allegory upon the pervasive narrative motif that itself relates the problematic dimension of rules to the mystery of destiny. It is particularly powerful to use in the critique of the

---

ANTINOMIANISM IN THE COLONY OF MASSACHUSETTS BAY, 1636–1638, at 285–336 (1894); G. HASKINS, *supra* note 41, at 48–50.

The phenomenon of the dangerous return to myths of origin has been most thoroughly noted with respect to religious eschatological movements and with respect to the challenge that prophecy and revelation present for a church. But there are secular examples as well. Consider the analysis of political oppression by the relatively staid Joseph Story in his *Commentaries on the Constitution:* "If there be any remedy at all . . . it is a remedy never provided for by human institutions. It is by a resort to the ultimate right of all human beings in extreme cases to resist oppression, and to apply force against ruinous injustice." 1 J. STORY, COMMENTARIES ON THE CONSTITUTION OF THE UNITED STATES § 395, at 374–75 (Boston 1833). Consider also Gary Wills' interesting discussion of Abraham Lincoln's tendency to appeal to the Declaration of Independence, often in contexts that, from the perspective of the "slave power," must have seemed an uncomfortable recalling of revolutionary overtones. *See* G. WILLS, INVENTING AMERICA: JEFFERSON'S DECLARATION OF INDEPENDENCE at xvi–xxi (1978).

67. In the American experience, the myth of social contract has led theorists to value both the right of expatriation (or withdrawal of the individual), *see* G. WILLS, *supra* note 66, at 82–84; Tucker, *Appendix* to 2 W. BLACKSTONE, COMMENTARIES at note K (S. Tucker ed. & comm., Philadelphia 1803), and the right of secession of the constituent polities, the states, *see* E. BAUER, COMMENTARIES ON THE CONSTITUTION 1790–1860, at 253–308 (1952).

68. *Galatians* 4:22–31. The allegory is discussed briefly in N. FRYE, *supra* note 57, at 186, and is given a more interesting treatment in S. HANDELMAN, THE SLAYERS OF MOSES 87–88 (1982).

law of Israel an allegory built on the theme that itself expresses the
extralegality of Israel's destiny.

Thus, to know the narratives is not only to know of the psycho-
familial complexities of succession, not only to see the motif of overturning the rule of succession as a vehicle for the problem of dynastic
succession, but also to understand that motif as an expressive vehicle
for the *unresolved* moral problems of geopolitics and as a potential
source of sectarian division.

I have used biblical material in this first pass at the problem of
legal meaning for several reasons. First, the material is conventionally
bounded. The canon establishes both that all biblical narrative is
relevant to normative meaning and that no other material is. Second,
it is familiar. Third, it demonstrates the irrelevance of genre to the
creation of legal meaning. The narratives in questions are relevant
to the meaning of the biblical *nomos* not because they are true, but
because they are biblical. That is, they are within a convention of
established materials for interpretation. In the discussion that follows,
I shall address problems of "meaning" within our own *nomos*. These
materials are less well bounded. There are no easy conventions for
the creation of meaning. Still, we must wade in to understand our
own dilemma.

C. The Creation of Constitutional Meaning

The biblical worlds of normative meaning were built around a sacred
text that included both precept and narrative. The text constituted
the paideic center for the interpretive traditions that grew from it.
Historically, the texts we know as the Bible did not always occupy
the uncontested, conventionally defined center of the tradition; but
in attempting to understand the creation of legal meaning, we can
treat the tradition from a distant perspective that simplifies analysis.
In our own normative world, there is no obvious central text, certainly none that exhaustively supplies both narrative and precept.
Nonetheless, the Constitution of the United States declares itself to
be "supreme Law."[69] Many of our necessarily uncanonical historical
narratives treat the Constitution as foundational—a beginning—and
generative of all that comes after. This is true even though the Con-

---

69. U.S. CONST. art. VI, § 2.

stitution must compete with natural law, the Declaration of Independence, the Articles of Confederation, and the Revolution itself for primacy in the narrative tradition. Finally, the Constitution is a widespread, though not universally accepted basis for interpretations; it is a center about which many communities teach, learn, and tell stories.

Most of the literature concerning constitutional meaning has focused primarily on the work of courts and secondarily on that of other state officials. I shall start with the work of nonofficials and deal only in conclusion with the ways in which officials create or destroy meaning. I take this approach because I believe that, in the domain of legal meaning, it is force and violence that are problematic. I shall explore the special status of meaning in a context accompanied by violence only after I have considered the processes through which meaning is created in contexts less clearly marked by force than are the state's decrees. This Section will first discuss the ways insular communities establish their own meanings for constitutional principles through their constant struggle to define and maintain the independence and authority of their *nomos*. Next, I shall consider the jurisgenerative processes of groups dedicated to radical transformations of constitutional meaning as it affects the application of state power. These subsections will then constitute the backdrop against which I shall discuss, in Section D, the work of courts, which commonly inhibit—but occasionally foster—the processes of creating legal meaning.

1. The Origin of Legal Meanings in Interpretive Communities

(a) Insular Autonomy

Among the briefs amici curiae submitted to the Supreme Court in *Bob Jones University v. United States*[70] is one in the form of a simple narrative written by the Church of God in Christ, Mennonite, and submitted by counsel on behalf of the church. It reads in part:

> There is in our consciousness a strong sense of an often torturous history, in which our predecessors passed through periods of

---

70. 103 S. Ct. 2017 (1983).

extreme hardship and suffering, a history that includes the records of many martyrs who suffered for those tenets that still constitute our confession of faith. A notable feature of our church history is that of a church in a migratory status, migrating from one place, or nation, to another in search of religious consideration or toleration, a defenseless people looking for a place to be. This has left within us an extremely high regard for religious liberty. We consider the religious liberty that this nation concedes as possibly its greatest virtue.[71]

In this narrative, a community of 7,700 believers identifies itself with more than 7,000 sixteenth century "brethren" put to death on the Continent,[72] and with wandering Mennonite communities during the intervening four centuries.[73]

The Mennonite brief in this respect is not unique. In the brief on behalf of the respondents in *Wisconsin v. Yoder*,[74] the following characterization appears:

The Amish of this case come before the Court in familiar role: the passive and peaceable objects of civil wrath. . . . [T]heir history . . . reaches back . . . to the Switzerland of 1525 where their ancestors sought a return to a Golden Age. These were the "Anabaptists" who attempted, not Church reform, but restoration of a lost and primitive Christianity. To be "First Century Christians" demanded . . . a *separated community of peaceableness and mutual aid.* . . .

The "separated community" implied not only separation from "the world" but also *the separation of church and state* as a safeguard of religious liberty.[75]

This common narrative generates three dimensions of the Anabaptist

---

71. Brief Amicus Curiae in Support of Petition for Writ of Certiorari on Behalf of Church of God in Christ, Mennonite at 1–2, *Bob Jones University* (No. 81-3) (footnotes and internal quotation marks omitted) [hereinafter cited as Mennonite Brief].

72. *See id.* at 1 & n. 1.

73. *See id.* at 1–2 & n. 2.

74. 406 U.S. 205 (1972).

75. Brief for Respondent at 12, *Yoder* (No. 70-110) (footnotes omitted).

nomos. First, it builds upon a vision of the insular community of first century Christianity. For the Anabaptist, the aspiration to life as a member of a first century primitive church has become a stronger referent than the external constraints imposed by contemporary reality. The vision is thus the fixed point in the Anabaptist's experience of history. Second, the narrative establishes a series of temporal "realities" in the dilemmas posed by various civil authorities. These "realities" are the historically contingent variable. Finally, the narrative creates a *people* dedicated to the vision—a people whose actions and norms for action render the vision a constant, with the various civil demands constituting shifting variables around it. It is the internal *law*[76] of the Anabaptist community that creates the bridge between the vision and the reality. And it is the character of that bridge that determines whether it will hold the vision steady.

The structure of the Anabaptist *nomos* determines the place within it, and therefore the meaning, of the principle of free exercise of religion enunciated in the United States Constitution. This principle, as a part of Mennonite belief, is eloquently presented in the Mennonite amicus brief in *Bob Jones University:*

> The tremendous stress that we have faced and face when we find ourselves in conflict between the will of secular government and what we understand as the will of God constitutes one of the most difficult aspects of our religious experience.
>
> Our faith and understanding of scripture enjoin respect and obedience to the secular governments under which we live. We recognize them as institutions established by God for order in society. For that reason alone, without the added distress of punitive action for failure to do so, we always exercise ourselves to be completely law abiding. Our religious beliefs, however, are very deeply held. When these beliefs collide with the demands

---

76. It is a fair question whether we ought to characterize a "primitive" Christian Church as a community living under a "law." The rejection of the "law" as the fundamental connection between God and the individual and between God and the Church is critical to the beliefs of this community. Nonetheless, from an external perspective, the community undoubtedly builds a normative world that it treasures and self-consciously preserves. Moreover, the rejection of "the covenant of law" for that of grace does not imply an absence of law from the internal functionings of earthly communities. Indeed, the coherent and normative force of Amish doctrine is argued forcefully in the Amish brief in *Yoder. See id.* at 14–26; *infra* pp. 29–30.

of society, our highest allegiance must be toward God, and we must say with men of God of the past, 'We must obey God rather than men', and *these are the crisis from which we would be spared.*[77]

The purpose of the first amendment free exercise clause for members of this church is constituted, in part, by a live sense of the crisis of obligation posed by their religious beliefs. Now logically, any person who considers his or her obligation to the law of the state to be measured by some standard—ethical, religious, or political—that is external to the law itself faces the same potential dilemma as do the Mennonites and the Old Order Amish. But not all of us who affirm an external limit to the obligation we owe the law identify ourselves with narratives in which just such a theoretically possible dilemma becomes the paradigmatic crisis—"one of the most difficult aspects of our religious experience." The Mennonite narratives, whether the quasi-sacred tales of martyrs[78] or the more recent stories of conscientious objectors,[79] help to create the identity of the believer and to establish the central commitment from which any law—and especially any organic law—of the state will be addressed. The hopes, fears, and possibilities that this point of identity and commitment brings into focus have, of course, major implications for the generality of the principle laid down in the *Bob Jones University* decision.

What troubled the Mennonites, the Amish, and various evangelical and other religious groups was not the specific loss of tax-exempt status for a religious school discriminating on the basis of race. Few, if any, of the amici curiae filing briefs in support of Bob Jones University or Goldsboro Christian Schools discriminate on the basis of race or face IRS action threatening their tax-exempt status.[80] The principle that troubled these amici was the broad assertion that

---

77. Mennonite Brief, *supra* note 71, at 3–4 (footnotes omitted).
78. *See id.* at 1 & n. 1.
79. *See id.* at 3 n. 4.
80. *See* Brief *Amici Curiae* of the American Baptist Churches in the U.S.A., joined by the United Presbyterian Church in the U.S.A. at 1, *Bob Jones University* (No. 81-3); Brief for the Center for Law and Religious Freedom of the Christian Legal Society, as *Amicus Curiae* in Support of a Petition for a Writ of Certiorari to the United States Court of Appeals for the Fourth Circuit at 2, *Bob Jones University* (No. 81-3); Brief of *Amicus Curiae* General Conference Mennonite Church in Support of Petition for a Writ of Certiorari at 1, *Bob Jones University* (No. 81-3).

a mere "public policy," however admirable, could triumph in the face of a claim to the first amendment's special shelter against the crisis of conscience.

I am making a very strong claim for the Mennonite understanding of the first amendment. That understanding is not to be taken as simply the "position" of an advocate—though it is that. I am asserting that within the domain of constitutional meaning, the understanding of the Mennonites assumes a status equal (or superior) to that accorded to the understanding of the Justices of the Supreme Court. In this realm of meaning—if not in the domain of social control— the Mennonite community creates law as fully as does the judge. First, the Mennonites inhabit an ongoing *nomos* that must be marked off by a normative boundary from the realm of civil coercion, just as the wielders of state power must establish their boundary with a religious community's resistance and autonomy. Each group must accommodate in its own normative world the objective reality of the other. There may or may not be synchronization or convergence in their respective understandings about the normative boundary and what it implies. But from a position that starts as neutral—that is, nonstatist—in its understanding of law, the interpretations offered by judges are not necessarily superior. The Mennonites are not simply advocates, for they are prepared to live and do live by their pro- claimed understandings of the Constitution. Moreover, they live within the complex encodings of commitments—their sacred narratives—that ground the understanding of the law that they offer.

The *Bob Jones University* case, of course, presented an oppor- tunity to explore other, very different and conflicting narratives and principles. I shall return to these later. For the moment, it is enough to mark the association of this one genre of central narrative with one of the understandings of constitutional meaning. This under- standing not only dictates a preferred rule—that a bona fide religious practice cannot be defeated by a claim of public policy—but also fits that rule into a more comprehensive view of legal/moral obligation and constitutional destiny:

> We believe that God has blessed in a very special way, the noble consideration toward sincere religious convictions that this nation has extended. . . .
> Our intense desire, or continual prayer is that this nation may

continue to enjoy the protection and blessing of Almighty God,
that it may ever be a safe place where people such as we may
have a place to life [sic] and search out the will of God for us
in tranquility.[81]

The principle of separateness is constitutive and jurisgenerative.
It is not only a principle limiting the state, but also one constitutive
of a distinct *nomos* within the domain left open. The Amish ham-
mered upon this point in their *Yoder* brief:

There exists no Amish religion apart from the concept of the
Amish community. A person cannot take up the Amish religion
and practice it individually. The community subsists spiritually
upon the bonds of a common, lived faith, sustained by "common
traditions and ideals which have been revered by the whole community from generation to generation."[82]

The Amish insist upon the essentially nomian character of the world
they construct:

To call their beliefs "non-doctrinal", or to infer that these beliefs
constitute eccentric but dispensable customs, merely because they
are not expressed on printed texts, decrees and regulations, is
misleading. Amish "doctrine" (*i.e.*, teaching) is supremely certain
and clearly known, being safeguarded to each generation by
means of an *oral tradition* which contains and repeats the essential teachings.[83]

Ultimately, it is the state's capacity to tolerate or destroy this
self-contained *nomos* that dictates the relation of the Amish community to its political host. The Amish and Mennonite narratives
are clear about the typologies of accommodation, oppression, and
resistance. The response of the Amish to attacks by civil authority
upon the nomian insulation of their world "has been to sell their

---

81. Mennonite Brief, *supra* note 71, at 4.
82. Brief for Respondent at 21, *Yoder* (No. 70–110) (quoting J. HOSTETLER, AMISH
SOCIETY 131 [2d ed. 1968].)
83. *Id.* at 14–15 (footnote omitted).

farms and to remove to jurisdictions, here or abroad, wherein hope-
fully they will be allowed peaceably to follow the will of God."[84]

There is a powerful, almost physical image at work in the conception to which the Amish and Mennonites implicitly appeal in their
constitutional confession. The image is one of a dedicated, sacred
space, a refuge carved out from the general secular, legal space of
the state. Within the dedicated nomic refuge, there is an accommodation to a religious rule of recognition expressed in Acts 5:29—
"We ought to obey God rather than men"—instead of submission to
the principle, embodied in article VI, section 2 of the Constitution,
that "[t]his Constitution, and the Laws of the United States which
shall be made in Pursuance thereof . . . shall be the supreme Law of
the land." The self-referential supremacy of each system is, of course,
mitigated by the partly principled, partly prudential rules of deference
that each manifests in relation to the other.[85]

The free exercise clause is only one of many principles that may
be employed to create boundaries for communities and their quasi-
autonomous law. Professor Carol Weisbrod's excellent study of nineteenth century utopian communities demonstrates the power of freedom of contract to create nomic insularity.[86] It is not surprising that
she finds that the voluntaristic character of the ideology of these
communities—especially the Shaker community—dominated their
constitutional thought, just as the vision of free exercise dominates
Amish and Mennonite constitutional theory.[87]

Property and corporation law have also been bases for claims
to creation of an insulated nomic reserve. The company town, mine,
or plant often asserts a right to law creation and enforcement with
respect to social relations. Such claims were a pervasive condition
of industrial life throughout the nineteenth and early twentieth centuries; they retain some importance today, even though the extreme
conditions of nineteenth century Pullman, Illinois, are seldom rep-

---

84. *Id.* at 26.

85. It is, of course, entirely in keeping with tradition to see the meaning of all
human history centered upon a remnant and a refuge for the remnant. From a secular
perspective on the Constitution, the free exercise clause's creation of small, dedicated,
nomic refuges may appear to be merely an (unimportant) accommodation to religious
autonomy. But for the Mennonites, the clause is the axis on which the wheel of
history turns.

86. C. WEISBROD, THE BOUNDARIES OF UTOPIA (1980).

87. *See id.* at 61–79 (discussion of Shaker contract ideology).

licated.[88] Perhaps the most compelling historical example of the use
of private law in the generation of a *nomos* was the creation of a
polity out of the corporate charter of Massachusetts Bay.[89] And
although such dramatic instances of the normative authority of the
corporate charter are rare, modern corporation law continues to bear
the formal character of a grant of norm-generating authority.[90]

The point that is relevant here is not only that private lawmaking
takes place through religious authority, contract, property, and corporate law (and of course through all private associational activity),
but also that from time to time various groups use these universally
accepted and well-understood devices to create an entire *nomos*—an
integrated world of obligation and reality from which the rest of the
world is perceived. At that point of radical transformation of perspective, the boundary rule—whether it be contract, free exercise of
religion, property, or corporation law—becomes more than a rule:
it becomes constitutive of a world. We witness normative mitosis. A
world is turned inside out; a wall begins to form, and its shape differs
depending upon which side of the wall our narratives place us on.

The constitutional visions of the Amish, the Mennonites, the
utopian communities, the early Mormons, the Pilgrims, and the emi-
grant Puritans elevated the importance of associational autonomy.
Although all these groups had a place in their normative worlds for
civil authority, and although some would transform civil authority
into an intolerant arm of their own substantive vision when the
chance arose, all, finding themselves within a state not under their
control, sought a refuge not simply *from* persecution, but *for* associational self-realization in nomian terms. This norm-generating
autonomy might be formally granted in charter language.[91] It might

88. Pullman was more than a town. It was an ideology, benevolent in origin
and intent if oppressive in effect. *See, e.g.,* S. LENS, THE LABOR WARS 85–87 (1973);
R. SENNETT, AUTHORITY 62–66 (1980).

89. Professor Barbara Black has eloquently described the processes by which a
private law document came to have overpowering effect as the public law of the
Massachusetts Bay Colony for the colony's entire first charter period. *See* B. Black,
The Judicial Power and the General Court in Early Massachusetts (1634–1686) ch.
1 (1975) (unpublished Ph.D. dissertation, Yale University Department of History).
See generally G. HASKINS, *supra* note 41, at 189–221 (discussing colonists' use of the
charter to develop an independent legal order).

90. The radical character of "corporations" and their basis in natural law thought
is explored in O. GIERKE, NATURAL LAW AND THE THEORY OF SOCIETY, 1500–1800, at
162–95 (E. Barker trans. 1957).

91. The Charter of the Massachusetts Bay Colony granted the colony authority

be implicit in a principle of religious liberty, freedom of contract, or protection of property. Typically, however, communities with a total life-vision, a *nomos* entirely of their own, find their own charters for the norm-generating aspects of their collective lives. The state's explicit or implicit acknowledgment of a limited sphere of autonomy is understood from within the association to be the state's accommodation to the extant reality of nomian separation. Such an acknowledgment is welcome as a preventative of suffering, but it does not create the inner world.

Freedom of association is the most general of the Constitution's doctrinal categories that speak to the creation and maintenance of a common life, the social precondition for a *nomos*.[92] From the point of view of state doctrine, the simplest way to generalize the points that I have made concerning the ways in which various groups have built their own normative worlds is to recognize that the norm-generating aspects of corporation law, contract, and free exercise of religion are all instances of associational liberty protected by the Constitution. Freedom of association implies a degree of norm-generating autonomy on the part of the association.[93] It is not a liberty to *be* but a liberty and capacity to create and interpret law— minimally to interpret the terms of the association's own being.[94]

"from tyme to tyme to make, ordeine, and establishe all manner of wholesome and reasonable orders, lawes, statutes, and ordinances, direccions, and instruccions not contrarie to the lawes of this our realme of England." CHARTER OF THE MASSACHUSETTS BAY COLONY (1629), *quoted in* G. HASKINS, *supra* note 41, at 27.

92. On the natural law of associational liberties, see O. GIERKE, *supra* note 90. For a fascinating contemporary exploration of the philosophical foundations of associational freedoms in American constitutional doctrine—or rather an exploration of the potential incorporation of such freedoms into American constitutional doctrine— see Garet, *Communality and Existence: The Rights of Groups*, 56 S. CAL. L. REV. 1001 (1983). There is, of course, a vast difference between the individual right of free association recognized in NAACP v. Alabarma *ex re* Patterson, 357 U.S. 449 (1958), and a group right to autonomous status. *Cf.* Fiss, *Groups and the Equal Protection Clause*, 5 PHIL. & PUB. AFF. 107 (1976) (contrasting individualistic and group-oriented approaches to equal protection analysis).

93. *See* Howe, *The Supreme Court, 1952 Term—Foreword: Political Theory and the Nature of Liberty*, 67 HARV. L. REV. 91, 91 (1953) ("[G]overnment must recognize that it is not the sole possessor of sovereignty, and that private groups within the community are entitled to lead their own free lives and exercise within the area of their competence an authority so effective as to justify labeling it a sovereign authority.").

94. The religion clauses of the Constitution seem to me unique in the clarity with which they presuppose a collective, norm-generating community whose status

To elaborate the doctrine of associated rights, however, is simply to assume for ourselves the perspective of the state official looking out. The center of the Amish *nomos* is the New Testament,[95] the center of the Shaker *nomos* is a vivid and literal social contract.[96] Groups assume different constitutional positions in order to create boundaries between the outside world and the community in which real law grows—in order to maintain the jurisgenerative capacity of the community's distinct law. We ought not lightly to assume a statist perspective here, for the *nomos* of officialdom is also "particular"— as particular as that of the Amish. And it, too, reaches out for validation and seeks to extend its legitimacy by gaining acceptance from the normative world that lies outside its core.

The principles that establish the nomian autonomy of a community must, of course, resonate within the community itself and within its sacred stories. But it is a great advantage to the community to have such principles resonate with the stories of other communities that establish overlapping or conflicting normative worlds. Neither religious churches, however small and dedicated, nor utopian communities, however isolated, nor cadres of judges, however independent, can ever manage a total break from other groups with other understandings of law. Thus it is that the Shaker understanding of "contract" is hardly independent of understandings of contract that were prevalent in the nineteenth century. The Amish concept of church-state relations is not entirely independent of secular, libertarian concepts of such relations. The interdependence of legal meanings makes it possible to say that the Amish, the Shakers, and the judge are all engaged in the task of constitutional understanding. But their

---

as a community and whose relationship with the individuals subject to its norms are entitled to constitutional recognition and protection.

Respect for a degree of norm-generating autonomy has also traditionally been incident to the federal government's relations with Indian tribes. *See, e.g.,* Santa Clara Pueblo v. Martinez, 436 U.S. 49 (1978).

95. *Cf.* J. HOSTETLER, *supra* note 82, at 21–23, 75–92 (explaining the influence of biblical precepts in the Amish normative order).

96. "A theological perspective on the covenant and a reference to Locke's view of the original consensual nature of government are found here together, in a single document, which provided the legal form of the Shaker community." C. WEISBROD, *supra* note 86, at 75–76. The Shakers took the position of strict insularity: they believed that civil law did not create the Shaker associations, though as a practical matter civil law had to be consulted to "see that we did not trespass upon [its] premises." *Id.* at 76 (internal quotation marks omitted).

distinct starting points, identifications, and stories make us realize that we cannot pretend to a unitary law.

Sectarian communities differ from most—but not all—other communities in the degree to which they establish a *nomos* of their own. They characteristically construct their own myths, lay down their own precepts, and presume to establish their own hierarchies of norms. More importantly, they identify their own paradigms for lawful behavior and reduce the state to just one element, albeit an important one, in the normative environment. Even an accommodationist sectarian position—one that goes to great lengths to avoid confrontation or the imposition upon adherents of demands that will in practice conflict with those imposed by the state—establishes its own meaning for the norms to which it and its members conform.

(b) Redemptive Constitutionalism

Liberty of association is not exhausted by a model of insular autonomy. People associate not only to transform themselves, but also to change the social world in which they live. Associations, then, are a sword as well as a shield. They include collective attempts to increase revenue from market transactions, to transform society through violent revolution, to make converts for Jesus, and to change the law or the understanding of the law. Despite the interactive quality that characterizes transformational associations, however, such groups necessarily have an inner life and some social boundary; otherwise, it would make no sense to think of them as distinct entities. It is this social organization, not the datum of identity of interest, that requires the idea of liberty of association.[97] Commonality of interests and objectives may lead to regularities in social, political, or economic behavior among numbers of individuals. Such regularities, however, can be accommodated within a framework of individual rights. When groups generate their own articulate normative orders concerning the world as they would transform it, as well as

---

97. One of the fundamental questions regarding group litigation is the extent to which and the circumstances in which mere commonality of interest ought to suffice to ground party status—that is, status as an entity for purposes of litigation as opposed to extralitigational social organization. Professor Stephen Yeazell has put this issue in historical context in a recent series of articles. *See* Yeazell, *From Group Litigation to Class Action* (pts. 1 & 2), 27 UCLA L. REV. 514, 1067 (1980); Yeazell, *Group Litigation and Social Context*, 77 COLUM. L. REV. 866 (1977).

the mode of transformation and their own place within the world, the situation is different—a new *nomos*, with its attendant claims to autonomy and respect, is created. Insofar as the vision and objectives of such a group are integrative, however, the structure of its *nomos* differs from that of the insular sectarian model.

Any group that seeks the transformation of the surrounding social world must evolve a mechanism for such change. There must be a theory and practice of apostolic ministry to the unconverted, a theory and practice of Leninist selection of cadres and a class-consciousness raising activity, or a theory and practice of legislation and deliberative politics. Of course, some associations—most limited-purpose ones—strive for small change in a world understood to be unproblematic if ill defined. This is less true of other associations. It is least true when the transforming association has its own vision, which it fits together with its conception of reality and its norms to create an integrated whole. The discontinuities between the respective visions, constructions of reality, and norms posited by some such associations and by the state's authoritative legal institutions may be considerable. I shall use "redemptive constitutionalism" as a label for the positions of associations whose sharply different visions of the social order require a transformational politics that cannot be contained within the autonomous insularity of the association itself.

I use the term "redemptive" to distinguish this phenomenon from the myriad reformist movements in our history. Redemption takes place within an eschatological schema that postulates: (1) the unredeemed character of reality as we know it, (2) the fundamentally different reality that should take its place, and (3) the replacement of the one with the other. The term "redemptive" also has the connotation of saving or freeing *persons*, not only "worlds" or understandings. I have chosen a word with the religious connotations of both personal and cosmic freedom and bondage, because the paradigmatic cases I have in mind require just such a heavy weight of meaning. I shall use the examples of radical antislavery constitutionalism and the civil rights movement to illustrate the phenomenon. Both movements set out to liberate persons and the law and to raise them from a fallen state. This way of thinking about law and liberty— shared as well by the women's movement and the right-to-life movement—is obviously tied to the religious traditions that invoke the vocabulary of redemption.

2. Antislavery Constitutionalism: The Competition Between Insular and Redemptive Models

If there was a fault line in the normative topography of American constitutionalism—akin in significance and expressive power to the principle of succession in biblical life—it was, for four score and ten years, the place of slavery within the union. Certain particular rules associated with that institution, such as the fugitive slave acts, came to assume an expressive potential comparable to that of Deuteronomy 21:15–17. Rescuing fugitives, and aiding and abetting them or their rescuers, were at once practical acts and symbolic ones. In context, such acts did much more than measure the relative strength of a person's commitments to liberty and to union. Constitutionalism was central to the meaning of the conflict over slavery because that conflict raised the ultimate question of authority versus meaning—the jurisprudential equivalent of theodicy in religion.[98] I and others have canvassed the constitutionalism of antislavery elsewhere at some length.[99] In this subsection, I want to focus on two groups in particular and on one aspect of their thought.

The position of Garrisonian abolitionists with respect to the United States Constitution is well known. It is best epitomized by Wendell Phillips' speech on the occasion of the seizure in Boston of George Latimer, a runaway slave: "There stands the bloody [fugitive slave] clause—you cannot fret the seal off the bond. The fault is in allowing such a Constitution to live an hour. . . . I say, my curse be on the Constitution of these United States."[100] I have argued elsewhere

---

98. In JUSTICE ACCUSED, see R. COVER, supra note 4, I discuss the way the authority structure of judicial jurisdiction put an end to the exploration of constitutional bases for an attack on the fugitive slave laws. Professor Dworkin constantly addresses the hermeneutic of the free judge, see Dworkin, The Law of the Slave-Catchers, 1975 TIMES LITERARY SUPP. (London) 1437 (Book Review) (reviewing R. Cover, supra note 4), without speaking to the constraints of jurisdiction. See infra pp. 160–63 (discussing hermeneutics of jurisdiction).

99. The leading work in antislavery constitutional thought is W. Wiecek, THE SOURCES OF ANTISLAVERY CONSTITUTIONALISM IN AMERICA, 1760–1848 (1977). For an analysis of the varieties of critical and synthetic antislavery thought, see R. Cover, supra note 4, at 149–58. On the apologetic functions of law, see id. at 119–23; M. Tushnet, THE AMERICAN LAW OF SLAVERY, 1810–1860 (1981). Of great value is placing the constitutional problems in the broader contexts of antislavery thought and action is D. Davis, THE PROBLEM OF SLAVERY IN THE AGE OF REVOLUTION, 1770–1823 (1975) (especially ch. 11).

100. W. Phillips, Speech at Faneuil Hall, Boston (Oct. 30, 1842), quoted in I. BARTLETT, WENDELL PHILLIPS: BRAHMIN RADICAL 117–18 (1961).

that the Garrisonians interpreted and analyzed the Constitution in a manner consistent with the dominant professional methods of their day (and of our day as well).[101] By these interpretive methods, the Garrisonians reached the conclusions that the Constitution permitted the states to create and perpetuate slavery as part of their municipal law, that the Constitution guaranteed certain national protections for slavery where it did exist, and that the Constitution imposed upon citizens of free states the obligation to cooperate in the corrupt national bargain to aid and perpetuate slavery. Of course, having reached these conclusions, Garrison, Phillips, and their followers opted for a radically different course from the one taken by the mainstream bench and bar. They eschewed participation in and renounced obligation to government under such a Constitution.[102]

The Garrisonian move, like that of religious sectarians, was a move toward nomian insularity—the rejection of participation in the creation of a general and public *nomos*. It is therefore not surprising to find that the insular quality of antislavery anticonstitutionalism was connected to a more general nomian insularity. Indeed, William Wiecek, the leading historian of antislavery constitutionalism, has argued that Garrisonian anticonstitutionalism is incomprehensible and absurd "[i]f not integrated with its nonconstitutional components."[103] Garrisonian "perfectionism," a millenial philosophy, held that each person had an obligation to attain perfection in this life by foreswearing sin. The withdrawal of perfectionists to their enclosed nomian island, the Garrisonians believed, would ultimately cause the dissolution of government. The immediate action required of perfectionists was therefore disengagement from participation in the state. This disengagement did not entail physical or social insularity, but a radical insularity of the normative world alone.

From such a perspective of committed insularity, the hermeneutic interest of the Garrisonian lay not in fitting the Constitution into the definition of a perfectionist community. Because the Constitution was a powerful symbol for most Americans, *renunciation* of constitutional obligation was an expressive act that created a boundary defining fidelity to the implications of perfectionist beliefs. When

---

101. *See* R. COVER, *supra* note 4, at 150–54.
102. *See id.* at 151; W. WIECEK, *supra* note 99, at 228–48.
103. W. WIECEK, *supra* note 99, at 228.

Wendell Phillips and Roger Taney "agreed" that the fugitive-from-labor clause of article IV of the Constitution dictated the return of runaway slaves, they agreed, in one sense, on the "meaning" of the Constitution. The more important "meaning" that Phillips sought to establish, however, was a denial of the self-referential norm of obligation found in the supremacy clause of article VI. Thus, it was Phillips' total normative world—his Garrisonian perfectionism—that made his constitutional stance intelligible within the community of resistance and within the *nomos* that supported it. Roger Taney's positivist interpretation, on the other hand, assumed a principle justifying obedience to the Constitution.[104]

The relationship among vision, reality, and norm in Garrisonianism needs to be explored. Garrisonian perfectionism, because of its comprehensive demand upon conduct, required a system of norms sharply delineating the distinctions between those who strove for Christ-like perfection and the rest of the world. Its own norms thus demarcated the distinctions found in the present reality. But reality is only one ground for norms. Vision is the other. By demarcating reality, perfectionist Garrisonian norms necessarily gave up any emphasis on the process of transformation itself.[105]

This trade-off is instructive, for it was made in a completely different manner by the archrivals of Garrisonian theorists—those whom Wiecek calls radical constitutionalists.[106] We can best understand the nature of the difference by attending to the normative journey of a person who passed from Garrisonianism to radical constitutionalism—Frederick Douglass. This is Douglass' own account of his change of heart with regard to constitutional interpretation:

---

104. *See* Scott v. Sandford, 60 U.S. (19 How.) 393 (1857). Imagine a simple world in which everyone took the position of Roger Taney, and contrast it with another simple world in which half the people took Taney's position and the other half the position of Wendell Phillips. In the first world, we would see a consensus on the meaning of the law of the fugitive slave. In the second world, no such consensus would form, because there would be disagreement about the law's justification and about how a person should behave in relation to the law. The two groups in the second world could only be said to agree on the meaning of the document abstracted from any need or desire to act upon it. But by its own terms the text is a ground for action. And no two people can be said to agree on what the text requires if they disagree on the circumstances in which it will warrant their actions.

105. *See* W. Wiecek, *supra* note 99, at 247.

106. Wiecek examines the philosophy, tactics, and influence of the radical constitutional antislavery movement in *id.* at 249–75.

Brought directly, when I escaped from slavery, into contact with abolitionists who regarded the Constitution as a slaveholding instrument, and finding their views supported by the united and entire history of every department of the government, it is not strange that I assumed the Constitution to be just what these friends made it seem to be. . . . But for the responsibility of conducting a public journal [in Western New York], and the necessity imposed upon me of meeting opposite views from abolitionists outside of New England, I should in all probability have remained firm in my disunion views. My new circumstances compelled me to re-think the whole subject, and to study with some care not only the just and proper rules of legal interpretation, but the origin, design, nature, rights, powers, and duties of civil governments, and also the relations which human beings sustain to it. By such a course of thought and reading I was conducted to the conclusion that the Constitution of the United States— inaugurated to "form a more perfect union, establish justice, insure domestic tranquility, provide for the common defense, promote the general welfare, and secure the blessings of liberty"—could not well have been designed at the same time to maintain and perpetuate a system of rapine and murder like slavery, especially as not one word can be found in the Constitution to authorize such a belief.[107]

Undoubtedly, Douglass is correct in his appreciation of the community as the source and sustenance of ideas about law. I have already suggested in what way the issue of constitutional interpretation was central to the definition of the Garrisonian community with its holistic vision of perfection on earth. For Frederick Douglass, more than for any other leading abolitionist, a different need was primary. Douglass was *the* escaped slave. His escape constituted a redemption and the beginning of his real life.[108] Douglass' greatest need was for a vision

---

107. F. DOUGLASS, LIFE AND TIMES OF FREDERICK DOUGLASS 261–62 (R. Logan ed. 1967).

108. Several times in his autobiography, Douglass invoked an image of the beginning of his life to describe his freedom. *See id.* at 202, 216, 259. And frequently he wrote and spoke of his fear of being returned to slavery. *See id.* at 218–19; Letter from Frederick Douglass to Henry C. Wright (Dec. 22, 1846), *reprinted in* 1 F. DOUGLASS, THE LIFE AND WRITINGS OF FREDERICK DOUGLASS 204 (P. Foner ed. 1975).

of law that both validated his freedom and integrated norms with a
future redemptive possibility for his people. The radical constitutionalists criticized the Garrisonians precisely for their failure to adopt
such a vision. The Garrisonian alternative seemed, to the constitutionalists, an abdication: "Dissolve the Union, on this issue, and you
delude the people of the free States with the false notion that their
responsibilities have ceased, though the slaves remain in bondage.
Who shall stand up as deliverers, then?"[109] When Frederick Douglass
asserted his psychological and political independence from his Boston
abolitionist benefactors, he chose, in part, to break with Garrisonian
anticonstitutionalism by embracing a vision—a vision of an alternative world in which the entire order of American slavery would
be without foundation in law.[110]

William Wiecek's assessment of radical constitutionalism is that,
"[i]n the short run, [it] was a failure."[111] He points out that the radicals
became increasingly sectarian, although he attributes a long-term
significance to their use of natural law in constitutional exegesis.[112]
The sectarian character of radical abolitionist normative thought,
however, is of a peculiar sort. Utopian constitutionalism such as that
envisioned by the radicals has as its raison d'être the transformation
of the conditions of social life. It arises out of the utopian's inability
to bear the dissonance of the lawfulness of the intolerable, and it is
therefore, like all nomic eschatology, extremely unstable. Its adherent
must either give up his connection with what is the case, including
the predictable patterns of behavior of other actors, or give up the
vision. The vision of slavery destroyed by the power of law requires
for its fulfillment the participation of the larger community that exercises state power. The logic of perfectionism permits the pursuit of
a pure *nomos* without a polis. But for a *nomos* to be redemptive in
the sense posited by Douglass' vision, more is necessary.

If law reflects a tension between what is and what might be, law
can be maintained only as long as the two are close enough to reveal

---

109. Convention of Radical Political Abolitionists, Proceedings of the
Convention of Radical Political Abolitionists 44 (New York 1855).

110. On Douglass' break with the Garrisonians, see 2 F. Douglass, *supra* note
108, at 48–66. For a forceful statement of Douglass' constitutional position, see his
speech, The Constitution of the United States: Is It Pro-Slavery or Anti-Slavery?
(Mar. 26, 1860), *reprinted in id.* at 46–80.

111. W. Wiecek, *supra* note 99, at 274.

112. *See id.*

a line of human endeavor that brings them into temporary or partial reconciliation. All utopian or eschatological movements that do not withdraw to insularity risk the failure of the conversion of vision into reality and, thus, the breaking of the tension. At that point, they may be movements, but they are no longer movements of the law.

While their movement lasted, the radical constitutionalists contributed to an immense growth of law. They worked out a constitutional attack upon slavery from the general structure of the Constitution; they evolved a literalist attack from the language of the due process clause and from the jury and grand jury provisions of the fifth and sixth amendments; they studied interpretive methodologies and self-consciously employed the one most favorable to their ends; they developed arguments for extending the range of constitutional sources to include at least the Declaration of Independence. Their pamphlets, arguments, columns, and books constitute an important part of the legal literature on slavery,[113] which, I believe, would substantially eclipse contemporaneous writings in, say, American tort law. Their work reveals a creative pulse that proliferates principle and precept, commentary and justification, even in the face of a state legal order less likely to hold slavery unconstitutional than to declare the imminent kingship of Jesus Christ on Earth.[114] In the workings of a committed community with common symbols and discourse, common narratives and interpretations, the law undeniably grew.

D. "Jurispathic" Courts

The reader may have tired by now of my insistence upon dignifying the internal norms, redemptive fantasies, briefs, positions, or argu-

---

113. Much of this antislavery literature is cited and discussed in R. COVER, *supra* note 4, at 149 n; W. WIECEK, *supra* note 99, at 249–75.

114. *Compare* Vidal v. Mayor of Philadelphia, 43 U.S. (2 How.) 127, 198 (1844) ("So that we are compelled to admit that although Christianity be a part of the common law of the State, yet it is so in this qualified sense, that its divine origin and truth are admitted, and therefore it is not to be maliciously and openly reviled and blasphemed against, to the annoyance of believers or the injury of the public.") *with* Scott v. Sandford, 60 U.S. (19 How.) 393, 411 (1857) ("[T]here are two clauses in the Constitution which point directly and specifically to the negro race as a separate class of persons, and show clearly that they were not regarded as a portion of the people or citizens of the Government then formed.").

ments of various groups with the word "law." In an imaginary world in which violence played no part in life, law would indeed grow exclusively from the hermeneutic impulse—the human need to create and interpret texts.[115] Law would develop within small communities of mutually committed individuals who cared about the text, about what each made of the text, and about one another and the common life they shared. Such communities might split over major issues of interpretation, but the bonds of social life and mutual concern would permit some interpretive divergence. I have played out a fantasy to some extent in suggesting that we can see the underlying reality of the jurisgenerative process in the way in which real communities do create law and do give meaning to law through their narratives and precepts, their somewhat distinct *nomos.*

But the jurisgenerative principle by which legal meaning proliferates in all communities never exists in isolation from violence. Interpretation always takes place in the shadow of coercion. And from this fact we may come to recognize a special role for courts. Courts, at least the courts of the state, are characteristically "jurispathic."

It is remarkable that in myth and history the origin of and justification for a court is rarely understood to be the need for law. Rather, it is understood to be the need to suppress law, to choose between two or more laws, to impose upon laws a hierarchy. It is the multiplicity of laws, the fecundity of the jurisgenerative principle, that creates the problem to which the court and the state are the solution. For example, in Aeschylus' literary re-creation of the mythic foundations of the Areopagus, Athena's establishment of the institutionalized law of the polis is addressed to the dilemma of the moral and legal indeterminacy created by two laws, one invoked by the Erinyes and the other by Apollo.[116]

---

115. By texts, I mean not only self-conscious, written verbal formulae, but also oral texts, *see e.g.,* S. LIEBERMAN, *The Publication of the Mishnah,* in HELLENISM IN JEWISH PALESTINE 83, 87 (2d ed. 1962); Tedlock, *The Spoken Word and the Work of Interpretation in American Indian Religion,* in TRADITIONAL AMERICAN INDIAN LITERATURES 45 (K. Kroeber ed. 1981), and "social texts," which entail the "reading" of meaning into complex social activity, *see, e.g.,* C. GEERTZ, THE INTERPRETATION OF CULTURES, *supra* note 7, at 3–30; C. GEERTZ, NEGARA, *supra* note 7.

116. *See* AESCHYLUS, ORESTEIA (R. Lattimore trans. 1953); *id.* at 133 (*The Eumenides*); R. KUHNS, THE HOUSE, THE CITY, AND THE JUDGE 63–94 (1962) (comparing attitudes toward law expressed by Athena, Apollo, and the Erinyes in the trial scene of *The Eumenides*). The Erinyes recognize the jurispathic element of the law of the

Just as there are myths in which courts arise out of "polynomia,"
so there are stories in which polynomia arises out of the loss of
courts. In a famous talmudic passage, Rabbi Jose re-creates the hal-
cyon days before the destruction of Jerusalem, where the Great Sanhedrin sat and whence the Law went out to all Israel. After the end
of that court, the Law became two laws.[117] The state of unredeemed
controversy, the problem of too much law, is thus seen to be either
solved by the authority of courts or caused by the failure or lack of
authority of courts.

We find a closely parallel set of arguments when we move from
antiquity to the foundations of our own Supreme Court. It, too, is
a solution to the problem of too much law. Consider, for example,
the classic apology for a national supreme court in *The Federalist:*

> To produce uniformity in these determinations, they ought to be
> submitted, in the last resort, to one SUPREME TRIBUNAL. . . . If there
> is in each State a court of final jurisdiction, there may be as
> many different final determinations on the same point as there
> are courts. There are endless diversities in the opinions of men.
> We often see not only different courts but the Judges of the came
> [*sic*] court differing from each other. To avoid the confusion which
> would unavoidably result from the contradictory decisions of a
> number of independent judicatories, all nations have found it
> necessary to establish one court paramount to the rest, possessing
> a general superintendence, and authorized to settle and declare
> in the last resort a uniform rule of civil justice.[118]

polis in their complaint: "Gods of the younger generation, you have ridden down
the laws of the elder time, torn them out of my hands." AESCHYLUS, *The Eumenides,*
lines 778–79, 808–09, in AESCHYLUS, ORESTEIA, *supra,* at 163–64. The transition from
the blood feud to civil justice is not a transition from "no law" to "law," or even,
necessarily, from greater to less total violence. On the ways in which law characterizes
the entire "meaning" of feuding behavior, see William Miller's extraordinary work,
Miller, *Choosing the Avenger,* 1 LAW & HIST. (1983).

117. *See* BABYLONIAN TALMUD, *Sanhedrin* 88b.

118. THE FEDERALIST No. 22, at 148–49 (A. Hamilton) (E. Bourne ed. 1947).
Strictly speaking, the passage quoted concerns the narrow issue of adjudication
respecting treaties. But the argument clearly applies more broadly, and elsewhere in
The Federalist Hamilton refers implicitly to the discussion quoted above as the justification for a single supreme tribunal. *See id.* No. 81, at 119 (A. Hamilton).

Sixteen years after *The Federalist,* William Cranch, justifying his first venture
into reprinting the decisions of the Supreme Court, wrote:

> Uniformity, in such cases [in which little information can be derived from
> English authority], can not be expected where the judicial authority is shared

Modern apologists for the jurispathic function of courts usually state the problem not as one of *too much* law, but as one of *unclear* law. The supreme tribunal removes uncertainty, lack of clarity, and difference of opinion about what the law is. This statist formulation is either question begging or misleading. To state, as I have done, that the problem is one of too much law is to acknowledge the nomic integrity of each of the communities that have generated principles and precepts. It is to posit that *each* "community of interpretation" that has achieved "law" has its own *nomos*—narratives, experiences, and visions to which the norm articulated is the right response. And it is to recognize that different interpretive communities will almost certainly exist and will generate distinctive responses to any normative problem of substantial complexity.

On the other hand, to state the problem as one of unclear law or difference of opinion about *the* law seems to presuppose that there is a hermeneutic that is methodologically superior to those employed by the communities that offer their own law. One might suppose that this assumption had been put to rest by Justice Jackson's famous aphorism: "We are not final because we are infallible, but we are infallible only because we are final."[119] Any claim to a privileged hermeneutic method appears unfashionable today, but it has ancient roots and tenaciously persists in the law. Chief Justice Edward Coke's response to King James' claim to exercise jurisdiction personally is one classic formulation of the privileged hermeneutic position:

[T]hen the King said, that he thought the law was founded upon reason, and that he and others had reason, as well as the Judges: to which it was answered by me, that true it was, that God had endowed His Majesty with excellent science, and great endow-

---

among such a vast number of independent tribunals, unless the decisions of the various courts are known to each other. Even in the same court, analogy of judgment can not be maintained if its adjudications are suffered to be forgotten. . . .
. . . One of the effects, expected from the establishment of a national judiciary, was the uniformity of a judicial decision; an attempt, therefore, to report the cases decided by the Supreme Court of the United States, can not need an apology.
Cranch, *Preface* to 5 U.S. (1 Cranch) at iii–iv (1804). Thus, hierarchical authority and an apparatus for communicating its decisions are alike prescribed as the solutions to the self-evidently problematic condition of polynomia.
119. Brown v. Allen, 344 U.S. 443, 540 (1953) (Jackson, J., concurring).

ments of nature; but His Majesty was not learned in the laws of his realm of England, and causes which concern the life . . . or fortunes of his subjects are not to be decided by natural reason but by the artificial reason and judgment of law, which law is an act which requires long study and experience. . . .[120]

And contemporary jurists who speak of special expertise are but mouthing a variant of this position.

Alternatively, the statist position may be understood to assert implicitly, not a superior interpretive method, but a convention of legal discourse: the state and its designated hierarchy are entitled to the exclusive or supreme jurisgenerative capacity. Everyone else offers suggestions or opinions about what the single normative world should look like, but only the state creates it. The position that only the state creates law thus confuses the status of interpretation with the status of political domination. It encourages us to think that the interpretive act of the court is privileged in the measure of its political ascendance.

Although this second position may be good state law—the Constitution proclaims itself supreme—the position is at best ambiguous when viewed as a description of what the various norm-generating communities understand themselves to be doing. Insular communities often have their own, competing, unambiguous rules of recognition. They frequently inhabit a *nomos* in which their distinct *Grundnorm* is supreme from its own perspective. The redemptive constitutional model offers a more ambiguous perspective on the conventions of constitutional discourse. At times, redemptive groups may adopt an oracular jurisprudence, or at least one that is not naively positivist in character. They may assert their constitutionalism as the true constitution and denounce that of the courts as not only misguided, but also "void." At the same time, it would be strange indeed to find the redemptive constitutionalist unwilling to concede the superior practical effects of securing the acquiescence of judges, legislators,

120. Prohibitions del Roy, 12 Co. 63, 64–65, 77 Eng. Rep. 1342, 1343 (K. B. 1655). Pocock sees the tension between natural reason and the technical knowledge of any specific law as an element in the dilemma of the status of the disciplines of practical action in the normative and intellectual worlds. It is a dilemma to which historicism and the associated hermeneutics are a proffered solution. *See* J. POCOCK, THE MACHIAVELLIAN MOMENT 3–30 (1975).

and governors in the radical revisions that he offers up as the only true constitutional meanings. It is surely possible to articulate a radical redemptive constitutionalism in which the statist convention—that the officials of the state make law—is accepted. The theoretical problems of the status of critical insight in such a positivist ordering will, for practical reasons, be ignored.

Theorists who appeal to the general justice of the political structure of which the courts are a part make a somewhat different sort of claim for the special position of judicial interpretation. Professor Owen Fiss has asserted such a claim:

> In what ways is the interpretation of the judge uniquely authoritative? There are two answers to this question. . . . [First, a] judicial interpretation is authoritative in the sense that it legitimates the use of force against those who refuse to accept or otherwise give effect to the meaning embodied in that interpretation.
>
> The second sense of authoritativeness . . . stresses not the use of state power, but an ethical claim to obedience—a claim that an individual has a moral duty to obey a judicial interpretation, not because of its particular intellectual authority . . . , but because the judge is part of an authority structure that is good to preserve.[121]

Fiss goes on to emphasize that the claim to institutional virtue and hence the claim to obedience through conscience depend on a rejection of the "nihilism" that would deny the possibility and the value of interpretation itself.[122]

By posing the question as one involving a choice between the judicial articulation of values (albeit contested) and nihilism, Fiss has made too easy the answer to his question about the institutional virtue of the judiciary and of the political system of which the judiciary is a part. The real challenge presented by those whom Fiss calls "nihilists" is not a looming void in which no interpretation would take place. Even those who deny the possibility of interpretation must constantly engage in the interpretive act. The challenge presented by the absence of a single, "objective" interpretation is, instead,

---

121. Fiss, *supra* note 7, at 755–56 (footnotes omitted).
122. *Id.* at 762–63.

the need to maintain a sense of legal meaning despite the destruction
of any pretense of superiority of one *nomos* over another. By exercising its superior brute force, however, the agency of state law shuts
down the creative hermeneutic of principle that is spread throughout
our communities. The question, then, is the extent to which coercion
is necessary to the maintenance of minimum conditions for the creation of legal meaning in autonomous interpretive communities.

The insular communities and redemptive movements that generate their own constitutional law have to this point been considered
almost as if they operated in a world in which opposing meanings
had no connection with force and violence. In the next Part, I shall
consider one of the elements that I have thus far ignored—the commitments essential to the living of a law in a violent world.

III. Commitment

In the normative universe, legal meaning is created by simultaneous
engagement and disengagement, identification and objectification.
Because the *nomos* is but the process of human action stretched
between vision and reality,[123] a legal interpretation cannot be valid
if no one is prepared to live by it. Certain thinkers may be dismissed
as "merely" utopian, not only because they posit standards for behavior radically different from those by which we are accustomed to
living, but also because they fail to posit alternative lives to which
we would commit ourselves by stretching from our reality toward
their vision.[124]

The transformation of interpretation into legal meaning begins
when someone accepts the demands of interpretation and, through
the personal act of commitment, affirms the position taken.[125] Such

---

123. I mean to evoke, without commitment to it, Nietzsche's aphorism: "Man
is a rope stretched between the animal and the Superman—a rope over an abyss."
F. NIETZSCHE, THUS SPAKE ZARATHUSTRA 9 (T. Common trans. 2d ed. 1911).

124. More's Utopia, *see* T. MORE, UTOPIA (London 1516), has no edge because
it is not, in context, a call to action. The Christian commonwealth of Calvin, on
the other hand, is fraught with action. *See* 2 Q. SKINNER, *supra* note 7, at 230–38.

125. I do not mean that valid interpretation always entails a present and uncon-
ditional commitment to the course of conduct posited by the interpretive act. I am
not articulating an ethic for enthusiasts. Nonetheless, the difference between speculation and practical interpretation—of which legal interpretation is one form—is that
practical interpretation entails commitment, however contingent or attenuated that

affirmation entails a commitment to projecting the understanding of the norm at work in our reality through all possible worlds into the teleological vision that the interpretation implies. From the Amish perspective, for example, the interpretation of the principle of separation of church and state begins with the affirmation that the Amish community will do whatever is necessary to maintain its first century Christian insularity. And the meaning of this affirmation must include the projection of the understanding of the primitive Church into the unrealized worlds that loom.

Creating legal meaning, however, requires not only the movement of dedication and commitment, but also the objectification of that to which one is committed. The community posits a law, external to itself, that it is committed to obeying and that it does obey in dedication to its understanding of that law. Objectification is crucial to the language games that can be played with the law and to the meanings that can be created out of it. If the Amish lived as they do because it was fun to do so, they might still fight for their insularity. They would not, however, be disobedient to any articulable principle were they to capitulate. And they could not hold someone blameworthy—lawless—were he to give in.

Creation of legal meaning entails, then, subjective commitment to an objectified understanding of a demand. It entails the disengagement of the self from the "object" of law, and at the same time requires an engagement to that object as a faithful "other." The metaphor of separation permits the allegory of dedication. This objectification of the norms to which one is committed frequently, perhaps always, entails a narrative—a story of how the law, now object, came to be, and more importantly, how it came to be one's own. Narrative is the literary genre for the objectification of value.

The range of meaning that may be given to every norm—the

commitment may be. The position I assert here is simply a weak perversion of Heidegger's far more general proposition about interpretation:

> As understanding, Dasein projects its Being upon possibilities. This *Being-towards-possibilities* which understands is itself a potentiality-for-Being, and it is so because of the way these possibilities, as disclosed, exert their counter-thrust [Rückschlag] upon Dasein. The projecting of the understanding has its own possibility—that of developing itself [sich auszubilden]. This development of the understanding we call "interpretation." . . . Nor is interpretation the acquiring of information about what is understood; it is rather the working-out of possibilities projected in understanding.

M. HEIDEGGER, BEING AND TIME 188–89 (J. Macquarrie & E. Robinson trans. 1962).

norm's interpretability—is defined, therefore, both by a legal text, which objectifies the demand, and by the multiplicity of implicit and explicit commitments that go with it. Some interpretations are writ in blood and run with a warranty of blood as part of their validating force. Other interpretations carry more conventional limits to what will be hazarded on their behalf. The narratives that any particular group associates with the law bespeak the range of the group's commitments. Those narratives also provide resources for justification, condemnation, and argument by actors within the group, who must struggle to live their law.

To know the law—and certainly to live the law—is to know not only the objectified dimension of validation, but also the commitments that warrant interpretations.

A. Unofficial Interpretation

In Part II, I wrote of the proliferation of legal meaning—the impossibility and undesirability of suppressing the jurisgenerative principle, the legal DNA. I have suggested that the proliferation of legal meaning is at odds, however, with the effort of every state to exercise strict superintendence over the articulation of law as a means of social control. Commitment, as a constitutive element of legal meaning, creates inevitable conflict between the state and the processes of jurisgenesis. I turn now to the problem of unofficial interpretation— the elaboration of norms by committed groups standing against the state.

I. The Special Case of Civil Disobedience

The decision to act in accord with an understanding of the law validated by the actor's own community but repudiated by the officialdom of the state, including its judges, is commonly understood as a decision to engage in justifiable disobedience. Even commentators whose general perspective on law is largely statist have argued that disobedience premised upon an interpretation of the law should have a special status.[126] This concession is said to depend upon the "plausible" character of the interpretation—plausible in terms of the prec-

---

126. *See* R. DWORKIN, *supra* note 44, at 206–22.

edents and activities of courts.[127] According to such a theory, the "disobedient" actor must take into account the pronouncements of courts because "no one can make a reasonable effort to follow the law unless he grants the courts the general power to alter it by their decisions."[128]

From its own point of view, however, the community that has created and proposed to live by its own, divergent understanding of law makes a claim not of justifiable disobedience, but rather of radical reinterpretation. If one addresses the status of "civil disobedients" from the perspective of the state's courts, one can hardly avoid framing the jurisprudential question as one of the individual's obligation to the state's law. From a general jurisprudential perspective, however, to concede so central a role to the courts (in any sense other than as a sociological datum—that is, a recognition that courts in the United States do wield the heaviest stick and, as a result, are often the voice most carefully attended to) is to deny to the jurisgenerative community out of which legal meaning arises the integrity of a law of its own.

Consider the case of the civil rights sit-in movement from 1961 until 1964. The movement's community affirmed that the Constitution of the United States has a valid moral claim to obedience from the members of the community. Yet the community also affirmed an understanding that the Constitution's guarantee of equal protection includes a right to be served in places of public accommodation without regard to race. In the face of official interpretations of the Constitution that permitted continued discriminatory practices in public accommodations, the movement had this choice: it could conform its public behavior to the official "law" while protesting that the law was "wrong," or it could conform its public behavior to its own interpretation of the Constitution. There is both "disobedience" and "obedience" in either case. But only obedience to the movement's own interpretation of the Constitution was fidelity to the understanding of law by which the movement's members would live uncoerced. Thus, in acting out their own, "free" interpretation of the Constitution, protestors say, "We *do* mean this in the medium of blood" (or in the medium of time in jail); "our lives constitute the bridges between the reality of present official declarations of law and the

127. See *id.* at 215.
128. *Id.* at 214.

vision of our law triumphant" (a vision that may, of course, never come to fruition).

By provoking the response of the state's courts, the act of civil disobedience changes the meaning of the law articulated by officialdom. For the courts, too, may or may not speak in blood. To be sure, judges characteristically do not have to use their own blood to create meaning; like most power wielders, they usually write their bloodier texts in the bodies of the inmates of the penal colony. But the fact that all judges are in some way people of violence does not mean they rejoice in that quality or write their texts lightly.

A community that acquiesces in the injustice of official law has created no law of its own. It is not sui juris. The community that writes law review articles has created a law—a law under which officialdom may maintain its interpretation merely by suffering the protest of the articles. The community that disobeys the criminal law upon the authority of its own constitutional interpretation, however, forces the judge to choose between affirming his interpretation of the official law through violence against the protesters and permitting the polynomia of legal meaning to extend to the domain of social practice and control. The judge's commitment is tested as he is asked what he intends to be the meaning of his law and whether his hand will be part of the bridge that links the official vision of the Constitution with the reality of people in jail.[129]

2. Commitment and the Problem of Violence

Justice Brandeis grasped the problem. Writing his own, rather slanted narrative of the founding fathers' commitment to free speech, he asserted: "Believing in the power of reason as applied through public discussion, they eschewed silence coerced by law—the argument of force in its worst form."[130] Brandeis recognized that the coercive dimension of law is itself destructive of the possibility of interpretation. If we think of interpretation, unrealistically, as the mere offer-

---

129. For an extraordinary instance of the failure of judicial commitment to the statist interpretation, see Hamm v. City of Rock Hill, 379 U.S. 306 (1964).

130. Whitney v. California, 274 U.S. 357, 375-76 (Brandeis, J., concurring). The quotation and its place within Brandeis' thought are discussed in Cover, *The Left, the Right, and the First Amendment: 1918-1928*, 40 MD. L. REV. 349, 385-87 (1981).

ing of disembodied doctrine, the coercion of silence of which Brandeis wrote would rest on a claim that courts ought to possess the unique and exclusive power to offer interpretations. This is "the argument of force in its worst form," illegitimate as interpretative method.

Brandeis' constitutional thought represents a valiant effort to solve the inherent difficulty presented by the violence of the state's law acting upon the free interpretive process. He would have attacked the problem of the law's violence by constitutionalizing the principles of an uncoerced politics, a free public space, which would generate a law legitimated even in its coercive dimensions by its uncoerced origins. Free speech was to be the linchpin of this legitimation—free speech conceived of as all the components of deliberative public life.[131] Brandeis combined this enshrinement of free speech with a strong decentralizing tendency in the structural dimension of his constitutionalism, and he thereby attempted to safeguard the practical preconditions for the exercise of the participatory rights guaranteed by his first amendment jurisprudence.[132]

Brandeis' approach, however, is not entirely successful. The statist appeal to the "free" conditions of political life seems strongly influenced by a somewhat romantic view of the Greek (or Athenian) polis. And although Brandeis' federalism responded to an acknowledged need for participation in a common life, by the mid-twentieth century the states had long since lost their character as political communities. Whether this loss is primarily attributable to scale or to more intractable problems of reconciling the community of meaning with the exercise of territorial domination based on violence, I do not know. In any event, American political life no longer occurs within a public space dominated by common mythologies and rites and occupied by neighbors and kin. Other bases are necessary to support the common life that generates legal traditions.

The creation of legal meaning cannot take place in silence. But neither can it take place without the committed action that distin-

---

131. *See* Cover, *supra* note 130, at 376–80.

132. On Brandeis' federalism, see, for example, New State Ice Co. v. Liebmann, 285 U.S. 262, 311 (1932) (Brandeis, J., dissenting); *see also* A. BICKEL, THE SUPREME COURT AND THE IDEA OF PROGRESS 116 (1970) (describing Brandeis as the prophet of a movement toward decentralization). An excellent analysis of Brandeis' federalism is to be found in a student paper. E. Steiner, A Progressive Creed: The Experimental Federalism of Mr. Justice Brandeis (unpublished manuscript on file in Harvard Law School Library).

guishes law from literature. Brandeis' enduring legacy is his realization that it is particularly problematic to coerce silence, for such
coercion destroys the element of reason that interpretation entails.
Yet it is also problematic, even if less so, to coerce the abandonment
of actions that arise from common life in a dedicated space within
the normative world. The effect of this latter form of coercion is to
destroy the experience and interpersonal faith that, as much as "reason," are constitutive of our understanding of normative worlds.
Those who would offer a law different from that of the state will not
be satisfied with a rule that permits them to speak without living
their law.

Whenever a community resists a rule of silence or some other
law of the state, it necessarily enters into a secondary hermeneutic—
the interpretation of the texts of resistance. For a group to live its
law in the face of the predictable employment of violence against it
requires a new elaboration of "law"—the development of an understanding of what is right and just in the violent contexts that the
group will encounter. The group must understand the normative
implications of struggle and the meaning of suffering and must accept
responsibility for the results of the confrontations that will ensue.[133]

One of the texts of resistance asserts that "all . . . are endowed
by their creator with certain unalienable Rights." But this text goes
on to concede to the dictates of prudence that we must "suffer, while
evils are sufferable" and to recognize that "a decent respect to the
opinions of mankind" imposes upon us an obligation carefully to
recount the reasons that led to the decision to resist.[134] The obligations
to engage in a prudential calculus of suffering and to justify resistance
before a common humanity are among the norms generated by interpreting the natural rights texts in a context of commitment to the

---

133. This "understanding" may include acceptance of responsibility for shedding
blood or for others' shedding of it. Consider Judaism's elaboration of a law governing
the conduct of the victim of oppressive violence, *see* D. DAUBE, COLLABORATION WITH
TYRANNY IN RABBINIC LAW (1965), and the narrative explication of the law of martyrdom in S. SPEIGEL, THE LAST TRIAL (J. Goldin trans. 1967). The Gandhian tradition
of nonviolence is also a law governing the resistant "victim."

134. The Declaration of Independence (U.S. 1776). On the Declaration of Independence as a revolutionary document, see G. WILLS, *supra* note 66, at 3–90. For
both Jefferson's original text and that of the Congress, see *id.* at 375–79; *see also*
C. BECKER, THE DECLARATION OF INDEPENDENCE (1922) (analyzing the Declaration of
Independence by focusing upon the document itself and the manner in which it
expresses a motivating idea).

course of resistance. Bentham could criticize natural rights phrase-ology as "nonsense upon stilts";[135] he could assert its tendency to "impel a man, by that force of conscience, to rise up in arms against any law whatever that he happens not to like,"[136] because, in char-acteristic fashion, Bentham failed to recognize that texts of resistance, like all texts, are always subject to an interpretative process that limits the situations in which resistance is a legitimate response. Any understanding of the texts is qualified when they are projected onto the future.

In interpreting a text of resistance, any community must come to grips with violence. It must think through the implications of living as a victim or perpetrator of violence in the contexts in which violence is likely to arise.[137] Violence—as a technique either to achieve or to suppress interpretations or the living of them—may be said to put a high price on those interpretations. But an "economic" approach here is misleading. For the understanding of law is the projection not only of what we would in fact do under different circumstances, but

---

135. J. BENTHAM, *A Critical Examination of the Declaration of Rights*, in BENTHAM'S POLITICAL THOUGHT 257, 269 (B. Parekh ed. 1973).

136. J. BENTHAM, A FRAGMENT ON GOVERNMENT 149 (London 1776).

137. Some theories of revolution idealize violence. Such theories should be distinguished from a theory of radical autonomy of juridical meaning such as the one I am proposing. Jurisgenesis is a process that takes place in communities that already have an identity. Their members are, in Sartre's terms, already bound by a "pledge" (*le serment*), *see* J. SARTRE, CRITIQUE OF DIALECTICAL REASON 419 (J. Rée ed. 1976), though such a vocabulary suggests too much in the way of contractarian processes and too little in the way of stable cultural understanding. The complexity of the mutual understandings at work in the community is, I believe, revealed and transmitted in the narratives of the group.

Theorists of revolution frequently concern themselves with the formation of group bonds—the development of "consciousness" or solidarity. Violence may well be a particularly powerful catalyst—arguably a necessary one—in the chemistry by which a collection of hitherto unrelated individuals becomes a self-conscious revo-lutionary force. And in many instances, such a group will ultimately offer rich contributions to legal meaning.

But such collective realizations of identity are not my concern here, however much they may interest theorists of revolution. The persistent effort to live a law other than that of the state's officials presupposes a community already self-conscious and lawful by its own lights—not a mass inarticulately seeking realization in the face of the brute fact of domination. The argument that violence is a necessary part of revolution does not apply to the interpretation of texts of resistance by an extant community living its law. But although resistant groups affirming their own laws need not realize themselves in violence, they always live in the shadow of the violence backing the state's claim to social control.

also of what we ought to do. And we commonly believe situations
of violent interaction to be dominated by special principles and values. The invocation of these special principles, values, and even myths
is a part of the hermeneutic of the texts of resistance.

Religious communities have a special jurisprudence of exile and
martyrdom; revolutionary cadres evolve special principles governing
life in prison or on the barricades. Most impressively, some persis-
tently antistatist but quintessentially lawful groups have evolved a
jurisprudence of nonviolence to govern interactions in the minefields
of active resistance to the violence of the state. This is what the
Amish promise in the event that their interpretation of religious liberty fails to converge with that of the state:

> [T]he Amish answer to forms of legal harassment, which would
> force them to violate their religion, has been to sell their farms
> and to remove. . . . [I]t would, if this Court sustains this prose-
> cution, sound the death knell, in this country, for an old, dis-
> tinctive and innocent culture.[138]

But not every divergent understanding of law is sufficient to
withstand the coercive power of the state. Bob Jones University once
interpreted its controlling biblical texts to require that no unmarried
black person be admitted to the school; but after the power of the
state was invoked to deny the University favorable tax status, that
interpretation was withdrawn.[139] I do not know the extent to which
the state's coercive action caused the interpretive change, but I suspect
that the change was at least partly attributable to weakness of commitment in the original interpretive act. That commitment was suf-

---

138. Brief for Respondents at 26, Wisconsin v. Yoder, 406 U.S. 205 (1972) (No.
70–110).

139. Bob Jones Univ. v. United States, 103 S. Ct. 2017, 2023 (1983). The Court
stated that Bob Jones University had changed its policies in response to the Fourth
Circuit decision in McCrary v. Runyon, 515 F.2d 1082 (4th Cir. 1975), aff'd, 427
U.S. 160 (1976), which had held that racially motivated exclusion of blacks by private
schools is proscribed by 42 U.S.C. § 1981 (1976). It must also be noted that on April
16, 1975, the IRS had notified Bob Jones University of the proposed revocation of
tax-exempt status effective December 1, 1970, the date on which the school received
general notification of the change in the IRS interpretation of I.R.C. § 501(c)(3)
(1976). The change in the school's admissions policies took place on May 29, 1975,
six weeks after both the IRS notification and the Fourth Circuit decision. See Bob
Jones Univ., 103 S. Ct. at 2023.

ficient to support the violence of racial exclusion only as long as the price of such violence was not hostile treatment by the IRS. The absence of commitment to the action dictated by an interpretation often produces a change in the interpretation itself.

Violence at the hands of the state escalates the stakes of the interpretive enterprise, but so does the violence of any nonstate community in defining its bounds or implementing its redemptive program.[140] The army of the Mormons at Nauvoo imposed a "law" upon the faithful that brooked neither exit nor effective dissent.[141] Violence within the community and an armed stance looking out, no less than the incarceration and murder of Joseph Smith, set the scene for the later constitutional history of Mormonism—a history in which a common hermeneutic between insular community and state always seemed impossible. The culmination, in *Late Corp. of the Church of Jesus Christ of Latter-Day Saints v. United States*,[142] was officialdom justifying its repression to itself. The long process leading to Utah's statehood was, from the Mormon perspective, an exploration of the degree of resistance demanded by religious obligation and the realities of power.[143]

Certain efforts to interpret the texts of resistance have a strange, almost doomed character. The state's claims over legal meaning are, at bottom, so closely tied to the state's imperfect monopoly over the domain of violence that the claim of a community to an autonomous

---

140. If the state treats the apostolic ministry or the enlistment of cadres for the revolution as a breach of the peace or criminal syndicalism, the groups involved must be prepared to generate their norms in the shadow of the potential violence of the criminal law. If officialdom chooses to understand with these groups that the apostolic ministry or recruitment of cadres is constitutionally protected, there is a convergence of hermeneutics.

The effect of the state on the autonomous community's jurisgenerative process is completely symmetrical with that of the community on the elaboration of statist legal meaning. A judge may often stand upon an understanding of the law that becomes increasingly problematic if actively resisted by groups in society. The reaction of the state to the Amish affects the law of the religious community in precisely the same way that the reaction of the Amish to the state affects the state's law. (Of course, this may be a bit like saying that the mass of my bean bag and the mass of the earth play an identical role in the formula determining how the bodies will behave with respect to each other.)

141. *See* D. OAKS & M. HILL, CARTHAGE CONSPIRACY: THE TRIAL OF THE ACCUSED ASSASSINS OF JOSEPH SMITH 6–23 (1975).

142. 136 U.S. 1 (1890), *modified,* 140 U.S. 665 (1891).

143. *See* C. WEISBROD, *supra* note 86, at 16–33 (citing sources).

meaning must be linked to the community's willingness to live out its meaning in defiance. Outright defiance, guerrilla warfare, and terrorism are, of course, the most direct responses. They are responses, however, that may—as in the United States—be unjustifiable and doomed to failure.

Our overriding temptation in the absence of substantial, direct, and immediate violent resistance to official law is to concede the state's principal claim to interpretation and to relegate the jurisgenerative processes of associations, communities, and movements to a delegated, secondary, or interstitial status. For those unwilling to conceive of law in such a state-bound framework, however, the law-creating processes of the Quakers, Amish, and other groups that have made their relation to the violence of the state a central normative question assume a special significance. This significance lies in the group's creation of a jurisprudence that orders the forms and occasions of confrontation, a jurisprudence of resistance that is necessarily also one of accommodation.[144]

One may choose to characterize the accommodations and capitulations of persons and communities under threat of the various nasty things the state might do as themselves integral parts of the normative world. Just as living in the economic world entails an understanding of price, so living in the normative world entails an understanding of the measures of commitment to norms in the face of contrary commitments of others. Such a view of the normative import of coercion avoids privileging the violence or the interpretations of the state. If there is a state and if it backs the interpretations of its courts with violence, those of us who participate in extrastate jurisgenesis must consider the question of resistance and must count the state's violence as part of our reality. But this is the sum of what the state has added. First, the state influences interpretation: for better or worse, most communities will avoid outright conflict with a judge's interpretations, at least when he will likely back them with violence. Second, when state and community offer conflicting interpretations, the community must elaborate the hermeneutics of resistance or of

---

144. See, e.g., A. WASKOW, FROM RACE RIOT TO SIT-IN 219–54 (1966). For a fascinating extended study of the evolution of sectarian doctrine concerning abstention from war and war-related obligations of the state, see R. MacMASTER, S. HORST & R. ULLE, CONSCIENCE IN CRISIS: MENNONITE AND OTHER PEACE CHURCHES IN AMERICA, 1739–1789 (Studies in Anabaptist and Mennonite History No. 20, 1979).

withdrawal—the justificatory enterprises of institutional stances chosen by or forced upon those who would make a *nomos* other than
that of the state.

B. The Act of Commitment from the Point of View
of the Judges: Jurisdiction as the Secondary Text

Judges are people of violence. Because of the violence they command,
judges characteristically do not create law, but kill it. Theirs is the
jurispathic office. Confronting the luxuriant growth of a hundred
legal traditions, they assert that *this one* is law and destroy or try
to destroy the rest.

But judges are also people of peace. Among warring sects, each
of which wraps itself in the mantle of a law of its own, they assert
a regulative function that permits a life of law rather than violence.
The range of the violence they could command (but generally do
not) measures the range of the peace and law they constitute.

The resistance of a community to the law of the judge, the
community's insistence upon living its own law or realizing its law
within the larger social world, raises the question of the judge's
commitment to the violence of his office.[145] A community's acquiescence in or accommodation to the judge's interpretation reinforces
the hermeneutic process offered by the judge and extends, in one way
or another, its social range. Confrontation, on the other hand, challenges the judge's implicit claim to authoritative interpretation.[146]

---

145. See *supra* pp. 147–48. For a discussion of judges who persevered in performing acts that they themselves found morally unpalatable and even, at times, illegal
or unconstitutional if judged against a "free" interpretation—acts that they nevertheless
believed were constitutionally required by the authoritative interpretations of superior
tribunals within the judicial hierarchy—see R. Cover, *supra* note 4.

146. In this respect, Abraham Lincoln's famous remarks on the *Dred Scott*
decision, Scott v. Sandford, 60 U.S. (19 How.) 393 (1857), made during the Lincoln-
Douglas debates, repay study. Lincoln's position strongly denies any obligation to
treat the Court's interpretation as a privileged or binding one. Because jurisdiction
is entirely case-specific, the only deference due the Court's authority is to refrain
from direct resistance to its specific edicts. We are under no obligation, according to
Lincoln, to relate our understanding of the law, and our projection of that understanding, to the Court's interpretation. Our future actions are to be governed by *our
own* understanding, not the Court's:

   I do not resist [*Dred Scott*]. If I wanted to take Dred Scott from his master,
   I would be interfering with property. . . . But I am doing no such thing as that,
   but all that I am doing is refusing to obey it as a political rule. If I were in

In the face of challenge, the judge—armed with no inherently superior interpretive insight, no necessarily better law—must separate the exercise of violence from his own person. The only way in which the employment of force is not revealed as a naked jurispathic act is through the judge's elaboration of the institutional privilege of force—that is, jurisdiction. Just as those who would live by the law of their community are led to the texts of resistance, the judge who would kill that law resorts to the texts of jurisdiction. The most basic of the texts of jurisdiction are the apologies for the state itself and for its violence—the ideology of social contract or the rationalizations of the welfare state.[147] The judge, however, rarely concedes that these

---

Congress, and a vote should come up on a question whether slavery should be prohibited in a new territory, in spite of that Dred Scott decision, I would vote that it should.

Speech by Abraham Lincoln at Chicago, Illinois (July 10, 1858), *reprinted in* 2 A. LINCOLN, THE COLLECTED WORKS OF ABRAHAM LINCOLN 484, 495 (R. Basler ed. 1953). Lincoln's position is an attempt to separate completely the projection of understanding from the decree that is the direct exercise of power. Such separation allows one to "acquiesce" by refraining from resistance while simultaneously refusing to extend the social range of the Court's hermeneutic. But Lincoln's solution is at best a limited one. Some decrees project consequences of interpretive processes into the future in ways that are far less circumscribed than the decision in *Dred Scott*. The injunction, with its prospective remedial ambitions, is the most obvious such decree. The future-oriented regulation of social life according to a controverted projection of a controverted understanding of the law is likely to raise the choice of acquiescence or resistance. See A. BICKEL, THE LEAST DANGEROUS BRANCH 254–72 (1962). Bickel correctly assimilates Lincoln's position to that of groups that resisted the ruling of Brown v. Board of Educ., 347 U.S. 483 (1954). Resistance, however, is not evil per se; its merits depend upon what is resisted and upon the quality of the rebel's hermeneutic of resistance. *See supra* pp. 150–55. For a sensitive treatment of the "therapeutic" promise of resistance, see Burt, *Constitutional Law and the Teaching of the Parables*, 93 YALE L.J. 455 (1984).

147. Nowhere is the connection clearer than in T. HOBBES, LEVIATHAN (W. Smith ed. 1909) (1st ed. London 1651). When the claim made for the state is as all-encompassing as it is for Hobbes, the role of jurisdiction is simply ancillary to the authority of the sovereign and derivative from the very concept of sovereignty:

And therefore the Interpretation of all Lawes dependeth on the Authority Soveraign; and the Interpreters can be none but those, which the Soveraign, (to whom only the Subject oweth obedience) shall appoint. For else, by the craft of an Interpreter, the Law may be made to beare a sense, contrary to that of the Soveraign; by which means the Interpreter becomes the Legislator.

Id. ch. XXVI, at 211–12. Hobbes thus directly connects the privileged character he accords official judicial interpretation with *Leviathan's* larger enterprise of justifying the sovereignty of the state.

Yet although the texts of jurisdiction justify and excuse the violence of the state, they may also act as a constraint upon it. Indeed, the legitimation of institutional

underlying questions are even at issue. Judicial consideration of the texts of jurisdiction starts with the justification for courts—in general or in particular.

The significance of the jurisdictional principles through which courts exercise violence is that they separate the exercise of the judge's authority or violence from the primary hermeneutic act that that exercise realizes. All such principles obscure the nature of the commitment entailed in adjudication. The commitment of the resister is seldom so clouded. For example, the jurisdictional rule of *Walker v. City of Birmingham*[148]—that an injunction is to be obeyed (that is, will be enforced through violence) even though found to be incorrect by an appellate court or on collateral review—justifies official violence by the very act of resistance to it. The court ultimately responsible for the interpretation need never commit itself separately to the proposition that the particular interpretation warrants violence. It is the regime of obedience—of state superiority—that warrants the violence.

Walker may also be said to stand for a strong view of equity. The court's authority derives ultimately from a conception of the equity judge as guarantor of the social order, who must have nearly absolute authority to put a stop to the "disorders" of collective action guided by law or interests other than those of the state.[149] *Walker* relies heavily on the reasoning of *Howat v. Kansas*,[150] a case that stands squarely within the philosophy of the Taft Court, which enshrined the labor injunction as a constitutionally required prop of public order.

The rule of *Walker v. City of Birmingham* subordinates the creation of legal meaning to the interest in public order. It is the rule of the judge, the insider, looking out. It speaks to the judge as agent of state violence and employer of that violence against the "private" disorder of movements, communities, unions, parties, "people," "mobs." When the judge, aligned with the state, looks out upon the

---

privilege through law may itself have a constraining effect on the state. *See, e.g.,* E. GENOVESE, ROLL, JORDAN, ROLL 25–49 (1974) (discussing "the hegemonic function of the law"); E. THOMPSON, WHIGS AND HUNTERS 258–69 (1975).

148. 388 U.S. 307 (1967).

149. From the 1880s through the 1920s, this view of equity was central to the conservative case for the labor injunction. The twin high points of this conservative doctrinal elaboration were *In re* Debs, 158 U.S. 564 (1895), and Truax v. Corrigan, 257 U.S. 312 (1921), which seemed to constitutionalize the labor injunction.

150. 258 U.S. 181 (1921).

committed acts of those whose law is other than the state's, *Walker* tells him that the court's authority is greater than its warrant in interpretation of the Constitution or the law. Even when wrong, the judge is to act and is entitled to be obeyed. The signal *Walker* sends the judge is to be aggressive in confronting private resistance, because his authority will be vindicated even if in error. *Walker* tells the resister, moreover, that authority counts for so much and legal meaning for so little that even were he to convince the judge that his interpretation was correct, he would still be punished for his persistent and active commitment to it.

Just as the *Walker* doctrine places a court's orders beyond their intrinsic support in substantive legal interpretation, *Rizzo v. Goode*,[151] *Younger v. Harris*,[152] and *City of Los Angeles v. Lyons*[153] invoke a weak conception of equity and, in the name of principles of deference that emerge from ideas of federalism or separation of powers, place the violence of administration beyond the reach of "law"—even court law. The rules of *Rizzo*, *Younger*, and *Lyons* are the rules of judges as potential outsiders looking in at state violence. When the question is whether judicial interpretations that *circumscribe* the authority of the wielders of state violence will be given full effect, jurisdictional principles require that the judges' interpretations be given *less than* their intrinsic authority. Even if the judge is considered to have been correct in holding that a police practice violated the constitutional rights of its victims[154] or that a prosecution poses a present threat to the exercise of constitutional rights,[155] some principle of deference— whether to states, administrators, or legislative majorities—requires that equity, the only effective remedy, stay its hand.

Thus, equity is "strong" when the court is aligned with state violence and "weak" when the court is a counterweight to that violence. The result in all cases is deference to the authoritarian application of violence, whether it originates in court orders or in systems of administration. Law, even constitutional law, succumbs to the hermeneutic of jurisdiction. The jurisgenerative impulse that led a

---

151. 423 U.S. 362 (1976).

152. 401 U.S. 37 (1971).

153. 103 S. Ct. 1660 (1983).

154. *Cf.* Rizzo v. Goode, 423 U.S. 362 (1976) (denying injunctive relief against practices of the Philadelphia police).

155. *Cf.* Younger v. Harris, 401 U.S. 37 (1971) (refusing to enjoin prosecution under allegedly unconstitutional state statute).

judge to find the chokehold practices of the Los Angeles Police Department unconstitutional,[156] the jurisgenerative impulse that compels the creation of law by forcing the court to grapple with substantive issues, is silenced. The apologetic and statist orientation of current jurisdictional understandings prevents courts from ever reaching the threatening questions.[157]

Contemporary federal equity doctrines, which legitimate judicial and administrative coercion without regard to its support in legal principle, are strongly linked to the general Thayerite principle of deference to the "majoritarian" branches. I do not mean to belittle the fundamental conundrum at the heart of the countermajoritarian difficulty. Admittedly, insofar as administration has a secure base in the legitimating factor of popular government, the veto exercised on the basis of constitutional principle by an unelected judge presents an insoluble confrontation between principle and process. But it is difficult to ignore the fact that the tie between administration and coercive violence is always present, while the relation between administration and popular politics may vary between close identity and the most attenuated of delegations.[158]

---

156. *See* Lyons v. City of Los Angeles, 656 F.2d 417 (9th Cir. 1981) (upholding injunction against use of chokehold by Los Angeles police), *rev'd*, 103 S. Ct 1660 (1983).

157. On the Supreme Court's use of jurisdictional concepts to insulate the decisions of state authorities from review, see, for example, Fiss, *Dombrowski*, 86 YALE L.J. 1103 (1977).

158. Even proponents of judicial deference acknowledge that administrative action may bear only an attenuated relation to majoritarian values. *See* A. BICKEL, *supra* note 145, at 202. The countermajoritarian difficulty has been one of the primary subjects of debate in American constitutional law, at least since James Thayer's criticism of judicial review, *see* Thayer, *The Origin and Scope of the American Doctrine of Constitutional Law*, 7 HARV. L. REV. 129 (1983), and Holmes' attack on substantive due process in his *Lochner* dissent, Lochner v. New York, 198 U.S. 45, 74 (1905) (Holmes, J., dissenting). The triumph of Thayerism in 1937 did not put an end to the debate but did transform its terms. For an historical and doctrinal treatment of the transformation, see Cover, *The Origins of Judicial Activism in the Protection of Minorities*, 91 YALE L.J. 1287 (1982). The doctrinal implications of a moderate defense of a limited judicial review shaped by the countermajoritarian difficulty itself—a defense that might be called the "footnote four solution" because of its derivation from United States v. Carolene Prods. Co., 304 U.S 144, 152 n.4 (1938)—are best elaborated in L. LUSKY, BY WHAT RIGHT? (1975), and more recently in J. ELY, DEMOCRACY AND DISTRUST (1980). The strongest claim for majoritarianism and the minimalist position on judicial review have been very ably presented, first by Learned Hand, *see* L. HAND, THE BILL OF RIGHTS (1958), then by Herbert Wechsler, *see* Wechsler,

The jurisdictional principles of deference are problematic precisely because, as currently articulated by the Supreme Court, they
align the interpretive acts of judges with the acts and interests of
those who control the means of violence. The more that judges use
their interpretive acts to oppose the violence of the governors, the
more nearly do they approximate a "least dangerous branch" with
neither sword nor purse, and the less clearly are they bound up in
the violent suppression of law. Indeed, the quality of their interpretive
acts and the justifications for their special role—that is, the hermeneutics of jurisdiction—are all that judges have to play against the
violence of administration. When they oppose the violence and coercion of the other organs of the state, judges begin to look more like
the other jurisgenerative communities of the world.[159]

It is not only "equity" and deference to "political branches" that
entail the substitution of the hermeneutic of jurisdiction for the hermeneutic of the text. Consider, for example, the lower court judge
supposedly constrained by superior authority to apply a rule that he

---

Toward Neutral Principles of Constitutional Law, 73 HARV. L. REV. 1 (1959), and
Alexander Bickel, *see* A. BICKEL, *supra* note 146, and most recently by Jesse Choper,
see J. CHOPER, JUDICIAL REVIEW AND THE NATIONAL POLITICAL PROCESS (1980). The
most eloquent defenders of the privileged position of judges as articulators of fundamental values have been Michael Perry, *see* M. PERRY, THE CONSTITUTION, THE
COURTS, AND HUMAN RIGHTS (1982), and Owen Fiss, *see* Fiss, *The Supreme Court,
1978 Term—Foreword: The Forms of Justice*, 93 HARV. L. REV. 1 (1979). Although
I advocate aggressive, articulate judicial review, my position differs fundamentally
from the positions of Fiss and Perry in that I accord no privileged character to the
work of the judges. I would have judges act on the basis of a committed constitutionalism in a world in which each of many communities acts out its own *nomos*
and is prepared to resist the work of the judges in many instances.
  159. Bickel's brief defense of the Court's dismissal of the appeal in Naim v.
Naim, 350 U.S. 985 (1956) (per curiam), a case that presented the issue of the
constitutionality of the Virginia miscegenation statute, raises the specter of a Court
stripped of the authority that distinguishes its legal interpretations from those of
other norm-generating communities:
    Actually a judgment legitimating such statutes would have been unthink-
    able.... But would it have been wise, at a time when the Court had just
    pronounced its new integration principle, when it was subject to scurrilous
    attack by men who predicted that integration of the schools would lead directly
    to "mongrelization of the race" . . . would it have been wise, just then, in the
    first case of its sort, on an issue that the Negro community as a whole can
    hardly be said to be pressing hard at the moment, to declare that the states
    may not prohibit racial intermarriage?
A. BICKEL, *supra* note 146, at 174.

believes to be wrong—not simply morally wrong, but wrong in law as well. In such a case, the lower court affirms a hierarchical principle in place of his interpretive convictions and thereby directly affirms his commitment to the triumph of the hierarchical order over meaning.[160] The extraordinary capacity of small shifts in membership of the Supreme Court to transform not only the decisional law of that Court, but also the strategic significance of the entire federal judiciary, is testimony to the commitment of judges to the hierarchical ordering of authority first, and to interpretive integrity only later.[161] The judge's commitments characteristically are supposed to be to the structure of authority. Absent this jurisdictional canon, the judge would have to measure the violence in each case against his own commitment to the meaning vindicated by it.

The logic of the judge's practice of justifying his violence through a commitment not to the end that the violence serves in the particular case, but to the structure of jurisdiction need not have the largely state-serving implications it generally has today. It is possible to conceive of a natural law of jurisdiction that might supplant the positivist version I have described. In elaborating such a law of jurisdiction, a judge might appeal to narratives of judicial resistance—Lord Coke's resistance to King James,[162] Taney's resistance to Lincoln,[163] or the incredibly courageous resistance of several Ghanaian judges to the perpetrators of a military coup.[164] He might thus defend his own

---

160. See R. Cover, supra note 4, at 252–56 (describing state court's refusal to use habeas corpus to free from federal custody aiders of fugitive slaves).

161. Of course, the notion that a 5–4 majority of the Supreme Court should bind the interpretive activity of all judges may superficially be said to have all the strengths and weaknesses of arguments for majority rule. The majority is certainly not always right, but it would surely make no sense to have interpretation governed by a 4–5 minority. What is important, however, is not the justifiability of the jurisdictional structure, but simply its existence.

162. Prohibitions del Roy, 12 Co. 63, 77 Eng. Rep. 1342 (K.B. 1655). For a somewhat debunking discussion of the case, see C. Bowen, The Lion and the Throne: The Life and Times of Sir Edward Coke 303–06 (1956).

163. Ex parte Merryman, 17 F. Cas. 144 (C.C.D. Md. 1861); see C. Swisher, The Taney Period, 1836–64, at 844–53 (Oliver Wendell Holmes Devise History of the Supreme Court of the United States No. 5, 1974); 3 C. Warren, The Supreme Court in United States History 90–96 (1924).

164. On June 4, 1979, one military government in Ghana succeeded another in a military coup. The new rulers, the Armed Forces Revolutionary Council (AFRC), promised a swift return to civilian government. The promise was, in a sense, fulfilled

authority to sit in judgment over those who exercise extralegal violence in the name of the state. In a truly violent, authoritarian situation, nothing is more revolutionary than the insistence of a judge that he exercises such a "jurisdiction"—but only if that jurisdiction implies the articulation of legal principle according to an independent hermeneutic. The commitment to a jurisgenerative process that does not defer to the violence of administration is the judge's only hope of partially extricating himself from the violence of the state.[165]

---

three months later with a formal return to civilian government under a new constitution. The Constitution of 1979 contained several special provisions, including article 15 of what are known as the transitional clauses—clauses designed to preclude, in effect, review of all acts perpetrated by the AFRC. In interpreting these clauses, several Ghanaian judges asserted a residual power of inquiry, whether upon petition for writ of habeas corpus or upon other writs seeking review. The judges varied in the degree to which they enunciated their manipulation of the constitutional denial of jurisdiction. Contrast the highly articulate, self-conscious appeal to English legal history in the opinion of Judge Taylor in *Ex parte* Forson (Accra High Ct. May 19, 1980) (opinion on file in Harvard Law School Library) with the somewhat more disingenuous approach of Judge Koranteng-Addow in *Ex parte* Shackleford (Accra High Ct. Aug. 8, 1980) (opinion on file in Harvard Law School Library). The Supreme Court of Ghana did not support the actions of Judges Taylor and Koranteng-Addow: in *Kwakye v. Attorney-General*, six justices denied relief; only Justice Taylor dissented. *See* Kwakye v. Attorney-General (Ghana Sup. Ct., Super. Ct. of Judicature Nov. 10, 1981) (opinions of Apaloo, Sowah, Archer, Crabbe, and Taylor, JJ., on file in Harvard Law School Library).

When the AFRC is watching over the shoulder of the deciding judge, both the direct and the disingenuous approaches to the maintenance of jurisdiction in the face of power may be fatal. On December 31, 1981, the AFRC again took control of the government of Ghana. In June, 1982, Judge Koranteng-Addow disappeared and was later found dead. Two other judges have been killed. A commission of inquiry has been appointed but has not reported.

I am indebted to Ms. Anne-Marie Ofori for bringing these events to my attention and for providing me with copies of the judgments of the Ghanaian courts in the above-mentioned cases. In her unpublished paper, A. Ofori, Continuity and Change in the Ghanaian Legal System: The Coup D'etat and After (1983) (on file in Harvard Law School Library), Ms. Ofori describes the courage of several Ghanaian judges in insisting upon the availability of habeas corpus; her account raises important jurisprudential questions for reigning positivist ideologies of law.

165. Consider, for example, the Court's decisions in Korematsu v. United States, 323 U.S. 214 (1944), and *Ex parte* Endo, 323 U.S. 283 (1944). Unlike *Ex parte* Merryman, 17 F. Cas. 144 (C.C.D. Md. 1861), these cases involved no explicit suspension of the writ of habeas corpus. Rather, the Court faced a situation similar to the one that the transition clauses presented to the Ghanaian judges. *See supra* note 164. The Court had jurisdiction, but the Executive argued for a virtually automatic ratification of actions effected through the application of patently unjust criteria in time of crisis. The value of Taney's courageous insistence upon jurisdiction in *Merryman* is vitiated by the kind of deference shown crisis authority in *Korematsu*.

Such a hermeneutic of jurisdiction, however, is risky. It entails commitment to a struggle, the outcome of which—moral and
physical—is always uncertain. It is easier by far to pursue the positivist hermeneutic of jurisdiction. Judges are surely right that the
issue of power will rarely be in doubt if they pursue the office of
jurisdictional helplessness before the violence of officials. The meaning
judges thus give to the law, however, is not privileged, not necessarily
worth any more than that of the resister they put in jail. In giving
the law *that* meaning, they destroy the worlds that might be built
upon the law of the communities that defer to the superior violence
of the state, and they escalate the commitments of those who remain
to resist.

IV. The Imperial Virtues

In Part II of this Foreword, I quoted Rabbi Simeon ben Gamaliel's
aphorism that the world persists on the bases of justice, truth, and
peace. These imperial characteristics are indeed, in some sense, jurispathic in contrast to the paideia of Torah that Simeon the Just
described. But the Temple *has* been destroyed—meaning *is* no longer
unitary; any hermeneutic implies another. Keeping the peace is no
simple or neutral task. For in the normative worlds created around
us, not all interpretive trajectories are insular. The worlds of law we
create are all, in part, redemptive. With respect to a world of redemptive constitutionalism, the court must either deny the redemptionists
the power of the state (and thereby either truncate the growth of
their law or force them into resistance) or share their interpretation.
The court will often employ the secondary hermeneutic of jurisdiction
to deny the redemptionist vision. Ultimately, however, it is precisely
the structure of jurisdiction that locates responsibility for constitutional vision with the courts.[166] The courts may well rely upon the
jurisdictional screen and rules of toleration to avoid killing the law
of the insular communities that dot our normative landscape. But

---

Indeed, *Ex Parte* McCardle, 74 U.S. (7 Wall.) 506 (1869), which upheld a congressional
restriction of Supreme Court jurisdiction, may also be understood to qualify the
import of the rule in *Merryman*.

166. This is a question of statist positive law. There are many forms other than
ours for apportioning specialized state functions of interpreting law. *See, e.g.,*
M. SHAPIRO, COURTS ch. 5 (1981) (discussing absence of appeal in Islamic law).

they cannot avoid responsibility for applying or refusing to apply power to fulfill a redemptionist vision.

The problem is exemplified in the Supreme Court's treatment of competing claims concerning the education of children and youth. The claims of both insular and redemptionist visions have particular force: the bond between group and individual is by definition paideic, and disputes over educational issues raise the question of the character of the paideia that will constitute the child's world. The American constitutional treatment of schooling has responded by assuming a twofold form. Certain decisions have acknowledged the dangerous tendencies of a statist paideia and marked its boundaries through formal specification of the limits of public meaning. *West Virginia v. Barnette*,[167] *Epperson v. Arkansas*,[168] and the *School Prayer Cases*[169] are the landmarks, though all proceed, in one sense, from *Meyer v. Nebraska*.[170] Although these decisions suggest that the state's specification of meaning is most dangerous when religion and politics are concerned, the issues in these cases are presented by every public curriculum.[171] No sharp line between the problems of *Epperson* and those of a typical history curriculum can be drawn. Similarly, the confessional or sacramental character of the utterances in *Barnette* and the *School Prayer Cases* distinguish them only in degree from the confessional character of all claims of truth and meaning.[172]

That the public curriculum is itself the core problem of which *Barnette* and *Epperson* mark the outer ring may be perceived in another way. The weakness of the state's claim to authority for its formal umpiring between visions of the good is evidenced by the state's willingness to abdicate the project of elaborating meaning. The public curriculum is an embarrassment, for it stands the state at the

---

167. 319 U.S. 624 (1943).

168. 393 U.S. 97 (1968).

169. School Dist. v. Schempp, 374 U.S. 203 (1963); Engel v. Vitale, 370 U.S. 421 (1962).

170. 262 U.S. 390 (1923). Although *Meyer* rests on the substantive due process rights of teachers, it nonetheless presupposes a constitutional determination that the curricular judgments that led to the exclusion of German language courses from the schools' curriculum were unjustified.

171. *See* Hirschoff, *Parents and the Public School Curriculum: Is There a Right to Have One's Child Excused From Objectionable Instruction?*, 50 S. CAL. L. REV. 871, 955 (1977).

172. For the element of personal commitment entailed in the assertion of truth, see M. POLANYI, *supra* note 10.

heart of the paideic enterprise and creates a statist basis for the meaning as well as for the stipulations of law. The recognition of this dilemma has led to the second dimension of constitutional precedent regarding schooling—a breathtaking acknowledgment of the privilege of insular autonomy for all sorts of groups and associations. The principle of *Pierce v. Society of Sisters*[173] was always grounded on a substantive due process that protected not only religious education, but also private education in general, and it has proved the single, solid survivor from the era of substantive due process. *Wisconsin v. Yoder*[174] recognized an even broader autonomy for religious community. The state's extended recognition of associational autonomy in education is the natural result of the understanding of the problematic character of the state's paideic role. There must, in sum, be limits to the state's prerogative to provide interpretive meaning when it exercises its educative function. But the exercise is itself troublesome; thus, the private, insular alternative is specially protected. Any alternative to these limits would invite a total crushing of the jurisgenerative character. The state might become committed to its own meaning and destroy the personal and educative bond that is the germ of meanings alternative to those of the power wielders.

The school's central place in the paideic order connects the liberty of educational association to the jurisgenerative impulse itself. To this principle Bob Jones University appealed in its attempt to establish itself as a normative community entitled to protection against statist encroachment:

> It is both a religious and educational institution. Its teachers are required to be devout Christians, and all courses at the University are taught according to the Bible. Entering students are screened as to their religious beliefs, and their public and private conduct is strictly regulated by standards promulgated by University authorities.[175]

The University's interpretations of scripture held interracial dating and marriage to be forbidden. Black persons were excluded from

---

173. 268 U.S. 510 (1925).
174. 406 U.S. 205 (1972).
175. Bob Jones Univ. v. United States, 103 S. Ct. 2017, 2022 (1983).

admission to Bob Jones University until 1971. From 1971 until 1975, the University accepted no applications from unmarried blacks. Since May 29, 1975, the University has admitted students without regard to race, but has forbidden, on pain of expulsion, interracial dating, interracial marriage, the espousal of violation of these prohibitions, and membership in groups that advocate interracial marriage.[176]

The University, in effect, claimed for itself a nomic insularity that would protect it from a general public law prohibiting racial discrimination. Implicitly, it claimed immunity from the effects of 42 U.S.C. § 1981,[177] held by the Court in *Runyon v. McCrary*[178] to prohibit racial discrimination in private education. The Court in *Runyon* explicitly avoided deciding whether its rule applied to religious schools.[179] The protection that Bob Jones University claimed is, as we have seen, well located in the manifold narratives of insularity. Bob Jones University was backed by (among others) the Amish, the Mennonites, and some Baptist and Jewish organizations, because the typology that its claim triggers is that of the paideic autonomy of the religious community in the education of the young.[180]

One's interpretive stance toward such a case may change drastically, however, when one fits the competing considerations involved into a narrative of constitutional redemption. In this respect, contrasting the treatment of claims to insularity in *NLRB v. Catholic Bishop*[181] and in *Bob Jones University*[182] is instructive.

In both *Catholic Bishop* and *Bob Jones University*, an administrative agency had interpreted very general statutory language to limit the nomic autonomy of a religious school. In *Catholic Bishop*, the NLRB had held lay teachers in a parochial seminary and high

---

176. *Id.* at 2022–23.

177. 42 U.S.C. § 1981 (1976).

178. 427 U.S. 160 (1976).

179. *Id.* at 167.

180. Among the amicus briefs supporting Bob Jones University were those of the General Conference of the Mennonite Church, the National Association of Evangelicals, the National Committee for Amish Religious Freedom, the American Baptist Churches, and the National Jewish Commission on Law and Public Affairs. *See* Briefs Amicus Curiae for Petitioner, *Bob Jones Univ.* (No. 81-3). The American Jewish Committee and the Anti-Defamation League of B'nai B'rith, however, filed briefs in support of the United States. *See* Briefs Amicus Curiae for Respondent, Goldsboro Christian Schools, Inc. v. United States, 103 S. Ct. 2017 (1983) (No. 81-1).

181. 440 U.S. 490 (1979).

182. *See* 103 S. Ct. at 2034–35.

school to be within the National Labor Relations Act's[183] jurisdiction and had thereby authorized procedures to establish a bargaining unit and triggered the requirement that the employer, the Catholic Bishop of Chicago, bargain in good faith. The Supreme Court recognized the religious school's interest in autonomy by holding that the agency should not have chosen an interpretation of the Act that so implicated values protected by the first amendment, unless a contrary interpretation was foreclosed by text or clear legislative history.[184] The majority found no strong redemptive narrative in which to locate the NLRB's assertion of jurisdiction. The central thrust of the redemptive story of the struggle for protection of labor's rights of organization and bargaining seemed to the Court to involve a religious school only marginally, whereas the Court perceived the norms of educational autonomy to be centrally related to the narratives of free exercise.

Bob Jones University formally parallels *Catholic Bishop.* The IRS had interpreted very broad statutory language that long antedated the particular public controversies at issue. It had ruled that section 501(c)(3) of the Internal Revenue Code,[185] which gives tax-exempt status to certain charitable organizations including qualifying religious and educational institutions, and section 170,[186] which permits taxpayers to deduct contributions to section 501(c)(3) organizations, must be interpreted to exclude from such preferential treatment schools that do not have a "racially nondiscriminatory policy as to students."[187] Neither the text of the Code nor the legislative history before the IRS' 1970 ruling seemed to compel such an interpretation.[188]

---

183. 29 U.S.C. §§ 151–169 (1976 & Supp. V 1981).

184. 440 U.S. at 507.

185. 26 U.S.C. § 501(c)(3) (1976).

186. 26 U.S.C. § 170 (1976 & Supp. V 1981).

187. Rev. Rul. 71-447, 1971-2 C.B. 230, *clarified in* Rev. Proc. 72-54, 1972-2 C.B. 834, *and superseded by* Rev. Proc. 75-50, 1975-2 C.B. 587.

188. The only support in legislative history for the *Bob Jones University* result was Congress' behavior after the IRS' 1970 ruling. *See Bob Jones Univ.,* 103 S. Ct. at 2032-34. The Court's reliance on congressional inaction is quite interesting in light of the Court's nearly simultaneous invalidation of the legislative veto. *See* Immigration & Naturalization Serv. v. Chadha, 103 S. Ct. 2764 (1983) *Chadha* seems to suggest that congressional behavior that manifests dissatisfaction with regulatory action cannot have the force of law unless it has the formal characteristics of legislation under article I of the Constitution. It is difficult, then, to see why congressional "acquiescence" in a regulatory move of the sort counted in *Bob Jones University, see* 101. S. Ct. at 2033, can have any legal force. Depending on the circumstances, congressional acquiescence in an administrative interpretation may be more or less

Thus, as in *Catholic Bishop*, the agency interpreted general language in a way that created a basis for substantial interference in the nomian insularity of a religious educational institution. (The original IRS ruling was not confined to religious schools, but the Service refused to exempt them from its general interpretation.)[189]

There are several possible bases for distinguishing the two cases. *Catholic Bishop* may be said to entail the imposition of direct federal regulation, whereas *Bob Jones University* entails "only" the denial of a tax subsidy. The Court's analysis of tax subsidization last Term in *Regan v. Taxation with Representation*[190] suggests that such a distinction might be important. This argument is uncompelling, however, and is not the tack taken by the Court.[191] Rather, the Court

---

probative evidence of what congressional intent was at the time the statute in question was passed. Given that § 501(c)(3) was enacted decades before the IRS' 1970 ruling and without consideration of the issues raised by that ruling, Congress' aquiescence in the ruling hardly demonstrates the *enacting* legislature's intent. Although I am not opposed to considering the interpretations and intentions of the current Congress in our reading of the law, I find it difficult to see why the conduct of a Congress that enacts nothing under article I formalities can have normative force in *Bob Jones University* but cannot have such force in the case of a legislative veto.

189. *See Bob Jones Univ.*, 103 S. Ct. at 2021–25.

190. 103 S. Ct. 1997 (1983). "We have held in several contexts that a legislature's decision not to subsidize the exercise of a fundamental right does not infringe that right, and thus is not subject to strict scrutiny." *Id.* at 2003 (citing Harris v. McRae, 448 U.S. 297 (1980); Maher v. Roe, 432 U.S. 464 (1977); and Buckley v. Valeo, 424 U.S. 1 (1976)); *see id.* at 2001 (discussing Cammarano v. United States, 358 U.S. 498 (1959)). Another generalization in the Court's opinion in *Taxation with Representation* suggests the distinction the Court sees between direct regulation and denial of tax subsidies: "Legislatures have especially broad latitude in creating classifications and distinctions in tax statutes." *Id.* at 2002.

191. It is difficult to maintain the distinction between a regulatory measure with primarily civil sanctions and the denial of a tax benefit to a taxpayer that has failed to conform its conduct to a regulatory condition. To be sure, *some* regulation—for example, safety standards for consumer products or the workplace— is intended to convey society's outright unwillingness to tolerate particular conduct, whereas the conditioning of preferred tax treatment on conformity to a rule of conduct indicates the legal system's willingness to permit nonconforming conduct—for a price. But this distinction dissolves if one conceptualizes a regulatory sanction as a price set upon the forbidden conduct. Holmes' theory of contract breach is the best-known instance of this approach, which also pervades the entire methodology of the economic analysis of law. For Holmes' thesis and a critique of it, see G. GILMORE, THE DEATH OF CONTRACT 14 (1974).

The special character of the tax benefit at stake in *Bob Jones University* makes the distinction between regulation and denial of tax benefits particularly problematic.

met the argument of protected insularity by asserting a compelling governmental interest "in eradicating racial discrimination in education."[192] Chief Justice Burger appealed to a variety of executive, legislative, and judicial efforts to eliminate such discrimination, and finally compressed them into a précis of the narrative:

> Given the stress and anguish of the history of efforts to escape from the shackles of the "separate but equal" doctrine . . . it cannot be said that educational institutions that, for whatever reasons, practice racial discrimination, are institutions exercising "beneficial and stabilizing influences in community life" . . . or should be encouraged by having all taxpayers share in their support by way of special tax status.[193]

Thus, the Chief Justice countered the claim of insularity with a narrative of redemption. Whereas the Court did not consider the

---

Denial of § 501(c)(3) status to a charitable organization may lead donors who are accordingly denied § 170 deductions to stop making gifts altogether rather than simply to reduce gifts to the point at which the after-tax cost of the donation remains constant. For the same price, a donor can give $1/(1-(\text{marginal tax rate}))$ times as much to an institution exempt under § 501(c)(3) as to a nonexempt organization. Assuming that the donor's satisfaction depends on the amount received by the donee rather than the cost of the gift, an additional gift dollar should thus be given to a nonexempt organization only if the marginal satisfaction obtained from a unit of gift to the nonexempt organizaiton is $1/(1-(\text{marginal tax rate}))$ times as great as the satisfaction obtained from a unit of gift to an exempt organization. Thus, the denial of § 501(c)(3) treatment may effectively cut off all donations from less loyal givers; for some organizations, the result may be the end of virtually all support. Admittedly, though, it is also possible that the loyalty of donors to an institution like Bob Jones University may be such that gift behavior is not particularly sensitive to price.

192. *Bob Jones Univ.*, 103 S. Ct. at 2035.

193. *Id.* at 2030. Significantly, Chief Justice Burger wrote of the "stress and anguish" of the attempt to escape from the "'separate but equal' doctrine." It seems to me a peculiarly court-centered characterization of the turmoil of the post-*Brown* era to write of that doctrine rather than the practices of racism and apartheid. The Court's stress and anguish may have been related to the shadow of Plessy v. Ferguson, 163 U.S. 537 (1896), and to the need to reconcile Brown v. Board of Educ., 347 U.S. 483 (1954), and post-*Brown* actions with customary principles of judicial neutrality, deference, and self-restraint. But for the true moving force, the civil rights movement, the stress and anguish have been and remain most acute when the movement must consider the "lawfulness" of disobedient and possibly violent tactics in the struggle to maintain a living law of equality in the face of state-sponsored violence or indifference.

treatment of teachers at Chicago Catholic schools to contradict the central redemptive message of the NLRA, the Court found that discrimination against blacks in an otherwise tax-exempt religious school contradicted the central redemptive narrative of the struggle for racial equality and for desegregation of the nation's schools. One could write a history in which the redemptive ideology of labor organization played a larger role. One *could* rewrite *Catholic Bishop;* given the outcome in that case, however, the critical factor explaining the decision in *Bob Jones University* is the power of a redemptive constitutionalism that stakes its own claim to reform the life of the schools.

Precisely because the school is the point of entry to the paideic and the locus of its creation, the school must be the target of any redemptive constitutional ideology. Through education, the social bonds form that give rise to autonomy, to the jurisgenerative process. In education are the origins of the processes in which "law" is given meaning. Were there a single, statist corpus, a state school, a state understanding—Spartan *eunomia*—we might imagine a rather simple participation-protecting rule to guarantee universal access to the process. In our own complex *nomos*, however, it is the manifold, equally dignified communal bases of legal meaning that constitute the array of commitments, realities, and visions extant at any given time. The judge must resolve the competing claims of the redemptive constitutionalism of an excluded race, on one hand, and of insularity, the protection of association, on the other.

Nonetheless, the force of the Court's interpretation in *Bob Jones University* is very weak. It is weak not because of the form of argument, but because of the failure of the Court's commitment—a failure that manifests itself in the designation of authority for the decision. The Court assumes a position that places nothing at risk and from which the Court makes no interpretive gesture at all, save the quintessential gesture to the jurisdictional canons: the statement that an exercise of political authority was not unconstitutional. The grand national travail against discrimination is given no normative status in the Court's opinion, save that it means the IRS was not wrong. The insular communities, the Mennonites and Amish, are rightly left to question the scope of the Court's decision: are we at the mercy of each public policy decision that is not wrong? If the public policy here has a special status, what is it? Can Congress change the policy? If not, there is of course a powerful response to the insular claim—

the counterclaim of constitutional redemption. Such a redemptive claim would pose no general threat to the insular community, no threat that rests on anything save the kind of commitment that goes with the articulation of the consitutional mandate.

This claim the Court did not make. Indeed, the Court explicitly avoided the question whether Congress could constitutionally grant tax exemption to a school that discriminates on the basis of race.[194] The Amish, the Mennonites, and all insular communities, whatever their stand on race, are right to be dissatisfied with *Bob Jones University v. United States*. It is a case that gives too much to the statist determination of the normative world by contributing too little to the statist understanding of the Constitution. It is a case in which authority is vindicated without the expression of judicial commitment to principle that is embodied in constitutional decision. In the impoverished commitment of Chief Justice Burger's opinion, the constitutional question was not unnecessary, but the Court avoided it by simply throwing the claim of protected insularity to the mercy of public policy. The insular communities deserved better—they deserved a constitutional hedge against mere administration. And the minority community deserved more—it deserved a constitutional commitment to avoiding public subsidization of racism.[195]

---

194. 103 S. Ct. at 2032 n. 24.

195. Such a commitment would necessarily have invited a host of problems. But that is as it should be. The invasion of the *nomos* of the insular community ought to be based on more than the passing will of the state. It ought to be grounded on an interpretive commitment that is as fundamental as that of the insular community. And any such commitment would entail massive potential change. In *Bob Jones University*, the Court would have challenged all public subsidization of private racist conduct. Such subsidization is not confined to the potential operation of § 501(c)(3) for the benefit of discriminatory charitable organizations. If the Constitution were read to mandate the result in *Bob Jones University*, we would soon be asking whether it also mandates the denial of investment tax credits or accelerated cost recovery to otherwise qualifying taxpayers who discriminate in employment or other business practices. Would discrimination in home real estate transactions disqualify a taxpayer from taking advantage of the home mortgage interest deduction? Would public tax subsidization of private discrimination based on gender, religion, national origin, or alienage similarly be subject to constitutional proscription?

There are answers to these questions—distinctions that can plausibly be drawn among the various cases I have put and the hundreds of others that might be put. The Court could not and would not have had to decide all those cases now, but a constitutional commitment to the *Bob Jones University* decision would certainly have invited an early encounter with them. Without such a commitment, we are left with no principled law at all, but only administrative fiat to govern the relation between public subsidy and permissible private discrimination.

Judges are like the rest of us. They interpret and they make law. They do so in a niche, and they have expectations about their own behavior in the future and about the behavior of others. It may be that the whole show in *Bob Jones University* was built on shoddy commitments, fake interpretations. Bob Jones University seemed uncommitted and lackadaisical in its racist interpretation—unwilling to put much on the line. The IRS ruling was left shamefully undefended by an administration unwilling to put *anything* on the line for the redemptive principle. The Justices responded in kind: they were unwilling to venture commitment of themselves, to make a firm promise and to project their understanding of the law onto the future. *Bob Jones University* is a play for 1983—wary and cautious actors, some eloquence, but no commitment.

The statist impasse in constitutional creation must soon come to an end. When the end comes, it is unlikely to arrive via the Justices, accustomed as they are to casting their cautious eyes about, ferreting out jurisdictional excuses to avoid disrupting the orderly deployment of state power and privilege. It will likely come in some unruly moment—some undisciplined jurisgenerative impulse, some movement prepared to hold a vision in the face of the indifference or opposition of the state. Perhaps such a resistance—redemptive or insular—will reach not only those of us prepared to see law grow, but the courts as well. The stories the resisters tell, the lives they live, the law they make in such a movement may force the judges, too, to face the commitments entailed in their judicial office and their law. It is not the romance of rebellion that should lead us to look to the law evolved by social movements and communities. Quite the opposite. Just as it is our distrust for and recognition of the state as reality that leads us to be constitutionalists with regard to the state, so it ought to be our recogition of and distrust for the reality of the power of social movements that leads us to examine the nomian worlds they create. And just as constitutionalism is part of what may legitimize the state, so constitutionalism may legitimize, within a different framework, communities and movements. Legal meaning is a challenging enrichment of social life, a potential restraint on arbitrary power and violence. We ought to stop circumscribing the *nomos*; we ought to invite new worlds.

Chapter 4

The Folktales of Justice: Tales of Jurisdiction

I. Introduction

The word "law" resonates richly in the language and mythology of western civilization. H.L.A. Hart began his great work, *The Concept of Law*, with an inquiry into the persistence of the question "what is law?" in our jurisprudence.[1] He argued that it is strange that such an apparently elementary question has persisted in jurisprudence while no analogous question such as "What is chemistry?" has occupied other areas of human inquiry.[2] Hart's answer to his own question is, in some sense, the book, itself. He stresses and illuminates the analytic perplexities that constitute the deep structure of our concept of law. But there is an historical and political answer to Hart's question which may be more to the point. The literature on the question "what is law?" is voluminous and continues to grow not because there are analytic difficulties in our conceptual apparatus—our categories—in this field. There are, indeed, such difficulties, but they are no greater than analogous problems in the categories of the sciences. In the sciences, however, the illumination of a deep structural ambiguity hitherto uncaptured by the "chemistry" paradigm does not lead to another round in a perpetual argument over "what is chemistry" but to the creation of new fields like "biochemistry" or "molecular biology." The new fields take as their standard cases the problematic case for "chemistry." The label itself is not the object of controversy.

A label may be the object of controversy, however, if the question

This paper was the basis for the 1984 John E. Sullivan Lecture given on November 15, 1984, at Capital University Law School.
    1. H. L. A. HART, THE CONCEPT OF LAW 1 (1961).
    2. *Id.*

is not "what is chemistry?", but rather, "what is science?"[3] For the word "science" is a heavily loaded one, freighted with normative significance. If one is doing "science"—which may or may not be chemistry—then the legitimacy of the enterprise is not in question, only the appropriate administrative label. Such labels are matters of convenience. But if one is not doing science at all, then the charge is that the enterprise itself is outside the scope of legitimate inquiry for a certain sort of truth.[4]

The word "law", itself, is always a primary object of contention. People argue and fight over "what is law" because the very term is a valuable resource in the enterprises that lead people to think and talk about law in the first place. "Law" evokes the law given on Sinai, Solon's legislative enterprise, Kant's categorical imperative. On a political level, it connotes legitimacy in the exercise of coercion and in the organization of authority and privilege.[5] On a philosophical plane it connotes universality and objectivity. Legal positivism may be seen, in one sense, as a massive effort that has gone on in a self-conscious way for over two centuries to strip the word "law" of these

3. The philosophy of science in recent decades is frequently a debate about what is science. Thomas S. Kuhn's *The Structure of Scientific Revolutions* (1962) has been enormously influential in defeating simplistic earlier models of "scientific method" as systems of observation, hypothesis, confirmation/disconfirmation. Michael Polanyi's brilliant work *Personal Knowledge* (1958) represents a still earlier and in some ways richer critique of what was then conventional philosophy of science.

4. Thus, the battle over the label science is fought out not only on the front of philosophy: what is science? what is scientific method? but also through various heavily loaded questions for particular fields: e.g., is Psychoanalysis a science? is its method scientific? *See, e.g.,* Coleman, *Pressure Mounts for Analysts to Prove a Theory is Scientific,* N.Y. Times, January 15, 1985, at C1. *See also* M. EDELSON, HYPOTHESIS AND EVIDENCE IN PSYCHOANALYSIS (1984).

Similarly, great heat and everlasting smoke may be generated over the question of whether "social science" is "science". More narrowly, still, consider the debates over the "scientific" character of IQ testing. And, also, the long debate over the issue of whether ESP studies can be called "scientific."

5. It is a resource in legitimation, in aspirations to ideas of justice and in ambition for social control. *See, e.g.,* E. P. THOMPSON, WHIGS AND HUNTERS 258–269, especially 260–64 (1975). "Most men have a strong sense of justice, at least with regard to their own interest. If law is evidently partial and unjust, then it will mask nothing, legitimize nothing, contribute nothing to any class's hegemony. The essential pre-condition for the effectiveness of law, in its function as ideology, is that it shall display an independence from gross manipulation and shall seem to be just. It cannot seem to be so without upholding its own logic and criteria of equity; indeed, on occasion, by actually *being* just." *Id.* at 263 (emphasis in original).

resonances.[6] But the sacred narratives of our world doom the positivist enterprise to failure, or, at best, to only imperfect success.[7]

Historicist and analytic debunking of "law" have, indeed, rendered the term problematic. There is now a counter-resonance. For law has also come to suggest the mask of privilege.[8] Nonetheless, the very meaning of law as an effective mask or ideology would be lost were the word to lose its primary mythic resonances.[9] The struggle over what is "law" is then a struggle over which social patterns can plausibly be coated with a veneer which changes the very nature of that which it covers up. There is not automatic legitimation of an institution by calling it or what it produces "law", but the label is a move, the staking out of a position in the complex social game of legitimation. The jurisprudential inquiry into the question "what is law" is an engagement at one remove in the struggle over what is legitimate.[10]

I have recently staked out a position about the nature of law that has obvious and consciously chosen political significance.[11] My position is very close to a classical anarchist one—with anarchy understood to mean the absence of rulers, not the absence of law.

6. *See* J. BENTHAM, FRAGMENT ON GOVERNMENT (1776). And see, especially, H. L. A. Hart's classic defense of positivism in the Hart-Fuller debate in the Harvard Law Review: H. L. A. Hart, *Positivism and the Separation of Law and Morals* 71 HARV. L. REV. 593 (1958).

7. The fact that "law" is located in our myths and stories as a powerful attribute of legitimate authority creates a potential ironic twist in the political consequences of positivist theory. The positivist assures us that evil "law" is "law" nonetheless, that the character of something as "law" cannot depend upon its moral qualities. Yet, the mythologies that we share *do* give that which is law legitimating force not by virtue of a sound analytic argument but by virtue of brute facts of culture, language and history. The result of the two vectors of positivism and cultural legitimation may be the unwanted greater legitimation of evil law. Positivism breaks down psychological barriers to outright conscription of the word "law" to nefarious purposes which natural law thinking might create. There remains, however, especially among the masses—sufficient cultural force to the symbolism of law that the evil law is given a substantial degree of legitimacy it would not otherwise have. Whether such a situation is "stable" is doubtful.

8. *See* Horwitz, *Review of Whigs and Hunter,* 86 YALE L.J. 561 (1977).

9. *See* E. P. THOMPSON, *supra* note 5.

10. *See* Unger, *The Critical Legal Studies Movement,* 96 HARV. L. REV. 561 (1983). The critical legal studies movement has certainly been a primary force in placing the ideological functions and the "legitimation" process at the heart of contemporary legal scholarship.

11. Cover, *Foreword: Nomos and Narrative,* 97 HARV. L. REV. 4 (1983).

Law, I argued, is a bridge in normative space connecting [our under-standing of] the "world-that-is" (including the norms that 'govern' and the gap between those norms and the present behavior of all actors) with our projections of alternative "worlds-that-might-be" (including alternative norms that might 'govern' and alternative jux-tapositions of imagined actions with those imagined systems of norms).[12] In this theory, law is neither to be wholly identified with the understanding of the present state of affairs nor with the imagined alternatives. It *is* the bridge—the committed social behavior which constitutes the way a group of people will attempt to get from here to there. Law connects "reality" to alternity[13] constituting a new reality with a bridge built out of committed social behavior. Thus, visions of the future are more or less strongly determinative of the bridge which is "law" depending upon the commitment and social organization of the people who hold them.

The above is not a definition of law; it is a plea to understand the legitimating force of the term in a certain way. It is a plea to grant all collective behavior entailing systematic understandings of our commitments to future worlds equal claim to the word "law." The upshot of such a claim, of course, is to deny to the nation state any special status for the collective behavior of its officials or for their systematic understandings of some special set of "governing" norms.[14] The status of such "official" behavior and "official" norms is not denied the dignity of "law." But it must share the dignity with thousands of other social understandings. In each case the question of what is law and for whom is a question of fact about what certain communities believe and with what commitments to those beliefs. The organized behavior of other groups and the commitments of actors within them have as sound a claim to the word "law" as does the behavior of state officials. The most important consequence of this radical relativization of law is that violence—a special problem in the analysis of any community's commitments to its future—must be viewed as problematic in much the same way whether it is being carried out by order of a federal district judge, a mafioso or a cor-porate vice-president.[15]

---

12. *Id.* at 9–10.
13. G. STEINER, AFTER BABEL 222 (1975).
14. Cover, *supra* note 11, at 25–41.
15. Please note well, here, that I am not saying that all violence is equally

I have argued not only that the nature of law is a bridge to the future, but also that each community builds its bridges with the materials of sacred narrative that take as their subject much more than what is commonly conceived as the "legal." The only way to segregate the legally relevant narrative from the general domain of sacred texts would be to trivialize the "legal" into a specialized subset of business or bureaucratic transactions.[16]

The commitments that are the material of our bridges to the future are learned and expressed through sacred stories. Paradigmatic gestures are rehearsed in them. Thus, the claim to a "law" is a claim as well to an understanding of a literature and a tradition. It doesn't matter how large the literature or how old the tradition. Sinai might have been yesterday or four thousand years ago; the text might be two tablets or the infinity of Borges' library of Babel.[17]

In my earlier work on this subject, I considered primarily the commitments and narratives of those communities who would make a law for themselves apart from that of the State. I believed and still believe that that emphasis is a necessary corrective to the imbalanced character of almost all contemporary legal theory. Nonetheless, I did consider briefly the commitments that are implicit in the assumption of jurisdiction by official judges of the state.[18] In that section of my earlier work I criticized most jurisdictional reasoning as largely apologetic, state-serving enterprises. I did conclude, however, with the following, undeveloped thought:

> It is possible to conceive of a natural law of jurisdiction. . . .
> In elaborating such a law . . . a judge might appeal to narratives
> of judicial resistance. . . . He might thus defend his own authority
> to sit in judgment over those who exercise extralegal violence in

---

justified or unjustified. I am claiming that it is problematic in the same way. By that I mean that the form of analysis that we enter into to determine whether or not the violence is justified is the same. That same method will, of course, if it is any good at all, not yield the same answer with respect to dissimilar cases.

16. Cover, *supra* note 11, at 19-25. *See also* the important work of James White arguing for the significance of such narrative materials in the "culture of argument." J. WHITE, WHEN WORDS LOSE THEIR MEANING (1984); White, *Law as Language: Reading Law and Reading Literature*, 60 TEX. L. REV. 415 (1982).

17. Borges, *The Library of Babel*, in LABYRINTH 51 (D. Yates & J. Irby eds. 1964).

18. Cover, *supra* note 11, at 53-60.

the name of the state. In a truly violent, authoritarian situation, nothing is more revolutionary than the insistence of a judge that he exercises such a "jurisdiction"—but only if that jurisdiction implies the articulation of legal principle according to an independent hermeneutic. . . .

Such a hermeneutic of jurisdiction [texts], however, is risky. It entails commitment to a struggle, the outcome of which— moral and physical—is always uncertain.[19]

In this article, I take up the task of elaborating on the idea that there are sacred narratives of jurisdiction that might constitute the texts to ground judicial commitments. In part II, I shall consider one category of such texts—the resistance to "Kings". In Part III, I shall consider another, more problematic category—bringing the Messiah. Part II treats of the minimal aspirations of our myths for autonomous "law." Part III treats of the place of law in more comprehensive Utopian reorderings of the world.

II. Of Judges and Kings

Leonard Koppett once wrote that the most important single fact about hitting a baseball and the one least mentioned explicitly is fear.[20] There is the archetype of an upright judge—as there is in the upright batter—an important element of having conquered a fear, a fear which is always present yet almost forgotten. To understand that fear and its significance we must tell the stories that remember the fear and rehearse the gestures we make in response to it.

There is in the Talmud, tractate Sanhedrin, a fascinating account. The law in the Talmud (Mishneh) seems clear: "The king does not judge and we do not judge him."[21] This rule appears to state a not unexpected norm of sovereign immunity and a perhaps unexpected norm of sovereign judicial incapacity. The rule was enunciated almost two thousand years ago and it will, as we shall explore, perhaps ring some bells concerning English law in the seventeenth century.[22] In

---

19. *Id.* at 58–60.
20. L. KOPPETT, A THINKING MAN'S GUIDE TO BASEBALL (1967).
21. MISHNEH SANHEDRIN, II, 3.
22. *See* notes 29–37 *infra* and accompanying text.

any event, the Talmud, having stated the rule in question, asks about its origin. Let me quote the answer in full:

> But why this prohibition? Because of an incident which happened with a slave (servant) of King Yannai, who killed a man. Simeon b. Shetah (head of Sanhedrin) said to the court of sages: Be bold and let us judge him. They sent for the king saying, your slave killed a man. The King sent the slave to them. They sent to the King saying you must appear with him. He appeared but sat down before the court. Then Simeon b. Shetah said, Stand on your feet, King Yannai, so witnesses may testify against thee. For you do not stand before us but before He who spoke and the World was created. The King replied, 'I will not act by your word but upon the words of the court as a whole. He then turned to the left and to the right, but all looked at the ground. Then Simeon said, Are you wrapped in thought? Let the Master of thoughts come and call you to account. Instantly, Gabriel came and smote them all and they died. Then it was enacted: The King may neither judge nor be judged, testify nor be testified against.[23]

What, we might ask, are we to make of this fabulous tale of a not altogether unreasonable king, a courageous, perhaps foolhardy and somewhat inflexible judge, and the Angel Gabriel? It seems clear enough that the taleteller and the redactor of the text consider it both a cautionary tale and a celebration of courage. Simeon b. Shetah is the hero. He is spared, and his castigation of his cravenly colleagues leads directly to their demise at the hand of the angel. At the same time the incident is put forward to account for a rule of law which, itself, seems to owe more to the cowardice of Simeon's colleagues than to the courage of their leader. The rule which results from the incident is not, after all, that Courts judge Kings courageously and impartially, but that they do not judge them at all. Before we begin an analysis of this very common paradox of jurisdiction, we should explore, for a bit, the historic episode that may lie behind this fabulous story.

The tales of the Talmud may be founded in myth or history.

---

23. BABYLONIAN TALMUD (hereinafter cited as B. J. Sanhedrin), 19a–19b.

They may owe their fabulous character to literary or religious imagination, to failure to appreciate and preserve scientific historicity, or
to the need—in some periods—to disguise a story with revolutionary
implications. In the case of the story of King Yannai and Simeon b.
Shetah we have another ancient source which tells a similar though
by no means identical tale. In his work, *Jewish Antiquities*, the hel-
lenized Jewish historian, Josephus, related a story which, if true, took
place in 47 B.C.E. almost forty years after the death of King Yannai.

Antipater the Idumite had been appointed the governor or proc-
urator of Judea by Caesar. He executed his office while Hyrcanus II,
the hereditary, legitimate, ruler of the Jews, descendant of the Has-
monean family of high priests, served as high priest and titular King
of the Jewish nation. Both Hyrcanus and Antipater strongly supported
Caesar and the Romans in their Egyptian campaign. In return, Caesar
supported Hyrcanus in his conflict with Aristobulus II over Has-
monean succession. Antipater, at least for a while, formed an alliance
with Hyrcanus. Antipater's second son, Herod, still very young, was
made governor of the Galilee. There, he succeeded in boldly putting
down a group of bandits or rebels, killing the leader and a number
of others. According to Josephus, this and other acts formed the basis
of a series of complaints from leading Jews that Antipater and his
sons had become the de facto rulers of Judea and that Hyrcanus and
the Jews were left with but a shadow.[24]

The complaints fastened upon the fact that Herod's execution
of the leader and some men of the band of brigands without judicial
trial violated Israel's law. They asked that Herod be brought to
account for this act. Hyrcanus, whether for political or personal
reasons, summoned Herod to be tried for the act. [The servant of
the king had killed a man]. Josephus suggests that Hyrcanus may
have then received some sort of instructions or requests from Sextus,
Roman governor of Syria, that Herod be acquitted.[25] In any event,

---

24. JOSEPHUS, JEWISH ANTIQUITIES, Book XIV 143–184 (Loeb Classical Library,
Josephus. VII, R. Marcus, trans. 1976). For the date of the event in question see
Loeb Edition, at 533 note d.

25. Id. at 170. *See also* Loeb Edition, at 539 note e. There is a somewhat more
abbreviated version of this event related in Josephus, I *The Jewish War*, 211 (reprinted
by Penguin, G. Williamson, at 48–49). In *The Jewish War*, Josephus attributes
Hyrcanus' motive in bringing Herod to trial entirely to jealousy. He sees the event
as one involving a play by Hyrcanus to regain real power which was blocked by
Sextus acting as ally and patron of Herod.

Josephus tells us that Herod arrived with a bodyguard of troops and stood before the Sanhedrin or Court with those troops, an act which had the desired effect:

> he overawed them all, and no one of those who had denounced him before his arrival dared to accuse him thereafter; instead there was silence and doubt about what was to be done.[26]

Josephus then goes on with a remarkable parallel to the Talmud's tale.

> While they were in this state, someone named Samaias, an upright man and for that reason superior to fear, arose and said, 'Fellow councillors and King, I do not myself know of, nor do I suppose that you can name, anyone who when summoned before you for trial has ever presented such an appearance. . . . But this fine fellow Herod, who is accused of murder . . . stands here clothed in purple, with the hair of his head carefully arranged and with his soldiers around him, in order to kill us if we condemn him as the law prescribes, and to save himself by outraging justice. But it is not Herod whom I should blame for this . . . but you and the King for giving him such great licence. Be assured, however, that God is great, and this man, whom you now wish to release for Hyrcanus' sake, will one day punish you and the King as well.' And he was not mistaken in either part of his prediction. For when Herod assumed royal power, he killed Hyrcanus and all the other members of the Sanhedrin with the exception of Samaias.[27]

Hyrcanus, by Josephus' account, saw that Samaias had moved

---

26. JOSEPHUS, *supra* note 24, at 171. *See also* JOSEPHUS, *supra* note 25, at 201 note ff. In *The Jewish War* the trial scene is not related but Josephus does say that Herod "presented himself in Jerusalem, accompanied by a strong escort—not so swollen a force as to suggest the intention of dethroning Hyrcanus, nor small enough to leave him helpless in face of jealousy." *Id.* at 211.

27. JOSEPHUS, *supra* note 24, at 172–76. The identity of Samaias is a matter of scholarly dispute. See Loeb Edition at 540–41 note a, for difficulties in piecing together the parallel accounts.

the Court and postponed any decision so that Herod could escape. At that point, Herod resolved not to answer any future summons.[28]

While there are difficulties and possible internal contradictions in Josephus' account, it plainly described an historical moment of great danger in the jurisdiction of the Sanhedrin—a moment the *moral* enormity of which is captured in the Talmud's tale. That the historical referent for both tales was the same event has long been recognized even by traditional Medieval Jewish commentators on the Talmud for whom Josephus was hardly a canonical text.[29]

---

28. JOSEPHUS, *supra* note 24, at 177–79.

29. *See* HIDUSHEI HALAHOTH VE. AGGADOT MAHARSHA (Novellae of Laws and Legends of Samuel Eliezer ben Judah Ha-Levi Edels, 1555–1631) *discussing* B. SAN-HEDRIN 19a:

> [T]he reason he (the King) did not send him (the servant) to them and emancipate him (thus removing his own legal responsibility to answer) may have been that the servant was dear to him and it was hard for him to put him to death. And when he first sent him before them he relied on the supposition that they would not judge him from fear of the King since he was the servant of the King as they say. And so it appears from Josephus that this murdering servant was Herod and the King wanted to save him.

(My translation).

See L. FINKELSTEIN, II THE PHARISEES, 684 n.6 (1938) for a discussion of some nineteenth and twentieth century critical scholarship on the event in question. The discussion of the MAHARSHA on this question, which I have translated above, shows that the identification of the two stories long antedates the Wissenschaft des Judentums sources cited by Finkelstein.

The persistent question concerning the identity of "Samaias" in the account of Josephus is of interest. Shammai the Elder—who is one of the candidates for the role—is said, by the Talmud, to have differed with the majority of the Sages in that he held that one who procures the murder of a third person at the hand of an agent is nonetheless completely responsible as a murderer. *See* B. KIDDUSHIN, 43a. While there is absolutely no basis in either the Talmud's account or the account of Josephus for believing that the trial of Herod ever got to the point of a discussion of legal principles grounding Herod's liability as commander for acts done at and under his command, it is nonetheless interesting that Shammai did advocate from a minority position the only rule of law which would have rendered Herod criminally liable. Moreover, Shammai's proof text is II Samuel c.12, v. 9: " . . . you killed him with the sword of the Ammonites," referring to David's sending Uriah to the front against the Ammonites.

The identification of Herod and Yannai occurs elsewhere in Rabbinic literature. I'm not sure what to make of it, but in Megillath Ta'anith, ch. 11., we find:

> "On the second of Shevat is a holiday and not for lamentations. And why is this different from, "that [the first day] for as to the first day, it is not written that there not be lamentations," and here it is written. On the first day (of Shevath) Herod died and on this (second) day Yannai the King died. And it is

Before we begin an analysis of this story, it is well to compare it to a striking counterpart in seventeenth century English legal history. The special, sacred history of the common law treats as one of its high moments the opinion supposedly enunciated by Chief Justice Coke in the matter reported by him and published posthumously under the style, *Prohibitions Del Roy.*[30] King James, you will remember, had become angry at the writs of prohibition emanating from the common law courts and directed at the Court of High Commission. Some of these prohibitions had issued with respect to the power of High Commission to punish puritans for breaches of ecclesiastical discipline. The culmination of a string of acrimonious disputes over the use of the writ of prohibition by the common law courts to restrain High Commission came in *Fuller's Case.*[31] Nicholas Fuller was a barrister who had defended puritan dissenters in trouble over breaches of discipline. In one case before High Commission, Fuller had overreached a bit in his rhetoric, complaining of the process before the Court of High Commission as "popish, under jurisdiction not of Christ but of anti-Christ." This inspired advocacy led contemporaries to remark that Nicholas Fuller had "pleaded so boldly for the enlargement of his clients that he procured his own confinement."[32]

The question of whether the common law courts could issue writs of prohibition to deny to High Commission the power to punish

---

a joy before the Holy One Blessed Be He when the wicked are removed from the world. They said: 'when Yanai got sick he captured 70 Sages of the elders of Israel, put them in prison, and commanded the officers of the prison: If I die, kill the Elders. So that to the extent that Israel is joyful (at my death) may they lament their teachers.' They said: 'He (Yannai) had a good wife, Salome by name. When he died she removed the ring from his hand and sent it to the officer of the prison. She said to him, your master in (by) a dream has freed these sages. He freed them and they went home. Afterward she said, Yannai, the King is dead. And on that day that he died they make a holiday.'"

Josephus tells almost exactly the same story concerning the death of Herod. JOSEPHUS, The Jewish War, Book I, 660 *et seq.* In JOSEPHUS, it is Herod's sister, Salome, who saves the Jewish leaders. (This is not the Salome of the New Testament.)

30. The story is told in very readable form in C. BOWEN, THE LION AND THE THRONE: THE LIFE AND TIMES OF SIR EDWARD COKE 291–306 (1959). Coke's report of *Prohibitions del Roy* is at 12 COKE 63. This twelfth volume of Coke's Reports was not published during Coke's lifetime. *See* Usher, *James I and Sir Edward Coke,* 18 ENGLISH HISTORICAL REV. 668–75 (1903).

31. *Nicholas Fuller's Case,* 12 COKE 41; *See also* BOWEN, *supra* note 30, at 293–301.

32. BOWEN, *supra* note 30, at 299.

a barrister for contempt was the context in which the greatest of the common law texts of jurisdiction was written. Fuller was finally committed to prison though not for contempt but for, *inter alia*, schism and heresy over which it was conceded that the ecclesiastical courts had jurisdiction. Nonetheless, the case had precipitated a showdown on the issue of who was to be the final arbiter of jurisdiction within the English legal system. Archbishop Bancroft argued that the final determination of the respective jurisdictions of courts could and should properly rest with the King, himself, since all judges derived authority from him.[33] Coke, if we are to believe his own account of the affair, answered not only the Archbishop, but the King, himself, with the ringing words that:

> true it was that God had endowed his Majesty with excellent science and great endowments of nature. But his Majesty was not learned in the Laws of his Realm of England; . . . With which the King was greatly offended, and said that then he should be under the Law, which was treason to affirm (as he said). To which I said, that Bracton saith, Quod Rex non debet esse sub homine, sed sub Deo et Lege—that the King should not be under man, but under God and the Law.[34]

It is striking that in this case, as in the case of Simeon b. Shetah, there is an alternative to the canonical version of the event. Contemporary historians have largely rejected Coke's self-serving account,[35] relying instead on other seventeenth century evidence including a letter from Sir Roger Boswell to Dr. Milborne which recites that:

> his Majestie fell into that hight indignation as the like was never knowne in him, looking and speaking fiercely with a bended fist, offering to strike him etc., which the Lo. Cooke perceiving fell flatt on all fower; humbly beseeching his Majestie to take compassion on him and to pardon him if he thought zeale had gone beyond his dutie and allegiance.[36]

---

33. *Prohibitions del Roy,* 12 COKE at 63; BOWEN, *supra* note 30, at 303–04.
34. *Prohibitions del Roy,* 12 COKE at 65.
35. BOWEN, *supra note* 30, at 305–06.
36. *Id. See also* Usher, *supra* note 30, at 673.

In both of our stories of judges and Kings we find an unambiguous canonical text in which the courageous judge challenges the
King, affirms the value of an impersonal law or source of law over
the King and places the authority of the Court to speak the law—
its jurisdiction—upon that impersonal foundation. The didactic power
of these stories inheres in part in the literary form—the compression
of the messages into a concentrated text which, itself, depicts a highly
focused and artificially circumscribed stage upon which the action
unfolds. In short, the classic "unities" are observed. History is rarely
so neat. The processes by which Courts acquire the concepts of
independence of jurisdiction and relate it to the autonomy of the law
are long and complex. Moreover, the acts by which judges resist
political subordination of themselves, their courts, and their law
almost always entail prudential as well as principled behavior.
Samaisas, in Josephus' account, may have simply seen more clearly
than did his colleagues, that Herod was a man to be unambiguously
crushed or else catered to. If Josephus is to be credited, Samaias may
have been principled in opposing Herod but he later became Herod's
political ally.[37] Similarly, according to Usher and Holdsworth following him,[38] Coke cowtowed to King James but lived to continue his
struggle on technical grounds in Common Pleas. Moreover, he completed his texts which became the canon after his death.

   These texts and countertexts provide an interesting context for
asking what the respective places of myth and history are in the
building of law. It is important to note that from an "inside" perspective it is Coke's report not Boswell's letter that is the "source of
law", the "priviliged" text, the citation for the future. From the
"inside" perspective of Jewish law it is the Talmud not Josephus that
is the privileged text. History certainly should provide cold water to
throw upon any overzealous inclination to read these canonical texts
uncritically. But the complex and circuitous paths of history ought
not be permitted to obscure the proper destination of our journey.
It is the canonical myths that supply *purpose* for history. They are
the stories we would write and would live if we could. If we *could*

---

   37. JOSEPHUS, *supra* note 24, at 176: "[Herod] held him in the greatest honour,
both because of his uprightness and because when the city was later besieged by
Herod and Sossius, he advised the people to admit Herod. . . ."
   38. *See* Usher, *supra* note 30. *See also* HOLDSWORTH, 5 HISTORY OF ENGLISH LAW
430-31 (1903).

we *would*, as judges, be the Lord Coke of the Reports, the Simeon b. Shetah of tractate Sanhedrin. The legitimating objective of jurisdiction, these canonical texts proclaim, is prophetic not bureaucratic. As a judge, one must be other than the King not because of the need for specialists in dispute resolution, but because of the need to institutionalize the office of the Prophet who would say to the King, as Nathan said to David, "You are that Man";[39] As Simeon b. Shetah said to Yannai, "Stand! before He who spoke and the World was created"; As, Coke said to James I, ". . . under no man, but under God and the Law." For that ultimate purpose—speaking truth to power—there must be a jurisdiction of the judge which the King cannot share.

At the moment the judge so speaks—if he so speaks—he is naked. Much, perhaps in one sense, all, of the complexity of jurisdictional lore from ancient times to our own day arises from a contra-motif produced in the tales through the awefulness of that very realization when it comes to both Judge and King. If the judge does not call the King to account—if the King is not judged—then the judge will not stand there, as Nathan, as Simeon, as Edward Coke, stripped of institutional protection against the power that ordinarily stands behind the Court. Prudential deference, thus, is the great temptation, and the final sin of judging.

In both the historical context for *Prohibitions del Roy* and in the case of King Yannai / Herod, the gesture of courage is conjoined with pragmatic concession. It may be that had the craven colleagues of Simeon been more courageous, they would all have survived. It may also be that they all would have died and Simeon with them as their leader. It may be that Lord Coke would have produced a greater gesture if we were left in no doubt as to his standing tall before the King. It may be that if, in fact, he kissed the royal feet, that gesture rescued both the author of his great texts and the texts themselves from destruction. We can never be sanguine about the capacity of courage to rescue itself. Still, the gesture of courage is the aspiration, perhaps fabricated by Coke, certainly rescued in the talmudic account by a deus ex machina—the Angel Gabriel, himself. Nonetheless, were the gesture and aspiration of resistance not the principal motif of these stories, *we* would have no reason to remember them or to make

---

39. II SAMUEL, ch. 12, v. 7.

them our own. We would need no myth to prepare us to cave in before violence and defer to the powerful. We must get the relative roles of myth and history straight. Myth is the part of reality we create and choose to remember in order to *reenact*. It is intensely personal and committed. History is a countermove bringing us back to reality, requiring that we test the aspiration objectively and pru- dentially. History corrects for the scale of heroics that we would otherwise project upon the past. Only myth tells us who we would become; only history can tell us how hard it will really be to become that.

III. Bringing the Messiah

I have spoken until now of the fearful act of speaking law to power and of the necessarily difficult tightrope act that judges must perform precisely in these most challenging of cases.

Imagine yourself a tribunal. Pretend you have an audience—a community of some sort that will recognize you as a tribunal. Now, go all the way. What grandeur of transformation of the normative universe would you perform? Will you simply issue a general writ of peace? A warrant for justice notwithstanding facts and law? Will you order everyone to be good? Perhaps, perhaps you will judge the dead? Or even bring God as a defendant? The possibilities are endless and the question arises whether or why one should or should not try something outlandish, impossible, or just plain daring. (Now, I am not speaking of jokes. If you are to try God you must believe in God.) If law, however, is a bridge from *reality* to a new world there must be some constraints on its engineering. Judges must dare, but what happens when they lose that reality?

I want to explore a couple of outlandish attempts to do more with a court then perhaps we would think might plausibly be done. Among the folktales of justice are a few serious comedies as well as the tragedies we always rehearse. The first of these tales is a serious enough attempt to create a Court to bring the Messiah in 1538 in the Holy Land. The second is more recent history: the Bertrand Russell/Jean Paul Sartre Vietnam war crimes tribunal in Sweden and Copenhagen in 1967. Both of these events had much about them that cannot be captured in the idea of courts and jurisdiction. But they each had something as well which approaches an idea of jurisdiction based on "pure" legal meaning divorced from power and coercion in every way. As such they are worth studying.

A. The Renewal of Semikhah at Safed, 1538

Jewish law has traditionally distinguished between the authority exercised by ordinary judges and that exercised by truly ordained judges. Ordination, or Semikhah, the laying on of hands, was a transference of authority that supposedly traced back through an uninterrupted chain to Moses, himself. Only a truly ordained judge could decide certain classes of cases, especially those involving fines or criminal penalties. Sometime, probably in the fifth century, the chain of ordination was broken.[40] Indeed, Roman authorities had tried to prohibit semikhah much earlier, though according to the Jewish sources they never totally wiped it out.[41] The end of the chain of Semikhah, shrouded in mystery, did not bring a sudden or catastrophic change in the actual practices of Jewish courts. For one thing, most elements of criminal jurisdiction had been taken from these courts by the Roman authorities centuries before the end of Semikhah. Moreover, to the extent that Non-Jewish authorities permitted a measure of criminal jurisdiction to the Jewish courts, Jewish law evolved doctrinal ways of permitting that power to be exercised by judges who did not have true Semikhah. Categories of penalties imposed by virtue of the exigency of the hour were exempted from the semikhah requirement. In short, as one might suppose would happen, legal fictions and categories were created to accommodate the formal requirements of the system to reality.[42]

The formal characteristics of the system continued, however, to have some impact. Certain penalties—those biblically mandated— were not carried out by unordained judges. Moreover, the cosmological significance of human jurisdiction was impaired. For example,

---

40. ENCYCLOPEDIA JUDAICA, sub nom. Semikhah.

41. B. SANHEDRIN, 13b–14a.

42. For an interesting compilation of these fictions and subterfuges *see* E. QUINT & N. HECHT, I JEWISH JURISPRUDENCE, ITS SOURCES AND MODERN APPLICATIONS, 139–213 (1980). The terms "fictions and subterfuges" is mine and would not, I think be an acceptable characterization of "exigency jurisdiction" to Quint and Hecht themselves. For a much more aggressive posture on the application of exigency jurisdiction, *see* J. GINZBERG, MISHPATIM LE' ISRAEL: A STUDY IN JEWISH CRIMINAL LAW (Hebrew) (1956).

according to the Talmud, many transgressions are punishable by "excision."[43] This penalty is signaled by the biblical phrase, "And he shall be cut off. . . ." Rabbinic law had taught that this penalty meant that the person who transgressed would either die an untimely death or, alternatively, that he would not have a place with Israel in the world to come after the Messiah.[44] But the penalty or excision could be avoided by the experience of the very this-worldly punishment of flogging for the violation in question.[45] But precisely in this respect the fictions surrounding the exercise of rabbinic authority cut deeply. For the floggings imposed by the Bible were among the true biblical penalties that unordained judges could not impose. On the other hand, they could impose flogging for rebellion against rabbinic authority. But were floggings imposed for rebellion efficacious in preventing the penalty of excision? Of such stuff are academic legal discussions made. And you can be sure that such academic discussions there were in the thousands. But even academic discussions may become pressing matters if conditions are ripe.

In 1492 the Jews were exiled from Spain, the home of the most important and brilliant of Jewish communities in the world. The disaster of that exile existed at several levels. Homelessness and economic losses were catastrophic. Cultural loss was equally great as the dominant scholars and artists of the Jewish world lost their communities and tried to start afresh as refugees and wanderers. If communities in Turkey and the East profited greatly from the dislocation, it was at a great cost to those who were themselves dislocated. Among the refugees were many who had undergone at least nominal conversion to Christianity during the disastrous years attending the exile. Those pseudo-Christians or Marranoes frequently viewed themselves as having committed a grievous sin—one punishable by excision—in the acts attending their conversion. Their attempt to find solace, or more precisely penitence, was an important phenomenon, particularly among the most religiously active and pious of the refugees. A second phenomenon of importance was the wave of Messianic anticipation that attended the disasters in the wake of the Exile.[46]

---

43. *See* MISHNEH K'RITOTH I, 1.
44. MAIMONIDES, MISHNEH TORAH, Laws of Repentance, ch. 8, ¶ 1.
45. B. MAKKOTH, 23a-b.
46. In particular, there was a major Messianic anticipation surrounding the life and martyrdom of Solomon Molcho (1500-1532). Molcho, himself, was a reconverted

Both of the phenomena mentioned above raised the problem of the true status of Jewish courts and judges. The penitents needed, or so some of them thought, a tribunal that could impose upon them the true biblical lashings that would absolve them from the penalty of excision, especially now that there were signs of the coming of the Messiah. The coming of the Messiah, itself, was related to the renewal of Semikhah. For, in Isaiah, Chapter 1, we have a Messianic proof text: "I will return your Judges as of Old, your counselors as at the beginning; And (then) you shall be called the faithful city. . . ."[47] All rabbinic authorities agreed that the return of the judges referred to true judges: namely those ordained in the tradition that went back to Moses. The text from Isaiah thus provided an occasion for the use of law to express powerfully needs and aspirations that are not themselves necessarily legal.[48]

The precise legal question that was raised was whether it was possible to reconstitute Semikhah—true ordination—once it had been lost, as all agreed it had been, long before the sixteenth century. For the position that such a bold act of jurisdiction creation was possible there was the word of the greatest of medieval Jewish authorities, Maimonides, himself. There were two texts in the Maimonidean corpus in which the issue was addressed as a legal question. In Maimonides' Commentary on the Mishnah, written while Maimonides was a young man and completed in 1168, the Great Eagle wrote that if all the sages of the Land of Israel should agree to reinstitute Semikhah and should all agree on one of their number to be the head of the academy, then that person would be truly ordained and would have the power to pass on the ordination to others.[49]

Marrano. He had predicted that a Messianic event would occur in 1540, and many of his followers believed he had been miraculously saved from the stake in 1532. For the Messianic background to the Safed events, see, e.g., R. WERBLOWSKI, JOSEPH KARO, LAWYER AND MYSTIC, 97–99 (1976); Y. MAIMON HIDUSH HA SANHEDRIN BE MEDINNATENU HA MEHUDESHETH (1967). See also ENCYCLOPEDIA JUDAICA, sub nom. Molcho, Solomon.

47. ISAIAH, ch. 1, v. 26.

48. For examples of law as a medium of expression, see Cover, supra note 11, at 8.

49. MAIMONIDES, MISHNEH COMMENTARY, SANHEDRIN, I, 3: "And I reason that if there be agreement from all the students and sages to appoint a man of the Academy—that is that they make him Head—on condition that this be in Israel— then behold that would make that person ordained and he could ordain whomever he wished."

In his great code, the Mishneh Torah, written in 1180, Maimonides takes a somewhat more equivocal position:

> It seems to me that if all the sages in the land of Israel agree to appoint judges and to ordain them then they would thereby be ordained and could judge matters of fines and could ordain others.... And the matter requires reflection.[50]

These texts suggested a blueprint for the reinstitution of ordination, even if it was not clear what the reflection on the matter would yield. Maimonides, himself, reasoned that there had to be a formal, legal process for reinstitution of Semikhah, in part because he was not prepared to take an apocalyptic perspective on Messianism. Indeed, Maimonides held that the Messiah himself could do nothing against the law. He would have no power to change or transform the law, but only to oversee its more perfect implementation. Thus, it was necessary that the verse "I will renew your judges ..." be amenable to realization without postulating any extra-legal act by the Messiah or by God.[51]

Maimonides' texts and the texts surrouding the renewal of Semikhah in Safed leave little doubt that for this legal civilization "true jurisdiction" was a sacred aspiration, a part of Messianic fulfillment. The justice that was rendered as part of their daily lives—and these Rabbis were all judges in their communities—was an inadequate and pallid reflection of the justice that could be rendered by true courts. The active approach to Messianism taken by many in the generation after 1492 included the view that those acts which were necessary preconditions to the Messiah which could be done by human beings should be done by them to hurry the Messiah on his way. Among those acts was the renewal of Semikhah—the return of the Judges.[52]

---

50. MAIMONIDES, MISHNEH TORAH, LAWS OF SANHEDRIN, ch. 4, ¶ 11.

51. MAIMONIDES, supra note 49. Maimonides' reasoning in this respect led later commentators to engage in elaborate textual exegesis to determine whether there were proof texts for a scenario in which Maimonides' requirement for a return of judges without abrogating the law could be satisfied without also postulating some concrete legal act for reinstituting semikhah. See, e.g., the commentary of Yom Tov Heller on Mishneh Sanhedrin I, 3 (Tosephoth Yom Tov) suggesting that Elijah the Prophet who undoubtedly has Semikhah will precede the Messiah and will ordain the judges.

52. On the connection between Messianism and the renewal of Semikhah see R. WERBLOWSKI, supra note 46, at 122–25.

By the 1530s there was a geographic center to the Messianic
yearnings, to the Kabbalistic approaches to manipulation of the cosmos and to the legal scholarship that in Judaism had never been
divorced from the esoteric approaches to religion. That center was
Safed, a small city in the Galilee. There probably had been speculation and preparation for a renewal of Semikhah in Safed for a year
or two prior to 1538.[53] Jacob Berab, the dominant scholar in the
town, seems to have attempted to create an academy of colleagues
that enacted his vision of what the Great Sanhedrin had been and
would be. Berab was able to mold a community out of such great
and often conflicting figures as Joseph Karo and Moses b. Isaac Trani
(The MaBIT).[54] While we do not know a lot about the communal
processes that led up to the fateful renewal of Semikhah, we can
guess that there must have been an intense interpersonal atmosphere
of moral energy and collegial pride to produce such an act. For, the
act was an act of supreme juridicial chutzpah (nerve). Rabbi Jacob
Berab, the head of the Academy in Safed,[55] the acknowledged leader
if not the acknowledged master among them, was made the head of
the academy as outlined by Maimonides and was given Semikhah.
The sages of Safed were unanimous in their appointment of Berab
and in their intent to renew Semikhah. They proclaimed their act
through a message sent to the sages of Jerusalem through one of their
number.[56] In the message sent to Jerusalem they also purported to
confer upon the leader of the sages of Jerusalem, Rabbi Levi Ibn
Habib, ordination by virtue of the new authority of Berab.[57]

The missive to Jerusalem was, of course, necessary from two

---

53. On Berab's role in creating the academy and its spirit, see H. Dimitrovsky,
Rabbi Ya'akou Berab's Academy, 7 SEFUNOT, ANNUAL FOR RESEARCH ON THE JEWISH
COMMUNITIES IN THE EAST, 41–102 (1983). See also R. WERBLOWSKI, *supra* note 46,
at 125.

54. On the later conflicts between Karo and Trani *see* H. Dimitrovsky, *A Dispute
Between Rabbi J. Caro and Rabbi Moshe Trani*, 6 SEFUNOT 71–134 (1962).

55. *See* H. Dimitrovsky, *supra* note 53.

56. The messenger was R. Solomon Hazzan or possibly Hasson.

57. The proclamation of Semikhah and the polemical literature between R. Levi
Ibn Habib and R. Jacob Berab were collected by Ibn Habib and published by him
as a sort of appendix to his responsa. It has become known as *Kunteres Ha Semikhah*
and may be most conveniently found as a separately numbered addendum to *She'eloth
U'Teshuvoth HaRaLBaH* reprinted, Jerusalem, 1975. Two additional items in the
controversy have been found and published by H. Dimitrovsky. 10 SEFUNOT 113–
192 (1966). These documents are also included in the modern reprint edition. *Some*
of the documents are also reprinted in Y. MAIMON, *supra* note 46.

perspectives. First, Maimonides had written of the necessity for the consent of all the sages in Israel. Outside of Safed, which was by the 1530s the dominant community in Israel, Jerusalem was the only town in the holy land which had a community of scholars worth noting. At the very least, the consent of Ibn Habib and of his colleagues appeared necessary to follow the outline that Maimonides had left. Quite apart from the legal validity of the acts in question without the assent of the Jerusalem sages, was the political force of the failure to secure their approval. It was hardly likely that the rest of Judaism would take the Safed experiment seriously without such assent.

In fact, Ibn Habib considered the missive from Safed and quickly concluded that it had no basis in law according to the normal canons of standard legal reasoning. A war of pamphlets ensued between Berab and Ibn Habib with some assistance from others on both sides. Eventually, a request for a formal opinion was also sent to Rabbi David Ibn Abi Zimra (RaDBaZ), one of the great authorities of the time, then residing in Egypt. He sided with the sages of Jerusalem and, by his own account, sent them a responsum denying the power to renew Semikhah.[58]

We can hardly ignore the fact that for the Rabbis of Safed this was not a case of standard legal reasoning. Indeed, the most eloquent testimony to this fact is a "dog that didn't bark." Rabbi Joseph Karo was, as I have said, among the academy that conferred Semikhah on Berab. Moreover, he, himself, was one of four disciples of Berab who received Semikhah from him when he had to leave the country a year later. Finally, we know that Karo used the authority of Semikhah he had received to ordain still a third "generation" of sages, his disciple Moses Alshekh.[59] None of this would be surprising in itself. However, in all of Karo's large legal corpus there is very little that indicates his opinion on the validity of this audacious act. Indeed, Karo wrote a commentary to the Mishneh Torah of Maimonides in which there is a gloss to practically every legal provision in the sections covered by the commentary. The provision in which Maimonides makes his creative and by no means uncontroversial sug-

---

58. See gloss of the RaDBaZ, in MAIMONIDES, *supra* note 50 C.4, ¶ 11 (printed ad loc. in standard editions).

59. On Karo, *see* R. WERBLOWSKI, *supra note 46*, at 122–29. On Alshekh, *see* PORGES, INTRODUCTION TO SHE'ELOTH U'TESHUBOTH MAHARAM ALSHEKH (1982).

gestion draws no substantive comment or expression of approval
from Karo. It is almost as if Karo managed to keep his legalistic
oeuvre mentally separated from this act, the reasons for which were
not standard legal reasoning but the necessity to hasten the Messiah.[60]

There is in the Act of Safed, a daring commitment and a risk
of madness. The daring commitment is in this: One of law's usual
functions is to hold off the Messiah. Messianism implies upheaval
and fairly total transformation. Law ordinarily requires a cautious
discernment among commitments: some of these we are prepared to
undertake *now* with total subordination of other values; some of
these we are prepared to undertake only after specified preconditions
shall be met; and some we are not prepared to undertake now but
subject to certain prior claims; some we are prepared to undertake
only after specified preconditions shall be met; and some we are not
prepared to commit ourselves to concretely though we may yet
acclaim their value. The readiness to move into a pre-Messianic mode
of judicature is a readiness to dramatically increase the range of
current legal commitment. It is to evince not only dramatic dissatisfaction with the world as it is, but a looming responsibility for
drastic change. Now the natural understanding for a Court confronting a gap between what is affirmed as right and the world as perceived, is that the *world* will be changed. Courts exercise power to
that end. But we know from the study of failed Messiahs that the
failure of inflated expectations may entail complex compensations in
the *perception* and understanding of a reality that cannot be brought
to coincide with the demand made upon it. The risk, in short, is that
the gulf between the redeemed world and the unredeemed will be
bridged not by our committed practical behavior, but by our "inner
life"—our spiritual and psychological realities. The Safed which was
to have been the home of the Great Court or Sanhedrin became the

---

60. R. WERBLOWSKI, *supra* note 46, at 124. There are several references, sometimes oblique, to the Semikhah incident in the strange work, *Maggid Mesharim*, a
sort of mystical diary attributed to Karo in which the Mishneh personified speaks
to and through Karo. The authenticity of the attribution was long in doubt though
Werblowski has established the work as Karo's to the satisfaction of those competent
to judge (of whom I am not one). *Id.* ch. 2–3. One must note that the Kesef Mishneh
was the last of Karo's major works to be completed and he must have looked back
at the Semikhah incident from a perspective of it having failed. On the other hand,
the MaBiT in his commentary on the Mishneh Torah does explicitly relate the incident.
Kiryath Sefer ad loc.

home of Lurianic Kabbalah, increasingly spiritual and esoteric; psychologically demanding; and powerfully expressive of the chasm between the unredeemed fractured world of mortal human kind and the hope and vision that could no longer be grasped through law. Such powerful, expressive movements of the inner life may have revolutionary potential, realized in this case in the Sabbatian Movement in the 1660's. But such movements, though they bring a Messiah, do not do so through law. Sabbatai Sevi was hardly the Messiah Maimonides, Berab, or Karo had projected for the world.[61]

b. Nuremberg and The Creation of A Modern Myth

As the allied victors in World War II set out to punish many of the leaders and other perpetrators of atrocities among the vanquished axis powers, a curious debate took shape about the character that should be given to the punishment proceedings. Almost nobody seriously maintained that the principal perpetrators of the axis war policies should go unpunished.[62] But there was vigorous debate about whether the forms of law and justice should be used.[63] Charles Wyzanski asked of the trials:

> For those who were not chargeable with ordinary crimes but only with political crimes such as planning an aggressive war, would it not have better to proceed by an executive determination— that is, a prescription directed at certain named individuals?...
>
> To be sure, [such an executive determination] is also an exhibition of power and not of restraint. But its very merit is its naked and unassumed character. It confesses itself to be not legal justice but political.[64]

---

61. *See, e.g.,* N. COHN, THE PURSUIT OF THE MILLENIUM (1961); L. FESTINGER, et al., WHEN PROPHECY FAILS (1956); See, more pointedly, the complex social responses to the collapse of the Sabbatian Messianic Expectations. G. SCHOLEM, SABBATAI SEVI: THE MYSTICAL MESSIAH (Werblowski: trans. 1973) especially at 689–93. *See also* G. SCHOLEM, *The Crypto-Jewish Sect of Donmeh (Sabbatians) in Turkey,* in THE MESSIANIC IDEA IN JUDAISM AND OTHER ESSAYS ON JEWISH SPIRITUALITY (1972).

62. *See* M. BELGION, VICTORS' JUSTICE (1949) for one view that no punishment was warranted for the "political" crimes.

63. *See, e.g.,* TUSA & TUSA, THE NUREMBERG TRIAL, ch. 1–5 (1983).

64. Wyzanski, *Nuremberg—A Fair Trial? Dangerous Precedent,* ATLANTIC MONTHLY, April 1946 *reprinted in* C. WYZANSKI, JR., THE NEW MEANING OF JUSTICE 125, 135 (1966).

Wyzanski's public challenge to the War Crimes Tribunal took place in April, 1946. We now know that a similar debate about whether to proceed in a juridical or purely political mode took place at the planning stages both within the American administration and among the allies.[65]

The defense of the Nuremberg Trials—a defense which Wyzanski, himself, came to accept in large part—was sounded at the outset in terms of the capacity of the event to project a new legal meaning into the future. Building a precedent which would be taken seriously was one of Robert Jackson's enuciated objectives.[66] And his retrospective judgment on the event included that objective as one of its principal achievements.[67] The fact of having shed blood in the juridical mode made the precedent one of special character. Wyzanski, by the end of 1946 acknowledged:

> But the outstanding accomplishment of the trial, which could never have been achieved by any more summary executive action, is that it has crystallized the concept that there already is inherent in the international community a machinery both of the expression of international criminal law and for its enforcement.[68]

It is important to note that while the unlawful and evil character of the Nazi War seemed self-evident to most, the "agressive war"

---

65. *See* R. SMITH, REACHING JUDGEMENT AT NUREMBERG (1977) for debate among allies and something of the debate within the American administration. The internal debate is more comprehensively canvassed in B. SMITH, THE ROAD TO NUREMBERG (1981). TUSA & TUSA, *supra* note 63, give a summary of this material.

66. For the significance of the "aggressive war precedent" to Jackson before Nuremberg, *see, e.g., Minutes of Conference Session of July 25, 1945* in U.S. DEPT. OF STATE, REPORT OF ROBERT H. JACKSON, U.S. REPRESENTATIVE TO THE INTERNATIONAL CONFERENCE ON MILITARY TRIALS, 376, 383–84 (1945), Doc. 1.

67. *Report to the President by Mr. Justice Jackson, October 7, 1946* in *Id.* at 437:
    "We have also incorporated its principles into a judicial precedent. 'The power of the precedent,' Mr. Justice Cardozo said, 'is the power of the beaten path.' One of the Chief obstacles to this trial was the lack of a beaten path. A judgement such as has been rendered shifts the power of the precedent to the support of these rules of law. No one can hereafter deny or fail to know that the principles on which the Nazi leaders are adjudged to forfeit their lives constitute law— and law with a sanction."

68. C. WYZANSKI, JR., *Nuremberg in Retrospect,* in THE NEW MEANING OF JUSTICE, 137, 144 (1966).

crime was also applied across the world in the trial, conviction and execution of Japanese defendants. In retrospect, the Tokyo tribunal judgments seem to have applied criminal sanctions to a range of conduct which was not discontinuous with "normal statecraft" in the way that Nazi policy had been.[69] Finally, in a series of trials by Military Commission, American tribunals undertook to punish Japanese General Officers for atrocities committed under their command on a theory of command responsibility which was breathtakingly broad and, as applied, seemed to some almost impossibly demanding.[70]

The War Crimes tribunals of 1946 and the Military Commissions that interpreted command responsibility in 1945 employed the forms of jurisdiction in the interests of power. They were, in our typology, instances of Kings using judges. That, indeed, was the essence of the critic's case. But these were also instances of judges using Kings. It is true that the particular proceedings at Nuremberg and Tokyo were limited to trials of axis defendants. But, the precedent that Jackson believed he was creating and that Wyzanski came to accept as a justification for the Trial was one which could not be so circumscribed.

As a matter of doctrine, the judgments at Nuremberg and Tokyo and the *Yamashita* enunciation of command responsibility *did* become part of the law of war of the United States of America.[71] However, the controversy about the trials in 1946 had not been so much a controversy over doctrine as one over jurisdiction and its exercise. The issue was not so much whether to make "law" as it was whether to make a Court. In making the Court in 1946 the interests of judges and of Kings converged. What would happen when they came to diverge?

The Vietnam War, twenty years after Nuremberg, created a protracted and complex case study of the life of legal ideas when they come to diverge from the exercise of power through state institutions. Millions of Americans took the Nuremberg principles as their guide for conduct in opposing the Vietnam conflict and in legitimating their large scale opposition to a national war. Those principles were par-

69. R. MINEAR, VICTOR'S JUSTICE, THE TOKYO WAR CRIMES TRIAL (1971).

70. *In re* Yamashita, 327 U.S. 1 (1946); R. LAEL, THE YAMASHITA PRECEDENT, WAR CRIMES AND COMMAND RESPONSIBILITY (1982).

71. T. TAYLOR, NUREMBERG AND VIETNAM: AN AMERICAN TRAGEDY 50–51, 77, 94 (1970).

ticularly well-suited for legitimating opposition without recourse to alternative loyalties (the old treason rubric) and without requiring any ideology of internationalism (such as WW I pacifist socialism). Moreover, once certain factual premises were accepted, the Nuremberg principles provided the basis for an *obligation* to oppose such a war.

There were a variety of texts for this application of principle. Richard Falk and Telford Taylor wrote major works legitimating the comparison of Nuremburg to Vietnam.[72] Taylor's small book was particularly important because of the weight of his own person—a chief prosecutor at the second round trials at Nuremburg itself.

With a few lonely exceptions that I shall not go into detail about here[73] the official courts of the United States, when confronted with a variety of challenges to the Vietnam War in terms of the Nuremberg principles, refused to challenge power with law. The courts played a deference game, averting their eyes from the wielders of violence like the sage colleagues of Simeon b. Shetah.[74] Can we expect more from the protected holders of life tenure? Is one of the preconditions for being given such a job the expectation that one will not take advantage of it to seriously discomfort the wielders of power?

The gesture of speaking truth to power was not often made within the official court system; but, it was inevitable that someone would think of institutionalizing the extraordinary popular feeling that Nuremburg was in fact applicable through creating a "court" just as the victorious powers had done in 1946.

In 1967 events took place first in Stockholm, then in Copenhagen

---

72. R. FALK, THE VIETNAM WAR AND INTERNATIONAL LAW (1968).

73. For an account of the exceptions and of the rule see BANNAN & BANNAN, LAW, MORALITY AND VIETNAM (1974); A. D'AMATO & R. O'NEIL, THE JUDICIARY AND VIETNAM (1972). Taylor, it should be noted, did feel the Nuremberg principles were directly relevant to Vietnam and argued eloquently that we should learn that lesson, but he did not think the domestic tribunals of the United States could or should stop the war. *See* T. TAYLOR, *supra* note 71 at 120–21. The author of this article has taken the position since 1968 that whether or not they could have stopped the war, judges should have removed themselves completely from the apparatus of complicity. *See* Cover, *Atrocious Judges: Lives of Judges Infamous as Tools of Tyrants and Instruments of Oppression,* 68 COLUMB. L. REV. 1003 (1968) (book review).

74. *See* Cover, *supra* note 73; the final and most grotesque instance of this averting of the eyes took place in the Howard Levy Case. Parker v. Levy, 417 U.S. 733 (1974).

which purported to be an "International War Crimes Tribunal."[75] The tribunal was under the "Honorary Presidency" of Bertrand Russell and the "Executive Presidency" of Jean Paul Sartre.[76] There were no individual defendants. The tribunal purported to adjudicate certain questions about the United States—Has the government of the United States committed acts of aggression against Vietnam under the terms of international law?—about the conduct of the war; and about the complicity of other governments. There can be little doubt that the tribunal passed a judgment that was in a sense a foregone conclusion.[77] There can also be no doubt that the tribunal was understood to be a tribunal manqué by the very organizers themselves. They disclaimed any intent to bring to justice or punish the perpetrators of the acts they condemned.[78] Yet, the event took the form of a trial and that form was not accidental. It did have force to others as well. The French government denied to some partipants the visas necessary to let them convene on French territory for the trial, thus requiring it to be moved to Stockholm. DeGaulle wrote to Sartre that:

> Neither is it [the right to hold the tribunal in France] a question of the right of assembly nor of free expression, but of duty, the more so for France, which has taken a widely known decision in this matter [of opposition to the war] and which must be on guard lest a state with which it is linked and which, despite all differences of opinion, remains its traditional friend, would on French territory become that subject of proceedings exceeding the limit of international law and custom. Now such would seem to be the case with regard to the activity envisaged by Lord Russell and his friends, since they intend to give a juridicial form to their investigations and the semblance of a verdict to their

---

75. See AGAINST THE CRIME OF SILENCE, PROCEEDINGS OF THE INTERNATIONAL WAR CRIMES TRIBUNAL (J. Duffett ed. 1968).

76. Id. at 17.

77. "At no time did we maintain that the Tribunal consisted of men who were agnostic about the war in Vietnam. On the contrary, we proclaimed our conviction that terrible crimes were occuring. . . . " Id. at 7 (Forward by Ralph Schoenman).

78. Opening statement of Jean Paul Sartre: "We are powerless: it is the guarantee of our independence. . . . What is certain, in any case, is that our powerlessness . . . makes it impossible for us to pass a sentence." quoted in id. at 43.

conclusions. I have no need to tell you that justice of any sort, in principle as in execution, emanates from the State.[79]

DeGaulle thus recognized a kind of force to the tribunal as such in denying it a French location. Needless to say, Sartre did not accept the characterization of the exclusive role of the State in justice which DeGaulle asserted. But in his answer to DeGaulle he went somewhat further than nonacceptance. He also answered the question of the mandate by which the tribunal created its own jurisdiction over the matter. In this Sartre recognized and quite correctly delineated a relation between the tribunal and the nonaction of the official world of law.

> There was Nuremburg, of course, but after having enforced the laws of the conqueror on the conquered—just laws, for once— the court was quickly disbanded by its creators for fear that one day they might find themselves brought before it. . . . Why did we appoint ourselves? For the precise reason that no one else did. Governments or peoples could have done it. But governments want to retain the ability to commit war crimes without running the risk of being judged; they are therefore not about to set up an international body responsible for judging them. As for the people, save in time of revolution they do not appoint tribunals; therefore they could not appoint us.[80]

Sartre expressed some hope that the tribunal either continue or be a precedent for similar bodies to take cognizance of other war crimes around the world. But the important thing to note here is that the act of utopian jurisdiction-making was, in simple terms, an anarchist variant of a state institutional response. For Sartre it is perhaps second best. But any response, whether by the courts of states, revolutionary tribunals, or the Russell tribunal would share the legal meaning created still earlier by the primal act of Nuremberg. It is an irony of the history of this age that Nuremburg—an act often characterized as a fig leaf for naked power, bore as offspring the attempt to empower the fig leaf standing alone. The "lynching party" of Robert Jackson,

---

79. Letter from DeGaulle to Sartre, April 19, 1967, *cited in id.*
80. *Id.* at 33.

to use Hugo Black's phrase becomes Lord Russell's affront to the dignity of the United States which France would not abide—an affront that had the juridical defects not of a lynching, but of a tea party.

IV. Conclusion

The Russell/Sartre tribunal, like the Sanhedrin that R. Jacob Berab tried to set up, was a philosopher's realization of an ideal type. But both "Courts" refrained from acts that might have tested definitively their capacity to transform their worlds. Had the Russell/Sartre tribunal purported to license or solicit political assassination against particular defendants it would certainly soon have confronted a test in blood concerning the legitimacy of the "trial" and conviction of the defendants. For reasons of principle as well as prudence the "Court" took only actions which could—in a liberal democracy—be characterized by others not as a "Court" but as dramatization, or instruction. Berab and the elders he ordained in Safed never acknowledged any defect in their ordination. But, they, too, so far as we know, refrained from taking specific action that would test either world Jewry's view of the legitimacy of their status or the Turkish overlord's authority. They used their "ordination" but probably only for purposes for which the defective, routine ordination of ordinary Rabbis would have sufficed.

The caution which the Utopian jurist exercises in this regard is parallel to the caution that the state's judge exercises before the King. Both thereby maintain the connection between law and reality. Both risk losing law to the overpowering force of what is and what is dominant. Integrity in both kinds of judges is the act of maintaining the vision that it is only that which redeems which is law.

Chapter 5

Violence and the Word

I. Introduction: The Violence of Legal Acts

Legal interpretation[1] takes place in a field of pain and death. This is true in several senses. Legal interpretive acts signal and occasion the imposition of violence upon others: A judge articulates her understanding of a text, and as a result, somebody loses his freedom, his property, his children, even his life. Interpretations in law also constitute justifications for violence which has already occurred or which is about to occur. When interpreters have finished their work, they frequently leave behind victims whose lives have been torn apart by these organized, social practices of violence. Neither legal interpretation nor the violence it occasions may be properly understood apart from one another. This much is obvious, though the growing literature

---

There are always legends of those who came first, who called things by their *right* names and thus founded the culture of meaning into which we latecomers are born. Charles Black has been such a legend, striding across the landscape of law naming things, speaking "with authority." And we who come after him are eternally grateful.

I wish to thank Harlon Dalton, Susan Koniak, and Harry Wellington for having read and commented upon drafts of this essay. Some of the ideas in this essay were developed earlier, in the Brown Lecture which I delivered at the Georgia School of Law Conference on Interpretation in March, 1986. I am grateful to Milner Ball, Avi Soifer, Richard Weisberg, and James Boyd White for comments made in response to that lecture which have helped me in reworking the ideas here.

I am particularly grateful to my summer research assistant, Tracy Fessenden, for research, editorial, and substantive assistance of the highest order.

1. I have used the term "legal interpretation" throughout this essay, though my argument is directed principally to the interpretive acts of judges. To this specifically *judicial* interpretation my analysis of institutional action applies with special force. Nonetheless, I believe the more general term "legal interpretation" is warranted, for it is my position that the violence which judges deploy as instruments of a modern nation-state necessarily engages anyone who interprets the law in a course of conduct that entails either the perpetration or the suffering of this violence.

that argues for the centrality of interpretive practices in law blithely ignores it.[2]

Taken by itself, the word "interpretation" may be misleading.

---

2. There has been a recent explosion of legal scholarship placing interpretation at the crux of the enterprise of law. A fair sampling of that work may be seen in the various articles that have appeared in two symposia. *Symposium: Law and Literature*, 60 TEX. L. REV. 373 (1982); *Interpretation Symposium*, 58 S. CALIF. L. REV. 1 (1985) (published in two issues). The intense interest in "interpretation" or "hermeneutics" in recent legal scholarship is quite a different phenomenon from the traditional set of questions about how a particular word, phrase, or instrument should be given effect in some particular context. It is, rather, the study of what I have called "a normative universe . . . held together by . . . interpretive commitments. . . ." Cover, *The Supreme Court, 1982 Term—Foreword: Nomos and Narrative*, 97 HARV. L. REV. 4, 7 (1983). Or, in Ronald Dworkin's words, it is the study of the effort "to impose *meaning* on the institution . . . and then to restructure it in the light of that meaning." R. DWORKIN, LAW'S EMPIRE 47 (1986) (emphasis in original). Dworkin, in *Law's Empire*, has written the most elaborate and sophisticated jurisprudence which places the meaning-giving, constructive dimension of interpretation at the heart of law. James Boyd White has been another eloquent voice claiming primacy for what he has called the "culture of argument." White has raised rhetoric to the pinnacle of jurisprudence. *See* J. B. WHITE, WHEN WORDS LOSE THEIR MEANING (1984); J. B. WHITE, HERACLES' BOW (1985).

The violent side of law and its connection to interpretation and rhetoric is systematically ignored or underplayed in the work of both Dworkin and White. White, in chapter nine of *Heracles' Bow*, comes closest to the concerns of this essay. He launches a critique of the practice of criminal law in terms of its unintelligibility as a "system of meaning" in the absence of significant reforms. White does not see violence as central to the breakdown of the system of meaning. But he does contrast what the judge says with what he does in the saying of it. Still, White reiterates in this book his central claim that "law . . . is best regarded not as a machine for social control, but as what I call a system of constitutive rhetoric: a set of resources for claiming, resisting, and declaring significance." *Id.* at 205. I do not deny that law is all those things that White claims, but I insist that it is those things in the context of the organized social practice of violence. And the "significance" or meaning that is achieved must be experienced or understood in vastly different ways depending upon whether one suffers that violence or not. In *Nomos and Narrative*, I also emphasized the world-building character of interpretive commitments in law. However, the thrust of *Nomos* was that the creation of legal meaning is an essentially cultural activity which takes place (or *best* takes place) among smallish groups. Such meaning-creating activity is not naturally coextensive with the range of effective violence used to achieve social control. Thus, because law is the attempt to build future worlds, the essential tension in law is between the elaboration of legal meaning and the exercise of or resistance to the violence of social control. Cover, *supra*, at 18: "[T]here is a radical dichotomy between the social organization of law as power and the organization of law as meaning." This essay elaborates the senses in which the traditional forms of legal decision cannot be easily captured by the idea of interpretation understood as interpretation normally is in literature, the arts, or the humanities.

"Interpretation" suggests a social construction of an interpersonal reality through language. But pain and death have quite other implications. Indeed, pain and death destroy the world that "interpretation" calls up. That one's ability to construct interpersonal realities is destroyed by death is obvious, but in this case, what is true of death is true of pain also, for pain destroys, among other things, language itself. Elaine Scarry's brilliant analysis of pain makes this point:

> [F]or the person, in pain, so incontestably and unnegotiably present is it that "having pain" may come to be thought of as the most vibrant example of what it is to "have certainty," while for the other person it is so elusive that hearing about pain may exist as the primary model of what it is "to have doubt." Thus pain comes unshareably into our midst as at once that which cannot be denied and that which cannot be confirmed. Whatever pain achieves, it achieves in part through its unshareability, and it ensures this unshareability in part through its resistance to language. . . . Prolonged pain does not simply resist language but actively destroys it, bringing about an immediate reversion to a state anterior to language, to the sounds and cries a human being makes before language is learned.[3]

The deliberate infliction of pain in order to destroy the victim's normative world and capacity to create shared realities we call torture. The interrogation that is part of torture, Scarry points out, is rarely designed to elicit information. More commonly, the torturer's interrogation is designed to demonstrate the end of the normative world of the victim—the end of what the victim values, the end of the bonds that constitute the community in which the values are grounded. Scarry thus concludes that "in compelling confession, the torturers compel the prisoner to record and objectify the fact that intense pain is world-destroying."[4] That is why torturers almost always require betrayal—a demonstration that the victim's intangible normative world has been crushed by the material reality of pain

---

3. E. SCARRY, THE BODY IN PAIN 4 (1985).
4. Id. at 29.

and its extension, fear.[5] The torturer and victim do end up creating their own terrible "world," but this world derives its meaning from being imposed upon the ashes of another.[6] The logic of that world is complete domination, though the objective may never be realized.

Whenever the normative world of a community survives fear, pain, and death in their more extreme forms, that very survival is understood to be literally miraculous both by those who have experienced and by those who vividly imagine or recreate the suffering. Thus, of the suffering of sainted Catholic martyrs it was written:

> We must include also . . . the deeds of the saints in which their triumph blazed forth through the many forms of torture that they underwent and *their marvelous confession of the faith*. For what Catholic can doubt that they suffered more than is possible for human beings to bear, and did not endure this by their own strength, but by the grace and help of God?[7]

And Jews, each year on Yom Kippur, remember—

---

5. *Id.*
Pain and interrogation inevitably occur together in part because the torturer and the prisoner each experience them as opposites. The very question that, within the political pretense, matters so much to the torturer that it occasions his grotesque brutality will matter so little to the prisoner experiencing the brutality that he will give the answer. For the torturers, the sheer and simple fact of human agony is made invisible, and the moral fact of inflicting that agony is made neutral by the feigned urgency and significance of the question. For the prisoner, the sheer, simple, overwhelming fact of his agony will make neutral and invisible the significance of any question as well as the significance of the world to which the question refers. . . . It is for this reason that while the content of the prisoner's answer is only sometimes important to the regime, the form of the answer, the fact of his answering, is always crucial. . . . [I]n confession, one betrays oneself and all those aspects of the world—friend, family, country, cause—that the self is made up of.

Id. While pain is the extreme form of world destruction, fear may be as potent, even if not connected to physical pain and torture. The fact of answering and the necessity for "world destruction" through betrayal were also central to the reign of fear of McCarthyism. *See, e.g.*, V. NAVASKY, NAMING NAMES 346 (1980) (informer destroys "the very possibility of a community . . . for the informer operates on the principle of betrayal and a community survives on the principle of trust").

6. On the "fiction of power" that torture creates, see E. SCARRY, *supra* note 3, at 56–58.

7. P. BROWN, THE CULT OF THE SAINTS 79 (1981) (emphasis added) (quoting from the DECRETUM GELASIANUM, PATROLOGIA LATINA 59.171).

Rabbi Akiba ... chose to continue teaching in spite of the decree [of the Romans forbidding it]. When they led him to the executioner, it was time for reciting the Sh'ma. With iron combs they scraped away his skin as he recited *Sh'ma Yisrael*, freely accepting the yoke of God's Kingship. "Even now?" his disciples asked. He replied: "All my life I have been troubled by a verse: 'Love the Lord your God with all your heart and with all your soul,' which means even if He take your life. I often wondered if I would ever fulfill that obligation. And now I can." He left the world while uttering, "The Lord is One."[8]

Martyrdom, for all its strangeness to the secular world of contemporary American Law, is a proper starting place for understanding the nature of legal interpretation. Precisely because it is so extreme a phenomenon, martyrdom helps us see what is present in lesser degree whenever interpretation is joined with the practice of violent domination. Martyrs insist in the face of overwhelming force that if there is to be continuing life, it will not be on the terms of the tyrant's law. Law is the projection of an imagined future upon reality. Martyrs require that any future they possess will be on the terms of the law to which they are committed (God's law). And the miracle of the suffering of the martyrs is their insistence on the law to which they are committed, even in the face of world-destroying pain.[9] Their triumph—which may well be partly imaginary—is the imagined triumph of the normative universe—of Torah, Nomos,—over the material world of death and pain.[10] Martyrdom is an extreme form of

---

8. The quotation is from the traditional Eileh Ezkerah or martyrology service of Yom Kippur. I have quoted from the translation used in MAHZOR FOR ROSH HASHANAH AND YOM KIPPUR, A PRAYER BOOK FOR THE DAYS OF AWE 555–57 (J. Harlow ed. 1972).

9. The word "martyr" stems from the Greek root *martys*, "witness," and from the Aryan root *smer*, "to remember." Martyrdom functions as a *re*-membering when the martyr, in the act of witnessing, sacrifices herself on behalf of the normative universe which is thereby reconstituted, regenerated, or recreated. One of the earliest sources dealing with martyrdom as a religious phenomenon, 2 MACCABEES, stresses the characteristic of the phenomenon as an insistence on the integrity of the Law of the martyr and of the obligation to it in the face of overpowering violence. At one point the book describes the horrible torture and killing of seven sons before their mother's eyes, each death more horrible than the one before. The last and youngest child, encouraged by his mother, answers the King's demand to eat pork with the words: "I will not submit to the King's command; I obey the command of the law given by Moses to our ancestors." 2 MACCABEES 7.30.

10. In extreme cases martyrdom may be affirmatively sought out, for it is the

resistance to domination. As such it reminds us that the normative world-building which constitutes "Law" is never just a mental or spiritual act. A legal world is built only to the extent that there are commitments that place bodies on the line. The torture of the martyr is an extreme and repulsive form of the organized violence of institutions. It reminds us that the interpretive commitments of officials are realized, indeed, in the flesh. As long as that is so, the interpretive commitments of a community which resists official law must also be realized in the flesh, even if it be the flesh of its own adherents.

Martyrdom is not the only possible response of a group that has failed to adjust to or accept domination while sharing a physical space. Rebellion and revolution are alternative responses when conditions make such acts feasible and when there is a willingness not only to die but also to kill for an understanding of the normative future that differs from that of the dominating power.[11]

Our own constitutional history begins with such an act of rebellion. The act was, in form, an essay in constitutional interpretation affirming the right of political independence from Great Britain:

> We therefore the representatives of the United States of America in General Congress assembled, appealing to the supreme judge of the world for the rectitude of our intentions, do in the name, and by the authority of the good people of these colonies, sol-

---

final proof of the capacity of the spirit to triumph over the body. That triumph may be seen as a triumph of love or of law or of both, depending upon the dominant motifs of the normative and religious world of the martyr and her community. The great jurist and mystic, Joseph Karo (1488–1578), had ecstatic dreams of martyrdom and was promised the privilege of dying a martyr by a "maggid"—a celestial messenger who spoke through his mouth and appeared to him in visions. (The promise was not fulfilled. He died of very old age.) See Z. WERBLOWSKI, JOSEPH KARO: LAWYER AND MYSTIC 151–54 (2d ed. 1977). Note also the phenomenon of communities slaughtering themselves in the face of an enemy. Compare the complex mythos of the Jewish martyrs before the crusaders, elaborated in S. SPIEGEL, THE LAST TRIAL: ON THE LEGENDS AND LORE OF THE COMMAND TO ABRAHAM TO OFFER ISSAC AS A SACRIFICE: THE AKEDAH (J. Goldin trans. 1969) with the myth of the White Night enacted by Jonestown in our own day, recounted in J. SMITH, IMAGINING RELIGION: FROM BABYLON TO JONESTOWN 102–20, 126–34 (1982).

11. The archetype for the transition from martyrdom to resistance is found in 1 MACCABEES, with the dramatic killing carried out by the Priest Matathias in Modi'in. 1 MACCABEES 2, 19–28. His act assumes dramatic significance in the work in part because it stands in marked contrast to the acts of heroic martyrdom described in 2 MACCABEES. See supra note 9.

emnly publish and declare that these United Colonies are and of right ought to be free and independent states; that they are absolved from all allegiance to the British crown, and that all political connection between them and the State of Great Britain is, and ought to be, totally dissolved.[12]

But this interpretive act also incorporated an awareness of the risk of pain and death that attends so momentous an interpretive occasion:

We mutually pledge to each other our lives, our fortunes and our sacred honour.[13]

Life, fortune, and sacred honour were, of course, precisely the price that would have been exacted from the conspirators were their act unsuccessful. We too often forget that the leaders of the rebellion had certainly committed treason from the English constitutional perspective. And conviction of treason carried with it a horrible and degrading death, forfeiture of estate, and corruption of the blood.[14] Great issues of constitutional interpretation that reflect fundamental questions of political allegiance—the American Revolution, the secession of the States of the Confederacy, or the uprising of the Plains Indians—clearly carry the seeds of violence (pain and death) at least

---

12. The Declaration of Independence (1776). For the senses in which the Declaration should be seen as interpretive of the constitutional position of America in the Empire, see Black, *The Constitution of Empire: The Case for the Colonists*, 124 U. PA. L. REV. 1157 (1976).

13. The Declaration of Independence (1776).

14. *See* IV BLACKSTONE'S COMMENTARIES *92–93:
    The punishment of high treason in general is very solemn and terrible. 1. That the offender be drawn to the gallows, and not be carried or walk; though usually (by connivance, at length ripened by humanity into law) a sledge or hurdle is allowed, to preserve the offender from the extreme torment of being dragged on the ground or pavement. 2. That he be hanged by the neck, and then cut down alive. 3. That his entrails be taken out, and burned, while yet he is alive. 4. That his head be cut off. 5. That his body be divided into four parts. 6. That his head and quarters be at the king's disposal.

On forfeiture and corruption of the blood, see *id.* at *388–96. It is, therefore, not unexpected that among the few specific protections incorporated into the body of the original Constitution were those which closely defined treason, set procedural safeguards for conviction of treason, and forbade the extension of attaint and corruption of the blood as vicarious punishment upon the family or descendants of those convicted of treason.

from the moment that the understanding of the political texts becomes embedded in the institutional capacity to take collective action. But it is precisely this embedding of an understanding of political text in institutional modes of action that distinguishes *legal* interpretation from the interpretation of literature, from political philosophy, and from constitutional criticism.[15] Legal interpretation is either played out on the field of pain and death or it is something less (or more) than law.

Revolutionary constitutional understandings are commonly staked in blood. In them, the violence of the law takes its most blatant form. But the relationship between legal interpretation and the infliction of pain remains operative even in the most routine of legal acts. The act of sentencing a convicted defendant is among these most routine of acts performed by judges.[16] Yet it is immensely revealing of the way in which interpretation is distinctively shaped by violence. First, examine the event from the perspective of the defendant. The defendant's world is threatened. But he sits, usually quietly,

---

15. Every interpretive practice takes place in some context. Among recent critics, Stanley Fish has been as insistent as any concerning the dominance of institutional contexts even in understanding literary texts. *See generally* S. FISH, IS THERE A TEXT IN THIS CLASS? (1980); Fish, *Fish v. Fiss*, 36 STAN. L. REV. 1325, 1332 (1984) ("To be ... 'deeply inside' a context is to be already and always thinking (and perceiving) with and within the norms, standards, definitions, routines, and understood goals that both define and are defined by that context."). I do not wish to dispute Fish's central point about literature. I do think, however, that the institutions that are designed to realize normative futures in part through the practice of collective violence stand on a somewhat different footing than do those which bear only a remote or incidental relation to the violence of society. I am prepared to entertain views such as those of Fredric Jameson, who argues for "the priority of the political interpretation of literary texts." F. JAMESON, THE POLITICAL UNCONSCIOUS: NARRATIVE AS A SOCIALLY SYMBOLIC ACT 17 (1981). But while asserting the special place of a political understanding of our social reality, such views do not in any way claim for literary interpretations what I am claiming about legal interpretation—that it is part of the *practice* of political violence.

16. I have used the criminal law for examples throughout this essay for a simple reason. The violence of the criminal law is relatively direct. If my argument is not persuasive in this context, it will be less persuasive in most other contexts. I would be prepared to argue that all law which concerns property, its use and its protection, has a similarly violent base. But in many, perhaps most, highly visible legal transactions concerning property rights, that violent foundation is not immediately at issue. My argument does not, I believe, require that every interpretive event in law have the kind of direct violent impact on participants that a criminal trial has. It is enough that it is the case that where people care passionately about outcomes and are prepared to act on their concern, the law officials of the nation state are usually willing and able to use either criminal or violent civil sanctions to control behavior.

as if engaged in a civil discourse. If convicted, the defendant cus-
tomarily walks—escorted—to prolonged confinement, usually without significant disturbance to the civil appearance of the event. It is,
of course, grotesque to assume that the civil facade is "voluntary"
except in the sense that it represents the defendant's autonomous
recognition of the overwhelming array of violence ranged against
him, and of the hopelessness of resistance or outcry.[17]

There are societies in which contrition or shame control defendants' behavior to a greater extent than does violence. Such societies
require and have received their own distinctive form of analysis.[18]
But I think it is unquestionably the case in the United States that
most prisoners walk into prison because they know they will be
dragged or beaten into prison if they do not walk. They do not
organize force against being dragged because they know that if they
wage this kind of battle they will lose—very possibly lose their lives.

If I have exhibited some sense of sympathy for the victims of
this violence it is misleading. Very often the balance of terror in this
regard is just as I would want it. But I do not wish us to pretend
that we talk our prisoners into jail. The "interpretations" or "conversations" that are the preconditions for violent incarceration are
themselves implements of violence. To obscure this fact is precisely
analogous to ignoring the background screams or visible instruments
of torture in an inquisitor's interrogation. The experience of the pris-

---

17. A few defendants who have reached their own understandings of the legal
order have overtly attempted to deny the fiction that the trial is a joint or communal
civil event where interpretations of facts and legal concepts are tested and refined.
The playing out of such an overt course of action ends with the defendant physically
bound and gagged. Bobby Seale taught those of us who lived through the 1960s that
the court's physical control over the defendant's body lies at the heart of the criminal
process. The defendant's "civil conduct," therefore, can never signify a shared understanding of the event; it may signify his fear that any public display of his interpretation of the event as "bullshit" will end in violence perpetrated against him, pain
inflicted upon him. Our constitutional law, quite naturally enough, provides for the
calibrated use of ascending degrees of overt violence to maintain the "order" of the
criminal trial. See, e.g., Illinois v. Allen, 397 U.S. 337 (1970); Tigar, *The Supreme
Court, 1969 Term—Forword: Waiver of Constitutional Rights: Disquiet in the Citadel*,
84 HARV. L. REV. 1, 1–3, 10–11 (1970) (commenting in part upon *Allen*).

18. On the distinction between "shame cultures" and "guilt cultures," see generally E. DODDS, THE GREEKS AND THE IRRATIONAL (1951) and J. REDFIELD, NATURE
AND CULTURE IN THE ILIAD (1975). For an analysis of a modern "shame culture," see
R. BENEDICT, THE CHRYSANTHEMUM AND THE SWORD: PATTERNS OF JAPANESE CULTURE
(1946).

oner is, from the outset, an experience of being violently dominated, and it is colored from the beginning by the fear of being violently treated.[19]

The violence of the act of sentencing is most obvious when observed from the defendant's perspective. Therefore, any account which seeks to downplay the violence or elevate the interpretive character or meaning of the event within a community of shared values will tend to ignore the prisoner or defendant and focus upon the judge and the judicial interpretive act. Beginning with broad interpretive categories such as "blame" or "punishment," meaning is created for the event which justifies the judge to herself and to others with respect to her role in the acts of violence. I do not wish to downplay the significance of such ideological functions of law. But the function of ideology is much more significant in justifying an order to those who principally benefit from it and who must defend it than it is in hiding the nature of the order from those who are its victims.

The ideology of punishment is not, of course, the exclusive property of judges. The concept operates in the general culture and is intelligible to and shared by prisoners, criminals and revolutionaries as well as judges. Why, then, should we not conclude that interpretation *is* the master concept of law, that the interpretive work of understanding "punishment" may be seen as mediating or making sense of the opposing acts and experiences of judge and defendant in the criminal trial? Naturally, one who is to be punished may have to be coerced. And punishment, if it is "just," supposedly legitimates the coercion or violence applied. The ideology of punishment may, then, operate successfully to justify our practices of criminal law to ourselves and, possibly, even to those who are or may come to be "punished" by the law.

There is, however, a fundamental difference between the way in which "punishment" operates as an ideology in popular or professional literature, in political debate, or in general discourse, and the way in which it operates in the context of the legal acts of trial, imposition of sentence, and execution. For as the judge interprets,

---

19. This point and others very similar to it are made routinely in the literature that comes out of prisons. *See, e.g.,* E. CLEAVER, SOUL ON ICE 128–30 (1968); J. WASHINGTON, A BRIGHT SPOT IN THE YARD: NOTES & STORIES FROM A PRISON JOURNAL 5 (1981).

using the concept of punishment, she also acts—through others—to restrain, hurt, render helpless, even kill the prisoner. Thus, any commonality of interpretation that may or may not be achieved is one that has its common meaning destroyed by the divergent experiences that constitute it. Just as the torturer and victim achieve a "shared" world only by virtue of their diametrically opposed experiences, so the judge and prisoner understand "punishment" through their diametrically opposed experiences of the punishing act. It is ultimately irrelevant whether the torturer and his victim share a common theoretical view on the justifications for torture—outside the torture room. They still have come to the confession through destroying in the one case and through having been destroyed in the other. Similarly, whether or not the judge and prisoner share the same philosophy of punishment, they arrive at the particular act of punishment having dominated and having been dominated with violence, respectively.

II. The Acts of Judges: Interpretations, Deeds and Roles

We begin, then, not with what the judges say, but with what they do.

The judges deal pain and death.

That is not all that they do. Perhaps that is not what they usually do. But they *do* deal death, and pain. From John Winthrop through Warren Burger they have sat atop a pyramid of violence, dealing . . .

In this they are different from poets, from critics, from artists. It will not do to insist on the violence of strong poetry, and strong poets. Even the violence of weak judges is utterly real—a naive but immediate reality, in need of no interpretation, no critic to reveal it.[20] Every prisoner displays its mark. Whether or not the violence

---

20. On the violence that strong poets do to their literary ancestors, see H. BLOOM, THE ANXIETY OF INFLUENCE (1973), H. BLOOM, THE BREAKING OF THE VESSELS (1982), and much of Bloom's other work since *Anxiety*. Judges, like all readers and writers of texts, do violence to their literary—i.e., judicial—forebearers. For an interesting application of Bloom's central thesis to law, see D. Cole, *Agon and Agora: Creative Misreadings in the First Amendment Tradition*, 95 YALE L.J. 857 (1986). Cole acknowledges that the connection of law to violence distinguishes legal from literary interpretation, though he does not, unfortunately, develop the point. *Id.*

of judges is justified is not now the point—only that it exists in fact and differs from the violence that exists in literature or in the metaphoric characterizations of literary critics and philosophers. I have written elsewhere that judges of the state are jurispathic—that they kill the diverse legal traditions that compete with the State.[21] Here, however, I am not writing of the jurispathic quality of the office, but of its homicidal potential.[22]

The dual emphasis on the *acts* of judges and on the violence of these acts leads to consideration of three characteristics of the interpretive dimension of judicial behavior. Legal interpretation is (1) a practical activity, (2) designed to generate credible threats and actual deeds of violence, (3) in an effective way. In order to explore the unseverable connection between legal interpretation and violence, each of these three elements must be examined in turn.

---

at 904.

The anxiety of juridical influence was rather aptly and nicely stated somewhat earlier by Learned Hand in his tribute to Cardozo, *Mr. Justice Cardozo*, 30 COLUM. L. REV. 9 (1939). My point here is not that judges do not do the kind of figurative violence to literary parents that poets do, but that they carry out—in addition—a far more literal form of violence through their interpretations that poets do not share. It is significant, and has been much noted, that the immediacy of the connection between judge and violence of punishment has changed over the centuries. *See, e.g.,* M. FOUCAULT, DISCIPLINE AND PUNISH: THE BIRTH OF THE PRISON (A. Sheridan trans. 1977). Certainly in the United States today, the judge's obvious responsibility for the violence of punishment requires an appreciation—which all who live in this society acquire—of the organizational form of action. In that sense "naive" reality should not be taken to signify too much. One need not be sophisticated to understand the violence of judging, but neither is it as naive a form of violence as it would be if judges carried out their own sentencing. On the implications of this point, *see infra* pp. 234–36.

21. Cover, *supra* note 2, at 40–44.

22. The violence of judges and officials of a posited constitutional order is generally understood to be implicit in the practice of law and government. Violence is so intrinsic to this activity, so taken for granted, that it need not be mentioned. For instance, read the Constitution. Nowhere does it state, as a general principle, the obvious—that the government thereby ordained and established has the power to practice violence over its people. That, as a general proposition, need not be stated, for it is understood in the very idea of government. It is, of course, also directly implicit in many of the specific powers granted to the general government or to some specified branch or official of it. *E.g.,* U.S. CONST. art. I, § 8, cl. 1 ("Power To lay and collect Taxes . . . and provide for the common Defence"); *id.,* cl. 6 ("To provide for the Punishment of counterfeiting"); *id.,* cl. 10 ("To define and punish Piracies"); *id.,* cl. 11 ("To declare War"); *id.,* cl. 15 ("To provide for calling forth the Militia to execute the Laws of the Union, suppress Insurrections and repel Invasions;"); *id.,* art. IV, § 2, cls. 2–3 (providing for rendition of fugitives from justice and service).

A. Legal Interpretation as a Practical Activity

Legal interpretation is a form of practical wisdom.[23] At its best it seeks to "impose *meaning* on the institution . . . and then to restructure it in the light of that meaning."[24] There is, however, a persistent

---

23. On practical wisdom, see ARISTOTLE, THE NICOMACHEAN ETHICS 1140a(24) to 1140b(30).

24. R. DWORKIN, *supra* note 2, at 47. Dworkin's opus, celebrating what he calls the "integrity" of coherent and consistent interpretation, stands within a long tradition of work elaborating on Aristotle's fundamental insight into the nature of deliberation. Aristotle assigned the broad area of normative deliberation, of which legal interpretation consists, to practical wisdom or *phronesis*, which he distinguished from speculative knowledge. ARISTOTLE, *supra* note 23, at 1139b(14) to 1140b(30). On *phronesis*, see also H. ARENDT, WILLING 59–62 (1977). Practical wisdom, according to Aristotle, is a form of applied understanding: it does not consist, like knowledge, of pre-existing truths. It entails deliberation—an activity which is senseless with respect to logical truth. Deliberation engages the relevance of past to present understandings through a reflexive "discovery" of what is implicit in past understanding. Technical knowledge also has applied character, but practical wisdom, being in the normative sphere, cannot be measured by an external standard such as usefulness, because it consists of the application of understanding to the shaping of self.

Hans Georg Gadamer elevated these characteristics of practical wisdom to the central place in what he called "the human sciences." H. GADAMER, TRUTH AND METHOD 5–10 and *passim* (G. Barden & J. Cummings eds., 2d ed. 1975). Gadamer found these interpersonal, constructive acts of understanding—hermeneutics or interpretations—most clearly exemplified in what he called "legal dogmatics." Gadamer's project may be understood in some measure as an attempt to comprehend all human understanding in terms of *phronesis;* that is, to take the category of applied thought that defines our situation as moral actors and generalize that situation to include all of life. "Understanding is, then, a particular case of the application of something universal to a particular situation." *Id.* at 278.

For Gadamer, Aristotle is the source—the one who places action and striving at the center of moral philosophy. "Aristotle's description of the ethical phenomenon and especially of the virtue of moral knowledge . . . is in fact a kind of model of the problems of hermeneutics. . . . Application is neither a subsequent nor a merely occasional part of the phenomenon of understanding, but codetermines it as a whole from the beginning." *Id.* at 289. Gadamer proceeds from Aristotle by incorporating Heidegger's fundamental insight that we are always situated in the world, building the future worlds we shall inhabit. We do this through interpretation which is simultaneously a discovery of what we know and a new understanding of this "known" that enables us to discover more about what we know. Building on Heidegger, Gadamer posits the unity of all hermeneutics, all interpretive activity. Because all understanding is a building of both self and the world, it is in some measure practical and social, and therefore never divorced from ethics.

The practice of legal interpretation by the judge is no different from any other hermeneutic exercise. It exemplifies the mutually and reflexively constructive effects of text, of prior understanding of text (tradition), of present application and understanding-as-applied, and of future commitment. And legal dogmatics are for

chasm between thought and action. It is one thing to understand what ought to be done, quite another thing to do it. Doing entails an act of will and may require courage and perseverance. In the case of an individual's actions, we commonly think such qualities are functions of motivation, character, or psychology.

Legal interpretation is practical activity in quite another sense, however. The judicial word is a mandate for the deeds of others. Were that not the case, the practical objectives of the deliberative process could be achieved, if at all, only through more indirect and risky means. The context of a judicial utterance is institutional behavior in which others, occupying preexisting roles, can be expected to act, to implement, or otherwise to respond in a specified way to the judge's interpretation. Thus, the institutional context ties the language act of practical understanding to the physical acts of others in a predictable, though not logically necessary, way.[25] These interpretations, then, are not only "practical," they are, themselves, practices.

Formally, on both a normative and descriptive level, there are or may be rules and principles which describe the relationship between the interpretive acts of judges and the deeds which may be expected to follow from them. These rules and principles are what H. L. A.

Gadamer the "model for the unity of dogmatic and historical interest and so also for the unity of hermeneutics as a whole." J. WEINSHEIMER, GADAMER'S HERMENEUTICS, A READING OF *Truth and Method* 194 (1985).

Gadamer's placement of legal dogmatics at the center of the general enterprise of understanding the human sciences represents an invitation—or perhaps a temptation—to those legal academics who conceive law as the building of a system of normative meaning. If one can begin to understand the entire world of the humanities, i.e., the many forms of interpretive activity, in terms of law, it should be possible to put this common element of interpretation at the heart of law itself. That, indeed, seems to have been the effect of the slow trickle down of ideas about interpretation to the legal academy in America.

Ronald Dworkin synthesizes these interpretativist ideas in his new work, *Law's Empire*. R. DWORKIN, *supra* note 2. *Law's Empire* is a major elaboration of the reflexive, deliberative form of practical wisdom rooted in Aristotle's *phronesis*. It also builds upon Dworkin's own earlier critique of legal positivism to render "interpretation" the central activity in the judicial act while keeping the judicial act central to law. I fully agree that the dominant form of legal thought ought to be interpretive in the extended sense of the term. However, the emergence of interpretation as a central motif does not, by itself, reflect upon the way in which the interpretive acts of judges are simultaneously performative utterances in an institutional setting for violent behavior.

25. One might say that institutions create the context for changing the contingent to the necessary. *See* H. ARENDT, *supra* note 24, at 14; *see also* J. SEARLE, SPEECH ACTS (1969).

Hart called "secondary rules."[26] At least some secondary rules and principles identify the terms of cooperation between interpretation specialists and other actors in a social organization. Prescriptive secondary materials purport to set the norms for what those relations ought to be; descriptive secondary rules and principles would generate an accurate prediction of what the terms of cooperation actually will be. Of course, in any given system there need be no particular degree of correspondence between these two sets of rules.

Secondary rules and principles provide the template for transforming language into action, word into deed. As such they occupy a critical place in the analysis of legal interpretation proposed here. The legal philosopher may hold up to us a model of a hypothetical judge who is able to achieve a Herculean understanding of the full body of legal and social texts relevant to a particular case, and from this understanding to arrive at the single legally correct decision.[27] But that mental interpretive act cannot give itself effect. The practice of interpretation requires an understanding of what others will do with such a judicial utterance and, in many instances, an adjustment to that understanding, regardless of how misguided one may think the likely institutional response will be. Failing this, the interpreter sacrifices the connection between understanding what ought to be done and the deed, itself. But bridging the chasm between thought and action in the legal system is never simply a matter of will. The gap between understanding and action roughly corresponds to differences in institutional roles and to the division of labor and of responsibility that these roles represent. Thus, what may be described as a problem of will with respect to the individual becomes, in an

---

26. H. L. A. HART, THE CONCEPT OF LAW 77–106 (1961). Dworkin has ably challenged the supposedly central role of secondary rules in a theory of law. R. DWORKIN, TAKING RIGHTS SERIOUSLY (1977). Dworkin's critique is most telling in undermining the idea that rules of recognition adequately account for certain principles which have the effect of law. See also Cover, supra note 2. However, some secondary rules of recognition are designed not to generate recognition of content of rules or principles but to recognize outcomes that are to be effectuated. That is, some secondary rules organize social cooperation in the violent deeds of the law. By and large the secondary rules that organize the law's violence are clearer and more hierarchical than those that organize the ideational content of the law. For an excellent review of the significance of Dworkin's position for the viability of legal positivism as a system, see Coleman, Negative and Positive Positivism, 11 J. LEG. STUD. 139 (1982).

27. See R. DWORKIN, supra note 26, at 105–30; see also infra note 61.

institutional context, primarily a problem in social organization. Elsewhere I have labeled the specialized understanding of this relation, between the interpretation of the judge and the social organization required to transform it into a reality, the hermeneutic of the texts of jurisdiction.[28] This specialized understanding must lie at the heart of official judging.

B. Interpretation within a System Designed to Generate Violence

The gulf between thought and action widens wherever serious violence is at issue, because for most of us, evolutionary, psychological, cultural and moral considerations inhibit the infliction of pain on other people. Of course, these constraints are neither absolute nor universal. There are some deviant individuals whose behavior is inconsistent with such inhibitions.[29] Furthermore, almost all people are fascinated and attracted by violence, even though they are at the same time repelled by it.[30] Finally, and most important for our purposes, in almost all people social cues may overcome or suppress the revulsion to violence under certain circumstances.[31] These limitations do not deny the force of inhibitions against violence. Indeed, both

---

28. Cover, *supra* note 2, at 53–60.

29. There are persons whose behavior is both violent toward others and apparently reckless in disregard of violent consequences to themselves. Moreover, this behavior is frequently accompanied by a strange lack of affect. The classification of such persons as suffering from mental illness is a matter of great dispute. Nonetheless, at the present time there are a variety of labels that may be appropriately applied on the basis of one authority or another. *See, e.g.,* AM. PSYCHIATRIC ASSOC., DIAGNOSTIC AND STATISTICAL MANUAL OF MENTAL DISORDERS 317–21 (3d ed. 1980) (diagnosing persons similar to those described above as suffering from "antisocial personality disorder"). For some earlier classifications, see W. McCORD & J. McCORD, THE PSYCHOPATH 39–55 (1964).

30. *See, e.g.,* C. FORD & F. BEACH, PATTERNS OF SEXUAL BEHAVIOR 64–65 (1951) (varying cultural responses to linking pain and sexuality). Whether there is a deeper sado-masochistic attraction to pain or violence involving more serious forms of imposition or suffering of pain that is similarly universal is a matter of dispute. The attaction to violence may also be accounted for in terms of an impulse of "aggression." *See generally* K. LORENZ, ON AGGRESSION (M. Wilson trans. 1966).

31. *See, e.g.,* S. MILGRAM, OBEDIENCE TO AUTHORITY (1974). The Milgram experiments are discussed and placed in the context of a much larger body of experimental work and anecdotal material on decisionmaking in I. JANIS & L. MANN, DECISION MAKING: A PSYCHOLOGICAL ANALYSIS OF CONFLICTS, CHOICE, AND COMMITMENT 268–71 (1977).

together create the conditions without which law would either be unnecessary or impossible. Were the inhibition against violence perfect, law would be unnecessary; were it not capable of being overcome through social signals, law would not be possible.

Because legal interpretation is as a practice incomplete without violence—because it depends upon the social practice of violence for its efficacy—it must be related in a strong way to the cues that operate to bypass or suppress the psycho-social mechanisms that usually inhibit people's actions causing pain and death. Interpretations which occasion violence are distinct from the violent acts they occasion. When judges interpret the law in an official context, we expect a close relationship to be revealed or established between their words and the acts that they mandate. That is, we expect the judges' words to serve as virtual triggers for action. We would not, for example, expect contemplations or deliberations on the part of jailers and wardens to interfere with the action authorized by judicial words. But such a routinization of violent behavior requires a form of organization that operates simultaneously in the domains of action and interpretation. In order to understand the violence of a judge's interpretive act, we must also understand the way in which it is transformed into a violent deed despite general resistance to such deeds; in order to comprehend the meaning of this violent deed, we must also understand in what way the judge's interpretive act authorizes and legitimates it.

While it is hardly possible to suggest a comprehensive review of the possible ways in which the organization of the legal system operates to facilitate overcoming inhibitions against intraspecific violence, I do wish to point to some of the social codes which limit these inhibitions. Here the literature of social psychology is helpful. The best known study and theory of social codes and their role in overcoming normal inhibitions against inflicting pain through violence is Milgram's *Obedience to Authority.*[32] In the Milgram experiments, subjects administered what they thought were actually painful electric shocks to persons who they thought were the experimental subjects. This was done under the direction or orders of supposed experimenters. The true experimental subjects—those who administered the shocks—showed a disturbingly high level of compliance with author-

---

32. S. Milgram, *supra* note 31.

ity figures despite the apparent pain evinced by the false experimental subjects. From the results of his experiment, Milgram has formulated a theory that is in some respects incomplete. The most developed part of the theory relies heavily on the distinction he draws between acting in an "autonomous" state and acting in an "agentic" state. Milgram posits the evolution of a human disposition to act "agentically" within hierarchies, since the members of organized hierarchies were traditionally more likely to survive than were members of less organized social groups. Concurrently, the "conscience" or "superego" evolved in response to the need for autonomous behavior or judgment given the evolution of social structures. It is this autonomous behavior which inhibits the infliction of pain on others. But the regulators for individual autonomous behavior had to be capable of being suppressed or subordinated to the characteristics of agentic behavior when individuals acted within an hierarchical structure.[33] In addition to his theories of species-specific evolutionary mechanisms, Milgram also points to the individual-specific and culture-specific forms of learning and conditioning for agentic behavior within hierarchical structures. Thus, in Milgram's explanation of the "agentic state," "institutional systems of authority" play a key role in providing the requisite cues for causing the shift from autonomous behavior to the agentic behavior cybernetically required to make hierarchies work.[34] According to Milgram, the cues for overcoming autonomous behavior or "conscience" consist of the institutionally sanctioned commands, orders, or signals of institutionally legitimated authorities characteristic of human hierarchical organization.[35]

There are, of course, a variety of alternative ways to conceptualize the facilitation of violence through institutional roles. One could point, for example, to the theory that human beings have a natural tendency, an instinctual drive, to aggression, and that a vari-

---

33. *Id.* at 135–38. Milgram even suggests that there may be chemoneurological regulators of that subordination.

34. *Id.* at 123–64.

35. *Id.* at 125–30, 143–48. Milgram also quite properly subjects his theory to the question of whether the behavior elicited in his experiments might be better explained by postulating a general impulse or tendency to aggression which is built into the human being and which is normally suppressed by social factors. The experiments might then be understood as opportunities created by the removal of the social constraints upon violence for the pre-existing aggression to emerge. *Id.* at 165–68. It is not clear that the two theories are mutually exclusive.

ety of learned behaviors keep aggression within bounds. The institutionally specified occasions for violence may then be seen as outlets
for the aggression that we ordinarily would seek to exercise but for
the restraints. Some scholars have, from a psychoanalytic perspective,
hypothesized that formal structures for the perpetration of violence
permit many individuals to deny themselves the fulfillment of aggressive wishes by "delegating" the violent activity to others.[36]

There is an enormous difference between Milgram's theory of
institutionalized violence and Anna Freud's or Konrad Lorenz's, and
between the assumptions about human nature which inform them.
But common to all of these theories is a behavioral observation in
need of explanation. Persons who act within social organizations that
exercise authority act violently without experiencing the normal inhibitions or the normal degree of inhibition which regulates the behavior
of those who act autonomously. When judges interpret, they trigger
agentic behavior within just such an institution or social organization.
On one level judges may appear to be, and may in fact be, offering
their understanding of the normative world to their intended audience.
But on another level they are engaging a violent mechanism through
which a substantial part of their audience loses its capacity to think
and act autonomously.

C. Interpretation and the Effective Organization
of Violence

A third factor separates the authorization of violence as a deliberative,
interpretive exercise from the deed. Deeds of violence are rarely
suffered by the victim apart from a setting of domination.[37] That

---

36. Anna Freud follows Stone in calling the phenomenon "delegation." "The
individual denies himself the fulfillment of aggressive wishes but concedes permission
for it to some higher agency such as the state, the police, the military or legal
authorities." A. Freud, *Comments on Aggression*, in PSYCHOANALYTIC PSYCHOLOGY
OF NORMAL DEVELOPMENT 161 (1981) (Vol. VIII of THE WRITINGS OF ANNA FREUD).
I am indebted to Diane Cover for this reference.

37. My colleague, Harlon Dalton, reports a view among some people who have
clerked for judges on the Second Circuit Court of Appeals that the judges seem
reluctant to affirm convictions from the bench when they believe the defendant to
be in the courtroom. Dalton suggests two reasons for the tendency to reserve decision
in such cases. First, the judges desire to give the appearance of deliberation in order
to minimize, to the extent possible, the loser's dissatisfaction with the outcome;
second, and more important, the judges desire to avoid having a disgruntled defendant

setting may be manifestly coercive and violent or it may be the product of a history of violence which conditions the expectations of the actors. The imposition of violence depends upon the satisfaction of the social preconditions for its effectiveness. Few of us are courageous or foolhardy enough to *act* violently in an uncompromisingly principled fashion without attention to the likely responses from those upon whom we would impose our wills.[38]

If legal interpretation entails action in a field of pain and death, we must expect, therefore, to find in the act of interpretation attention to the *conditions of effective domination.* To the extent that effective domination is not present, either our understanding of the law will be adjusted so that it will require only that which can reasonably be expected from people in conditions of reprisal, resistance and revenge,[39] or there will be a crisis of credibility. The law may come

(whose inhibitions against perpetrating violence are not what they might be) decide to "approach the bench," as it were. Dalton relates the scene he witnessed when clerking for a then-quite-new district judge who made the mistake of pronouncing sentence in the small robing room behind the courtroom. (The courtroom was temporarily unavailable for one reason or another.) The defendant's request that his family be present during sentencing was of course granted. As a result, the judge had to confront a weeping wife, dejected children, a lawyer who was now able to emote on an intimate stage, and a defendant who was able to give his allocution eye-to-eye with the judge from a distance of, at most, ten feet. It was impossible, therefore, for the judge to hide or insulate himself from the violence that would flow from the words he was about to utter, and he was visibly shaken as he pronounced sentence. Even so, neither he nor Dalton was prepared for what followed. The defendant began alternately shouting and begging the judge to change his mind; his wife began sobbing loudly; the defendant lurched forward with no apparent purpose in mind except, literally, to get to the judge who was doing this awful thing to him. Because the seating in the robing room was not designed with security in mind, it took the marshall a moment or two—a long moment or two—to restrain the defendant. Then, because the room's only exit was behind where the defendant and his family had been seated, the judge had to wait until they were, respectively, forced and importuned to leave before he could make his exit, thus witnessing first hand how his words were translated into deeds. I am grateful to Harlon Dalton for these accounts.

38. It is the fantasy of so acting which accounts for the attraction of so many violent heroes. Where systems of deterrence and justice do in fact depend, or have depended, upon high risk acts of violence, there have been great temptations to avoid too high principles. In many feuding societies the principle social problem appears not to have been how to stop feuds, but how to get reluctant protagonists to act in such a manner as to protect vulnerable members or avenge them. Miller, *Choosing the Avenger: Some Aspects of the Bloodfeud in Medieval Iceland and England,* 1 LAW AND HIST. REV. 159, 160–62, 175 (1983).

39. See the corpus of Miller's work on the Icelandic feuds. *Id.* at 175–94. *See*

over time to bear only an uncertain relation to the institutionally implemented deeds it authorizes. Some systems, especially religious ones, can perpetuate and even profit from a dichotomy between an ideal law and a realizable one.[40] But such a dichotomy has immense implications *if built into* the law. In our own secular legal system, one must assume this to be an undesirable development.

D. Legal Interpretation as Bonded Interpretation

Legal interpretation, therefore, can never be "free;" it can never be the function of an understanding of the text or word alone. Nor can it be a simple function of what the interpreter conceives to be merely a reading of the "social text," a reading of all relevant social data. Legal interpretation must be capable of transforming itself into action; it must be capable of overcoming inhibitions against violence in order to generate its requisite deeds; it must be capable of massing a sufficient degree of violence to deter reprisal and revenge.

In order to maintain these critical links to effective violent behavior, legal interpretation must reflexively consider its own social organization. In so reflecting, the interpreter thereby surrenders something of his independence of mind and autonomy of judgment, since the legal meaning that some hypothetical Hercules (Hyporcules) might construct out of the sea of our legal and social texts is only one element in the institutional practice we call law. Coherent legal meaning is an element in legal interpretation. But it is an element potentially in tension with the need to generate effective action in a violent context. And neither effective action nor coherent meaning can be maintained, separately or together, without an entire structure of social cooperation. Thus, legal interpretation is a form of bonded interpretation, bound at once to practical application (to the deeds

---

also W. Miller, *Gift, Sale, Payment, Raid: Case Studies in the Negotiation and Classification of Exchange in Medieval Iceland*, 61 SPECULUM 18–50 (1986); *cf.* E. AYERS, VENGEANCE AND JUSTICE: CRIME AND PUNISHMENT IN THE 19TH CENTURY AMERICAN SOUTH 18 (1984) ("Honor and legalism . . . are incompatible. . . .").

40. For example, the account of the dispute within Shi'ite legal theory as to whether it was permissible to set up an avowedly Shiah government before the advent of the Twelfth Imam reflects this dichotomy in a religious context. *See* R. MOTTAHEDEH, THE MANTLE OF THE PROPHET: RELIGION AND POLITICS IN IRAN 172–73 (1985). According to Shi'ite belief, only the advent of this "Imam of the age" would bring the possibility of a perfect Islamic political community. *Id.* at 92–93.

it implies) and to the ecology of jurisdictional roles (the conditions of effective domination). The bonds are reciprocal. For the deeds of social violence as we know them also require that they be rendered intelligible—that they be both subject to interpretation and to the specialized and constrained forms of behavior that are "roles." And the behavior within roles that we expect can neither exist without the interpretations which explain the otherwise meaningless patterns of strong action and inaction, nor be intelligible without understanding the deeds they are designed to effectuate.

Legal interpretation may be the act of judges or citizens, legislators or presidents, draft resisters or right-to-life protesters. Each kind of interpreter speaks from a distinct institutional location. Each has a differing perspective on factual and moral implications of any given understanding of the Constitution. The understanding of each will vary as roles and moral commitments vary. But considerations of word, deed, and role will always be present in some degree. The relationships among these three considerations are created by the practical, violent context of the practice of legal interpretation, and therefore constitute the most significant aspect of the legal interpretive process.

III. Interpretation and Effective Action: The Case of Criminal Sentencing

The bonded character of legal interpretation can be better appreciated by further unpacking a standard judicial act—the imposition of a sentence in a criminal case—this time from the judge's perspective. Such an act has few of the problematic remedial and role complications that have occupied commentators on the judicial role with regard to affirmative relief in institutional reform litigation or complex "political questions" cases.[41] In imposing sentences in criminal cases, judges are doing something clearly within their province. I do not mean to suggest that there are not disagreements about how the act should be carried out—whether with much or little discretion,

---

41. My argument is not simply that there are prudential considerations in some sub-class of cases that render it wise or politic or necessary for the judge to defer to supposed wishes or policies of other political actors. Rather, my point here is that in every act—even one thought to "belong" to judges—there is a necessary element of deference to the requirements of transforming judicial thought into violent action.

whether attending more to objective and quantifiable criteria or to subjective and qualitative ones. But the act is and long has been a judicial one, and one which requires no strange or new modes of interaction with other officials or citizens.

Taken for granted in this judicial act is the structure of cooperation that ensures, we hope, the effective domination of the present and prospective victim of state violence—the convicted defendant. The role of judge becomes dangerous, indeed, whenever the conditions for domination of the prisoner and his allies are absent. Throughout history we have seen the products of ineffective domination in occasional trials in our country and in many instances in other nations.[42] The imposition of a sentence thus involves the roles of police, jailers or other enforcers who will restrain the prisoner (or set him free subject to effective conditions for future restraint) upon the order of the judge, and guards who will secure the prisoner from rescue and who will protect the judge, prosecutors, witnesses and jailers from revenge.

The judge in imposing a sentence normally takes for granted the role structure which might be analogized to the "transmission" of the engine of justice. The judge's interpretive authorization of the "proper" sentence can be carried out as a deed only because of these others; a bond between word and deed obtains only because a system of social cooperation exists. That system guarantees the judge massive amounts of force—the conditions of effective domination—if necessary. It guarantees—or is supposed to—a relatively faithful adherence to the word of the judge in the deeds carried out against the prisoner.

A. Revealing Latent Role Factors

If the institutional structure—the system of roles—gives the judge's understanding its effect, thereby transforming understanding into

---

42. Ineffective domination has resulted, for example, in the extraordinary security precautions that take place in the more significant mafia trials in Italy. It is reflected in the failures of Weimar justice. *See* P. GAY, WEIMAR CULTURE: THE OUTSIDER AS INSIDER 20–21 (1968). We ought not to assume that our own legal system is entirely free from such problems. While judges, on the whole, have fared remarkably well given the number of people whom they injure, there are occasional instances of violence directed at judges. And the problem of protecting witnesses is a persistent and serious one for the criminal justice system.

"law," so it confers meaning on the deeds which effect this transformation, thereby legitimating them as "lawful." A central task of the legal interpreter is to attend to the problematic aspects of the integration of role, deed, and word, not only where the violence (i.e., enforcement) is lacking for meaning, but also where meaning is lacking for violence.

In a nation like ours, in which the conditions of state domination are rarely absent, it is too easy to assume that there will be faithful officials to carry out what the judges decree, and judges available to render their acts lawful. Just how crucial this taken-for-granted structure is may be appreciated by examining a case in which it is lacking. The decisions by Judge Herbert Stern in *United States v. Tiede*[43] display an unusually lucid appreciation of the significance of the institutional connections between the judicial word and the violent deeds it authorizes.

Judge Stern was (and is) a federal district judge in New Jersey. In 1979 he was appointed an Article II judge for the United States Court for Berlin. This unique event, the only convening of the Court for Berlin, was a response to the reluctance of West Germany to prosecute two skyjackers who had used a toy gun to threaten the crew of a Polish airliner en route from Gdansk to East Berlin and had forced it to land in West Berlin. The formal status of Berlin as an "occupied" city enabled the Germans to place the responsibility for prosecution of the skyjacker-refugees upon the Americans.[44]

Stern wrote a moving account of the unusual trial which ensued, including his long struggle with the United States government over the general question of whether the Constitution of the United States would govern the proceedings. After a jury trial, opposed by the prosecution, and a verdict of guilty on one of the charges, Stern was required to perform the "simple" interpretive act of imposing the appropriate sentence. As a matter of interpreting the governing materials on sentencing it might indeed have been a "simple" act—one in which relatively unambiguous German law was relatively unambig-

---

43. 86 F.R.D. 227 (U.S. Ct. for Berlin 1979). The reported opinion encompasses only certain procedural questions that arose in the trial, primarily the question of whether the defendants were entitled to a jury trial. A comprehensive account of the trial and the various rulings made during its course can be found in H. STERN, JUDGMENT IN BERLIN (1984).

44. H. STERN, *supra* note 43, at 3–61.

uously to be applied by virtue of American law governing a court of occupation.[45]

Stern brilliantly illuminated the defects in such a chain of reasoning. The judicial interpretive act in sentencing issues in a deed—the actual performance of the violence of punishment upon a defendant. But these two—judicial word and punitive deed—are connected only by the social cooperation of many others, who in their roles as lawyers, police, jailers, wardens, and magistrates perform the deeds which judicial words authorize. Cooperation among these officials is usually simply assumed to be present, but, of course, the conditions which normally ensure the success of this cooperation may fail in a variety of ways.

This is Judge Stern's account of his sentencing of the defendant, Hans Detlef Alexander Tiede:

> Gentlemen [addressing the State Department and Justice Department lawyers], I will not give you this defendant. . . . I have kept him in your custody now for nine months, nearly. . . . You have persuaded me. I believe, now, that you recognize no limitations of due process. . . .
>
> I don't have to be a great prophet to understand that there is probably not a great future for the United States Court for Berlin here. [Stern had just been officially "ordered" not to proceed with a civil case brought against the United States in Stern's Court. The case was a last ditch attempt in a complicated proceeding in which the West Berlin government had acquired park land—allegedly in violation of German law—for construction of a housing complex for the United States Army Command in Berlin. The American occupation officials had refused to permit the German courts to decide the case as it affected the interests of the occupation authority. American Ambassador Walter Stoessel had officially written Stern on the day before the sen-

---

45. There were several significant interpretive issues involved in the sentencing other than the one treated below: for example, whether an offer of a deal by the prosecution to the defendant in return for not persisting with the demand for a jury trial should operate to limit any sentence imposed to one no more severe than the proffered deal, *id.* at 344–45, and whether the judge was obligated to apply German law which carried a mandatory minimum sentence of three years for the offense of which Tiede was convicted, *id.* at 350–55.

tencing that "your appointment as a Judge of the United States
Court for Berlin does not extend to this matter."[46]

. . . .

Under those circumstances, who will be here to protect Tiede
if I give him to you for four years? Viewing the Constitution as
nonexistent, considering yourselves not restrained in any way,
who will stand between you and him? What judge? What independent magistrate do you have here? What independent magistrate will you permit here?

When a judge sentences, he commits a defendant to the
custody—in the United States he says, 'I commit to the custody
of the Attorney General of the United States'—et cetera. Here I
suppose he says, I commit to the custody of the Commandant,
or the Secretary of State, or whatever. . . . I will not do it. Not
under these circumstances. . . .

I sentence this defendant to time served. You . . . are a free man
right now.[47]

Herbert Stern's remarkable sentence is not simply an effective,
moving plea for judicial independence, a plea against the subservience
which Stern's government tried to impose. It is a dissection of the
anatomy of criminal punishment in a constitutional system. As such,
it reveals the interior role of the judicial word in sentencing. It reveals
the necessity of a latent role structure to render the judicial utterance
morally intelligible. And it proclaims the moral unintelligibility of
routine judicial utterance when the structure is no longer there.
Almost all judicial utterance becomes deed through the acts of
others—acts embedded in roles. The judge must see, as Stern did,
that the meaning of her words may change when the roles of these
others change. We tend overwhelmingly to assume that constitutional
violence is always performed within institutionally sanctioned limits
and subject to the institutionally circumscribed, role-bound action of
others. Stern uncovered the unreliability of that assumption in the
Berlin context and "reinterpreted" his sentence accordingly.[48]

---

46. *Id.* at 353.

47. *Id.* at 370.

48. Judge Stern confronted an unusual situation—no independent system of
courts, and no *explicit* denial by those in control of official violence that their power
was constitutionally limited. In a sense the situation was one of *de jure* lawlessness.

B. The Death Sentence as an Interpretive Act
of Violence

The questions of whether the death sentence is constitutionally permissible and, if it is, whether to impose it, are among the most difficult problems a judge encounters. While the grammar of the capital sentence may appear to be similar to that of any other criminal sentence, the capital sentence as interpretive act is unique in at least three ways. The judge must interpret those constitutional and other legal texts which speak to the question of the proper or permissible occasions for imposition of a capital sentence. She must understand the texts in the context of an application that prescribes the killing of another person. And she must act to set in motion the acts of others which will in the normal course of events end with someone killing the convicted defendant. Our judges do not *ever* kill the defendants themselves. They do not witness the execution. Yet, they are intensely aware of the deed their words authorize.[49]

The confused and emotional situation which now prevails with respect to capital punishment in the United States is in several ways a product of what I have described as the bonded character of legal interpretation—the complex structure of relationships between word and deed. To any person endowed with the normal inhibitions against the imposition of pain and death, the deed of capital punishment entails a special measure of the reluctance and abhorrence which constitute the gulf that must be bridged between interpretation and

---

But Stern's reasoning reaches beyond the case at hand; it may be extended to include, for example, the *de facto* state of lawlessness that attends life in many United States prisons. Institutional reform litigation—whether applied to prisons, schools, or hospitals—entails complex questions of judicial remedial power. Very often these questions are framed around problems of discretion in the administration of remedies. When deciding whether to issue an injunction, judges often "interpret" the law in light of the difficulties involved in effectuating their judgments. But Stern's decision in *Tiede* pursues a different path. A judge may or may not be able to change the deeds of official violence, but she may always withhold the justification for this violence. She may or may not be able to bring a good prison into being, but she can refrain from sentencing anyone to a constitutionally inadequate one. Some judges have in fact followed this course. *See, e.g.,* Barnes v. Government of the Virgin Islands, 415 F. Supp. 1218 (D.V.I. 1976).

49. Contrast the discreet distance judges now keep from capital sentences with the pageant of capital punishment in Hay, *Property, Authority and the Criminal Law,* in ALBION'S FATAL TREE: CRIME AND SOCIETY IN EIGHTEENTH-CENTURY ENGLAND 28–29 (1975).

action. Because in capital punishment the action or *deed* is extreme and irrevocable, there is pressure placed on the *word*—the interpretation that establishes the legal justification for the act.[50] At the same time, the fact that capital punishment constitutes the most plain, the most deliberate, and the most thoughtful manifestation of legal interpretation as violence makes the imposition of the sentence an especially powerful test of the faith and commitment of the interpreters.[51] Not even the facade of civility, where it exists, can obscure the violence of a death sentence.

Capital cases, thus, disclose far more of the structure of judicial interpretation than do other cases. Aiding this disclosure is the agonistic character of law: The defendant and his counsel search for and exploit any part of the structure that may work to their advantage. And they do so to an extreme degree in a matter of life and death.[52]

Thus, in the typical capital case in the United States, the judge is constantly reminded of that which the defense constantly seeks to exploit: The structure of interdependent roles that Judge Stern found to be potentially lacking in Berlin in the *Tiede* case. Consider. Not only do the actors in these roles carry out the judicial decision—they await it! All of them know that the judges will be called upon, time and again, to consider exhaustively all interpretive avenues that the defense counsel might take to avoid the sentence. And they expect

---

50. This pressure for more certain justification of the death sentence lies behind the development of the "super due process" position with regard to death penalty cases. *See, e.g.,* Radin, *Cruel Punishment and Respect for Persons: Super Due Process for Death,* 53 S. CAL. L. REV. 1143 (1980) (describing Supreme Court's Eighth Amendment procedural safeguards). No more powerful statement of the ultimate implications of this position is to be found than in C. BLACK, CAPITAL PUNISHMENT: THE INEVITABILITY OF CAPRICE AND MISTAKE (2d ed. 1981).

51. The decade-long moratorium on death sentences may quite intelligibly be understood as a failure of will on the part of a majority of the Court which had, at some point in that period, decided *both* that there was to be no general constitutional impediment to the imposition of the death sentence, *and* that they were not yet prepared to see the states begin a series of executions. Of course, throughout the period, new procedural issues were arising. But it does not seem far-fetched to suppose that there was also a certain squeamishness about facing the implications of the majority position on the constitutional issue. *See* Note, *Summary Processes and the Rule of Law: Expediting Death Penalty Cases in the Federal Courts,* 95 YALE L.J. 349, 354 (1985) (citing Court's "often uncertain and tortuous" death penalty jurisprudence during this period).

52. *See, e.g.,* Sullivan v. Wainwright, 464 U.S. 109, 112 (1983) (Burger, C.J., concurring in denial of stay) (Chief Justice Burger accused death penalty lawyers of turning "the administration of justice into a sporting contest").

that no capital sentence will in fact be carried out without several substantial delays during which judges consider some defense not yet fully decided by that or other courts.[53] The almost stylized action of the drama requires that the jailers stand visibly ready to receive intelligence of the judicial act—even if it be only the act of deciding to take future action. The stay of execution, though it be nothing— literally nothing—as an act of *textual* exegesis, nonetheless constitutes an important form of constitutional interpretation. For it shows the violence of the warden and executioner to be linked to the judge's deliberative act of understanding. The stay of execution, the special line open, permits, or more accurately, requires the inference to be drawn from the failure of the stay of execution. That too is the visible tie between word and deed.[54] These wardens, these guards, these doctors, jump to the judge's tune. If the deed is done, it is a con- stitutional deed—one integrated to and justifiable under the proper understanding of the word. In short, it is the stay, the drama of the possibility of the stay, that renders the execution constitutional vio- lence, that makes the deed an act of interpretation.

For, after all, executions I can find almost anywhere. If people disappear, if they die suddenly and without ceremony in prison, quite apart from any articulated justification and authorization for their demise, then we do not have constitutional interpretation at the heart of this deed, nor do we have the deed, the death, at the heart of the Constitution. The problem of incapacity or unwillingness to ensure a strong, virtually certain link between judicial utterance and violent deed in this respect characterizes certain legal systems at certain times.[55] It characterized much of the American legal system well into

---

53. The current Court (or a majority of it) is very hostile to such delays. Barefoot v. Estelle, 463 U.S. 880 (1983), Zant v. Stephens, 462 U.S. 862 (1983), California v. Ramos, 463 U.S. 992 (1983), and Barclay v. Florida, 463 U.S. 939 (1983), mark a reversal of the trend to permit or encourage a full hearing of all plausible claims or defenses. Nonetheless, even with this new impatience to be on with the execution, there are usually substantial delays at some point before execution.

54. Consider the opinions of the various Justices in Rosenberg v. United States, 346 U.S. 273 (1953), vacating, in special term, the stay of the sentence of death that had been granted by Justice Douglas. For an analysis of the deliberations, see Parrish, *Cold War Justice: The Supreme Court and the Rosenbergs*, 82 AM. HIST. REV. 805– 42 (1977).

55. *See, e.g.,* R. BROWN, STRAIN OF VIOLENCE, HISTORICAL STUDIES OF AMERICAN VIOLENCE AND VIGILANTISM 144–79 (1975) (discussing legal attitudes toward American vigilantism).

the twentieth century; lynching, for example, was long thought to be a peculiarly American scandal.[56] It was a scandal which took many forms. Often it entailed taking the punishment of alleged offenders out of the hands of courts entirely. But sometimes it entailed the carrying out of death sentences without abiding by the ordered processes of appeals and post-conviction remedies. Such was the outcome, for example, of the notorious "Leo Frank" case.[57]

The plain fact is that we have come a good way since 1914 with respect to our expectations that persons accused of capital crimes will be given a trial, will be sentenced properly, and will live to see the appointed time of the execution of their sentence. In fact, we have come to expect near perfect coordination of those whose role it is to inflict violence subject to the interpretive decisions of the judges. We have even come to expect coordinated cooperation in securing all plausible judicial interpretations on the subject.[58]

Such a well-coordinated form of violence is an achievement. The careful social understandings designed to accomplish the violence that is capital punishment, or to refrain from that act, are not fortuitous or casual products of circumstance. Rather, they are the products of design, tied closely to the secondary rules and principles which provide clear criteria for the recognition of these and other interpretive acts as, first and foremost, *judicial* acts. Their "meaning" is always secondary to their provenance. No wardens, guards or executioners wait for a telephone call from the latest constitutional law scholar,

56. *See* R. ZANGRANDO, THE NAACP CRUSADE AGAINST LYNCHING, 1909–1950, at 9–11 (1980).

57. Leo Frank was a Jewish New Yorker managing a pencil factory in Georgia. He was accused of having raped and murdered a 14-year-old employee of the factory. The trial (and conviction) took place amidst a mob atmosphere in which the Court was required to warn the defendant and his counsel not to be present in the courtroom at the rendering of the verdict lest they be violently harmed. After Frank's conviction he was forcibly removed from a prison labor gang and lynched. The case was instrumental in the formation of the B'nai Brith Anti-Defamation League. Collateral relief was denied by the Supreme Court in Frank v. Mangum, 237 U.S. 309 (1915), over the strong dissent of Justice Holmes and Justice Hughes.

58. I am not, of course, suggesting that unauthorized violence on the part of police, jailers, etc., no longer exists. But the quasi-public position that the "justice" of the mob should supplant the ordered process of the courts is no longer prevalent. See the extraordinary article by Charles Bonaparte, *Lynch Law and its Remedy*, 8 YALE L.J. 335, 336 (1899) (arguing that underlying purpose of lynching is "not to violate, but to vindicate, the law; or, to speak more accurately, . . . its 'adjective' part . . . is disregarded that its 'substantiative' [*sic*] part may be preserved").

jurisprude or critic before executing prisoners, no matter how com- pelling the interpretations of these others may be. And, indeed, they await the word of judges only insofar as that word carries with it the formal indicia of having been spoken in the judicial capacity. The social cooperation critical to the constitutional form of cooperation in violence is, therefore, also predicated upon the recognition of the judicial role and the recognition of the one whose utterance per- forms it.

There are, of course, some situations in which the judicial role is not well-defined but is contested. Nonetheless, social cooperation in constitutional violence as we know it requires at least that it be very clear who speaks as a judge and when. The hierarchical ordering among judicial voices must also be clear or subject to clarification. We have established, then, the necessity for rules and principles that locate authoritative interpreters and prescribe action on the basis of what they say. The rules and principles that locate authoritative voices for the purposes of action point to the defect in a model of judicial interpretation that centers around a single coherent and consistent mind at work. For here in the United States there is no set of secondary rules and principles more fundamental than those which make it impossible for any single judge, however Herculean her understanding of the law, ever to have the last word on legal meaning as it affects real cases. In the United States—with only trivial exceptions—no judge sitting alone on a significant legal issue is immune from appel- late review. Conversely, whenever any judge sits on the court of last resort on a significant legal issue, that judge does not sit alone. A complex of secondary rules determines this situation. These rules range from the statutes which generally give a right to at least one appeal from final judgments of trial courts, to special statutes which require that there be appellate review of death sentences, to the constitutional guarantee that the writ of habeas corpus not be sus- pended.[59] Final appellate courts in the United States have always had at least three judges. Some state constitutions specify the number. No explicit provision in the United States Constitution defines the Supreme Court in such a way that requires that it be made up of

---

59. See, e.g., 28 U.S.C. § 1291 (1982) (providing for appeals as of right from final decisions of district courts); id §§ 46(b), 46(c) (providing for hearing of cases by U.S. Courts of Appeals in panels of three judges unless rehearing en banc is ordered); U.S. CONST. art I, § 9, cl. 2 (protecting writ of habeus corpus).

more than a single judge. But both invariant practice and basic
understandings since 1789 have made the idea of a single-Justice
Supreme Court a practical absurdity. Given the clarity of the expectation that Supreme judicial bodies be plural, it seems doubtful to
me whether such an imaginary Court should be held to satisfy the
constitutional requirement that there be a Supreme Court.[60]

If some hypothetical Herculean judge should achieve an understanding of constitutional and social texts—an interpretation—such
that she felt the death penalty to be a permissible and appropriate
punishment in a particular case, she would be confronted at once
with the problem of translating that conviction into a deed. Her very
understanding of the constitutionality of the death penalty and the
appropriateness of its imposition would carry with it—as part of the
understanding—the knowledge that she could not carry out the sentence herself. The most elementary understanding of our social practice of violence ensures that a judge know that she herself cannot
actually pull the switch. This is not a trivial convention. For it means
that someone else will have the duty and opportunity to pass upon
what the judge has done. Were the judge a trial judge, and should
she hand down an order to execute, there would be another judge
to whom application could be made to stay or reverse her decision.
The fact that *someone else* has to carry out the execution means that
this someone else may be confronted with two pieces of paper: let
us say a warrant for execution of the sentence of death at a specified
time and place and a stay of execution from an appellate tribunal.
The someone else—the warden, for simplicity's sake—is expected to
determine which of these two pieces of paper to act upon according
to some highly arbitrary, hierarchical principles which have nothing
to do with the relative merits or demerits of the arguments which
justify the respective substantive positions.

It is crucial to note here that if the warden should cease paying
relatively automatic heed to the pieces of paper which flow in from
the judges according to these arbitrary and sometimes rigid hierar-

---

60. 28 U.S.C. § 1 (1982) (providing for Supreme Court of nine Justices, of whom
six constitute a quorum). The one rather significant historical exception to the generalization in the text gives me some pause with respect to the conclusion about the
constitutionality of a single-Justice Supreme Court. It is true, of course, that the
Chancellor was, in form, a single-justice high court. And, while it has not been the
rule, some American court systems have preserved a chancery, though often with
multi-judge appellate courts in equity.

chical rules and principles, the judges would lose their capacity to do violence. They would be left with only the opportunity to persuade the warden and his men to do violence. Conversely, the warden and his men would lose their capacity to shift to the judge primary moral responsibility for the violence which they themselves carry out. They would have to pass upon the justifications for violence in every case themselves, thereby turning the trial into a sort of preliminary hearing. There are, indeed, many prisons in this world that bear some resemblance to this hypothetical situation. There are systems in which the most significant punishment decisions are made by those who either perform or have direct supervisory authority over the performance of the violence itself.

We have done something strange in our system. We have rigidly separated the act of interpretation—of understanding what ought to be done—from the carrying out of this "ought to be done" through violence. At the same time we have, at least in the criminal law, rigidly linked the carrying out of judicial orders to the act of judicial interpretation by relatively inflexible hierarchies of judicial utterances and firm obligations on the part of penal officials to heed them. Judges are both separated from, and inextricably linked to, the acts they authorize.

This strange yet familiar attribute of judging in America has the effect of ensuring that no judge *acts* alone. Ronald Dworkin's "Judge as Hercules"[61] may appear to be a useful construct for understanding how a judge's mind ought to work. But it is misleading precisely because it suggests, if it does not require, a context which, in America, is never present. There may or may not be any sense in thinking about a judicial understanding of the law apart from its application. But one thing is near certain. The application of legal understanding in our domain of pain and death will always require the active or passive acquiescence of other judicial minds. It is possible to wear this point down to the most trite observation of professional practice. A judge who wishes to transform her understanding into deed must, if located on a trial court, attend to ensuring that her decision not

---

61. Dworkin's Hercules appears first in the article "Hard Cases." Dworkin, *Hard Cases*, 89 HARV. L. REV. 1057 (1975). Hercules lives on in LAW'S EMPIRE, *supra* note 2, at 239–75, wherein he assumes the mantle of a model judge of "integrity," which seems not to be primarily a personal quality for Dworkin but an interpretive posture which values intellectual consistency and coherence. *Id.* at 164–67.

be reversed. If on an appellate court, she must attend to getting at least one other judge to go along. It is a commonplace that many "majority" opinions bear the scars or marks of having been written primarily to keep the majority. Many a trial court opinion bears the scars of having been written primarily to avoid reversal.

Now the question arises, which is the true act of legal interpretation? The hypothetical understanding of a single mind placed in the admittedly hypothetical position of being able to render final judgments sitting alone? Or the actual products of judges acting under the constraint of potential group oversight of all decisions that are to be made real through collective violence? The single decision of a hypothetical Hercules is likely to be more articulate and coherent than the collective decision of many judges who may make compromises to arrive at that decision. But Hyporcules does not and cannot carry the force of collective violence. This defect is intrinsic to the definition of legal interpretation as a mental activity of a person rather than as the violent activity of an organization of people.

So let us be explicit. If it seems a nasty thought that death and pain are at the center of legal interpretation, so be it. It would not be better were there only a community of argument, of readers and writers of texts, of interpreters. As long as death and pain are part of our political world, it is essential that they be at the center of the law. The alternative is truly unacceptable—that they be within our polity but outside the discipline of the *collective* decision rules and the individual efforts to achieve outcomes through those rules. The fact that we require many voices is not, then, an accident or peculiarity of our jurisdictional rules. It is intrinsic to whatever achievement is possible in the domesticating of violence.

Conclusion

There is a worthy tradition that would have us hear the judge as a voice of reason; see her as the embodiment of principle. The current academic interest in interpretation, the attention to community of meaning and commitment, is apologetic neither in its intent or effect. The trend is, by and large, an attempt to hold a worthy ideal before what all would agree is an unredeemed reality. I would not quarrel with the impulse that leads us to this form of criticism.

There is, however, danger in forgetting the limits which are intrin-

sic to this activity of legal interpretation; in exaggerating the extent
to which any interpretation rendered as part of the act of state violence can ever constitute a common and coherent meaning. I have
emphasized two rather different kinds of limits to the commonality
and coherence of meaning that can be achieved. One kind of limit
is a practical one which follows from the social organization of legal
violence. We have seen that in order to do that violence safely and
effectively, responsibility for the violence must be shared; law must
operate as a system of cues and signals to many actors who would
otherwise be unwilling, incapable or irresponsible in their violent
acts. This social organization of violence manifests itself in the secondary rules and principles which generally ensure that no single
mind and no single will can generate the violent outcomes that follow
from interpretive commitments. No single individual can render any
interpretation operative as law—as authority for the violent act.
While a convergence of understandings on the part of all relevant
legal actors is not necessarily impossible, it is, in fact, very unlikely.
And, of course, we cannot flee from the multiplicity of minds and
voices that the social organization of law-as-violence requires to some
hypothetical decision process that would aggregate the many voices
into one. We know that—aside from dictatorship—there is no aggre-
gation rule that will necessarily meet elementary conditions for rationality in the relationships among the social choices made.[62]

While our social decision rules cannot guarantee coherence and
rationality of meaning, they can and do generate violent action which
may well have a distinct coherent meaning for at least one of the
relevant actors. We are left, then, in this actual world of the organization of law-as-violence with decisions whose meaning is not likely
to be coherent if it is common, and not likely to be common if it is
coherent.

This practical, contingent limit upon legal interpretation is, however, the less important and less profound of the two kinds of limits
I have presented. For if we truly attend to legal interpretation as it
is practiced on the field of fear, pain, and death, we find that the
principal impediment to the achievement of common and coherent
meaning is a necessary limit, intrinsic to the activity. Judges, officials,
resisters, martyrs, wardens, convicts, may or may not share common

---

62. K. Arrow, Social Choice and Individual Values (1951).

texts; they may or may not share a common vocabulary, a common cultural store of gestures and rituals; they may or may not share a common philosophical framework. There will be in the immense human panorama a continuum of degrees of commonality in all of the above. But as long as legal interpretation is constitutive of violent behavior as well as meaning, as long as people are committed to using or resisting the social organizations of violence in making their interpretations real, there will always be a tragic limit to the common meaning that can be achieved.

The perpetrator and victim of organized violence will undergo achingly disparate significant experiences. For the perpetrator, the pain and fear are remote, unreal, and largely unshared. They are, therefore, almost never made a part of the interpretive artifact, such as the judicial opinion. On the other hand, for those who impose the violence the justification is important, real and carefully culti- vated. Conversely, for the victim, the justification for the violence recedes in reality and significance in proportion to the overwhelming reality of the pain and fear that is suffered.

Between the idea and the reality of common meaning falls the shadow of the violence of law, itself.

Chapter 6

Obligation: A Jewish Jurisprudence of the Social Order

I. Fundamental Words

Every legal culture has its fundamental words. When we define our subject this weekend as human rights, we also locate ourselves in a normative universe at a particular place. The word "rights" is a highly evocative one for those of us who have grown up in the post-enlightenment secular society of the West. Even those among us who have been graced with a deep and abiding religious background can hardly have escaped the evocations that the terminology of "rights" carries. Indeed, we try in this conference to take a little credit here and there for the lustre which the edifice of rights reflects, perhaps suggesting now and again that the fine reflection owes something to some ultimate source of the light.

Judaism is, itself, a legal culture of great antiquity. It has hardly led a wholly autonomous existence these past three millennia. Yet, I suppose it can lay as much claim as any of the other great legal cultures to have an integrity to its basic categories. When I am asked to reflect upon Judaism and human rights, therefore, the first thought that comes to mind is that the categories are wrong. I do not mean, of course, that basic ideas of human dignity and worth are not powerfully expressed in the Jewish legal and literary traditions. Rather, I mean that because it is a legal tradition Judaism has its own categories for expressing through law the worth and dignity of each human being. And the categories are not closely analogous to "human rights." The principal word in Jewish law, which occupies a place equivalent in evocative force to the American legal system's "rights," is the word "mitzvah" which literally means commandment but has a general meaning closer to "incumbent obligation."

239

Before I begin an analysis of the differing implications of these two rather different key words, I should like to put the two words in a context—the contexts of their respective myths. For both of us these words are connected to fundamental stories and receive their force from those stories as much as from the denotative meaning of the words themselves. The story behind the term "rights" is the story of social contract. The myth postulates free and independent if highly vulnerable beings who voluntarily trade a portion of their autonomy for a measure of collective security. The myth makes the collective arrangement the product of individual choice and thus secondary to the individual. "Rights" are the fundamental category because it is the normative category which most nearly approximates that which is the source of the legitimacy of everything else. Rights are traded for collective security. But some rights are retained and, in some theories, some rights are inalienable. In any event the first and fundamental unit is the individual and "rights" locate him as an individual separate and apart form every other individual.

I must stress that I do not mean to suggest that all or even most theories that are founded upon rights are "individualistic" or "atomistic." Nor would I suggest for a moment that with a starting point of "rights" and social contract one must get to a certain end. Hobbes as well as Locke is part of this tradition. And, of course, so is Rousseau. Collective solutions as well as individualistic ones are possible but, it is the case that even the collective solutions are solutions which arrive at their destination by way of a theory which derives the authority of the collective from the individual. It is necessarily a theory which posits that that which was "given up" and therefore, at least implicitly, that which is desired, is a perfect freedom with all the alienated rights returned and the contradictions resolved.

The basic word of Judaism is obligation or mitzvah. It, too, is intrinsically bound up in a myth—the myth of Sinai. Just as the myth of social contract is essentially a myth of autonomy, so the myth of Sinai is essentially a myth of heteronomy. Sinai is a collective—indeed, a corporate—experience. The experience at Sinai is not chosen. The event gives forth the words which are commandments. In all Rabbinic and post-Rabbinic embellishment upon the Biblical account of Sinai this event is the Code for all Law. All law was given at Sinai and therefore all law is related back to the ultimate heteronomous event in which we were chosen—passive voice.

Now, just as the social contract theories generated Hobbes and others who bore a monstrous and powerful collective engine from the myth of individualism, so the Sinaitic myth has given rise to counter myths and accounts which stress human autonomy. The Rabbinic accounts of law-making autonomy are very powerful indeed, though they all conclude by suggesting that everything, even the questions yet to be asked by the brilliant students of the future and the answers to those questions—everything was given at Sinai. And, of course, therefore, all is, was, and has been commanded—and we are obligated to this command.

What have these stories to do with the ways in which the law languages of these respective legal cultures are spoken? Social movements in the United States organize around rights. When there is some urgently felt need to change the law or keep it in one way or another a "Rights" movement is started. Civil rights, the right to life, welfare rights, etc. The premium that is to be put upon an entitlement is so coded. When we "take rights seriously" we understand them to be trumps in the legal game. In Jewish law, an entitlement without an obligation is a sad, almost pathetic thing. There were, in ancient Rabbinic Judaism, many obligations from which a blind person was excused. One of the great Rabbis of the fourth century, Rabbi Joseph, who was blind, asked the great question of his colleagues: Is it greater to do the commandments out of love when one is not obligated to do them or is it greater to do the commandments out of obligation? He had at first assumed that to voluntarily comply with the commandments though not obligated to do so entailed a greater merit. But his colleagues held that to do the commandments out of obligation—more correctly, to do them as obligated—was the act which entailed greater merit. He then offered a feast for the Scholars if any could demonstrate that the great figure, Rabbi Judah's position that the blind were not obligated to do the commandments was erroneous.

Indeed, to be one who acts out of obligation is the closest thing there is to a Jewish definition of completion as a person within the community. A child does not become emancipated or "free" when he or she reaches maturity. Nor does she/he become *sui juris*. No, the child becomes bar or bat mitzvah, literally one who is of the obligations. Traditionally, the parent at that time says a blessing. Blessed is He that has exonerated me from the punishment of this child. The primary legal distinction between Jew and non-Jew is that the non-Jew is only obligated to the 7 Noachide commandments. Where women have been denied by traditional Judaism an equal participation in ritual, the reasoning of the traditional legist has been that women are not obligated in the same way as are men with respect to those ritual matters (public prayer). It is almost a sure sign of a nontraditional background for someone to argue that women in Judaism should have the right to be counted in the prayer quorum, to lead prayer services or be called to the Torah. Traditionalists who do argue for women's participation (and there are some who do), do so not on the basis of the rights. They argue rather that the law, properly understood, does or ought to impose on women the obligation of public prayer, of study of Torah, etc. For the logic of Jewish Law is such that once the obligation is understood as falling upon women, or whomever, then there is no question of "right" of participation. Indeed, the public role is a responsibility.

II. The Uses of Rights and Obligations

The Jewish legal system has evolved for the past 1900 years without a state and largely without much in the way of coercive powers to be exercised upon the adherents of the faith. I do not mean to idealize the situation. The Jewish communities over the millennia have wielded power. Communal sanctions of banning and shunning have been regularly and occasionally cruelly imposed on individuals or groups. Less frequently, but frequently enough, Jewish communities granted quasi-autonomy by gentile rulers, have used the power of the gentile state to discipline dissidents and deviants. Nonetheless, there remains a difference between wielding a power which draws on but also depends on pre-existing social solidarity, and, wielding one which depends on violence. There is also a difference between controlling the violence that is wielded autonomously and being dependent upon a potentially hostile power for that force. The Jewish legal apparatus had not had the autonomous use of violence at its disposal for two millennia which are, indeed, for all practical purposes the period in which Jewish Law as we know it came to be.

In a situation in which there is no centralized power and little in the way of coercive violence, it is critical that the mythic center of the Law reinforce the bonds of solidarity. Common, mutual, reciprocal obligation is necessary. The myth of divine commandment creates that web. It must also be pointed out that through most of the past two millennia there has been no well defined hierarchy of law articulating voices in Judaism. There have been times when great figures have lamented the cacophony of laws, and have understood it to be a condition imposed upon us for our sins. But another strain has almost rejoiced in the plethora of laws and has drawn strength from the traditional solution given by the Talmud to the question of whether the School of Hillel or the School of Shammai was truly correct. "Both are the words of the Living God." The acceptance of the idea that the single great mythic event of lawgiving can issue in apparently inconsistent precepts and understandings but that the apparent inconsistency can, itself, be the product of two correct readings of a larger understanding—that way of looking at the normative world—was immensely useful to a people doomed to live without an hierarchically determined authoritative voice. It was a myth that created legitimacy for a radically diffuse and coordinate system of authority. But while it created room for the diffusion of authority it did not have a place for individualism. One might have independent and divergent understandings of the obligations imposed by God through his chosen people, but one could not have a world view which denied the obligations.

The jurisprudence of rights, on the other hand, has gained ascendance in the Western world together with the rise of the national state with its almost unique mastery of violence over extensive territories. Certainly, it may be argued, it has been essential to counterbalance the development of the state with a myth which a) establishes the State as legitimate only in so far as it can be derived from the autonomous creatures who trade in their rights for security— i.e., one must tell a story about the State's utility or service to us, and b) potentially justifies individual and communal resistance to the Behemoth. It may be true as Bentham so aptly pointed out that natural rights may be used either apologetically or in revolutionary fashion, and there is nothing in the concept powerful enough analytically to constrain which use it shall be put to. Nevertheless, it is the case that natural right apologies are of a sort that in their articulation they limit the most far-reaching claims of the State, and the revolutionary ideology that can be generated is also of a sort which is particularly effective in countering organic statist claims.

Thus, there is a sense in which the ideology of rights has been a useful counter to the centrifugal forces of the western nation state while the ideology of mitzvoth or obligation has been equally useful as a counter to the centripetal forces that have beset Judaism over the centuries. But, in a sense, this kind of speculation is beside the point. The primary function of basic words is not to be found in so simple a functional explanation. We must look to the internal organization of normative thought, not to the external political results in the first instance.

III. The Nature of the Jurisprudence of Mitzvoth

The leading Maimonides scholar of this generation, Professor Isadore Twersky, has attributed to Maimonides' philosophy of law a thorough-going teleological understanding of the mitzvoth. Maimonides is generally thought of as being at the rationalist end of the spectrum of Jewish thinkers, so perhaps this attribution is natural. In any event, the position of Twersky is that Maimonides understood the rationale for the obligations of mitzvoth not only in terms of the bases for each of the commandments understood alone, but more important as a system with a systemic telos as well. In particular, Maimonides' system contrasts the normative world of mitzvoth with the world of vanity—hebel. It seems that Maimonides, in this respect, as in so many others, has hit the mark. A world centered upon obligation is not, really cannot be, an empty or vain world. Rights, as an organizing principle, are indifferent to the vanity of varying ends. But mitzvoth because they so strongly bind and locate the individual must make a strong claim for the substantive content of that which they dictate. The system, if its content be vain, can hardly claim to be a system. The rights system is indifferent to ends and in its indifference can claim systemic coherence without making any strong claims about the fullness or vanity of the ends it permits.

Maimonides' claim is more specific than the above. In the Epistle to Yemen he writes:

> If he could only fathom the inner intent of the law, he would realize that the essence of the true divine religion lies in the deeper meaning of its positive and negative precepts [mitzvoth],

every one of which will aid man in his striving after perfection, and remove every impediment to the attainment of excellence.

It is difficult in the light of such a claim to apply certain familiar categories of jurisprudence such as the distinction between a morality of duty and one of aspiration. It is certainly true that Judaism like every other normative system recognizes degrees of attainment in moral or legal excellence. However, the mitzvoth generally do not distinguish between precepts of duty and those of aspiration. And, indeed, the element of aspiration comes into the picture in part as a natural growth from the discipline of the duty imposed upon all. In any event, purpose and divine purpose are located in the basic word.

IV. The Natural Domains of Rights and Mitzvoth

There are certain kinds of problems which a jurisprudence of mitzvoth manages to solve rather naturally. There are others which present conceptual difficulties of the first order. Similarly, a jurisprudence of rights naturally solves certain problems while stumbling over others. It seems interesting to me that these dissimilarities have not been much explored. The claim I am making is not a very strong one. It is not, I will stress, that particular problems cannot be solved, in one system or the other—only that the solution entails a sort of rhetorical or philosophical strain.

The jurisprudence of rights has proved singularly weak in providing for the material guarantees of life and dignity flowing from the community to the individual. While we may talk of the right to medical care, the right to subsistence, the right to an education, we are constantly met by the realization that such rhetorical tropes are empty in a way that the right to freedom of expression or the right to due process are not. When the issue is restraint upon power it is intelligible to simply state the principle of restraint. Of course, whether the restraint will be effective depends on many things, not least of which is the good faith of those restrained. However, the intelligibility of the principle remains because it is always clear who is being addressed—whoever it is that acts to threaten the right in question. However, the "right to an education" is not even an intelligible principle unless we know to whom it is addressed. Taken alone it only speaks to a need. A distributional premise is missing which can only be supplied through a principle of "obligation."

In a system of mitzvoth this problem does not arise. Jewish law is very firm in its guarantee of an education. Something approaching universal male schooling was pursued perhaps two millennia ago. In any event, it is clear that throughout the middle ages it was the obligation of families and communities to provide schooling to all male children. I do not mean to imply that this principle was not often honored in the breach. But it was a principle and a clear one. And it did give rise to a system of schooling unrivaled in its time for educational opportunity. Yet, it is striking that the Jewish legal materials never speak of the right or entitlement of the child to an education. Rather, they speak of the obligation incumbent upon various providers to make the education available. It is a mitzvah for a father to educate his son, or grandson. It is a mitzvah for a teacher under certain circumstances to teach even without remuneration. It is a mitzvah for the community to make certain provisions for education and its institutions. It is a mitzvah for householders to board poor scholars and support them, etc.

Now, of course, in the United States with its rhetoric of rights, we too have statutes and provisions which allocate the responsibilities, fiscal and administrative, for the provision of education to children. As I said at the outset, we are comparing rhetorics not results. What is the case, however, is that these provisions concerning school districts and property taxes carry very little in the way of rhetorical freight. They do not move us or provide slogans or organizing ideologies. The provisions exist because if we are to carry on certain functions we need them. They neither move nor dignify in themselves. If we want to leap forward providing a kind or degree of education heretofore unprovided, we usually gravitate to the rhetoric of rights— declaring a campaign for the rights of the retarded to special education. "For every child has a right to an education." Then, the evocative force of the rights rhetoric having done its work we leave to the technicians the allocation of fiscal responsibility. If past experience is any indication, there will be a series of attempts to foist the responsibility off on someone else.

In a jurisprudence of mitzvoth the loaded, evocative edge is at the assignment of responsibility. It is to the parent paying tuition, the householder paying his assessment, that the Law speaks eloquently and persuasively. It is for him / her that the myth resonates. This is true for all welfare functions and for ritual ones as well.

There are procedural issues as well in which the rhetorical edge of mitzvoth as opposed to rights seems to make a difference. Consider for example the problem of the dress of litigants before a tribunal. In *Estelle v. Williams* the Supreme Court held that defendant had a right to appear at his trial (a jury trial) dressed in civilian garb of his choice rather than the convict garb in which he had spent the past days in jail. But, the Court concluded, in the absence of timely objection by counsel the right was deemed waived or not exercised. Now contrast Maimonides' treatment of a very similar though not identical issue:

1. A positive commandment enjoins upon the judge the duty to judge righteously . . .
2. If one of the parties to a suit is well clad and the other ill clad, the judge should say to the former, "either dress him like yourself before the trial is held or dress like him, then the trial will take place." (MT., Laws of Sanhedrin, c.21.)

It is, of course, the case that the rights-centered system of jurisprudence does frequently place affirmative obligations upon a judge to see to the protection of the "rights" of the parties. In that sense the kind of obligation evoked in Maimonides' Code is not completely strange. Moreover, the ethics of certain roles, like the roles of judges or even lawyers, do carry with them an evocative capacity associated with obligation and responsibility. Nevertheless, it is the case that even with respect to these areas we tend to have a system which is almost uniquely dependent upon parties and their representatives asserting their "fairness rights" rather than judges fulfilling their fairness obligations.

If there is a comparative rhetorical advantage to mitzvoth in the realm of communal entitlements, there is, it seems to me, a corresponding comparative rhetorical advantage to rights in the area of political participation. The myth of social contract is a myth of coequal autonomous, voluntary acts. It is a myth which posits participation because the legitimacy of what is generated depends upon the moral force of participation. The argument, for example, for the equal participation of women in political affairs or for their legal

equality is very straightforward under a rights jurisprudence, once
the parties to the argument accept the moral or biological equality
of the sexes. However, in a jurisprudence of mitzvoth one must first
create an argument for equality of obligation and only as a result of
that come to equality of participation. The fact is that there might
be important reasons which justify distinctions in obligations (e.g.,
the capacity to bear children) which nonetheless do not in any
straightforward way mitigate against complete equality of participation. The rights rhetoric goes to the nub of this matter because it
is keyed to the projection of personality among indifferent or hostile
others. The reality of such indifference, hostility or oppression is
what the rhetoric of responsibility obscures. At its best it obscures
it by, in fact, removing or mitigating the causes. At its worst it is
the ideological mask of familiar oppressions.

V. Conclusions

The struggle for universal human dignity and equality still proceeds
on many levels all over the world. There is no question that we can
use as many good myths in that struggle as we can find. Sinai and
social contract both have their place. Yet, as I scan my own—our
own—privileged position in the world social order and the national
social order, as I attend the spiritual and material blessings of my
life and the rather obvious connection that some of these have with
the suffering of others—it seems to me that the rhetoric of obligation
speaks more sharply to me than that of rights. Of course, I believe
that every child has a right to decent education and shelter, food and
medical care; of course, I believe that refugees from political oppression have a right to a haven in a free land; of course, I believe that
every person has a right to work in dignity and for a decent wage.
I do believe and affirm the social contract that grounds those rights.
But more to the point I also believe that I am commanded—that we
are obligated—to realize those rights.

Coda

Your Law-Baseball Quiz

The names of four major league baseball personalities appear after the name of a Supreme Court Justice. Circle the name of the baseball figure who bears the same relationship to baseball as the Justice bears to law.

EXAMPLE:

1. John Marshall

(a) Enos Slaughter
(b) Babe Ruth
(c) Dizzy Dean
(d) Cookie Lavagetto

The correct answer is (b) Babe Ruth. Both Marshall and Ruth transformed the games they played. Both became symbols of their institutions, and both are understood to be originators of their professions' modern age. This judgment holds regardless of whether their records are ever broken.

Questions

1. Earl Warren

(a) Yogi Berra
(b) Roberto Clemente
(c) Tris Speaker
(d) Willie Mays

2. Byron White

(a) Tommy Henrich
(b) Don Newcombe
(c) Jackie Jensen
(d) Steve Garvey

3. Oliver Wendell Holmes Jr.

(a) Stan Musial
(b) Mickey Mantle
(c) Ty Cobb
(d) Casey Stengel

4. Felix Frankfurter

(a) Ted Williams
(b) Wayne Terwilliger
(c) Bobby Murcer
(d) Cleon Jones

5. Robert Jackson

(a) Joe DiMaggio
(b) Marty Marion
(c) Duke Snider
(d) Ernie Banks

6. Louis Brandeis

(a) Pie Traynor
(b) Lou Gehrig
(c) Jim Rice
(d) Clyde Vollmer

Answers

1. Earl Warren. The correct answer is (a) Yogi Berra.

Both Warren and Berra were enormously effective performers on teams with many stars. Despite the presence of players such as Mantle, Maris, Frankfurter, Douglas and Black in the same lineup—

all of whom appeared to have a more elegant swing or style—Berra and Warren were the truly most valuable players. Both would frequently swing at bad pitches, but both were capable of hitting them for extra bases, especially in the clutch. Both saw through excessive thought to the true essence of their game:

"Theorists beset us with other definitions of law:... But the ideal of justice survives all such myopic views, for as Cicero said, 'We are born to it,'" said Warren. Or as Yogi said more succinctly, "How can you think and bat at the same time?"

2. Byron White. The correct answer is (c) Jackie Jensen.

Both were better as running backs. Despite a Golden-Boy buildup, Jensen failed to win a place on the great Yankee dynasty teams. However, on the mediocre and poor Washington and Boston Red Sox teams of the 50's he was a star. Similarly White, despite a big buildup, failed to achieve special distinction on the Warren Court. But in the context of the Burger Court he has achieved a measure of real stardom.

3. Oliver Wendell Holmes Jr. The correct answer is (d) Casey Stengel.

Both Holmes and Stengel had enormously varied and long careers, in each case serving the game for 50 years. Despite great success in purely legal or baseball terms, each achieved immortality for his use of the English language. Both men put the game they loved in the perspective of the skeptic's view of the eternal search for truth:

"Logical method and form flatter that longing for certainty and for repose which is in every human mind. But certainty is illusion and repose is not the destiny of man. . . ."

"So it's possible a college education doesn't always help you if you can't hit a left handed changeup as far as the shortstop. . . ."

4. Felix Frankfurter. The correct answer is (c) Bobby Murcer.

Frankfurter was in reality a rather ordinary Justice with good skills. However, many so-called experts had expected him to follow in the footsteps of the Mantles and DiMaggios of the law. Some people think Frankfurter was really Ted Williams. This kind of failure of expertise simply *cannot* happen in baseball and this demonstrates a weakness of this Law-Sport Aptitude Test. Experts may argue Mantle v. Mays or Williams v. Musial but there cannot be disagreement over whether Bobby Murcer is really Ted Williams.

5. Robert Jackson. The correct answer is (c) Duke Snider.

Both Jackson and Snider had the classic swing and style much appreciated by purists of the game. Both were men of enormous ability who were outstanding performers in their day. Yet both also seemed to disappoint their fans in failing, somehow, to achieve all-time super-star status. It has been written of Snider that he was always relieved to get a base on balls and Jackson is perhaps best remembered for his opinion in the Japanese-relocation cases that it would be best for the Court not to decide the case at all.

6. Louis Brandeis. The correct answer is (b) Lou Gehrig.

Brandeis and Gehrig had enormous ability and belong on the all-time All-Star team. Both had careers marked by outstanding, iron-man diligence. Gehrig's record of playing in 2,136 straight games may never be broken. Similarly, the Court may never have another Justice of whom it would be suggested that recreational reading consists of the reports of the Interstate Commerce Commission.

Note: Some have argued that this Law-Sport Aptitude Test discriminates against women. Unquestionably, there are few opportunities for women to identify with and become interested in either major league baseball or the Supreme Court. Neither game has ever had a woman player. Unfortunately, given the Court's role in the legal order, knowledge of such exclusively male preserves may be a bona fide job-related necessity for a career as a lawyer.

Afterwords

Robert Cover on Law and Violence

Austin Sarat

Robert Cover called himself an "anarchist" and, in so doing, sought to distance himself from conventional approaches to, and understandings of, law and its role in society.[1] While Cover succeeded in that effort in many ways, when he confronted the problem of law's relationship to violence, his anarchism was submerged and displaced. There, Cover found himself caught up in one of the central problematics of liberal political thought—namely, the problem of freedom and order.[2] He criticized and worried about the violence of law, about its pain-imposing, destructive qualities, yet, because he could see nothing but opposition between freedom and order, he reconciled himself to law's violence as a tragic necessity. Violence without law was, for him, an all-too-frightening possibility; as a result, law without violence was simply inconceivable.[3]

Portions of this essay are revised from an essay in *Law's Violence*, edited by Austin Sarat and Thomas R. Kearns (Ann Arbor: University of Michigan Press, 1992).

1. See Cover, "The Folktales of Justice: Tales of Jurisdiction," 14 *Capital University Law Review* 179, 181 (1985).

2. See R. Unger, *Knowledge and Politics* 66–67 (1975). See also R. Wolff, *The Poverty of Liberalism* (1968); H. Mansfield, *The Spirit of Liberalism* (1978); J. Gray, *Liberalism* (1986).

3. For a fuller statement of the argument, see Austin Sarat and Thomas Kearns, "Making Peace With Violence: Robert Cover on Law and Legal Theory" in *Law's Violence*, edited by Austin Sarat and Thomas R. Kearns (Ann Arbor: University of Michigan Press, 1992). On the tie between law and violence, see Walter Benjamin, "Critique of Violence," in *Reflections* (trans. Edmund Jepchott 1978). It is important to note that Cover embraced the most dramatic example of law's violence—capital punishment. See "The Bonds of Constitutional Interpretation: Of the Word, the Deed, and the Role," 20 *Georgia Law Review* 815, 831 (1986). For an interesting discussion of Cover's position see M. Tushnet, "Reflections on Capital Punishment: One Side of an Uncompleted Discussion," 27 *Journal of Law and Religion* 21 (1989).

"Legal interpretation," Cover wrote, "takes place on a field of pain and death."[4] "Legal interpretive acts," he continued, "signal and occasion the imposition of violence upon others: A judge articulates her understanding of a text, and as a result, somebody loses his freedom, his property, his children, even his life."[5] These sentences reveal, with great simplicity and directness, Cover's awareness of the tragic character of law's enterprise, the world-altering reality of legal meaning, and the way law and meaning are inextricably linked to violence. Because of law's tie to violence, because of the painful consequences of all legal activity, because its interpretations and meanings are inscribed on bodies, law, Cover claimed, could never be just another domain of meaning making and interpretation; law is, in this way, fundamentally different from poetry and philosophy.[6]

---

4. R. Cover, "Violence and the Word," 95 Yale Law Journal 1601 (1986).

5. Cover, "Violence," 1601.

6. "In this," Cover insisted, judges and others who wield the power of the state "are different from poets, from critics, from artists" (818). Showing a rare bit of impatience with those who insist that there is a strong resemblance between the violence done by judges and the interpretive violence done by poets, critics, and artists, Cover warned that ". . . it will not do to get precious—to insist on the violence of strong poetry, and strong poets. Even the violence of weak judges is utterly real— in need of no interpretation, no critic to reveal it—a naive but immediate reality. Take a short trip to your local prison and see" (818).

Yet this announcement is certainly not news to even the most casual observer of the legal system. As Karl Olivecrona put it almost fifty years before Cover,

According to an old and well-known line of thought law and force are regarded as opposite things. Force as such is put in opposition to law. In view of the extensive use of force, under the name of law, in the state organization, the contrast is, however, obviously false. Law as applied in real life includes a certain kind of force. It is organized, regulated force used against criminals, debtors and others according to patterns laid down by law-givers. . . . The real situation is that law . . . consists chiefly of rules about force, rules which contain patterns of conduct for the exercise of force. (K. Olivecrona, Law As Fact, 126, 134 (1939))

Indeed, by Cover's own account, to observe that "neither legal interpretation nor the violence it occasions may be properly understood apart from one another" (Violence," 1601) is merely to state the "obvious."

It was, however, such a statement that Cover repeated and elaborated in three separate articles published over a three year period (see "Nomos and Narrative," 97 Harvard Law Review, 4 [1983]; "Violence"; "The Bonds of Constitutional Interpretation: Of the Word, the Deed, and the Role"), articles written to correct what he saw as the all-too-easy assimilation of law and other interpretive enterprises. He wrote about violence, about the violence in and around law, and its inseparable connection to interpretation ("In law to be an interpreter is to be a force, an actor who creates effects even though or in the face of violence" ["Constitutional Inter-

In Cover's work, the everyday reality of law's violence is set against the utopian possibility of common meanings binding and inspiring human communities; meaning-destroying violence is juxtaposed with visionary imaginings of a norm-generating, normatively integrated group-life,[7] a rich pluralism of groups in a flourishing nomos.[8] Thus when Cover contemplated law's violence from the perspective of the plural communities that he so valued, that violence initially appeared deeply threatening and somewhat anomalous. It is, in Cover's account, potentially destructive, and unnecessarily so, of the world-affirming, world-building normative activities and commitments of communities and associations outside the state. It is, in addition, incompatible with narrativity, with the evolving network of beliefs, practices, and understandings that constitute or make possible a nomos. Violence, no matter what its source, puts an end to interpretation and meaning construction; it cuts off conversation. It does not elicit and evolve; it concludes.[9]

Law's violence is, as a result, a continuous threat to law's principal involvement in the production and maintenance of meaning in diverse normative communities. State law especially, because of its peacemaking and boundary-keeping roles, threatens to become imperial in character; it is easy for statist judges to become so intent on order, so insistent that only one law, the state's own, shall prevail,

---

pretation," 833]) as a bracing reminder of what he knew would seem obvious once stated; he wrote to bring to mind what he feared would be too easily forgotten in the rush to assimilate law into humanistic scholarship.

Cover's exploration of differences between law and other interpretive enterprises, and the nature of his disagreement with others in the effort to promote interdisciplinary legal scholarship, are perhaps best glimpsed in a long footnote to "Violence" (1601-2, n. 2). In that footnote, Cover begins by observing that "there has been a recent explosion of legal scholarship placing interpretation at the crux of law," acknowledging the rhetorical, interpretive, meaning-making quality of law, and, in this way, allying himself with Ronald Dworkin (see "Law as Interpretation," 60 *Texas Law Review* 527 [1982]), James Boyd White (*Heracles' Bow*), and other humanist scholars of law. At the same time, however, he notes, with some alarm, that "the violent side of law and its connection to interpretation and rhetoric is systematically ignored or underplayed" in humanist scholarship.

7. For a discussion of the way violence destroys meaning, see E. Scarry, *The Body in Pain* (1985).

8. Cover defined nomos as a "normative world" in which "we constantly create and maintain a world of right and wrong, of lawful and unlawful, of valid and void" (see "Nomos and Narrative," 4).

9. As Cover put it, "the coercive dimension of law is itself destructive of the possibility of interpretation" ("Nomos and Narrative," 48).

that the efforts and commitments of other rich sources of meaning, other normative enclaves, are needlessly limited or destroyed. Here, law's violence threatens law itself by being immoderate in its regulation of the sources of law.[10]

Nevertheless, Cover could not imagine law without violence. Despite its destructive, tragic character, Cover acknowledged and embraced the force of law. He insisted that "the jurisgenerative principle by which legal meaning proliferates in all communities never exists in isolation from violence."[11] And the shadow of that violence is cast as much by the "radical instability" of contesting, meaning-

---

10. Sometimes law's violence damages the source of law by being excessively deferential to the claims of state bureaucracy. In so doing legal actors condone the violence of administration. While, with regard to the normative communities outside the state, Cover calls for modesty and restraint, with regard to the state bureaucracy, Cover allows himself to imagine the judge as resister already inscribed in the sanctuaries of power, as a privileged rescuer of meaning and freedom from the forces of violence and order. In this imagining he works through what seems like a rather familiar argument about the rule of law in which the office of judge is set apart from the rest of the state's administrative apparatus (see John Norton Moore, "The Rule of Law: An Overview" [unpublished manuscript]) and he reminds us of Lord Coke's resistance to King James, Taney's resistance to Lincoln, and the resistance of judges in Ghana to the perpetrators of a military coup in the late 1970s. He urges judges to commit themselves to a "jurisgenerative process that does not defer to the violence of administration" ("Nomos and Narrative," 59) as the only way to temper law's all-too-close association with violence.

Law's violence signals, at some level and to some degree, a normative insufficiency, an inability of the controlling narratives to control. But the employment of force to retain control immediately raises questions about the normative basis, the justification, for that force. For if the use of force is required because of an indeterminacy or erosion in normative understandings, it would appear that those understandings are unavailable to ground and justify violence.

11. Cover, "Nomos and Narrative," 40. As he wrote about the organization of law's violence, and, in particular, about the way "judicial authority is transmitted through the inferior layers of the administration of justice," Cover, Douglas Hay has recently claimed, "celebrated . . . the fact of the integrity of that power of command of violence" ("Time, Inequality, and Law's Violence," in *Law's Violence*, ed. Austin Sarat and Thomas R. Kearns [Ann Arbor: University of Michigan Press, 1992]). Though Hay is onto something important about Cover's work, "celebrate" seems not quite right as a way of describing Cover's attitude toward the internal organization of law's violence. While continuing to press the analytic point about the relationship of violence and legal interpretation that animated his critique of others in the law and humanities movement, Cover's contemplation of the internal organization of law's violence is the contemplation of the sociologist simply investigating the facts rather than of the enthusiast celebrating what he has found. Yet it is nonetheless true that, in his sociological guise, Cover expressed much less regret about the fact of violence than he did in his reconstructive/utopian mood, and much more resigned acceptance of the need for law to do violence.

producing normative communities as by self-interested actors in an imaginary state of nature. He saw it as indispensable, albeit tragically so, in a world in which nomos is more aspiration than achievement, diversity is all-too-often accompanied by intolerance, and violence is too much the currency of human relations unregulated by law.

The language Cover used to describe a nomos that was unregulated and ungoverned makes his fear of such a place unmistakable; "Let loose, unfettered, the worlds created would be unstable and sectarian in their social organization, dissociative and incoherent in their discourse, wary and *violent* in their interactions."[12] Note too how he described "(w)*arring* sects" that wrap themselves in their own special law, in normative worlds where ". . . not all interpretive trajectories are insular."[13] In such a world, conflict, chaos, violence always threatens. Too much freedom and diversity appear to be the antithesis of order just as too much order would be the death of freedom and diversity.

Thus, law, and more precisely state law, is, according to Cover, always pulled in two directions, and, as a result, there is "an essential tension in law."[14] On the one hand, state law participates in the generation of normative meaning; on the other, state law plays in the domain of social control, and uses violence to enforce just one (namely its own) concept of order.[15] Meaning-making, meaning-generating normative activity in plural communities and associations sits uneasily and complicates the task of maintaining order. Thus, as Cover put it, "there is a radical dichotomy between the social organization of law as power and the organization of law as meaning. . . . The uncontrolled character of meaning exercises a destabilizing influence upon power."[16]

This formulation is, in many ways, quite typical of Cover's work. Meaning is, by definition, "uncontrolled"; power, left to itself, is stable. Thus, meaning and power, or interpretation and violence, exist separately, as forces in tension, working on and against each

---

12. Cover, "Nomos and Narrative," 16; italics added.

13. Cover, "Nomos and Narrative," 60; italics added.

14. Cover, "Violence," 1602, n. 2.

15. This is not to say that violence is only the province of the state. Cover seems to grant that *some* imposition, *some* force, is always a feature of law. Even the largely paideic Massachusetts Bay Colony sought to maintain its "holistic integrity" by forcefully *excluding* such heretics as Roger Williams and Ann Hutchinson.

16. Cover, "Nomos and Narrative," 18.

other. Meaning, because it is "uncontrolled," is the domain of free-dom; "the social organization of law as power" is the domain of *order*. The basic problem of society, politics, and law remains—despite Cover's effort to distance himself from this formulation—the problem as defined by liberalism, the problem of freedom and order, restated and redescribed no doubt, but reinscribed nonetheless.[17]

The internal coherence of systems of meaning and the order already within freedom, as well as the fragility of power and the possibilities of freedom already within the domain of order, seem to escape Cover's gaze just as they escape the gaze of liberalism. Because only the realm of meaning and interpretation is fluid, it, and only it, is or can be the realm of the plural, the possible, the imagined, the free. And because, despite Cover's own efforts to interpret and give meaning to the domain of legal violence, power and violence seem, in his account, to exist outside meaning and interpretation, the social, political, and legal world can only be a world in tension, moving now toward one pole, and then toward another, a world where meaning is always a threat to power, and where power is always the death of meaning.

Cover hoped that law's violence could be, despite the tragic shadow it casts, different than and preferable to other forms of violence—the violence of the lynch mob or the lawless state—which, in their own way, cast even more destructive shadows. Law's vio-lence is to be reluctantly preferred as a way of containing intolerance and counteracting that other violence, as a way of saving us from the darkest possibilities of human existence.[18] Here, Cover, the self-proclaimed anarchist, legitimates external imposition and coercive restraint as a way of preserving freedom, diversity, and pluralism. Like many liberal theorists, he does so by imagining the world without that ordering violence as a disorderly world and by describing the world of law's violence as an orderly and ordering one.[19] In this process, judges, even as they deploy violence, become, for Cover, "people of peace."[20]

---

17. See Unger, *Knowledge and Politics*.

18. See A. Sarat and T. R. Kearns, "A Journey through Forgetting: Toward a Jurisprudence of Violence," in *The Fate of Law* (Sarat and Kearns ed. 1991).

19. Sarat and Kearns, "Journey." See Peter Fitzpatrick, "Violence and Legal Subjection" (unpublished manuscript, 1991).

20. Cover, "Nomos and Narrative," 53.

Thus, the legal violence that initially seemed so inhospitable to the nomos and to the jurisgenerative work of communities and associations within that nomos is imaginatively tamed and transformed. The danger is dissipated and no price is paid for law's intimacy with violence.[21] In this imagined transformation of violence into peace, Cover moves away from critique to restate the liberal apology for the law and its reliance on force.[22]

Having imaginatively transformed violence into peace, Cover could further imagine that he had made peace between law's violence and the restraint and toleration he thought was so essential to law. Thus it is not surprising that Cover's other two treatments of law's violence—"Violence and the Word" and "The Bonds of Constitutional Interpretation"—would identify the conditions that make it effective in the world. If, in "Nomos and Narrative," Cover seems to ally himself with meaning against power, in "Violence" and "Constitutional Interpretation" the alliance is at the least destabilized and perhaps reversed. "So let us be explicit," Cover states,

> if it seems a nasty thought that death and pain are at the center of legal interpretation, so be it. It would not be better were there only a community of argument, of readers and writers of texts, of interpreters. As long as death and pain are part of our political world, it is essential that they be at the center of law. The alternative is truly unacceptable—that they be within our polity but outside the discipline of *collective* decision rules and the individual efforts to achieve outcomes through those rules.[23]

In these sentences we see no glimpse of the nomos, no bold assertion of the possibilities and virtues of a plural society where the threat of conflict is relegated to interactions at the boundaries separating normatively integrated communities. Instead, we see how a

---

21. By appealing to judges to resist "mere administration," to avoid acceding to the violence done by others, Cover hoped that he could reconcile law's violence with a legal order hospitable to diverse normative worlds. Here, the concern is that judges will violently and *unnecessarily* impose themselves against critique, vision, and aspiration in the normative world beyond state law and, in doing so, will destroy the nomos and narrative on which law itself deeply depends.

22. See Shklar, "The Liberalism of Fear," in *Liberalism and the Moral Life* (N. Rosenblum ed. 1989); see also Unger, *Knowledge and Politics.*

23. Cover, "Violence," 1628.

Hobbesian nightmare, death and pain undisciplined, inside the body polity but outside the reach of rules asserts itself in Cover's work.[24] Order and some semblance of peace can only be achieved where legal interpretation is embedded in, and is attentive to, what Cover called conditions of "effective domination."[25] Where such domination is not achieved, we face the prospect that people will find themselves in "conditions of reprisal, resistance, and revenge."[26]

That domination depends upon a structure of coordination and cooperation between those who authorize and control law's violence—namely judges—and those who carry it out, for example, police, prison guards, wardens, or executioners. Because judges do not themselves do the deeds that their acts authorize, they are dependent on others in preexisting institutional roles to carry out their orders and make their decisions work in the world.[27] Judges do the interpretive work that renders law's deeds of violence "intelligible," and, in return for their "relatively automatic heed" of the orders of judges, those who carry out those orders are able ". . . to shift to the judge primary moral responsibility for the violence which they themselves carry out."[28] Cover believed that the institutional context within which legal interpretation occurs provides, and should provide, a predictable, "though not logically necessary,"[29] set of responses to judicial decisions. Judges in the usual, ordinary performance of their duty seek to insure that predictability because, in Cover's view, interpretive acts mean nothing in a legal sense if they have no purchase in the world.[30]

---

24. For a similar analysis in a different context, see Peller, "Reason and the Mob," 2 *Tikkun* 28 (1987).

25. Cover, "Violence," 1616.

26. Cover, "Violence," 1616. See also S. Jacoby, *Wild Justice: The Evolution of Revenge* (1983).

27. Cover illustrates this familiar fact by considering the act of criminal sentencing, an act in which judges are "doing something clearly within their province" ("Violence," 1618). That act, however, depends upon a "structure of cooperation" in which "police, jailers or other enforcers . . . restrain the prisoner . . . upon the order of the judge, and guards who will secure the prisoner from rescue and who will protect the judge, prosecutors, witnesses, and jailers from revenge" ("Violence," 1619).

28. Cover, "Violence," 1617, 1626–27.

29. Cover, "Violence," 1611.

30. Thus judges ordinarily are not free ("Violence," 1617). They can never engage in poetic inattention to things outside the text. Judicial interpretation and the justifications judges provide are always, and must always be, attentive to the organizational context in which they will be received and translated into action. As Cover argued, "The practice of interpretation requires an understanding of what others will

When he considers the vertical organization of law, the lower ranges of the pyramid that judges rule from the top, anarchist Cover sounds suspiciously Weberian. "When judges interpret the law in an official context, we expect a close relationship to be revealed or established between their words and the acts that they mandate. That is, we expect the judges' words to serve as virtual triggers for action. We would not, for example, expect contemplations or deliberations on the part of jailers and wardens to interfere with the actions authorized by judicial words."[31] Judges who take into account the likely reaction of others in the chain of command, "regardless of how misguided" can, in this picture, expect the favor to be returned.

> When judges interpret, they trigger agentic behavior within . . . an institution or social organization. On one level judges may appear to be, and may in fact be, offering their understanding of the normative world to their intended audience. But on another level they are engaging a violent mechanism through which a substantial part of their audience loses its capacity to think and act autonomously.[32]

At this point, in the face of his own image of such rigid and unthinking bureaucratic behavior, one might almost expect that Cover would have rebelled against his own insights, rebelled against any use of interpretive authority to suspend the "capacity to think and act autonomously." Cover the anarchist or Cover the normative pluralist might have been expected to embrace and to praise a theory of social organization that allowed for and encouraged multiple sites of interpretation, sites in which alternative readings might prevail, sites of resistance. In this way the deployment of violence would be greatly tempered by problems of coordination within law's complex chain of command. To the extent that interpretive authority is fragmented and dispersed, that rival centers of power enter competing interpretations, the literal violence of the law might be reduced.

---

do with . . . a judicial utterance and, in many instances, an adjustment of that understanding, regardless of how misguided one may think the likely institutional response will be. Failing this, the interpreter sacrifices the connection between understanding what ought to be done and the deed, itself" ("Violence," 1612).
    31. "Violence," 1613–14.
    32. Cover, "Violence," 1615.

But there is, in fact, no rebellion, no endorsement of a loosely coupled bureaucratic structure; there is, instead, first, silence and, later, an approving, if stark, description of wardens, guards, and doctors engaged in the process of carrying out a death sentence who "jump to the judge's tune."[33] The world of interpretation is altered by a consideration of the requisites of order; meaning (freedom) gives way to insure that an orderly, a disciplined violence is done. Meaning is disciplined, in Cover's analysis, by the requisites of discipline itself. From the inside of law, and against the possibilities of undisciplined force and aggression, legal interpretation and law's social organization are looked to by Cover as the domain to achieve "whatever achievement is possible in the domesticating of violence."[34]

Violence domesticated, force turned into persuasion, war turned into peace, given this hope it is not particularly surprising that Cover accepts law's violence.[35] Combined, the instructions regarding state law expressed in "Nomos" and "Violence" appear to be: "Wherever possible, withhold violence; let new worlds flourish. But, for the sake of life, do not forget that law's violence is sometimes necessary and that its availability is not automatic but must be provided for. And finally, effective violence that is also temperate and controlled is a considerable achievement, requiring 'an organization of people' that is as complex as it is fragile."[36] To do its job, then, law *must* be violent, but as little as possible. Cover's attention to law's violence (in "Violence") signals his recognition that, despite the normativity that precedes law and partly because of it, there is need for law's violence and need also to secure the conditions of its effective use.

Cover was, in truth, no anarchist. If labels matter, then we would

33. Cover, "Violence," 1623–24.
34. Cover, "Violence," 1628.
35. It is apparent, then, that Cover was not so much of an anarchist that he was indifferent to the distinction between a lynching (or runaway police machinery) and an execution authorized after a trial and review on appeal. And this is precisely the point; Cover had neither such a romantic aversion to violence, nor such an unqualified sympathy for freedom over order, that he rejected violence entirely.
36. The insistence that legal violence should be used sparingly is explained by his conviction that "we inhabit a nomos—a normative universe" that is easily destroyed by such violence even though some measure of it is needed to maintain normativity. The restraint called for at the end of "Nomos" refers principally to instances or kinds of instances in which the use of force is justifiable or appropriate; to insist that such instances are relatively rare and that legal force should be used sparingly is, of course, perfectly compatible with the conviction that *some* use is actually necessary and, on those occasions, it should be applied efficiently.

label his thought about law and violence the thought of a reluctant liberal. In his mournful embrace of the violence of law, Cover allies himself, albeit not fully, with the intellectual project of liberal political thought. While Cover called himself an "anarchist," as a way of announcing his sympathy for freedom, diversity, and meaning, like any liberal he acknowledged the need for the state and its ferocious law. His work restates and redescribes what Roberto Unger has labeled the "antimonies of liberal thought."[37] Instead of radically departing from liberal political thought to reconceive the domain of law, Cover remained firmly within its hold, and, like many others similarly situated, moved uncertainly from one mood to another, first imagining a world of freedom, diversity, and meaning, and then embracing, albeit reluctantly, the necessity of the ordering force of law.[38]

And yet when Cover contemplated law's violence he was surely not just any liberal. While liberalism traditionally has been the major philosophical doctrine defending individualism, individual differences and the priority of the individual against what are seen as the suffocating demands of community and society,[39] Cover prized the life of communities, groups, and associations and worried about the effect of violence on them. But he was no communitarian.[40] For him there could be no single community, no well-ordered understanding of virtue. If law's violence had any constructive purpose or possibility, it was to make possible a community that was plural, diverse, and contentious in its articulation of normative ideals without, at the same time, being self-destructive.

---

37. See Unger, *Knowledge and Politics*, 6–7.

38. For a fuller exploration of these perplexities and uncertainties, see Unger, *Knowledge and Politics*. See also Kennedy, "The Structure of Blackstone's Commentaries," 28 *Buffalo Law Review* 28 (1979); Tushnet, "An Essay on Rights," 62 *Texas Law Review* 1363 (1984).

39. For a particularly vivid example of this tendency, see Kateb, "Nuclear Weapons and Individual Rights," 33 *Dissent* 161 (1986).

40. For a useful discussion of the difference between liberals and communitarians, see Taylor, "Cross-Purposes: The Liberal-Communitarian Debate," in *Liberalism and the Moral Life* (N. Rosenblum ed. 1989).

Meaning and Alternity

Michael Ryan

Reading Robert Cover's work, one feels that he would have been a good judge. He would have been sensitive to the dilemma between loyalty to law and the commitments of conscience that he so ably analyzed in *Justice Accused* and in his essays collected here. But he would also have been capable of a judicial courage tinged with the messianic, the kind of courage he admired so much in Judge Herbert Stern, whose Berlin decision rebuking the state and pledging a higher commitment to the care of victims of legal violence earned Cover's respect.[1]

What I admire as well about Cover is that, as I read through his work, it eventually answered all the objections that arose in my mind as I read. I began by feeling uncomfortable with his statist emphasis in *Justice Accused*, his examination of the moral travails of northern judges faced with enforcing the Fugitive Slave Law, as if the psychological troubles of whites merited more scrupulous attention than the physical and emotional pains of blacks under slavery (I should say that I was reading Jacobs's *Incidents in the Life of a Slave Girl* at the same time—perhaps an unfair comparison), but I ended by acknowledging and respecting Cover's strong sense of empathy for the victims of legal violence as well as his sense of the necessary difference of perspective between a judge's justifications of such violence and the pain of those on whom it is inflicted.

I initially questioned his use of the imperial "we" to describe a nomos or community of shared norms, as if the dispossessed and the disempowered could be summoned to a communal podium from

---

1. See "Violence and the Word."

which they are never allowed to speak and whose rules of procedure occur in a language they are never allowed to learn. But I found as I read that Cover, rather than being an apologist for an unexamined ideal of community that refuses to acknowledge the workings of inequality and power, was, if anything, a celebrant of radical divergences from nomic imperiums.

At first, Cover's concept of nomic narratives troubled me; my schooling in literary criticism has taught me to be suspicious of anyone who thinks highly of national narratives that embody communal norms. Those of us who teach the history of American culture are too aware of how easily a failed massacre of Indians by whites can become "Custer's Last Stand" under such narrational auspices. For every constitution, there is an epic, Cover writes, yet we are taught to think of such imposed stories as ideology, the deployment in culture of ideals of submission and obedience that make power more economical by making expenditures of violence less necessary. But as I read, I realized that Cover shared our sense of how the power of the state is exercised through narrative and of how alternate narratives can disrupt that power either by undermining narrative itself or by generating new visions and alternate world constructions.

Finally, I began by wondering how so much respect could accrue to someone who spent fifty pages discussing jurisdictional redundancy, not for me a terribly exciting topic—until I read the piece with that title and learned that at issue were crucial questions of creating or blocking the creation of norms and until I read further and learned that Cover conceived of such norm creation as the high road of law, something akin to the messianic risk that brings new worlds of normativity into being.

Cover's great virtue resides in his delineation of (and refusal to ideologically resolve) dilemmas that are integral to the very institution of law, at least at this point in history. Those dilemmas are between the conservative role of the state and the potential of law to serve as a bridge to "alternity," between legal meaning as that which provides unity and the essentially contested character of all meaning, and between the perspective of the victim of law and the perspective of the judge, which is also the necessary dilemma between a community of different perspectives and the aspiration to normative and legal coherence. In discussing these dilemmas, I will begin with a narrative: to plagiarize Bob Cover, for every critical introduction, an anecdote.

When I finished reviewing Cover's articles for this collection, I turned on the television and caught a few minutes of an old episode of the "Ed Asner Show." It concerned the son of orthodox Jews who survived the Nazi camps. He grew up thinking of himself as a victim, and, as an adult, he sought to escape that self-definition by repudiating his heritage and becoming a member of the American Nazi Party. The newspaper reporter who uncovers this hidden history of the seemingly anti-Semitic party leader was about to confront him with the possibility of exposure when a crying infant obliged me to turn off the show. But it made me think, nonetheless, of Cover's description of the way communities outside the state generate alternate normative possibilities.

Law is a bridge to alternity, he writes, and yet law destroys alternate worlds of legal meaning. It does so out of fear. The nomos or normative universe we inhabit must be maintained. The possibility of building an alternate world of meaning and value entails the risk of loss and madness for what can only be imagined. This messianic impulse, the jurisgenerative potential, resides in law, but law must also stand against the messianic precisely because it would mean a total transformation, a revolution in norms that destroys as much as it creates. The antislavery judges could have taken such a risk; one senses that Cover thinks they should have done so. They would have helped bring about another world, but, in doing so, they would have destroyed the nomos they inhabited, one founded on the idea that laws should be obeyed and that the duty of judges is to respect them. The task is easier outside the realm of institutional law, in the communities, often religious ones, that Cover sees as also possessing jurisgenerative potentials.

I wondered as I watched the television show if Cover would have considered communities like the Nazis as jurisgenerative. Are all normative alternities equally creative? Or are certain norms (the liberal one of respect for person, for example) required as standards of measure? As an anarchist, Cover sees what he calls the "pressure to imperialize"[2] as emanating from the state, but liberal statists see that

---

2. See "Nomos and Narrative."

pressure as emanating from the "extremes" of left and right that threaten a tolerant and pluralist liberal government. A witness to the violence of the state exercised through law, Cover has no trouble perceiving the mythic character of the liberal self-description. But it is nonetheless true that those who make strong substantive claims for their own visions usually conceive of the state as the appropriate instrument for realizing them.

That alternate communities like the Nazis do indeed become the state exposes both the shortcoming and the great virtue of Cover's thinking on this matter. There is a danger in certain kinds of messianic alternity; I suspect Cover does not explicitly take this possibility sufficiently into account. But to an extent he did so implicitly by arguing for a commitment to constitutionalism in the face of the racism of such an alternate community as Bob Jones University. His alternative to state jurisgenerativity is a legality that exists or could exist above or outside the state, either in the formal promises of constitutions or in communities and movements without either statist aspirations or harmful internal structures.

The wisdom of this position becomes clear when one considers that the Nazis began as an insular nomic community, only to very quickly become the state. Despite the protests of liberal political thinkers that such putschism is aberrant, the example is telling, for it suggests that the state might always be the legal expression of one insular community that has gained ascendancy over all others. Cover seems to have something like this in mind when he suggests that the state cannot be a locus of alternity because of its imperial, world-maintaining function. What he means by the "social control" function of law is essentially the putschist reality of all state governance of even the liberal variety—that it must restrain jurisgenerative alternatives to its own lawmaking power by quelling the messianic impulse of nomic communities other than itself.

Cover accurately describes the conceptual and functional short-comings of statism. But he cannot escape the dilemma posed by statist alternities and by the lack of an alternative to the state as a way of dealing with them. Because the state exercises a stabilizing power through the authority of law, it cannot be made a locus for jurisgeneration, but for all its functional shortcomings, the state cannot be abandoned altogether because not all communities are communities of virtue. Some aspire to state power and to the exercise of legal violence against others. While messianic alternity can, therefore, never be a pure good, that which limits its potential as well as its threat—the state in its world-maintaining role—can never be a pure good either.

The second dilemma was between the necessary unity of legal meaning and the necessarily contested character of all meaning. Cover's ideal of a nonstatist jurisgeneration leaves unanswered the question of the clash of substantive norms. We are plagued by an incommensurability of visions, what Cover refers to as the "problem of the multiplicity of meaning."[3] At times, especially in his description of a community nomos of shared norms, he seems to align himself with Ronald Dworkin's overly placid picture of a normative tradition that guides adjudication in the manner of a serial novel toward congenial and coherent ends. Cover avoids that possibility by refusing to grant unity to any one legal narrative. Legal meaning, he writes, is essentially contested. Our narratives, epics, and stories embody our norms, while locating and giving meaning to our legal institutions, but narratives, especially alternate narratives developed by communities and movements, contest the unity of law. They are the open doors at the other end of the hallway, pointing in their trajectories toward other meanings, other possible worlds.

To the traditionalist leanings of contemporary liberal legal theory in the Dworkin vein, Cover adds more potentially radical understanding of narrative as an ongoing story whose ending is less determined by what has already been conceived than by choices made regarding what has yet to be imagined. And the storytellers are numerous: not only judges, but also normmakers who take issue with the state and depart from its precepts. These practitioners of what Cover calls a "hermeneutic of resistance or withdrawal" confront the state with counternarratives,[4] other imaginings of human development than those sanctioned and enforced by the judicial servants of state power. They contest the imperial unity of legal meaning and help lay the foundation for that bridge to the future, between reality and alternity, that Cover thought law could and should be.

Cover chooses his examples of counternarrative carefully. It's hard not to see virtue in the civil rights narrative or in the Russell Tribunal on the Vietnam War's efforts to create an alternate source

---

3. See "Nomos and Narrative."
4. See "Nomos and Narrative."

of adjudication than the state. One easily grasps how fitting the present inequalities in the treatment and station of blacks in the United States into a narrative that moves from the deracination of enslavement to the continued hostility of a white-powered society leads to a different, more enabling interpretation than is possible if the narrative is one that draws on a conservative paradigm which tells the story of inequality as one of loss and gain amongst equally empowered individual competitors, none of whom are structurally disabled. In adjudication particularly, a choice between such narratives clearly gives rise to either liberatory or oppressive results.

But if not all alternities are alike, neither do all counternarratives tell equally worthy stories. For example, as I thought about Cover's work, I began thinking about the antiabortion protesters in Wichita, Kansas, who have been in the news so much lately. They constitute an insular nomic community of the kind Cover praises for their ability to resist the imperial mode of state law and to generate alternate narratives to the narrative of power. Granted, their antinomianism is qualified by the support lent by a conservative administration that takes the form of an intervention over jurisdiction whose significance as an attempt to insulate prejudice against redemption Cover would have appreciated. But they nonetheless invite comparison to the antiwar demonstrators of several decades past. Each instantiates the contradiction between loyalty to existing law and the commitments of conscience, and each constitutes an attempt to write an alternate narrative, one that would reinterpret events in such a way as to give them a different meaning—either "the war is unjust and must be stopped by any means" or "life begins at conception and must be preserved by any means." In each case, the narrative justifies the breaking of law for the sake of higher moral ends.

Yet although each movement places itself at odds with the state, each one's goal is to have its meaning become the state meaning. Once a meaning or narrative is made legally dominant by the state, as in the *Roe* abortion decision, which told the story of fetal life as one among many possible narratives, all other meanings are placed in opposition to both the law and the state. As a result, their proponents risk becoming victims of legal violence if they seek to make their meanings dominant against the will of the state. Law, Cover writes, "rescues us from the eschatology that is the collision in this

material social world of the constructions of our minds."⁵ But it must
do so through force, and it places us all in a conundrum. We claim
the right of civil disobedience for our own substantive ends, but we
(I, at least) also silently applaud the application of state force to
restrain the antistatist attempts of our ideological adversaries to
impose their particular meanings on the world. Like the slavery
judges, we live out the conflict between formal legal commitments
and substantive social desires, claiming the legal right to disobey the
state even as we aspire to nationalize our meanings.

Meaning is never simply contested, then, in the world picture
Cover draws for us. It must aspire to incontestability because meaning
is as much emotion as it is ideation. We always mean what we say
when we say what we mean. Private conviction regarding such issues
as abortion is only fulfilled when it becomes public authority.

One of the doors Cover opens allows us to see that it may be
the false unity of the state that makes decisions between contradictory
meanings necessary. Perhaps there should be a plurality of narratives,
a multiple jurisgenerativity that exceeds any singular nomos or any
decision between meanings. At times, Cover seems to think so. But
there is a problem lurking in this praiseworthy ideal, and that is the
emergence of insulated regions of prejudice, the tacit goal of the
conservative drive to separate jurisdictions, state from federal, in the
antiabortion controversy. Not all narratives tell nice stories; some
include women only in subordinate clauses. And some communities
(states) will, in all probability, impose the meaning the abortion
protestors favor on women's lives and bodies. At issue, in other words,
is something more than narratives, even if narration is the mode in
which the stakes involved must be played out. More than many who
are sensitive to the importance of interpretation, meaning, and rhetoric to law, Cover is aware of the pain beyond the words, the violence,
both actual and potential, inscribed in the stories.

In the face of the potential for insulated prejudice, we do perhaps
need the kind of judicial courage Cover recommends to impose
redemptive narratives paternalistically from above. The judge in
Wichita would no doubt satisfy Cover's standard in this regard, since
he put aside his own opposition to abortion in order to enforce the

5. See "Nomos and Narrative."

law. But Cover has more confidence in the good judge to prevent the multiplicity of meanings from becoming harmful than I myself can muster. The messianic narrative is one that is as much worth questioning as the one that allows states to tell our stories for us—how we won the war, for example, or why life begins at conception. Like the concept of the state, the notion of the Messiah has a particularly strong male ring to it. A distanced projection that embodies our most dangerous desires and aspirations in a safely alienated external site, it allows us to avoid the engagements and commitments with each other that might take us beyond the stasis of power. It tells a story of redemption that we are afraid to act out ourselves.

Moreover, the multiplicity of meaning itself should teach us that an individualist solution may not be sufficient. Such solutions limit an understanding of meaning to a choice of narratives that are not perceived as being inextricably embedded in material circumstances whose complexity is resistant to one good judge's fiat, regardless of how courageous. Meanings and interpretations emerge from a multiplicity of sites. And those sites are themselves temporary stabilizations of dynamic situations, of intersecting lines of determination that are social, psychological, economic, sexual, and so on. Each singular meaning conceals a multiplicity, and there is a multiplicity of meaning as much because there is a multiplicity of social locations as because there is a multiplicity of semantic possibilities. Law imposes coherent, uncontestable narratives only because the incoherence and contestation of the social world requires legal narratives to give it order. And that incoherence is not cognitive; it is rather the differences of inequality, the scaling of power, the misallocation of rewards, the skewing of educational and cultural possibilities, the disproportions of psychological well-being, and so forth—things whose meanings are not singular and whose solutions require a renegotiation of the fundamental rules of property, sexual and racial socialization, cultural and educational distribution, and the like in our society.

I'm not certain Cover's brave judge is a match for such an undertaking. I can imagine a judge ruling that everyone must undergo training in the best that modern liberal humanist ethics has to offer in order to take part in the abortion controversy, but I'm not sure I want to. Good judges and singular courageous acts may be necessary, but so will be a long and difficult labor of remaking that extends from the negotiation of differences to the fabrication of new consti-

tutions to the diagnosis and cure of contextual situations that breed
narrowness and kill souls to the promulgation of new values to the
elaboration of new habits of living and understanding to . . . Beyond
the multiplicity of meaning lies the possibility and the necessity of
remaking our worlds of meaning by remaking the social universe in
which meaning takes on shape and has its existence.

The final dilemma I wish to describe in Cover's work is between
judicial justification and the pain law inflicts. Cover's approach to
the dilemma is more empirical than theoretical, and for good reason.
Theory distances; it removes the pain. And perhaps this explains
why legal justification must, to a large degree, be theoretical. The
coherence of either statutory design or precedent, administration or
jurisdiction, gives reason and meaning to judicial violence. But, for
Cover, this very coherence makes law incompatible with community.
So long as coherence excuses the exercise of legal violence, there will
always be a radical, unhealable divergence of experience that prevents
legal coherence from attaining the identity with community to which
it aspires. "The perpetrator and victim of organized violence will
undergo achingly disparate significant experiences," Cover writes.
"[T]here will always be a tragic limit to the common meaning that
can be achieved."[6]

For Cover, the dilemma of coherence and community appears
most vividly in the personalized, if emblematic, encounter between
judge and criminal, and so it seems an unbridgeable divide, a tragic
limit. And yet his own communitarian vocabulary suggests different,
more "social" alternatives. Can we imagine a legal structure that
assesses conduct in a nonviolent manner? Is it possible to foresee
social arrangements characterized by a greater coherence of distribution, position, and power so that the coherence of law can more
readily be experienced as shared agreements of the kind Cover's ideal
communities would create? For law to cease to be violent in the
manner he describes, would it not be necessary for adjudication to
cease to be individualistic or paternalistic and to become a dramatic
equivalent of community and to offer a cognitive or narrative version
of structural complexity? If, indeed, we assume the victim's perspective instead of the judge's, might it not be necessary to move away
from adjudication as the focus of attention and concentrate instead

6. See "Violence and the Word."

on the acts that bring people before the bench, to begin perceiving those acts as effects whose causes must be cured by a somewhat different, more shaped legal messianism than is available to the singular model of the judge? And finally, given these dilemmas, is it not time for law to acknowledge the fruitful and promising undecidability of the issues that come before it, issues that might make it necessary, within such a new framework of understanding, different results—not decisions, but projects of negotiation and reconstruction?

Law as it exists and is practiced obliges Cover to think in terms of a one-on-one encounter and to request redemption from within the same framework. I cannot question the importance of the ideals of judicial courage and resistance that he proposes. Within the existing framework, they make sense. But like Auden's Brueghel, Cover's work invites us to look in a different way, to cast our glance into the corner of pictures, away from the grand figures and large events. There we find not only small acts of courage and violence that otherwise might pass unnoticed, but also glimpses of what might be called an implied alternity. The negativities Cover notices all suggest an alternate world-picture, what he perhaps means by the messianic. In that world-picture, the dilemmas I have described are resolved, and they are so by a change in the framework in which they are posed. The state, the dominant narratives, the relationship between judge and criminal all become different. The state no longer quells alternate visions, because it is nothing more than a loose ensemble of connected jurisgenerative alternities that nonetheless share a commitment to a fundamental nomos; dominant meanings no longer impose unity on contested issues; rather, negotiations work through differences to the point of mediation, while a long labor of reconstruction addresses the contextual sources of semantic difference; and, finally, the judge and the criminal find nonviolent alternatives to punishment through communal processes that are more redemptive than punitive.

Robert Cover's work is saved from the note of tragedy that usually accompanies a strong sense of the dilemma of social existence by such elements of hope. "We ought to stop circumscribing the nomos," he writes. "We ought to invite new worlds."[7]

---

7. See "Nomos and Narrative."

Subject Index

Aaron, domination of, by Moses, 116

Abel, story of Cain and. *See* Deuteronomy, inheritance laws of

Abolitionist movement, 133–38. *See also* Garrisonian abolitionists and the Constitution

Abortion. See *Roe v. Wade* in case index

Abstention doctrine. *See* Complex concurrency, "synchronic redundancy"

Aeschylus: *Orestia* and the treatment of legal and moral indeterminacy, 139

Arendt, Hannah, on Jewish self-consciousness, 44

Alshekh, Moses, 193. *See also* Semikhah, renewal of, at Safed

Alternity, 101

Amish: and associational/educational freedoms, 127, 128, 166; interpretation of constitutional rights, 145; New Testament and, 130; and nonviolence, 152, 154; *Wisconsin v. Yoder*, 122–23, 124, 125

Anabaptist, vision of internal laws, 122–23. *See also* Amish

Anarchy: and jurisdictional redundancy, 54; and the nature of law, 175; and utopian jurisdiction-making, 200

Anti-injunction statute. *See* Labor injunctions

Antipater, 180–82. See also *Jewish Antiquities* (Josephus)

Anti-slavery movement. *See* Abolitionist movement

Anti-war movement, Cover's participation in, 1

Apartheid in America, 29–30; and court's activist protection of minority participation in political process, 38, 39, 45–56; local politics and continuation of, 39–40; President's and Congress's role in combatting, 48. *See also* Voting rights; White primaries

Appellate review and legal interpretation, 223–24, 235–36

Articles of the Confederation competing with constitutional narrative, 121

Associational freedom, 127–30: natural law of, 129n.92; as precondition for *nomos*, 129; in private and parochial education (see *Bob Jones University v. United States*; *Wisconsin v. Yoder* in case index); relationship of corporation law, contract law, and free exercise of religion to, 129

Babel: Library of, 177; multiplicity of systems in, 111n.45

Bancroft, Archbishop. See *Fuller's Case*

Barth, Karl, on church versus civil society, 106–7

Index of Statutes and Cases